STRUCTURES FOR COMPOSITION

STRUCTURES
FOR
COMPOSITION

Bernard A. Drabeck

Helen E. Ellis

Virginia Low

Hartley Pfeil

Greenfield Community College, Greenfield, Massachusetts

Houghton Mifflin Company   Boston
Atlanta   Dallas   Geneva, Illinois   Hopewell, New Jersey   Palo Alto   London

Photograph Acknowledgments

Page 12, Jack Prelutsky. Page 19, Dennis Stock / Magnum. Page 26, Salem Witch Trial: Accusation of Bedeviled Girl. Engraving by Howard Pyle. The Bettmann Archive, Inc. Page 29, Patricia Hollander Gross / Stock, Boston.

Page 56, Daniel S. Brody / Stock, Boston. Page 72, Jack Prelutsky. Page 84, A Slave Auction in Virginia. From The Illustrated London News, Feb. 16, 1861. Courtesy of Boston Public Library. Page 91, Andrew Newell Wyeth, Ground Hog Day. 1959. Egg Tempera on Board — 31 x 31 inches. Philadelphia Museum of Art: Given by Henry F. DuPont and Mrs. John Wintersteen.

Page 111, Mark Chester. Page 112, William Thompson. Page 115, Paul Conklin.

Page 126, Margaret Bourke-White, Life Magazine © 1972 Time Inc. Page 157, Robert Rapelye. Page 160, David Kelley. Page 165, André Kertész / Magnum. Page 169, Paris, 1926 André Kertész / Magnum.

Page 216, George Krause. Page 182, F. Kirkman. The Wits (frontispiece). 1662. By permission of the Folger Shakespeare Library, Washington, D.C.

Page 226, Medieval Doctor's Office. The Bettmann Archive, Inc. Page 229, William Thompson. Page 231, Charles Gatewood. Page 241, Kentucky. Charles Harbutt / Magnum. Page 273, Ron Benvenisti / Magnum. Page 281, Peter Menzel / Stock, Boston. Page 293, Jack Prelutsky. Page 309, Clif Garboden / Stock, Boston.

Printed in the U.S.A.

Library of Congress Catalog Card Number: 73–10232

ISBN: 0-395-16967-4

Contents

Preface

This book contains a course in freshman composition. Like other composition texts, it attempts to help students solve the reading and writing problems they encounter not only in their English courses but whenever they have to cope with expository prose — that is, prose that attempts to convey information. Unlike most other rhetoric books, however, the focus here is on *structures* in composition. As you progress through the assignments, you will learn some very practical devices for sorting out your thoughts, arranging them in chronological or logical sequence, and communicating them with maximum clarity and impact. These devices will be of immediate use in all sorts of everyday and classroom situations — as you write letters home, as you attempt to influence voters, as you write applications for summer work, as you plan talks for student activities, and as you write papers and exams for all your college courses.

Problems in reading and writing

Much expository prose (the kind found in most texts) remains a dull mystery to many students, even when they read and re-read passages. Sometimes the problem with reading has to do with lack of interest or involvement, since the absence of these makes attention almost impossible to sustain. At other times, however, a student has trouble reading because he cannot follow what is being said. Problems with comprehension are compounded when the writing is intricate and the subject is complicated or abstract. In these cases, *some* of the obstacles to comprehension are due to the complexity of the material the student is attempting to understand; but much of the problem often lies in the reader's own mental disarray, especially as it influences the reading process itself. For reading is a time art. When a person reads, his eyes take in words singly or in groups; and as he moves from word to word, he has to remember what he has read and connect it to what he is reading, observing how words are put together to form sentences, how sentences are linked to form paragraphs, and how paragraphs are joined to form the entire essay. The problem in reading, then, is one not only of understanding individual words, but also of seeing and remembering how they are related to one another to present a statement of ideas. Until he learns to make such connections as he reads, the student will find most college level reading assignments very difficult.

Similarly, essay writing is to many students a pointless exercise in obscurity. Again, there may be a lack of interest and involvement, which affects both what is said and the way it is expressed. Many students do not possess sufficient information about what they are writing, nor do they feel impelled to discover what they do not know. As a result students have trouble finding concrete or specific things to say, their papers tend to be vague, abstract, and general, or they resort finally to filler and repetition.

Often, however, difficulty in writing, like difficulty in reading, has to do with fuzzy thinking, an unhappy condition which is usually due to an inability to organize. Ironically, those who have trouble with the paper as a whole can frequently compose reasonably grammatical sentences and perhaps even well developed paragraphs, but when they are faced with putting it all together, using a chain of paragraphs for extended communication, they fail to cover the subject adequately and in a way that is clear as well as accurate.

What this course can do for you

If you are aware of a need to improve your communication skills, if you can see how improvement in your reading and writing can increase your chances for success not only in English composition but in your other studies as well, then you should take this course seriously. And if you do, the results should be both noteworthy and gratifying. As you realize that reading can be simplified by observing how ideas are put together, as you become aware that writing is not a chore but a project which can be systematically and sensibly approached, you will gain both skill and confidence in all your studies.

Some texts in composition contain a collection of essays dealing with today's major issues. And although we agree that the vital problems of the world are matters with which every student should be concerned, the conditions of textbook publication are such that a book that tries to look like today inevitably looks like last year instead. Other texts try to achieve relevance by appealing to the inner need of many students to express their own feelings. Unfortunately, while these books do encourage self expression and perhaps even succeed in prompting the student to construct a chronicle of his own immediate responses to situations and events, most of these do not develop abilities which the student can universally apply to his reading and writing problems.

Our definition of relevant, as we have implied, is "of practical usefulness here and now," and therefore we are concerned in this course with what will help you deal most easily and directly with the difficulties inherent in receiving and transmitting information. We have not ignored contemporary issues; for our sample essays include many that deal with matters of perennial concern. Neither have we ignored the central need of the student to express himself — but we are convinced that if you know how to go about gathering information and organizing it, you will be in a better position to understand what you read, to know what you want to say, and to be able to put it into words. Perception of the internal and over-all structure of an essay will result in quicker and easier comprehension of the parts and the whole of what you read. And at the same time, familiarity with structures for composition will help you to arrange your own knowledge into patterns for writing that will allow you to do justice to that knowledge. By possessing these skills, you will be much more likely to satisfy your listener as well as your own need for self expression.

How to use this book

What you will find in this text is a carefully planned series of writing and reading exercises, beginning with comparatively concrete material and moving step by step to more complicated and abstract composition. The first two chapters explore chronological order as it is found in directions or process papers and the report. The rest of the book is concerned with logical order; Chapters Three and Four offer two applications of classification and division — definition and comparison —, and Chapters Five and Six deal with argumentation and persuasion, both of which also employ the principles of classification and division in determining the structure of part or all of the essay.

Each of the six chapters consists of three parts:

First are the introductions, in which you will find an explanation of the ideas central to each assignment, suggestions about the scope and range of writing possibilities, and a discussion of the ways in which the material in the chapter relates to your other studies.

Next you will find the guidelines proper. These offer step-by-step instructions on how to complete a given assignment. As you will notice, these detailed instructions tell you how to begin a writing assignment, how to organize your information, preliminary work, and how to turn your rough draft into a final paper. The guidelines are so constructed that if you follow them carefully, you will be guaranteed success in your writing. To help you follow them, each chapter includes with the guidelines a preliminary worksheet and an evaluation guide which you can use in the process of writing and assessing your own work.

After the guidelines is a collection of essays illustrating each structure. Some of these essays were written by students, so you can see what your peers have done with these assignments. The rest have been written by professionals, so you can observe how their work is put together. We have tried to include sample essays that cover a broad range of topics as well as provide concrete examples of the organizational patterns discussed in the introduction and guidelines.

How you use each chapter will, of course, be up to you and your instructor, but we would like to suggest the following method:

1. Read through the introductory comments.
2. Read through the guidelines to get some idea of the nature of the writing problems being covered in that chapter.
3. Look through the essays and read some of them carefully, particularly the student samples.
4. Select your topic, and as you reread the guidelines plan and write your essay.
5. Finally, and while you are working on Step 4, refer once more to the essays. Study them, and try to observe ways in which other writers have employed particular structures in their own writing. In Chapter One, for example, you should expect to find in the essays a chronological order, and you should further be able to assess each essay in terms of the rules for clarity and attention to detail that you find in the guidelines. You should also notice that if you are aware of the broad structural principles which govern the organization of the sample essays, you can read them with increased ease and understanding.

If you pay careful attention to the guidelines for each assignment, following the instructions closely, your work will be quite acceptable. One of our students remarked recently, "I don't understand why I'm doing so well. I had a terrible time with writing before this. But now all I have to do is read the guidelines, do some thinking, and spend time enough to write my papers carefully. And they turn out pretty well."

But, and we hope this is true of you, some students want to do better than simply "pretty well." You will notice that the guidelines for each chapter are flexible enough to allow you to set your own goal and measure up to it. By choosing to carry out the guidelines in an advanced way, by writing effectively on a difficult topic, you can make the assignments as demanding as you wish. You may prefer, especially at the beginning, to approach the assignments on a very simple and concrete level, but even if you do, your preliminary successes should increase your sense of security and thereby allow you a greater range of expression in later papers. There are no restrictions on your choice of subject or on the range of complexity you may explore, except that the topic you choose must be one that will work well in terms of the structures specified in each chapter.

How much you get out of this book will, of course, be up to you. But we promise that if you do the work as outlined with care and attention, your reading, writing and thinking will all improve — and that is what we think any course in composition should be all about.

THE AUTHORS

STRUCTURES FOR COMPOSITION

1   Chronology: Directions or Process

INTRODUCTORY COMMENTS

Successful written communication requires accurate, complete, and clear details which are at the same time organized effectively. Many students are frustrated in their attempts to write because it is difficult to manage both content and order simultaneously. The first two assignments in this text are therefore designed to enable you to focus your attention on only one problem at a time. The content—that is, the accurate, complete, and clear details—will be your chief concern in both papers, since directions or process in the first chapter and the report in the second involve structuring your information around a simple and natural time sequence. When a paper is so organized, it employs *chronological order*, an order in which the subject itself determines the structure of the paper.

Chronological order

If events are sequential in time, taking place one after another, they constitute a chronological order. As you should be aware, all of life is chronological, since everything that you do takes place in time, moments following one another and melting into days and years. Such a progression is what we mean by chronological order in its most basic sense, but it is the same order that underlies the organization of most of your activities. When you make plans for the day, when you undertake a project for the semester, when you envision a career and the steps that will make it possible, you are in each case making use of a chronological arrangement to determine appropriate procedure. Similarly, when you write a record of your day's events in your diary, when you contemplate your history or that of the world, you are also dealing with chronological order, since these activities, like those mentioned previously, involve investigating or noting a progression in time—what is first, second, third, etc. Of course, since you cannot always tell what came first, it may be difficult to decide on the proper and correct sequence. Usually, however, chronological order is either obvious or easy to discover if you possess pertinent facts. Be-

1

cause such an arrangement is dependent upon a series of steps in the order of their happening and because order of time is a natural part of all our lives, it is the simplest kind of order to learn and therefore offers the student a suitable and accessible introduction to the study of structures of composition.

Problems in directions or process papers

A paper whose purpose is to give directions or describe a process is easy to write if you have accurate and complete knowledge of the procedure you are trying to describe. This means that before you write anything at all, you must be aware of the step-by-step process involved—or at least know where to find information if you are unsure of order or method. Equally important, you must add those details which give a thorough description of procedure, so thorough, in fact, that your directions can be followed. As we have said, you will not have to be very much concerned with the organization of your paper, since that will be largely determined by the procedure you are describing. The body of your paper will be made up of this description. To it you will prefix a general, brief introduction, add a short conclusion, and your paper will be complete.

You should note, however, that the guidelines work for both simple and sophisticated topics. If you write on "Cleaning a Bridle" or "Braiding Hair," the principles of the guidelines can be literally applied, because these subjects obviously intend to give directions or analyze a process. The guidelines can also be used for such topics as "The Establishment of a Commune," "The Evolution of a Performer," "How to Psych-Out a Teacher," or "Learning a Foreign Language," which also require the application of a chronological order, but an order imposed on a set of generalizations rather than on clear-cut steps in a mechanical operation.

How long should your paper be? You will notice that the guidelines for this and all other assignments give no directions concerning length. Throughout this course, the same rule applies: the assigned structure and your chosen topic will determine how much you should write. Your paper should simply be long enough to cover your topic adequately, without filler but with all necessary material included.

Uses of directions or process structure

Whether you write directions for a simple task or a more complex description of a long-range process, your work on this assignment will make you more fully aware of the structure of such a paper and its usefulness as a means of organizing a wide variety of subjects. Once you are familiar with this structure, you will find that you can more easily read and understand text materials (including the samples in this book), instructions for laboratory projects, and many other kinds of material. You should also be able to follow lectures more readily and take better notes on them, provided, of course, that the lecture involves either directions or process. And finally, you will learn an organizational tool that you can employ repeatedly in your own writing, even when, as you will see, you are concerned with logical patterns of organization.

GUIDELINES

1. Choose a topic.

For this paper you can select a subject about which you know little and consult proper authorities, or you can describe something you already know how to do. Your topic may involve a specific and detailed set of directions, or you may write about a more general and complex procedure. Sample topics include "How to Detect Counterfeit Money," "The Electoral System—How It Works," "Training Your Dog for Obedience," "A Recipe for Spaghetti Sauce," "Building a Library of Folk Music," and "The Production of Antivenine."

2. Make a list and amplify it.

The common practice of placing a blank sheet of paper in front of you and staring into space for inspiration can be avoided by compiling notes. These notes should take the form of a list of the procedures involved and the details necessary to make the explanation of each step of the process both clear and complete. If you are dealing with something like "A Recipe for Spaghetti Sauce," a list of steps in their proper order would be expanded with details about *equipment, ingredients,* and the *process* of preparation, including information about time, temperature, and anything else the reader must know to be able to follow your directions. A similar list should be compiled for an operation which takes place over a more extended period of time. If you were to write on "The Production of Antivenine," for instance, you would discover that there are three major procedures involved, in this order:

> obtaining venom
> producing serum
> collecting serum

These would constitute the three main headings of your list. Each one would then be expanded by the addition of appropriate information, again in order of occurrence and in sufficient detail to explain each part:

   a. Venom is obtained
      1) two persons collect the venom by milking a snake (if the snake is exceptionally dangerous or active, it is anesthetized or chilled into helplessness)
         a) the collector pins down the snake's head and grasps it just behind the jaws, while his assistant controls its body
         b) because of the pressure, the snake will open its mouth; if not, the collector pulls it open with a small, blunt hook and places the fangs over the edge of a vial or tube
      2) the reptile ejects venom into the tube; the operator can squeeze out more by gently pressing on the venom-producing glands located in the snake's head
      3) the collector stores the venom, which may be kept separate or pooled with venom from others of the same species
      4) his assistant frees the snake or returns it to its cage to replenish its supply of venom

   b. Serum is produced
      1) the collector injects fresh venom into an animal, usually a horse
      2) the horse's system manufactures a substance called an antibody to resist or destroy the harmful agent
      3) when the animal has recovered from the ill effects of the poison (and sometimes the horse will die, no matter how carefully the dose is measured), the collector injects another, larger dose
      4) again the horse's system will produce antibodies to combat the poison
      5) the collector continues injecting progressively larger amounts of venom into the animal until a saturation point has been reached and the animal has developed immunity to the poison, no matter how large a dose he is given

   c. Serum is collected
      1) the collector bleeds the horse and allows the blood to run into sterile containers and clot
      2) he lets the blood sit until a clear liquid rises to the surface
      3) he collects the clear liquid, decants it, and stores it in a cool place

You will notice that the above list does not include technical information about a number of variables involved in the production of serum, such as the amounts of venom that might be collected from a single snake, how venom might be stored, or how much venom should be administered to the subject in the series of inoculations. If, however, you are writing about a project which the reader can do himself, your list must include every item or ingredient needed and all the steps required. In either case, since you are writing to inform, you must check over your list to see that it is accurate, in order, and as complete as it must be to tell the reader what he must know to follow your directions or understand the process you are describing.

3. Compose an introduction which includes a main-idea sentence.

Usually the purpose of an introduction is twofold: to describe what the subject of your paper is and to get the reader interested in it. Some kind of introduction is therefore as necessary for a directions or process paper as it is for any other essay. In addition, your introduction should contain a topic or main-idea sentence.

Introduction. To construct a lively and informative introduction, it is a good idea to include information that will not appear in the body of your essay. An introduction to a paper on antivenine might be based on information that answers the following questions:

What is snake venom? Why is it dangerous? How is it injected?

How many people get bitten by snakes in this country? How many die?

What are the two main types of venom?

How does antivenine work? Is it always effective?

Where is snakebite serum kept?

What is the principle behind the use of animals for manufacturing serum? (The blood of an animal made resistant to venom confers resistance to poison.)

What about dangers to injected animals? What about dangers to collectors of venom?

Although there are other areas of information you could investigate, the preceding ones constitute more than enough from which to formulate an introductory paragraph. As your next step in putting this paragraph together, select the material you want to use (you obviously can't use all of it), and then arrange it into a paragraph that contains a main-idea sentence.

Main-idea Sentence. A good main-idea sentence states the subject of the composition and in this way tells the reader (and incidentally reminds the writer) precisely what is to be communicated. Often it is helpful, even in directions or process papers, if the main-idea sentence also gives a clue to the structure of the body of the paper:

> Antivenine is a clear, liquid substance prepared under strict laboratory surveillance according to a process which utilizes the principle of antibody development and which involves several distinct steps.

The subject is the preparation of antivenine, and the sentence makes clear that the composition is structured around the sequence of operations in its production.

Note: a main-idea sentence may be placed anywhere within the introductory paragraph. In the sample, it serves to summarize the materials on which the rest of the introduction is based and therefore appears at the end, immediately before the body of the paper.

> When someone is bitten by a poisonous snake, venom is injected through the fangs into the victim's body. Whether the venom is neurotoxic (attacking the nerves) or haemolytic (destroying the blood), it is extremely dangerous to man, even in such small amounts as a single drop from a cobra. Treatment of snakebite should therefore include the injection of a suitable antivenine or serum, since the body by itself cannot produce sufficient counteragents to combat or nullify the effects of the poison. *Antivenine is a clear, liquid substance prepared under strict laboratory surveillance according to a process which utilizes the principle of antibody development and which involves several distinct steps.*

4. Write the body of your paper.

It has already been said that the body will consist of either directions for a project or the description of a process, and you have already done the preliminary work for this section by compiling your list of steps and details. To compose the middle paragraphs, determine first what paragraph arrangement can be made. In the sample, you will note that the list of steps includes three major parts which are relatively separate from one another. It seems reasonable, then, to plan three developed paragraphs in the body of a paper on antivenine. To compose these paragraphs, simply expand the list (including information on equipment, ingredients, and procedure) into sentence form, leading the reader from one step to another by using appropriate transitions.

Transitions are words, phrases, or sentence patterns that establish a connection or link between sentences within each paragraph and between the paragraphs themselves. There are many types of transitions, but in the body of the paper for this assignment and the next, you will be concerned largely with words and expressions that help the reader keep in mind the chronological sequence you are describing (other kinds of transitions will be discussed in detail in the third chapter). Building the actual body from your chronological list consists to a great extent in the use of such transitions to join the steps together.

Transitions Within Paragraphs. The movement or flow between one sentence and another must be clarified by the use of words or phrases which establish a connection or link. Since in this assignment your concern is with chronology, words which specify a time sequence will enable you to construct a series of sentences which are clearly connected. The first paragraph of the body below, for instance, begins with a statement about the collection of venom, and it is that process which is described in most of the following sentences, each step linked *in time* and *in the paper* by words which indicate the time/thought connection: "One of the collectors carefully lifts the snake." "He *then* pins down the snake's head and grasps it . . . *while* his assistant controls its body." "*Then* the fangs are placed. . . ." "*At this point*, the snake ejects. . . ."

Transitions Between Paragraphs. Just as smooth flow from one sentence to another requires use of connecting words or phrases, the movement from one paragraph to another and the way in which paragraphs are related to the overall structure must be clarified by the use of appropriate transitions. Such between-paragraph chronological transitions should therefore appear near the beginning of the first (usually topic) sentence of the new paragraph, reminding the reader that a major step in the process is being discussed and that the step is part of a sequence:

> The process of making antivenine *begins* with the collection of the venom itself.
>
> The *second step* of the procedure involves injecting a controlled amount of the venom into a large animal, usually a horse.
>
> *When* the animal has developed an immunity, the *third stage*, or the actual collection of antivenine, begins.

You can strengthen your awareness of chronological transitions and how they work by analyzing the italicized words or phrases in the sample body.

> The process of making antivenine *begins* with the collection of the venom itself. Sometimes the poison is purchased by a laboratory from individuals who extract and sell it, but it is usually obtained from reptiles (rattlers, cobras, etc.) kept in the laboratory. In either case, however, the procedure of milking the snake, as it is called, is the same. Often, especially if the snake is extremely active or dangerous, it is first anesthetized or chilled into helplessness; but in any case, two persons cooperate to extract the venom. The collector carefully lifts the snake with tongs or with a hook slid under its body. Just as carefully, he *then* pins down the snake's head and grasps it just behind the jaws *while* his assistant controls its body. Because of the pressure on its head, the snake will open its mouth; if not, the collector pulls it

open with a small, blunt hook. *Then* the fangs are placed over the edge of a vial or tube. *At this point,* the snake ejects a liberal amount of venom, and the collector often squeezes out more by applying gentle pressure on the venom-producing glands located in the snake's head. *After* the venom is extracted, the collector stores it separately in its vial or tube (under the proper conditions, it keeps its potency for months) or perhaps pools it with venom collected from other snakes of the same species; *meanwhile* his assistant either frees the snake or places it in its cage, where it rests, and replenishes its venom supply, a process that takes about three weeks, depending on the temperature and the snake's general condition. *Throughout* the operation, of course, both persons must guard against being bitten; for no matter what kind of snake they are handling, it is a live instrument of death and is potentially destructive even after having been milked, since the extraction of its venom does not necessarily render a snake even temporarily harmless.

The *second* step of the procedure involves injecting a controlled amount of the venom into a large animal, usually a horse. *After* the injection the horse's system will proceed to manufacture antibodies to resist or destroy the venom. *When* the animal has recovered from the ill effects of the poison (and it does not always: the horse sometimes dies, no matter how carefully the doses are measured), another, larger dose of venom is injected, and *again* the horse will produce antibodies to combat the poison. The process of injection and recovery is continued with progressively larger amounts of venom each time until a saturation point is reached and the animal has developed an immunity to the poison, no matter how large a dose he is given.

When the animal has developed such an immunity, the *third stage,* or the actual collection of antivenine, begins. In this stage blood is taken from the immunized animal and run into sterile containers. There the blood sits until it clots and a clear liquid rises to the surface. The clear liquid is the serum; and *after* it has separated from the blood, it is collected, decanted, and stored or distributed in snake-bite kits to doctors. Suitably contained, the serum keeps from two to three years without losing its effectiveness.

5. Write your conclusion.

The conclusion in a paper giving directions does not need to be very lengthy or complicated. It should, however, bring matters to a close and give the reader the feeling of completeness that all good endings supply. What to include in the conclusion is a matter of choice, with these limitations:

a. You must not introduce totally new material.

b. It is not enough simply to paraphrase something you have already said.

c. The paragraph should consist of more than one sentence.

Material for your final paragraph can include matters that you have touched on but not expanded anywhere else in your essay. It might be helpful, therefore, to consult the list of ideas drawn up for your introduction to see if there is anything there which might be dealt with in the conclusion. If we look at the questions which served as the basis for our opening paragraph on antivenine, we can see that we have not yet dealt in any detail with the following topics:

a. the incidence of snakebite in this country

b. the two types of snake venom—the neurotoxic and the haemolytic

c. the plight of the injected horse

d. is snakebite serum always effective?

Since the body of the paper has been concerned with a dangerous process, it might be well to begin the conclusions with a reminder of the risks involved. Other and related ideas expressed in suitably connected sentences will follow, bringing your essay to a close:

> The production of antivenine, then, is a complex enterprise. It is also a risky one, both to venom collectors and to the animals used in producing the serum. Even *after* these dangers are surmounted, however, what is produced is not a foolproof medication. For one thing, snakebite serum will work to counteract only that type of venom from which it is produced: thus, antivenine that is effective against the neurotoxic venom of the cobra or coral snake will not neutralize haemolytic or viperine poison. And there are other problems as well. Since snake poison is quick-acting, someone who is bitten must be inoculated quickly. Even then antivenine only checks further damage by the venom; it does not cure the damage already done. Moreover, antivenine is not always effective, for death from snakebite has occurred even after serum has been administered. In spite of all these drawbacks, however, antivenine remains the best treatment for snakebite.

As with the introduction, it may be necessary to omit from your conclusion material that will not fit into what you have written. You should not regard the accumulation of such information as wasted effort, however, since you may find an opportunity to use it in another paper— and besides, it is always better to work from an excess of material than to try to piece out fragments.

6. Prepare your final draft.

When you have finished your rough draft, you should turn your attention to the following matters.

Accuracy, Completeness, and Clarity. Make sure that what you want to say is clear in your mind first. If you are confused about something, that confusion will immediately reveal itself in your writing; on the other hand, if your thoughts are clear, your writing should be too.

Make sure that you express yourself as simply as possible. As a general rule, use short and concise sentences in preference to long and convoluted ones. It is easy to become more complex after you have mastered the essentials.

Do not include any information that is either unnecessary or beside the point.

Do not take too much for granted. Just as it is annoying when a writer "jumps to a conclusion," eliminating or passing over necessary steps in logic, it is also bothersome when he omits or fails to explain important information. This is another reason for making sentences as simple and direct as possible; precision of statement will result in accurate descriptions.

If you choose to write directions for a simple task, you will have the advantage of an immediate practical check on the contents of your paper. You may ask a friend to *try out* your directions to see whether they really work. If you have left out a step, put it out of order, or not given sufficient detail to make it clear, your friend will not be able to follow your directions, and you will know that your paper needs work.

Use of Pronouns. In the sample paragraphs the word "you" does not appear. The elimination of "you" from a theme on antivenine does not constitute, as it may seem, unfair discrimination. The point is merely that since the author preferred to keep references in the third person he had to be consistent about it.

In a paper giving directions, you may use "you" and talk directly to the reader if you wish. In fact, it is rather difficult and sometimes awkward (as the sample theme indicates) to avoid this usage in a paper giving directions, since such a paper is usually informal—that is, addressed directly to the reader.

There are two things to remember about pronouns: check to be sure that you do not shift from one person to another in the course of your paper. Do not begin talking to "you," change to "we," and then switch over to "he," "one," or "they." Be consistent. Check to be sure that pronouns stand for something. The reader will be confused if you shift pronouns from one person to another. He will be equally perplexed if the pronouns don't stand for anything at all.

Proofreading. After you have typed or written your composition, double spaced in either instance, with title and margins, read it through for those errors which are usually a matter of carelessness, especially if you type. If you can get yourself into the habit of writing a practice copy and proofreading your final one, your writing will almost automatically improve.

If you have read through the above directions carefully and if you follow them in your first paper, you should turn in a satisfactory essay. Complying with instructions obviously does not mean picking and choosing among items in the guidelines, however much you may be fond of some and dislike others. Accuracy, completeness, consistency, and concern for the reader are good habits for any writer to develop; and the successful completion of a paper giving directions or describing a process means paying attention to all of the guidelines.

SAMPLE ESSAYS

Diaper Changing   STUDENT SAMPLE

Interest-catching introduction, leading up to the main-idea sentence.

In the beginning you have a baby—a wet baby. This necessarily leads to the task of changing a wet, soggy diaper. Though this relatively simple procedure takes only a few moments to perform, it usually strikes fear in the hearts of the uninitiated. Trying to secure a strip of cloth around the tummy of a tiny and fragile bit of humanity can make you feel as if you had two hams in place of hands. However, with a bit of patience and practice, along with the observance of a few basics, the task of diaper changing can be accomplished with a minimum of effort.

First major step: preparing the materials for the task. List of necessary equipment smoothly worded in full sentence form.

For a simple start, fold the diaper. Use the standard thirty-six-by eighteen-inch size; although other variations such as the square diaper and paper disposable diaper are available, they are not as convenient or economical. To fold the standard size, hold the diaper lengthwise and fold it in half twice which will reduce it to a size of approximately nine by eighteen inches. Now that the diaper is folded and ready, proceed to the next step, which is to assemble all the other articles necessary for the change including a soak pad, diaper pail, a soapy cloth, a dry towel, pins, powder or cream, and rubber pants. Select a safe flat surface such as a bathinette, bed, or table on which to change the baby and set all the necessary items

Used by permission.

within easy reach. This is very important as a baby can move with lightning speed and therefore should never be left unattended even for a moment.

Place a soak pad on the changing surface in case of a wet accident during the change, and position the baby on the pad with his feet toward you. Begin by removing the outer clothing and rubber pants. Unpin the diaper pins and attach them to a safe spot, such as your shirt, where they will be easy to locate the moment you need them again. Now remove the diaper and drop it into a diaper pail to prevent stains on floors or rugs. With a soapy cloth, cleanse the baby well to prevent a rash or burn. Then wipe off all soap with a dry towel and pat the baby dry. Everything is now ready for the application of a fresh diaper.

With one hand grasp the baby's feet gently but firmly, and with the other hand take the diaper and slide it lengthwise halfway under the baby. Now release the baby's feet and apply powder or cream to protect the baby's sensitive skin. After powdering, bring the front half of the diaper up over the baby's tummy and overlap the corners on each side. At one side, with fingers between the diaper and the baby's skin to prevent stabbing the baby, join the edges through all thicknesses with the safety pin and secure the pin. If the pin stubbornly refuses to penetrate the diaper, run the pointed shaft of the pin either over a cake of soap or through your hair. This serves to coat the pin with a light film of oil which allows it to slide easily through the diaper. Repeat the pinning procedure on the other side, making sure the diaper is stretched firmly across the tummy. If it is fitted too tightly, the baby will be uncomfortable; too loosely, and the diaper will reduce to a soggy lump around his knees. Finally, slide on the rubber pants, making sure no diaper ends poke out at the waist or legs because an untucked edge will act as a wick and shortly everything will be wet. At last, the change is completed.

If you don't yet feel confident about changing a diaper, don't fret. The baby will soon give you an opportunity to try again. As proficiency increases in diaper changing, the baby also will be gaining proficiency in his art of squirming, rolling, kicking, and being generally uncooperative. At this point, a necessary addition to your list of supplies would be a series of funny faces, unusual noises, and a lot more patience. Or you can begin potty training.

Margin notes:

Second major step: preparing the baby.

Transitional sentence leading to final major step.

Third step: applying the fresh diaper. Note that all details within the step are in chronological order, reinforced by links and transitions.

Concluding paragraph brings paper to a smooth and amusing close.

How Dictionaries Are Made

S. I. HAYAKAWA

It is widely believed that every word has a correct meaning, that we learn these meanings principally from teachers and grammarians (except that most of the time we don't bother to, so that we ordinarily speak "sloppy English"), and that dictionaries and grammars are the supreme authority in matters of meaning and usage. Few people ask by what authority the writers of dictionaries and grammars say what they say. The writer once got into a dispute with an Englishwoman over the pronunciation of a word and offered to look it up in the dictionary. The Englishwoman said firmly, "What for? I am English. I was born and brought up in England. The way I speak *is* English." Such self-assurance about one's own language is not uncommon among the English. In the United States, however, anyone who is willing to quarrel with the dictionary is regarded as either eccentric or mad.

Let us see how dictionaries are made and how the editors arrive at definitions. What follows applies, incidentally, only to those dictionary offices where first-hand, original research goes on—not those in which editors simply copy existing dictionaries. The task of writing a dictionary begins with reading vast amounts of the literature of the period or subject that the dictionary is to cover. As the editors read, they copy on cards every interesting or rare word, every unusual or peculiar occurrence of a common word, a large number of common words in their ordinary uses, and also the sentences in which each of these words appears, thus:

> pail
> The dairy *pails* bring home increase of milk
> Keats, *Endymion* I, 44–45

That is to say, the context of each word is collected, along with the word itself. For a really big job of dictionary writing, such as the *Oxford English Dictionary* (usually bound in about twenty-five volumes), millions of such cards are collected, and the task of editing occupies decades. As the cards are collected, they are alphabetized and sorted. When the sorting is completed, there will be for each word anywhere from two or three to several hundred illustrative quotations, each on its card.

To define a word, then, the dictionary editor places before him the stack of cards illustrating that word; each of the cards represents an actual use of the word by a writer of some literary or historical importance. He reads the cards carefully, discards some, rereads the rest, and divides up the stack according to what he thinks are the several senses of the word. Finally, he writes his definitions, following the hard-and-fast rule that each definition *must* be based on what the quotations in front of him reveal about the meaning of the word.

The editor cannot be influenced by what *he* thinks a given word *ought* to mean. He must work according to the cards or not at all.

The writing of a dictionary, therefore, is not a task of setting up authoritative statements about the "true meanings" of words, but a task of *recording*, to the best of one's ability, what various words *have meant* to authors in the distant or immediate past. *The writer of a dictionary is a historian, not a lawgiver.* If, for example, we had been writing a dictionary in 1890, or even as late as 1919, we could have said that the word "broadcast" means "to scatter" (seed and so on) but we could not have decreed that from 1921 on, the commonest meaning of the word should become "to disseminate audible messages, etc., by radio transmission." To regard the dictionary as an "authority," therefore, is to credit the dictionary writer with gifts of prophecy which neither he nor anyone else possesses. In choosing our words when we speak or write, we can be *guided* by the historical record afforded us by the dictionary, but we cannot be *bound* by it, because new situations, new experiences, new inventions, new feelings, are always compelling us to give new uses to old words. Looking under a "hood," we should ordinarily have found, five hundred years ago, a monk; today, we find a motorcar engine.[1]

Study Questions

1. State in a single sentence each major step explained in the essay.
2. The introduction and conclusion of the essay say very little about the *process* of making a dictionary, but rather concern themselves with the nature of a dictionary. What is the purpose of these two paragraphs in relation to the rest of the essay?
3. As an individual or group project, compile a dictionary of current slang expressions. Begin by listing a number of words which have recently come into slang usage. Then collect examples of these words in context. Finally, write definitions stating what the words appear to mean to the people who use them.
4. At the time (1961) when *Webster's Third New International Dictionary* appeared, various writers attacked it on the ground that it did not give authoritative judgments about how words should be used. Other writers defended the *Third*, saying that a dictionary should merely report current usage, not set standards. Using the *Reader's Guide to Periodical Literature* in your library, locate and read some of these articles. What would be Hayakawa's position in this dispute?

[1]*Webster's Third New International Dictionary* lists the word "hood" also as a shortened form of "hoodlum."

The time that elapsed between *Webster's Second Edition* (1934) and the *Third* (1961) indicates the enormous amount of reading and labor entailed in the preparation of a really thorough dictionary of a language as rapidly changing and as rich in vocabulary as English.

Fake Fi

While you're waiting for the time you can assemble a really good hi-fi system, you can take a few simple steps to make everybody think you have one already. And you don't have to be an electronics expert to climb on the low-cost, fake-fi bandwagon.

The secret of fake fi is clutter. The more parts you have around the room —lying on the floor, perched on tables, peeking out of bookshelves—the more professional it looks. Never put components in a cabinet. A man whose FM tuner, tape deck, amplifier, and turntable are neatly concealed in a cabinet may have hi-fi and he may have stereo, but nobody will be impressed. When equipment is hidden in furniture behind little doors, people don't know where the music is coming from. To hear stereo, you've got to see it.

You can change an ordinary table radio into a fake-fi component simply by taking the case off and putting it on a bookshelf. It should be placed just below eye level, so that parts can be seen and tubes can give off a warm glow in the evening.

The next step is to add components, the weirder-looking the better. They should have dials or knobs or switches, or a combination of all three. Stick them here and there and string wire from one to the other. Don't conceal the wire; in fact, it's a good idea to position one wire so that visitors must step over it. Make some professionally apologetic comment like, "Watch the pre-amp lead, I haven't had a chance to finish winding the core."

Components are easy to find. Junk shops and junk yards offer a wealth of material. Almost any electronic-looking thing will do. If it can be made to light up, so much the better. Old radios are excellent, and so are old TV sets without the picture tube. (Even with no cabinet, a picture tube looks too much like a TV set.) Extremely impressive is a car speedometer wedged between your books and connected to another component with a spiral telephone cord. Anchor the speedometer pointer on the dial just to the right of center, about 65 mph on most GM cars. This gives you a steady "plus" reading, attesting to the soundness of your music system.

Genuine electronics experts build their own components in aluminum boxes, available in all shapes and sizes at radio supply stores. Get some of these boxes and glue knobs on them. Electronics catalogues offer packages of miscellaneous knobs, some even with pointers. If you want to get fancy you can get rotary switches with shafts. Drill holes in the boxes, install the switches, and fasten the knobs to the shafts.

Stretching your arms to turn two knobs at the same time—one way high up on the shelf and the other at knee level—has a good visual effect on guests, especially if you do it with your eyes closed. The fact that listeners can't tell the difference in the sound quality works to your advantage. Your ear is very sensitive; their ears aren't.

Labeling knobs and switches is a matter of personal choice, and you'll have to decide whether you belong to the "No Information" or the "Obscure Information" school.

Real electronics experimenter-builders never label which knob does what because they *know*. You can create that same impression. The No Information technique works best with a long, low aluminum box containing at least a dozen identical round brown knobs shoulder to shoulder with nary a hint as to what they do. If you want to bug the eyes and boggle the minds of friends, put another long box on top, this one full of unmarked toggle switches. Don't worry about anyone touching it; nobody will come near the thing.

Members of the Obscure Information school label knobs and switches, but with electronics terms that make no sense to the layman. Simple terms such as "Volume" and "On-Off" are never used. Borrow one of those label-makers and print terms like "Impedance Circuit," "Grid Leak," "Null Adj."

Whether or not your equipment is labeled, it may be improved by adding pilot lights. These are red, green, white, or amber jewels that light up when something is not working and should be; is working and shouldn't be; or is supposed to be working and is. You can buy pilot lights that run on house current. You put them into little aluminum boxes and then run wires to the wall socket. These actually serve a practical purpose. When your lights go off in a power failure the pilot light will go out, telling you that there's a power failure and your lights are off.

Just as your electronic equipment should be in plain sight, so must be your speakers. Don't hide them. They should be in boxes, carefully placed so that people have to walk around them. They should look crummy. A splintered, dirty speaker box means that there is a very expensive speaker inside and that the box was built for its acoustical properties, not for looks.

If you have a monaural system, it can be turned into an excellent stereo system merely by adding a second dummy speaker. A stereo set has two speakers, one on each side of the room. They should look alike. Run wires from each speaker to one of the other components, or into the books.

To make a speaker box, tack a piece of dark cloth tightly over a frame and then wedge a large embroidery hoop behind it so you can see a circular outline. To make a multiple-speaker box, put a series of one-pound coffee cans behind the cloth. The best-looking speakers have both large and small circles against the front cloth, and beer-glass marks on top. Each speaker should have a knob on the side. When somebody falls over the box, give a tight smile and spend several minutes with the knob "readjusting the balance."

Setting the proper volume is important. Music should be played just loudly enough so nobody can think. Properly distorted, music from one speaker sounds as if it's coming from ten. Put little wads of cotton deep in each ear before your guests arrive, turn the gain all the way up, and greet people while nodding and snapping your fingers. Everybody will know you've got a great music system. And you'll never have to worry about conversational lulls.

Study Questions

1. Is chronology an important factor in Williamson's essay? If not, to what extent is chronology involved in the procedure described? What factors other than time order determine the organization of the essay?
2. List the transitions which help to establish chronology in "Fake Fi."
3. What is Williamson's main-idea sentence? Where is it found in the essay?
4. How does the conclusion round off the essay? Does it add new material or does it relate mainly to the main-idea sentence?

Companion Planting   HARTLEY A. PFEIL

For many years, vegetable gardeners have been using poisonous sprays to control insect pests. Only recently have we begun to realize how much harm such sprays may cause: they kill beneficial insects such as bees and ladybugs as well as the pests they are supposed to kill; they cause long-range harm to birds, toads, and other garden helpers that feed on insects; and they may leave residues on the vegetables brought to the table, causing damage to human health as well. For these reasons, many gardeners are now learning to rely on natural biological means of controlling insect pests. One easy and completely safe way to limit the damage done by harmful insects is called companion planting, putting side by side in the garden certain different kinds of plants that actually help each other get rid of undesirable insects.

Companion planting can be started very early in the spring, with your first vegetable crops. As soon as the ground can be worked, vegetables that can stand some frost should be planted. Just when this planting time occurs depends on the climate where you live, but it is likely to be early April in New England and other states near the Canadian border, early March in the middle states, and early February in the South. Begin by setting out a double row of telephone peas, one row on each side of a chicken wire fence. Good hybrid varieties of seed do very well in humus-rich soil and are not subject to many diseases or predators except aphids. To discourage the aphids, plant onions, garlic, or chives in rows about two feet away from the peas. Use onion sets rather than seed, because the onion seed is slow to germinate, and you will want healthy, growing plants as soon as the nearby peas come up. The halitosis of the onions seems to drive aphids away from all nearby areas, so the pea plants will be well protected. You can take further advantage of your onion crop by planting lettuce, also frost-resistant but also subject to aphids, alongside the onion rows,

about eighteen inches away. These early crops will do very well together, and you can continue planting these particular companions at two-or-three-week intervals as long as the weather is cool.

In warmer weather, but while there is still some danger of frost, you can set out another plant companionship. Bush beans, either the green or the yellow wax variety, should be planted in company with potatoes. Both beans and potatoes can stand light frost while they are still young plants, so they can be started in late May in the northernmost states and earlier farther south. Somehow or other these plants protect each other. There are fewer Mexican bean beetles on the beans and fewer Colorado potato beetles on the potatoes where these crops grow side by side. Perhaps the adult beetles become confused and don't know where to lay their eggs.

A third companion planting, which must wait until the ground is warm and there is no danger of frost, involves four different kinds of plants. Begin with hills of cucumber or squash in a line along the center of a fairly large garden rectangle. For best results with these cucurbits, dig a hole six inches deep and work some well-rotted manure into the soil. Then fill up the hole until it is about three inches deep and scatter a few cucumber or squash seeds on the surface. Now cover with fine soil until the hole is only an inch deep. Radish seeds planted on top and covered with an inch of soil will come up quite soon, marking where the hills are. They will also drive away striped or spotted cucumber beetles, which do not like the smell of radishes. On each side of the cucumber or squash hills, plant a row of nasturtiums, and beyond the nasturtiums, set out your cabbage plants. Squash bugs and white cabbage butterflies are attracted to nasturtiums and will lay their eggs there instead of on the vegetable plants. Besides, you will have a supply of attractive flowers for your table; and, if your taste runs that way, you can make nasturtium leaf sandwiches for lunch. If you don't want all four of these plants in your garden, you can get good results with just radishes in the cucumber hills or nasturtiums near your cabbages.

These companion plantings will not give 100 percent protection against insect pests, but neither will sprays, unless you use extremely dangerous poisons and spray often and heavily. However, if you don't want the danger and disadvantages of poisonous sprays, try companion planting. Just put the proper vegetable companions together in your garden, and plant enough so that you can afford to share your crop with those few insect pests that still show up.

Study Questions

1. Which sentence in the essay is the main-idea sentence?
2. The writer states in his introduction that companion planting is an easy and safe way to grow vegetables. What part or parts of the essay lead to the idea that it is safe and what parts support the idea that it is easy?
3. The chronology of this essay is fairly complex since it involves the

chronology of both time (the season's progress) and labor (the planting process). Show how the writer successfully manages his organization so that there are no lapses in chronology.

How to Get Things Done   ROBERT BENCHLEY

A great many people have come up to me and asked me how I manage to get
so much work done and still keep looking so dissipated. My answer is "Don't
you wish you knew?" and a pretty good answer it is, too, when you consider
that nine times out of ten I didn't hear the original question.

But the fact remains that hundreds of thousands of people throughout the
country are wondering how I have time to do all my painting, engineering,
writing and philanthropic work when, according to the rotogravure sections
and society notes I spend all my time riding to hounds, going to fancy-dress
balls disguised as Louis XIV or spelling out GREETINGS TO CALIFORNIA in formation with three thousand Los Angeles school children. "All work and all play,"
they say.

The secret of my incredible energy and efficiency in getting work done is a
simple one. I have based it very deliberately on a well-known psychological
principle and have refined it so that it is now almost *too* refined. I shall have
to begin coarsening it up again pretty soon.

The psychological principle is this: anyone can do any amount of work,
provided it isn't the work he is *supposed* to be doing at that moment.

Let us see how this works out in practice. Let us say that I have five things
which have to be done before the end of the week: (1) a basketful of letters to
be answered, some of them dating from October, 1928 (2) some bookshelves
to be put up and arranged with books (3) a hair-cut to get (4) a pile of scientific
magazines to go through and clip (I am collecting all references to tropical fish
that I can find, with the idea of some day buying myself one) and (5) an article
to write for this paper.

Now. With these five tasks staring me in the face on Monday morning,
it is little wonder that I go right back to bed as soon as I have had breakfast,
in order to store up health and strength for the almost superhuman expenditure of energy that is to come. *Mens sana in corpore sano* is my motto, and,
not even to be funny, am I going to make believe that I don't know what the
Latin means. I feel that the least that I can do is to treat my body right when
it has to supply fuel for an insatiable mind like mine.

"How to Get Things Done" by Robert C. Benchley, from *The Benchley Roundup*.
Selected by Nathaniel Benchley. Copyright 1930 by Chicago Tribune–New York News
Syndicate, Inc. Reprinted by permission of Harper & Row, Publishers, Inc.

As I lie in bed on Monday morning storing up strength, I make out a schedule. "What do I have to do first?" I ask myself. Well, those letters really should be answered and the pile of scientific magazines should be clipped. And here is where my secret process comes in. Instead of putting them first on the list of things which have to be done, I put them last. I practice a little deception on myself and say, "First you must write that article for the newspaper." I even say this out loud (being careful that nobody hears me, otherwise they would *keep* me in bed) and try to fool myself into really believing that I must do the article that day and that the other things can wait. I sometimes go so far in this self-deception as to make out a list in pencil, with "No. 1. Newspaper article" underlined in red. (The underlining in red is rather difficult, as there is never a red pencil on the table beside the bed, unless I have taken one to bed with me on Sunday night.)

Then, when everything is lined up, I bound out of bed and have lunch. I find that a good, heavy lunch, with some sort of glutinous dessert, is good preparation for the day's work as it keeps one from getting nervous and excitable. We workers must keep cool and calm, otherwise we would just throw away our time in jumping about and fidgeting.

I then seat myself at my desk with my typewriter before me, and sharpen five pencils. (The sharp pencils are for poking holes in the desk-blotter, and a pencil has to be pretty sharp to do that. I find that I can't get more than six holes out of one pencil.) Following this I say to myself (again out loud, if it is practical), "Now, old man! Get at this article!"

Gradually the scheme begins to work. My eye catches the pile of magazines, which I have artfully placed on a nearby table beforehand. I write my name and address at the top of the sheet of paper in the typewriter and then sink back. The magazines being within reach (also part of the plot) I look to see if anyone is watching me and get one off the top of the pile. Hello, what's this! In the very first one is an article by Dr. William Beebe, illustrated by horrifying photographs! Pushing my chair away from my desk, I am soon hard at work clipping.

One of the interesting things about the *Argyopelius*, or "Silver Hatchet" fish, I find, is that it has eyes in its wrists. I would have been sufficiently surprised just to find out that a fish had wrists, but to learn that it has eyes in them is a discovery so astounding that I am hardly able to cut out the picture. What a lot one learns simply by thumbing through the illustrated weeklies! It is hard work, though, and many a weaker spirit would give it up half-done, but when there is something else of "more importance" to be finished (you see, I still keep up the deception, letting myself go on thinking that the newspaper article is of more importance) no work is too hard or too onerous to keep one busy.

Thus, before the afternoon is half over, I have gone through the scientific magazines and have a neat pile of clippings (including one of a Viper Fish which I wish you could see. You would die laughing). Then it is back to the grind of the newspaper article.

This time I get as far as the title, which I write down with considerable satisfaction until I find that I have misspelled one word terribly, so that the whole sheet of paper has to come out and a fresh one be inserted. As I am doing this, my eye catches the basket of letters.

Now, if there is one thing that I hate to do (and there is, you may be sure) it is to write letters. But somehow, with the magazine article before me waiting to be done, I am seized with an epistolary fervor that amounts to a craving, and I slyly sneak the first of the unanswered letters out of the basket. I figure out in my mind that I will get more into the swing of writing the article if I practice a little on a few letters. This first one, anyway, I really must answer. True, it is from a friend in Antwerp asking me to look him up when I am in Europe in the summer of 1929, so he can't actually be watching the incoming boats for an answer, but I owe something to politeness after all. So instead of putting a fresh sheet of copy-paper into the typewriter, I slip in one of my handsome bits of personal stationery and dash off a note to my friend in Antwerp. Then, being well in the letter-writing mood, I clean up the entire batch. I feel a little guilty about the article, but the pile of freshly stamped envelopes and the neat bundle of clippings on tropical fish do much to salve my conscience. Tomorrow I will do the article, and no fooling this time, either.

When tomorrow comes I am up with one of the older and more sluggish larks. A fresh sheet of copy-paper in the machine, and my name and address neatly printed at the top, and all before 11:00 A.M.! "A human dynamo" is the name I think up for myself. I have decided to write something about snake-charming and am already more than satisfied with the title "These Snake-Charming People." But, in order to write about snake-charming, one has to know a little about its history, and where should one go to find history but to a book? Maybe in that pile of books in the corner is one on snake-charming! Nobody could point the finger of scorn at me if I went over to those books for the avowed purpose of research work for the matter at hand. No writer could be supposed to carry all that information in his head.

So, with a perfectly clear conscience, I leave my desk for a few minutes and begin glancing over the titles of the books. Of course, it is difficult to find any book, much less one on snake-charming, in a pile which has been standing in the corner for weeks. What really is needed is for them to be on a shelf where their titles will be visible at a glance. And there is the shelf, standing beside the pile of books! It seems almost like a divine command written in the sky: "If you want to finish that article, first put up the shelf and arrange the books on it!" Nothing could be clearer or more logical.

In order to put up the shelf, the laws of physics have decreed that there must be nails, a hammer and some sort of brackets to hold it up on the wall. You can't just wet a shelf with your tongue and stick it up. And, as there are no nails or brackets in the house (or, if there are, they are probably hidden somewhere) the next thing to do is put on my hat and go out to buy them. Much as it disturbs me to put off the actual start of the article, I feel that I am doing only what is in the line of duty to put on my hat and go out to buy nails and brackets. And, as I put on my hat, I realize to my chagrin that I need a hair-cut badly. I can kill two birds with one stone, or at least with two, and stop in at the barber's on the way back. I will feel all the more like writing after a turn in the fresh air. Any doctor would tell me that.

So in a few hours I return, spick and span and smelling of lilac, bearing nails, brackets, the evening papers and some crackers and peanut butter. Then it's ho! for a quick snack and a glance through the evening papers (there might be something in them which would alter what I was going to write about snake-charming) and in no time at all the shelf is up, slightly crooked but up, and the books are arranged in a neat row in alphabetical order and all ready for almost instantaneous reference. There does not happen to be one on snake-charming among them, but there is a very interesting one containing some Hogarth prints and one which will bear even closer inspection dealing with the growth of the Motion Picture, illustrated with "stills" from famous productions. A really remarkable industry, the motion pictures. I might want to write an article on it sometime. Not today, probably, for it is six o'clock and there is still the one on snake-charming to finish up first. Tomorrow morning sharp! Yes, *sir!*

And so, you see, in two days I have done four of the things I had to do, simply by making believe that it was the fifth that I *must* do. And the next day, I fix up something else, like taking down the bookshelf and putting it somewhere else, that I *have* to do, and then I get the fifth one done.

The only trouble is that, at this rate, I will soon run out of things to do, and will be forced to get at that newspaper article the first thing Monday morning.

Study Questions

1. Benchley's introduction seems to serve at least two purposes. Considering what the introduction accomplishes, as the reader what would you suggest these purposes are?
2. Is Benchley's main-idea statement clearly stated in the essay or is it implied? Find the main-idea sentence if there is one, or write what you would consider to be a complete main-idea sentence for the essay.
3. "How to Get Things Done" humorously details a system for getting work accomplished, utilizing a chronological organization. What are the steps Benchley first outlines? What are the steps he follows in the essay?
4. What transitional words or phrases does Benchley use to establish chronology? List examples of how he also establishes chronology by devices other than transitions.

How to Catch a Witch
CHADWICK HANSEN

If Lawson, like Cotton Mather with the Goodwin children, thought prayer a more certain cure for witchcraft than anything the magistrates might do, it was partly because it was so difficult to catch a witch. She would not, after all, sign her pact with Satan on Main Street in broad daylight, nor practice her black arts there. Witchcraft was by its nature secret, and hard to be found out. Yet witches had been caught, and many examples were a matter of record, as were many theories on catching them.

There were, to begin with, commonly recognized grounds for investigation. If an apparition was appearing to the citizenry and afflicting them, one would surely want to investigate the person represented in that apparition. One would also look for evidence of malice, since witchcraft was an expression of ultimate malice, the diametrical opposite to Christian charity. And one could hope that an investigation would produce credible confessions. Confessions were often easy to obtain, particularly if one used the technique of "cross and swift questions" recommended by virtually all authorities from *Malleus Maleficarum* to Cotton Mather, but it was not always easy to judge whether they were credible. Satan was the Prince of Lies and witches were his servants; the word of confessed witches was therefore suspect in their accusations both of others and themselves. Furthermore, it was known that desperate persons had sometimes confessed to witchcraft as a bizarre means of committing suicide. And the mentally disturbed had also been known to imagine themselves witches and confess. In spite of all these difficulties, however, confession was often the best evidence one could hope for.

More concrete evidence was occasionally to be had. A diligent search, for example, might turn up some of the tools of the witch's trade: images with pins on them, ointments and potions, books of instruction in the magical arts. And one could search the body of the accused for the so-called Devil's Mark. It was believed that when a pact was made the Devil placed upon the witch's body a piece of flesh from which He, in His own person or that of a familiar, might suck the blood of the witch. (The blood has traditionally been thought to be the carrier of the spirit; in sucking blood the Devil was feeding on the witch's soul.) Since this "witch's tit" was created by the Devil rather than by God it lacked the warmth of normal flesh (hence the still-current expression about being cold as a witch's tit). It also lacked sensation, and one could test for that by running a pin through it to see whether it was a genuinely preternatural excrescence or only a wart or a hemorrhoid.

This "pricking" as a test for witchcraft sometimes had a kind of rough validity, as the psychologist Pierre Janet observed. Witches were often hysterics, like their victims, and one common symptom of hysteria is local anesthesia,

particularly if the limits of the anesthetic area make no sense in terms of nerve structure. Thus both Charcot and Janet probed for anesthetic areas in testing for hysteria, and Janet remarked that

> in our clinics, we are somewhat like the [medieval] woman who sought for witches. We blindfold the subject, we turn his head away, rub his skin with our nail, prick it suddenly with a hidden pin, watch his answers or starts of pain; the picture has not changed.[1]

Yet pricking for the Devil's Mark was most haphazard and uncertain. It was common for examiners, physicians included, to disagree over whether an excrescence was natural or prenatural. And it was not unheard of for them to find what they thought to be a Devil's Mark on one occasion, only to discover that there was nothing left of it but a piece of dried skin on a second examination.

The common people believed in a number of tests for witches. The best known was the water-ordeal, in which the suspect was bound and "swum": thrown into or dragged by a rope through the nearest body of water. If she floated she was a witch; the water was rejecting her as she had rejected Christian baptism. If she sank, she was innocent; the mob would try to drag her out before she drowned and profess to be sorry if they failed. (It *was* generally mob-action when a witch was swum; the courts seldom countenanced it, even when the accused requested it as a means of proving her innocence.)

Another such test was asking the accused to repeat the Lord's Prayer. It was believed that a witch could not say it correctly, even after prompting, since she regularly said it backwards at her witches' Sabbaths. It was also believed that a witch could not weep. Because she had rejected Christian charity in favor of demonic malice she would remain dry-eyed at the most heart-rending spectacles. Many of the learned, including Increase Mather and Deodat Lawson, rejected such tests outright as superstitions or as white magic or both. Others, like Cotton Mather, were willing to countenance experiments with them but refused to accept them as certain evidence.

There was one test for witchcraft that had a wide following among the learned as well as the common people. This was a kind of laying-on-of-hands in which the suspected person was made to touch an afflicted person in the midst of a fit. If the touch seemed to cure, the theory was that the spell had been taken back into the body of the witch from whom it came. Laying-on-of-hands, is, of course, one of the commonest kinds of faith-healing. It was practiced by Christ, and anyone who wishes to can watch it being practiced on television today by an evangelist with the surprising name of Oral Roberts. When the disease is psychosomatic and the sick person believes in the power of the healer there is no question that laying-on-of-hands frequently works. As a test for witchcraft it had been admitted as valid evidence by no less a person than Sir Matthew Hale, Chief Baron of the Exchequer, who presided at the witchcraft trial at Bury St. Edmunds in 1664 (where Sir Thomas Browne provided the expert medical opinion noted in the first chapter). Cotton Mather

[1] Pierre Janet, *The Major Symptoms of Hysteria* (New York, 1907), p. 273.

tells us that the accounts of this trial were "much considered by the judges of New England."[2]

All things considered, however, it was clearly more difficult to prove witchcraft than to prove most other crimes. It is hardly surprising that the Reverend Deodat Lawson thought prayer more efficacious than the law.

Study Questions

1. While a directions essay has a built-in chronology, a process paper generally requires imposing a chronology on the material based on an intellectual decision concerning the order of that process. What order has Hansen decided is most chronological?
2. To which step in the process of catching a witch does Hansen devote the most space? Why?
3. The essay begins and ends with references to Rev. Deodat Lawson, the writer of two books, *Brief and True Narrative* and *Christ's Fidelity: The Only Shield Against Satan's Malignity*, both published in 1692, and to Rev. Cotton Mather, who published *The Wonders of the Invisible World* in 1693. How do these references move the essay beyond a description of the process of catching a witch to argument? What has Hansen "proved"?

[2]Cotton Mather, *The Wonders of the Invisible World* (Boston, 1693), p. 83.

Be Your Own Interpreter   JACOB ORNSTEIN

"I'd like to learn a foreign language but I'm just no good at it." Thanks to this bromide, tens of thousands of Americans are denying themselves the benefits of learning and knowing a second language. And as a result, a language barrier complicates our international relations, and prevents Americans abroad from establishing friendly person-to-person contacts. In the Soviet Union, for example, no less than 10 million persons of all ages are studying English, while in our colleges less than 5,000 students are learning Russian.

There has been, of course, a genuine boom, since World War II, in textbook sales and in private and public school enrollments in foreign language courses. Despite this thousands of individuals remain eager to join the language march but hesitate because they lack confidence.

Reprinted by permission from *Think*, February 1960, pp. 29–31.

For these potential do-it-yourselfers there is a practical plan of language mastery. First of all, they have to get rid of certain misconceptions. One of the most deadly of these is that Americans are by nature poor at languages. This is nonsense. There is no RH factor predisposing Americans or anyone else to being linguistic ignoramuses.

Another harmful myth is that it is impossible to learn a language without living in the country where it is spoken. Desirable though this may be, it is not essential. One of the very best linguists I have ever met had lived all his life in the Pittsburgh area and had never been west of Gary, Indiana. He learned to speak eight languages so convincingly that he was often mistaken for a native by various nationalities. As an insurance agent, he also found that his hobby paid off handsomely in an increased volume of sales.

Another old chestnut is the I'm-too-old-to-learn-a-language routine. When told this, my favorite rejoinder is to cite the case of Queen Victoria, who learned Hindustani in her seventies.

And still another misconception is that only geniuses can hope to become linguists. As a matter of fact, persons of extreme brilliance sometimes do poorly at languages, while others of average IQ achieve impressive results.

Finally, let's dispose of the allegation that linguistic study is only for millionaires. About all you need is ten dollars for some books and a phonograph record, a pencil, paper—and the time and inclination. Now that we've cleared up these misconceptions, it is time to offer a simple aptitude test to determine fitness for language study. If you answer four out of the five following questions

affirmatively you may consider yourself a potentially satisfactory student.

(1) Are you of at least average intelligence? (2) Do you have the normal ability to remember? (3) Have you a genuine desire to learn a foreign language? (4) Are you willing to spend at least fifteen minutes a day in language study? (5) Do you have enough stick-to-itiveness to keep trying when the novelty has worn off and results seem slow?

Nine chances out of ten, you have passed the test and are ready to enroll in the Do-It-Yourself College of Linguistic Knowledge.

First comes the matter of choosing a language. The choice is incredibly wide. There are no less than 2,800 languages in the world, ranging from Mandarin Chinese, spoken by about 300 million persons, to Wichita, the tongue of an Indian tribe of 500 members in Oklahoma. Unless you have a special reason for doing otherwise, it is best to choose a language of international importance.

Among the "easiest" are Spanish, Italian, French, Portuguese, German, Dutch, Norwegian, Swedish, and Danish.

Among the "moderately difficult" are Russian, Polish, Czech, Bulgarian, Serbo-Croatian, Hungarian, Finnish, Turkish, Indonesian, and Gaelic.

How long will it take to gain a working knowledge of one of these? For the "easiest" category, the learner should allow a minimum of six months. This means acquiring an active vocabulary of about 1,000 words and being able to recognize another 1,000. With these and a knowledge of the rudiments of grammar, you should have little trouble carrying on a simple conversation on everyday topics and reading a newspaper with the aid of a dictionary. For the moderately difficult group, increase the time by one third.

You are now ready to procure your working tools. The basic do-it-yourself kit should include: a pronunciation record, a grammar or manual, a dictionary, a phrase book, and a reader. In selecting the reader it is best to choose a book containing present-day short stories and light selections on daily life in the country whose language you are studying. Classical masterpieces should be reserved for a more advanced stage of learning.

While no hard and fast rules can be given regarding length of study periods, it will be found that short periods at frequent intervals are far superior to long stretches, no matter how intensive, at widely spaced intervals. Fifteen minutes to one hour, six days a week, is an excellent program.

Step One: Learn the Symbols and the Sounds

The introduction to most manuals provides a description of the sounds of the language. This has to be used with caution as the symbols of most languages, or the alphabet, give only a partial idea of the exact pronunciation. Your best bet is to imitate painstakingly the voice on the pronunciation record. This is precisely the way a child learns to pronounce—by aping what he hears his parents say.

In practicing pronunciation, it is good to make full use of the principle of contrast. In every language there are sounds and words almost exactly alike, except for one distinguishing feature. Make special lists of words which are very similar except for one distinguishing sound, and devote extra drill to them. For example, in studying Spanish, pay special attention to words like *pero* and *perro.* The first of these, pronounced with only one roll or trill of the tip of the tongue, means *but,* while the second, uttered with two or three trills, is the Spanish word for *dog.*

Step Two: Acquire Vocabulary, the Building Blocks of Language

Words are the minimum units of human communication. There is no sacrosanct way of learning them, and each person is to a large extent free to plan his own strategy of vocabulary mastery. Whichever procedure he follows, he will succeed if he makes the learning as active an experience as possible.

Set yourself a goal of, perhaps, forty words a week, exceeding but never falling below this. These words will be found in the vocabulary portion of each lesson and may be supplemented by the use of the dictionary.

Since learning a language depends heavily on repetition you can use your ingenuity to invent ways to add variety and zest to this process. One very effective device, used extensively by Army and Navy students of Oriental languages during World War II, is the flash card idea. Obtain a supply of 3 × 5 cards. On one side, enter the English word; on the other, write the foreign language equivalent. If you are an amateur artist, sketch in the object or idea which the word suggests.

These cards help you to make use of odd moments while waiting for a bus, in the doctor's office, cooking a roast, or in thousands of other similar situations. Bombard your consciousness with language stimuli. Post linguistic pin-ups, consisting of words which you have difficulty in remembering, in various rooms —your kitchen, bedroom, and bathroom.

In learning vocabulary, it is helpful also to employ the principle of contrast by drawing up lists of words of opposite meanings. Here, too, the flash cards with accompanying drawings are useful.

Step Three: Know the Traffic Rules

The word "grammar" is about as popular as five-o'clock shadow. Unfortunately, dull and uninspired methods of teaching have made it a bugaboo. Actually, the rules needed for most languages can be presented on a page or two of charts. However, unless you know these rules of usage, you cannot drive along the foreign language highway.

Read each rule carefully to understand the principle involved, examine the illustrative sentences given, and commit to memory one of the sentences in which the functioning of the rule is particularly clear. Next, drive the principle home by working the exercises which the book gives. Substitution drill is a device which adds impact to this task. It consists merely of substituting words for those given in the book.

In studying French, for example, let us assume that the student encounters the sentence, *Mon père est allé au cinéma.* (My father went to the movies.) He can first substitute *venu* (came) for *allé* (went), and replace the *au* (to the) by *du* (from the), to form the new sentence, *Mon père est venu du cinéma.* (My father came from the movies.)

The flash-card principle is useful here, too. A series of closely related sentences can be written on each card, with "action" sketches to aid in their learning.

Step Four: Start Communicating; Speak and Read Whole Sentences

People everywhere, be it in Iran, Cambodia, or Spain, speak not in isolated words but in entire sentences. Again, the child's approach is useful. Children first learn a small number of simple but useful sentences, and by substituting and adding words they come to express the basic notions of everyday living. Similarly, you need to master actively a supply of basic sentences, which you will modify in hundreds of ways to increase your range of expressions.

Each lesson of your manual contains a number of basic sentences which you can supplement by sentences from your phrase book. First read each sentence to make sure of its meaning, then repeat it until you can reproduce it with little or no hesitation. The late Leonard Bloomfield, dean of American linguists, once commented to the effect that "All language learning is over-learning. Anything else is sheer nonsense."

Step Five: Read for Added Word Power

Reading is one of the most rewarding and yet most neglected activities in the language game. It will entertain you and at the same time increase your vocabulary and help fix in your mind the working rules of grammar.

In reading, you will find the meanings of unfamiliar words in the vocabulary at the end of the reader, or in the dictionary. Do not try to remember all the new words, but only note those words which you consider most important in a to-be-remembered list.

A particularly useful and inexpensive addition to the reader is a foreign language newspaper. A large number of these are published right in this country, or overseas subscription is possible. The front page is the best starting point, as it gives you news which should already be familiar to you from the English language radio and press.

Step Six: Operation "Recap"

As a do-it-yourself you must be your own drill sergeant. Since language learning involves so much detail, recapitulation or "recap" is of special importance. A good rule of thumb is to review after each five lessons.

Devise some simple tests for yourself or your family circle. Make up a vocabulary quiz with twenty words. Take off five points for each item missed. You don't like your score? Then copy out the words missed and give them additional drill.

Pick out ten basic sentences, put them into English and see if you can repeat them with no major errors. If not, the prescription is more repetition.

Step Seven: Go Social; Cultivate Linguistic Conviviality

Languages are meant to be spoken, and the sooner you put your new-found knowledge to the test the better. In most large cities there are various types of language clubs.

Join such a club or start one yourself. The club meetings can include a brief talk by a native speaker, followed by a social hour with refreshments and the chance to engage in chit-chat in the foreign tongue. Real zest is also added by playing records and singing songs in the language.

Other auxiliary activities with social possibilities include the viewing of foreign films and individual or group listening to short-wave radio broadcasts.

These social and extra-curricular activities will help you add a fourth dimension to language study, orienting you to the dynamics of foreign cultures and enabling you to penetrate the subtle complex of forces often described as the spirit of a people.

Now that you have gained a practical working knowledge of a foreign language and have some understanding of a foreign culture as well, you are ready to join that elite corps of Americans who are not tongue-tied once they leave our monolingual shores.

And if you are the quiet, retiring type who does not shuttle between Capetown and San Francisco, but prefers to settle down with a good book every weekend, your gift is far from wasted. You will not need to be told that *mucho dinero* means not "much dinner" but "much money." And when one of the characters of the novel uses the term *hors de combat* you will know that this does not refer to a "combat horse" but means "out of commission." Or if someone looks into your eyes and says, *Je t'adore*, you'll know that it definitely does not mean "Shut the door."

Study Questions

1. Many directions or process essays contain little or no introduction. Support Ornstein's use of a very lengthy introduction. Is it effective? Is it necessary? Explain the reasons for your answers.
2. How does Ornstein use chronological arrangement?
3. Discuss the chronology of the directions Ornstein gives. Is there a strict chronology in the process of language learning as he describes it? Could the steps be presented in a different order? Explain.
4. In his introduction, the author appeals to persons who want to understand a foreign language in order to make traveling more beneficial. His conclusion, however, is concerned mainly with the advantages of knowing a language for those who will never travel. Explain why you do or do not consider this change of appeal a flaw in the essay.

Rules by Which a Great Empire
May Be Reduced to a Small One   BENJAMIN FRANKLIN

An ancient Sage boasted, that, tho' he could not fiddle, he knew how to make a *great city* of a *little one*. The science that I, a modern simpleton, am about to communicate, is the very reverse.

I address myself to all ministers who have the management of extensive dominions, which from their very greatness are become troublesome to govern, because the multiplicity of their affairs leaves no time for *fiddling*.

I. In the first place, gentlemen, you are to consider, that a great empire, like a great cake, is most easily diminished at the edges. Turn your attention, therefore, first to your *remotest* provinces; that, as you get rid of them, the next may follow in order.

II. That the possibility of this separation may always exist, take special care the provinces are never incorporated with the mother country; that they do not enjoy the same common rights, the same privileges in commerce; and that they are governed by *severer* laws, all of *your enacting,* without allowing them any share in the choice of the legislators. By carefully making and preserving such distinctions, you will (to keep to my simile of the cake) act like a wise gingerbread-baker, who, to facilitate a division, cuts his dough half through in those places where, when baked, he would have it *broken to pieces.*

III. Those remote provinces have perhaps been acquired, purchased, or conquered, at the *sole expence* of the settlers, or their ancestors, without the aid of the mother country. If this should happen to increase her *strength*, by their growing numbers, ready to join in her wars; her *commerce*, by their growing demand for her manufactures; or her *naval power*, by greater employment for her ships and seamen, they may probably suppose some merit in this, and that it entitles them to some favour; you are therefore to *forget it all, or resent it,* as if they had done you injury. If they happen to be zealous whigs, friends of liberty, nurtured in revolution principles, *remember all that* to their prejudice, and resolve to punish it; for such principles, after a revolution is thoroughly established, are of *no more use*; they are even *odious* and *abominable.*

IV. However peaceably your colonies have submitted to your government, shewn their affection to your interests, and patiently borne their grievances; you are to *suppose* them always inclined to revolt, and treat them accordingly. Quarter troops among them, who by their insolence may *provoke* the rising of mobs, and by their bullets and bayonets *suppress* them. By this means, like the husband who uses his wife ill *from suspicion*, you may in time convert your *suspicions* into *realities.*

V. Remote provinces must have *Governors* and *Judges,* to represent the Royal Person, and execute everywhere the delegated parts of his office and authority. You ministers know, that much of the strength of government depends on the *opinion* of the people; and much of that opinion on the *choice of rulers placed* immediately over them. If you send them wise and good men for governors, who study the interest of the colonists, and advance their prosperity, they will think their King wise and good, and that he wishes the welfare of his subjects. If you send them learned and upright men for Judges, they will think him a lover of justice. This may attach your provinces more to his government. You are therefore to be careful whom you recommend for those offices. If you can find prodigals, who have ruined their fortunes, broken gamesters or stock-jobbers, these may do well as *governors;* for they will probably be rapacious, and provoke the people by their extortions. Wrangling proctors and pettifog-ging lawyers, too, are not amiss; for they will be for ever disputing and quarrelling with their little parliaments. If withal they should be ignorant, wrong-headed, and insolent, so much the better. Attornies' clerks and Newgate solicitors will do for *Chief Justices,* especially if they hold their places *during your pleasure;* and all will contribute to impress those ideas of your govern-ment, that are proper for a people *you would wish to renounce it.*

VI. To confirm these impressions, and strike them deeper, whenever the injured come to the capital with complaints of mal-administration, oppression, or injustice, punish such suitors with long delay, enormous expence, and a final judgment in favour of the oppressor. This will have an admirable effect every way. The trouble of future complaints will be prevented, and Governors and Judges will be encouraged to farther acts of oppression and injustice; and thence the people may become more disaffected, and at length desperate.

VII. When such Governors have crammed their coffers, and made them-selves so odious to the people that they can no longer remain among them, with safety to their persons, *recall and reward* them with pensions. You may make them *baronets* too, if that respectable order should not think fit to resent it. All will contribute to encourage new governors in the same practice, and make the supreme government, *detestable.*

VIII. If, when you are engaged in war, your colonies should vie in liberal aids of men and money against the common enemy, upon your simple requisi-tion, and give far beyond their abilities, reflect that a penny taken from them by your power is more honourable to you, than a pound presented by their benevolence; despise therefore their voluntary grants, and resolve to harass them with novel taxes. They will probably complain to your parliaments, that they are taxed by a body in which they have no representative, and that this is contrary to common right. They will petition for redress. Let the Parliaments flout their claims, reject their petitions, refuse even to suffer the reading of them, and treat the petitioners with the utmost contempt. Nothing can have a better effect in producing the alienation proposed; for though many can forgive injuries, *none ever forgave contempt.*

IX. In laying these taxes, never regard the heavy burthens those remote people already undergo, in defending their own frontiers, supporting their own provincial governments, making new roads, building bridges, churches, and other public edifices, which in old countries have been done to your hands by your ancestors, but which occasion constant calls and demands on the purses of a new people. Forget the *restraints* you lay on their trade for *your own* benefit, and the advantage a *monopoly* of this trade gives your exacting mer-chants. Think nothing of the wealth those merchants and your manufacturers acquire by the colony commerce; their encreased ability thereby to pay taxes at home; their accumulating, in the price of their commodities, most of those taxes, and so levying them from their consuming customers; all this, and the employment and support of thousands of your poor by the colonists, you are *intirely to forget*. But remember to make your arbitrary tax more grievous to your provinces, by public declarations importing that your power of taxing them has *no limits;* so that when you take from them without their consent one shilling in the pound, you have a clear right to the other nineteen. This will probably weaken every idea of *security in their property*, and convince them, that under such a government they *have nothing they can call their own;* which can scarce fail of producing the *happiest consequence!*

X. Possibly, indeed, some of them might still comfort themselves, and say, "Though we have no property, we have yet *something* left that is valuable; we have constitutional *liberty*, both of person and of conscience. This King, these Lords, and these Commons, who it seems are too remote from us to know us, and feel for us, cannot take from us our *Habeas Corpus* right, or our right of trial *by a jury of our neighbours;* they cannot deprive us of the exercise of our religion, alter our ecclesiastical constitution, and compel us to be Papists, if they please, or Mahometans." To annihilate this comfort, begin by laws to perplex their commerce with infinite regulations, impossible to be remembered and observed; ordain seizures of their property for every failure; take away the trial of such property by Jury, and give it to arbitrary Judges of your own appointing, and of the lowest characters in the country, whose salaries and emoluments are to arise out of the duties or condemnations, and whose appointments are *during pleasure*. Then let there be a formal declaration of both Houses, that opposition to your edicts is *treason,* and that any person suspected of treason in the provinces may, according to some obsolete law, be seized and sent to the metropolis of the empire for trial; and pass an act, that those there charged with certain other offences, shall be sent away in chains from their friends and country to be tried in the same manner for felony. Then erect a new Court of Inquisition among them, accompanied by an armed force, with instructions to transport all such suspected persons; to be ruined by the expence, if they bring over evidences to prove their innocence, or be found guilty and hanged, if they cannot afford it. And, lest the people should think you cannot possibly go any farther, pass another solemn declaratory act, "that King, Lords, Commons had, hath, and of right ought to have, full power and authority to make statutes of sufficient force and validity to bind the unrepresented provinces IN ALL CASES WHATSOEVER." This will include *spiritual* with temporal, and, taken together, must operate wonderfully to your purpose; by convincing them, that they are at present under a power something like that spoken of in the scriptures, which can not only *kill their bodies,* but *damn their souls* to all eternity, by compelling them, if it pleases, *to worship the Devil.*

XI. To make your taxes more odious, and more likely to procure resistance, send from the capital a board of officers to superintend the collection, composed of the most *indiscreet, ill-bred,* and *insolent* you can find. Let these have large salaries out of the extorted revenue, and live in open, grating luxury upon the sweat and blood of the industrious; whom they are to worry continually with groundless and expensive prosecutions before the abovementioned arbitrary revenue Judges; *all at the cost of the party prosecuted,* tho' acquitted, because *the King is to pay no costs.* Let these men, *by your order,* be exempted from all the common taxes and burthens of the province, though they and their property are protected by its laws. If any revenue officers are *suspected* of the least tenderness for the people, discard them. If others are justly complained of, protect and reward them. If any of the under officers behave so as to provoke the people to drub them, promote those to better offices: this will encourage others to procure for themselves such profitable drubbings, by multiplying and enlarging such provocations, and *all will work towards the end you aim at.*

XII. Another way to make your tax odious, is to misapply the produce of it. If it was originally appropriated for the *defence* of the provinces, the better support of government, and the administration of justice, where it may be *necessary,* then apply none of it to that *defence,* but bestow it where it is *not necessary,* in augmented salaries or pensions to every governor, who has distinguished himself by his enmity to the people, and by calumniating them to their sovereign. This will make them pay it more unwillingly, and be more apt to quarrel with those that collect it and those that imposed it, who will quarrel again with them, and all shall contribute to your *main purpose,* of making them *weary of your government.*

XIII. If the people of any province have been accustomed to support their own Governors and Judges to satisfaction, you are to apprehend that such Governors and Judges may be thereby influenced to treat the people kindly, and to do them justice. This is another reason for applying part of that revenue in larger salaries to such Governors and Judges, given, as their commissions are, *during your pleasure* only; forbidding them to take any salaries from their provinces; that thus the people may no longer hope any kindness from their Governors, or (in Crown cases) any justice from their Judges. And, as the money thus misapplied in one province is extorted from all, probably *all will resent the misapplication.*

XIV. If the parliaments of your provinces should dare to claim rights, or complain of your administration, order them to be harassed with *repeated dissolutions.* If the same men are continually returned by new elections, adjourn their meetings to some country village, where they cannot be accommodated, and there keep them *during pleasure;* for this, you know, is your PREROGATIVE; and an excellent one it is, as you may manage it to promote discontents among the people, diminish their respect, and *increase their disaffection.*

XV. Convert the brave, honest officers of your *navy* into pimping tidewaiters and colony officers of the *customs.* Let those, who in time of war fought gallantly in defence of the commerce of their countrymen, in peace be taught to prey upon it. Let them learn to be corrupted by great and real smugglers; but (to shew their diligence) scour with armed boats every bay, harbour, river, creek, cove, or nook throughout the coast of your colonies; stop and detain every coaster, every wood-boat, every fisherman, tumble their cargoes and even their ballast inside out and upside down; and, if a penn'orth of pins is found un-entered, let the whole be seized and confiscated. Thus shall the trade of your colonists suffer more from their friends in time of peace, than it did from their enemies in war. Then let these boats crews land upon every farm in their way, rob the orchards, steal the pigs and the poultry, and insult the inhabitants. If the injured and exasperated farmers, unable to procure other justice, should attack the aggressors, drub them, and burn their boats; you are to call this *high treason and rebellion*, order fleets and armies into their country, and threaten to carry all the offenders three thousand miles to be hanged, drawn, and quartered. *O! this will work admirably!*

XVI. If you are told of discontents in your colonies, never believe that they are general, or that you have given occasion for them; therefore do not think of applying any remedy, or of changing any offensive measure. Redress no grievance, lest they should be encouraged to demand the redress of some other grievance. Grant no request that is just and reasonable, lest they should make another that is unreasonable. Take all your informations of the state of the colonies from your Governors and officers in enmity with them. Encourage and reward these *leasing-makers*; secrete their lying accusations, lest they should be confuted; but act upon them as the clearest evidence; and believe nothing you hear from the friends of the people: suppose all *their* complaints to be invented and promoted by a few factious demagogues, whom if you could catch and hang, all would be quiet. Catch and hang a few of them accordingly; and the *blood of the Martyrs* shall *work miracles* in favour of your purpose.

XVII. If you see *rival nations* rejoicing at the prospect of your disunion with your provinces, and endeavouring to promote it; if they translate, publish, and applaud all the complaints of your discontented colonists, at the same time privately stimulating you to severer measures, let not that *alarm* or offend you. Why should it, since you all mean *the same thing?*

XVIII. If any colony should at their own charge erect a fortress to secure their port against the fleets of a foreign enemy, get your Governor to betray that fortress into your hands. Never think of paying what it cost the country, for that would look, at least, like some regard for justice; but turn it into a citadel to awe the inhabitants and curb their commerce. If they should have lodged in such fortress the very arms they bought and used to aid you in your conquests, seize them all; it will provoke like *ingratitude* added to *robbery*. One admirable effect of these operations will be, to discourage every other colony from erecting such defences, and so your enemies may more easily invade them; to the great disgrace of your government, and of course *the furtherance of your project.*

XIX. Send armies into their country under pretence of protecting the inhabitants; but, instead of garrisoning the forts on their frontiers with those troops, to prevent incursions, demolish those forts, and order the troops into the heart of the country, that the savages may be encouraged to attack the frontiers, and that the troops may be protected by the inhabitants. This will seem to proceed from your ill will or your ignorance, and contribute farther to produce and strengthen an opinion among them, *that you are no longer fit to govern them.*

XX. Lastly, invest the General of your army in the provinces, with great and unconstitutional powers, and free him from the controul of even your own Civil Governors. Let him have troops enow under his command, with all the fortresses in his possession; and who knows but (like some provincial Generals in the Roman empire, and encouraged by the universal discontent you have produced) he may take it into his head to set up for himself? If he should, and you have carefully practised these few *excellent rules* of mine, take my word for it, all the provinces will immediately join him; and you will that day (if you have not done it sooner) get rid of the trouble of governing them, and all the *plagues* attending their *commerce* and connection from henceforth and for ever.

Q. E. D.

Study Questions

1. Franklin calls his list of injunctions "rules." How do these rules describe a process? Are they arranged in a truly chronological order? If not, what governs their order?
2. This essay is a satire in which the writer's real views of governing colonies is quite different from what he actually states. Quote several sentences where the satirical element is most obvious to you.
3. Franklin, an important figure in America at the time of the American Revolution, clearly attacks Great Britain for its methods of ruling the American colonies. At whom does he direct his essay?

PRELIMINARY WORKSHEET

1. Topic _____

2. Source of information

   a. personal knowledge

   _____

   _____

   _____

   b. library resources

   _____

   _____

   _____

   _____

   _____

3. Complete list of major steps in chronological order _____

4. Main-idea sentence_____

5. Supplementary information for introduction _____

6. Concluding material _____

EVALUATION GUIDE

Name _____

Topic _____

Introduction

    1.   Does the introduction name the topic? _____

    2.   How could the introduction be strengthened to capture the reader's

        interest? _____

        _____

        _____

        _____

    3.   State the main-idea sentence. _____

        _____

        _____

        _____

Body

    1.   What steps are missing? _____

        _____

        _____

    2.   What steps need clarification or further explanation? _____

        _____

        _____

    3.   What steps appear to be out of order? _____

        _____

        _____

    4.   What transitions are used to lead the reader from one step to another?

        _____

        _____

5. What definitions of equipment and steps are included? _____

_____

_____

_____

_____

_____

Conclusion

1. Does the conclusion contain more than two sentences? _____

2. Does it contain totally new material? _____

3. How does this section draw the paper to a satisfactory close? _____

_____

_____

_____

Rating

___ This paper should be rewritten completely or in part.

___ This paper is acceptable but needs some minor revisions.

___ This is an outstandingly good paper.

2   Chronology: The Report

INTRODUCTORY COMMENTS

A report is a paper in which the writer presents an account of some experience or event in the order in which it happened. Hence, like the directions or process paper which you studied in the first chapter, the report uses chronological arrangement. The report also resembles the directions or process paper in that it must be complete, with no important details omitted; it must be unified, sticking to the point and not including information that has little relation to what actually happened; and it requires precise details so that the reader can know exactly the particulars of the subject. The directions or process paper, however, told *how to do* something; this paper will focus instead on *what was done, what took place* at some event. In general there are two broad types of report, and the one you choose will depend largely on your purpose in writing. If you wish to explore your personal feelings and reactions to the event you are reporting, you will write what might be called a *subjective* or *personal report*. If, on the other hand, your purpose is to reveal certain facts so that the reader can form his own reactions or judgments, you will probably write an *objective report*. While it is hardly possible for a report to be either purely subjective or purely objective, it is important that you choose a perspective consistent with your purpose, and therefore important that you be aware of the difference between objective and subjective material as you write.

Objective and subjective reality

Whenever you are a witness to or a participant in an event, there are two distinct realities of which you should be aware. One is the reality of the experience itself and its existence outside your own consciousness. The other is your personal response to and interpretation of the incident. The first is what we mean by objective reality—the *facts* of the experience. The second is called subjective reality—your individual reaction to those facts. When you deliberately try to detach yourself from what happened and look at an event for what it is, not for what it means to you, you are being *objective;* when, on the other hand, you allow your involvement to color your reaction to an experience so that you are aware only of your personal viewpoint, your perceptions are largely *subjective* in nature.

Perhaps an example will help to clarify the difference between the two perspectives. Suppose, for instance, that you have gone to the dentist for a filling, and a friend has gone along to keep you company. The process of having the tooth worked on has its own external reality, involving the dentist's hands, the drill and other instruments, certain noises, the odor of medications, and the altered surface of the tooth. As far as you, the dentist, and your friend are able to observe these external matters of fact *objectively,* you will agree on what they are. They exist in much the same form, and would be described in much the same way, by any one of you, *provided your description is objective.* But obviously there are some *subjective* experiences involved as well. For you as patient, there may be anxiety, pain, and eventual relief when the filling is completed. For the dentist, there may be concern about your possible pain mingled with pride in the quality of his work. For your waiting friend, there may be sympathy for you as well as happiness at not being in your place. These are subjective reactions, and they will vary from one person to another: you and the dentist and your friend could not possibly agree on *what it felt like* to have your tooth filled.

Generally, the more you are involved as a participant in an event rather than as an observer—the closer you are to the event—the more difficult it is for you to state the objective reality and, in fact, the more difficult it is for you to recognize the truth as the facts reveal it. The victims of and the witnesses to a holdup, for example, may confuse the police with their varying descriptions of the robbers, the getaway car, and other pertinent details, even though all those concerned may agree on the time and the place of the occurrence. The victims, terrified by the event, may describe the thieves as enormous and singularly ugly, when in fact the men were average in both size and appearance. The victims' fear may limit their objectivity. Moreover, while some witnesses may be able to describe the event accurately, others may respond with varying degrees of sub-jectivity, depending on such things as their physical proximity to the event, their own fears of being victimized, their past experiences with crimes of this sort, and so on.

Why be concerned with the difference?

While subjective experiences can be very important, and there are times when it is vital for you to try to communicate your feelings and your re-actions, it is also essential that you be able to distinguish between the two attitudes: to know when you are being subjective and when you are approaching the objective facts. It is also important to distinguish ob-jectivity from subjectivity as you read or listen. For while you cannot be completely objective, in that whatever you see or know is determined in some measure by the self (or subject) through which you perceive, you can attempt to see things for what they are, not just for what they mean to you. Such an attempt is especially important if you have to assess not only your observations of an experience (are you a reliable—that is, a perceptive and impartial—witness?) but also the observations of others (are their accounts trustworthy?). On these occasions, when someone is asked to relate the *facts* of the matter, relatively objective reporting is called for; it is essential to tell what happened without editorializing, without imposing personal interpretations on the data. Even when you write in your diary or tell a friend about a movie you have seen, effective reporting demands that you present the facts in the order in which they happened and let them speak for themselves, although you may wish to add comments about your own reactions as well.

But it is not for personal communication alone that your knowledge of the difference between objective and subjective reality is crucial; effective thinking and reading also require the ability to make this distinction. After all, you are constantly being bombarded with reports: communications from your friends, news broadcasts, magazine articles, film documentaries, books, and newspaper stories. It is therefore essential for you to be able to assess the factual value of these reports. Look, for example, at this pair of headlines:

BRITAIN REDUCES IMMIGRATION QUOTAS
BRITAIN SNUBS BLACKS

Both of these headlines cover the same news, but the first one states a fact, while the second reveals an opinion, an editor's interpretation. Careful reading of the news story may lead you to agree with that editor, but you should not mistake his judgment for a statement of fact. Similarly, you should be able to separate the objective from the subjective in any report, and your ability to do so will put you in a much better position to evaluate what you read or hear.

A report, then, is the documentation of an event or a succession of events in a larger process. It tells the reader *what happened*. It is therefore primarily based on factual material, organized chronologically. Whether it is largely objective or to some extent subjective and personal depends partly on the experience or event being described, but more on the knowledge, attitude, and purposes of the writer. In order to do this assignment, you may write any kind of report you wish, but with the following restrictions: you must organize your material chronologically; and you must either keep your personal feelings out of the chronicle or present them quite frankly, without confusing them with the objective facts.

Uses of the report structure

Familiarity with the use of chronological order in organizing accounts of experiences or events, and the ability to recognize the difference between factual (objective) material and personal (subjective) interpretations, should help you read as well as write better. Since the report and the order which governs its structure serve as the basis for most of the writing that appears in newspapers, periodicals, and many texts (especially in history), you should find yourself reading such materials more critically after you become familiar with the rules for constructing a report and distinguishing in it between objective and subjective material. In addition, your writing should benefit if you are aware of how to organize and present your material. First, you should find yourself in a better position to control what you write. Second, you should also learn a skill which you can use frequently in your own writing, both in and out of college. If you have to compose minutes for a meeting, if you write for the school newspaper, if you report on an experiment, you will be putting into practice what you learn in this chapter. Similarly, if you are asked to write the history of some past event—for example, the evolution of campus unrest, the growth of the two-party system in this country, or the development of architecture—you will find your work easier and more successful if you immediately apply the procedures enumerated and explained in the guidelines.

GUIDELINES

1. Choose a topic.

If you wish, you may write about some single event in which you were a participant or spectator and about which you therefore have firsthand knowledge, such as an accident you were involved in, a meeting you attended, or an incident in your personal life. Or, you may apply these guidelines to a long-range activity or complex process, like the growth of community service credit programs in your college or the development of a major ski area. In either case, however, keep in mind the necessity of obtaining sufficient factual material to make your account both true and complete. One way to obtain material for a report might be to attend some meeting or event such as a rock concert or a political demonstration, and take detailed notes. Similarly, if you decide to do library research or conduct interviews on a more general topic, make sure to obtain all the pertinent facts to make your report fully informed. Of course, the purpose of your report will determine whether or not the focus will be on the event itself or your responses to it, but even if you plan to write from a subjective point of view, you should have accurate information on the facts as well as notes about your reactions. In choosing a topic, then, consider the purpose of your report, how extensive it will be, and the kind of effort you will have to make to obtain the necessary data.

2. Make a list and amplify it.

The list should enumerate all the major events in the episode or experience you are describing. It should be constructed with particular attention to the following:

Order. The right order for a report is of course the order in which events actually happened, that is, *chronological order.* To be sure that you follow the natural and proper order in writing your report, list details as they actually happened, one after the other, the correct sequence carefully observed and documented. Suppose you have decided to write about the events of your first weekend at home from college. A list of details such as the following would only confuse the reader about chronology:

arriving home Saturday morning

getting into a fight with Dad about hitchhiking

deciding to hitchhike home from college

Saturday night date

Obviously, if your decision to hitchhike belongs in the list at all, you should list it first rather than third, in order to make the report chronological.

Completeness. Your list, like the report itself, must include all the details the reader needs to understand just what happened. The sample list above contains nothing about Saturday afternoon or Sunday. Perhaps you feel that nothing happened at those times worth including in the report; but if so, you should at least say so—if this is to be a report of the entire weekend rather than of two apparently separate events during it. Check your list to make sure you have included all the material for a complete report on your topic.

Unity. You must be equally careful, on the other hand, not to clutter up your list with details that really don't matter. The sample list includes "deciding to hitchhike." This detail *may* be important—but perhaps it is not. Since the weekend includes a "fight with Dad about hitchhiking," the fact that you *traveled* that way is pertinent, but your *decision* to travel that way may not necessarily have anything to do with the events of the weekend. Consider each detail carefully to make sure it belongs in a fully unified report. The list of incidents below is in chronological order and is reasonably complete and unified, so that it might form the basis for a satisfactory report:

> hitchhiking home Saturday morning
>
> arriving before my parents left to meet the bus
>
> argument about hitchhiking
>
> argument about clothes
>
> lunch and questions from parents
>
> phone calls to Tom and girlfriends
>
> Mother does my laundry
>
> argument with Dad about clothes for date
>
> argument with Dad about Tom's hair and beard
>
> Dad tells me what time to come in
>
> date with Tom: dinner and movie
>
> Sunday morning church and people's questions
>
> Sunday dinner at home
>
> to the bus station for the return trip

3. Compose an introduction which includes a main-idea sentence.

After you have compiled your list and checked it for order, completeness, and unity, you are ready to begin writing the first draft of your paper. As you did in the directions or process paper, you should begin by writing an introduction which leads the reader into your topic, by announcing your subject and by providing lively material to catch and hold the reader's interest. Your introduction should of course include a topic or main-idea sentence as well.

Introduction. The introduction to a report should be as straightforward as the report itself. Unlike the introduction to the directions or process paper, it need not include generalized and supplementary material, but should instead supply a brief, informative beginning to the body of the paper. Since a report is usually directed to a specific audience that is already interested in your topic, you may wish simply to begin with some action, perhaps the very first incident in your chronological list. You should make sure, however, to introduce early in the report the main-idea sentence.

Main-idea Sentence. The one essential for a *main-idea sentence* for a report is that it state the topic of the report. The details included in any report are organized around a single event, and just what that event is should be clearly stated in the main-idea sentence. Beyond this essential, the sentence may be of various types, depending in part on the purpose and emphasis of the report. In a largely subjective report whose purpose is to examine how the author *felt* about an event, the main-idea sentence might simply summarize that feeling. In a more objective type of report, the principles of the lead for a newspaper story may apply. Such a lead tells the reader what the report is about and answers the basic questions who, what, when, and where. In the sample below, this general type of main-idea sentence is used. It happens in this instance to be the second sentence of the paragraph, but it could appear anywhere in the paragraph, depending on its relationship to the rest of the introductory material.

> The elderly man in the Ford Torino drove me all the way to my parents' house, 40.1 miles from my apartment at M.Y.U. to 19 Dover Street, Hampshire. It was not quite noon on Saturday, September 21, and my first trip home since the start of college. I pulled my suitcase and laundry bag out of the back seat, thanked the man, and walked up the sidewalk. Neither my parents nor my eleven-year-old brother Peter was visible as I stumbled up the steps with the two bags, but just as I was about to kick open the door, Mother appeared in the doorway.

4. Write the body of your report.

The body of your paper will follow your introduction and main-idea sentence. As before, this section (of two or three paragraphs in reporting a single incident, longer if you're composing a more extended chronicle) will consist of the details in your list, expanded, and linked by transitions such as "next," "afterwards," and "then" to help the reader move from one step in the chronological sequence to another. To refresh your memory about transitions in a chronologically organized paper, you may wish to refer back to the guidelines in Chapter One. Then make careful note of the transitions and their use in the sample body of a report below. This sample body proceeds directly and in chronological order from the introduction above:

> "Janie!" she gasped. "Where did you come from? We were just getting ready to meet the bus."
> "I hitchhiked," I said.
> I heard my father explode, "What?" *Then* he appeared behind my mother.

> My mother pushed open the door and I brushed by her, dropping the bags inside the hallway. <u>For a minute</u> there were quick hugs and kisses followed by a torrent of questions and reproofs: why hadn't I taken the bus, it was so much safer; hitchhiking is very dangerous,

especially for a young girl; was the driver a very nice man? It was several minutes before they really looked at me. Then my father demanded, "What happened to the $453.00 wardrobe you left with two weeks ago?" He glared at my faded denims, skinny rib shirt, and sandals. Mother just sighed.

"Come out to the kitchen. Lunch is almost ready," she said.

Throughout the meal both of my parents were full of questions about my three roommates, my dates, my courses, my whole life at college. Pete, who'd arrived just in time to eat, kept calling me "hippie" and "frosh." Like he'd say, "Pass the sugar, dear hippie." I ignored him.

When dessert was over, I gathered my bags from the hallway, dropping the laundry bag by the washer and taking the suitcase upstairs to my room. By then it was almost two o'clock, and I still hadn't called my boyfriend, Tom. I hadn't seen him for two weeks either because he went to school at Hampshire Community College right in town. Lying on the bed, I dialed his number. We had a nice leisurely conversation and planned to meet for dinner and a movie at 6:00. with plenty of time until then, I called two girlfriends and got filled in on all the gossip. A lot had happened in just two weeks.

Later I went downstairs to tell my mother about the date. I could hear the washing machine churning.

"Haven't you washed any clothes while you've been gone?" she asked. "There must be at least four machine loads here."

"Of course," I answered indignantly. "These are just for the last couple of days. You want me to save money, don't you? The machines at the laundromat are expensive."

She just sighed, so I told her about dinner with Tom. She didn't make any response to that either. I went back upstairs to dress. When I came down at 5:45, Dad was hidden behind the newspaper, Pete was sprawled on the floor in front of the television, and Mom was in the kitchen. Dad peered around the paper at me, then dropped it completely.

"You're not planning to go out like that, are you?"

Since I had on my best hot-pants outfit, I simply answered yes.

Pete turned to look and started giggling. "She's knock-kneed. Hey, did you know that? She's knock-kneed!"

I kicked at him, but missed.

"Well," I said to my father, "you complained about my jeans."

He ignored that statement and asked where I was going.

"Out with Tom."

"Tom? That long-haired, bearded boy that hung around here all summer?"

"Yes."

"I thought by now you'd have met some nice, clean-cut, short-haired boy at college."

"There aren't any," I answered.

"Anyway, you get home at a decent hour. No daughter of mine, even if she is a college freshman, is going to be on the streets after midnight. You be home before twelve."

I groaned loudly.

The doorbell rang <u>just then</u> and I hurried out of the room, slamming the door behind me.

Tom and I had dinner at the pizza shop, <u>then</u> went to the drive-in movie. <u>It was 1:30 when</u> we came home. Only the light in the kitchen was still on, but no one was up. In my bedroom clean clothes were folded and stacked on my bed. I moved them to the dresser, stripped off my clothes, and got under the covers.

<u>The next morning</u> I was awakened by my mother and we all went to church. As usual we sat in the fourth pew from the back. I listened to the music, spoke the responses, half-heard the sermon, and bowed my head for the benediction. Outside the sun was bright and warm, and soon I was surrounded by old friends and family relations. All of them asked the same questions: How's the college girl? Studying hard? Is it true all the students are long-haired radicals and the professors are just as bad? All of them gave the same advice: Don't take any cigarettes or pills from anyone. Don't walk alone when it's dark. Study hard!

It was after noon when we got into the car and headed home. Mom had dinner started in the oven, so we were soon able to eat.

"The only bus today leaves at 2:00," Dad said. "We'll take you to the bus station right after dinner. No more of this hitchhiking."

I just kept eating. When we were through, I gathered up my bags, took a last look around my room, made a quick good-bye call to Tom and went down to the car. At the bus stop there was another round of kisses just as the bus arrived.

"When will you be home again, dear?" Mother asked.

It was my turn to sigh. "I don't know, Mother. I'm terribly busy at school. But I'll be home. I'll be home."

5. Write your conclusion.

Like the introduction, the conclusion of your report may be brief and direct. It should clearly indicate the end of the event—and that should be the end of the report. Especially in an objective report, make sure that you do not use the conclusion as an opportunity to make judgments or interpretations that should be left to the reader. The writer of the sample report might have been tempted to end with a judgment such as:

What a miserable weekend that was! I don't think I'll go home again very soon.

However, the actual conclusion of the report is more objective, and still manages to convey the writer's feelings very well:

I climbed aboard the bus, dragging my bags with me. When I'd found a seat, I looked back at them, the three of them waving, and I waved too. I had been home 26 hours and 20 minutes. Only 1 day, 2 hours and 20 minutes!

6. Revise your first draft.

Don't worry if your first draft is not as polished and successful as the sample above. You should expect to do some rewriting before preparing your final copy, and as you rewrite you should make sure the language of your report is *precise* and your material is *factual*.

Precision. To enable your reader to follow clearly and easily just what happened, you must use precise language. Precise language is specific and definite; it enables the reader to imagine the events as they happened. The rough first draft of the sample essay above perhaps included some such sentence as the following:

He looked at my comfortable old clothes.

This sentence may *look* specific and definite, but instead it is general and vague, as you can see if you attempt to visualize the scene. *How* did he look? Admiringly? Disparagingly? Angrily? What *were* the clothes? A cotton dress? Slacks and a sweater? And *how old* were they? Worn out? Threadbare? Or simply old-fashioned? Specific and definite language would answer such questions, in a sentence something like this:

He glared at my faded denims, skinny rib shirt, and sandals.

"Looked" and "clothes" are relatively general terms, as compared to "glared" and "denims." It is often possible, however, to be even more specific and therefore give even more help to the reader, who is trying to imagine what happened.
Suppose the report had included this sentence:

When I came down later on, somebody was reading, and somebody else was lying on the floor.

The reader would have a right to complain that this sentence is too general. If each member of the class drew a picture of what the sentence brings to mind, there would be a wide variety of pictures, no two really alike.

> When I came down the stairs around dinner time, a middle-aged man was intently reading the newspaper, and a boy was lying lazily spread out on the floor in front of the television.

Adding adjectives and adverbs to a general sentence may help make the picture clear; unfortunately, the sentence is likely to become heavy and clumsy as well. Really specific nouns and verbs do not need to be explained, however:

> When I came down at 5:45, Dad was hidden behind the newspaper and Pete was sprawled on the floor in front of the television.

Notice that numbers and proper nouns are highly specific. Notice, too, that a concrete verb like "sprawled" really provides a clearer picture than "lying lazily spread out." Precision in your report means paying careful attention to your nouns and verbs to make them specific and concrete.

Factual Material. Whether you are writing from a largely objective or largely subjective point of view, you should make sure that your report contains ample factual material. Factual material is information that can, at least in theory, be verified—by experimentation or by reference to another witness. Because it can be verified, and also because it is necessarily precise and specific, a factual statement is different from a subjective generalization. Note the difference between these two samples:

> 1. Dad said, "You be home before twelve."
> I groaned loudly. The doorbell rang just then and I hurried out of the room, slamming the door behind me.
> 2. Dad made a fuss about what time I should come in.

The first of these is a factual statement: "Dad" and anyone else who was present would presumably agree with the account of what happened. The second sample, however, interprets what happened. Like all interpretation, however, it is open to dispute. Perhaps "Dad" would not agree that he was the one who "made a fuss." In any case, the writer of the second sample was trying to express *how he felt* about what happened as well as tell what occurred. In a report, then, it is important to know the purpose of the writer which will enable you to distinguish carefully between facts, on the one hand, and feelings, or interpretations of the facts, on the other.

Sometimes the desire to express feelings or interpretations may lead to the use of so-called slanted language. The sample report above begins:

> The elderly man in the Ford Torino drove me all the way to my parents' house . . .

Not only the content but also the wording of the passage is factual; the author simply wishes to show that hitchhiking home was safe and simple. Suppose, instead, that she had wanted to express her attitude toward the driver:

> The doddering old geezer in the Ford Torino . . .

To some readers, this version will appear more interesting—but just what is a geezer? And how do you distinguish a *doddering* one from any other? While these words *appear* to have a factual content, they are actually *slanted*: the purpose of such writing is to instill an opinion, often with deliberate intent to mislead the reader. Sometimes, in order to evoke an emotional response in the relative absence of facts, some propagandists and advertisers can even use slanted language to make an interpretation *look like* factual material.

Since most language carries with it emotional overtones and is to some extent slanted, what is desirable or possible for the writer of a subjective report? If your purpose is to explore or express your feelings in relation to an event, avoid words which not only contain a bias but also attempt to persuade others to share your judgment. Instead, you should choose language which reveals your feelings directly:

> While I appreciated having a ride, I was nervous all the way home because the driver was old and seemed somewhat senile.

If you have chosen to write an objective report, you should take care to avoid using slanted or emotive language. Even in a frankly subjective account, you should make sure that both purpose and vocabulary involve honest response to experience rather than a promotion of prejudice:

7. Prepare your final draft.

When you have carefully revised your first draft, making sure your report follows chronological order, is complete, and has no unnecessary or extraneous information, and when you have checked your language for precision and factual content, then you are ready to prepare your final copy. Proofread it carefully before you hand it in.

SAMPLE ESSAYS

First Day in the Waves

Introductory paragraph clearly identifies who, where, what, and when, but without subjective comment on the event and without announcing its outcome.

Three years ago, on the morning of December 1, I traveled with my family to Connecticut and there I left them, peering from behind the chain-link fence, to board a turbo prop of Delta Airlines. My destination was Recruit Training Command, Bainbridge, Maryland, via Baltimore and Perryville. Upon arrival at the Baltimore airport, I plunged through the crowd, gathered my luggage, and hesitantly searched for transport to the "whistle stop" in Perryville.

Vividly concrete details emphasize the writer's discomfort and anxiety, though the passage is largely objective.

After a bus ride and limousine ride I arrived at the whistle stop, which was a restaurant parking lot. At the time of my arrival, the lot was as empty as my neglected stomach. It was by then 11:30 P.M., and thirty minutes passed by there in the parking lot while the snow and ice chewed at my feet. I considered that I might easily die of exposure if unable to gain entrance to the restaurant. Walking up to the window, I prepared my blanched knuckles to strike. The humming of a motor interrupted my action. My eyes stared up to a bus coated with battleship-grey paint, its exhaust floating heavily in the air and on its side the insignia of the United States Navy.

Direct quotation gives flavor of barracks language; for contrast, the author gives the same material in ordinary civilian language.

The short drive from Perryville to Recruit Training Command completely escapes my memory. I found myself inside the WAVES (Women Accepted for Voluntary Emergency Service) barracks, reporting my arrival to the Recruit Security Watchstander at the base, when the notion occurred to me that I might still have a chance to escape. I immediately blocked the thought and fumbled to retrieve my papers. "Advance to the second deck, choose a bunk, and hit the sack!" were my first verbal orders. Not completely understanding, I walked up the stairs, took a bed, and prepared myself for sleep.

Concrete and objective details convey mood (note especially the underlined words).

I had been in transit for almost sixteen hours prior to reporting for duty. As I lay in the bed, my body was denying my mind's calculations and adding at least twelve more hours. Yet, <u>I could not sleep</u>. The barracks was quiet except for the occasional whispers or <u>sobs</u> that <u>filtered</u> through the <u>stillness of the night</u>.

I was wondering what adventure the following day might offer, when an additional sound came to my ears: "clunk-creak, clunk-creak, clunk-creak." I stretched my neck to see beyond the seven-

Reprinted by permission.

by three-foot monstrosity that hugged the foot of my bed. A piercing light was thrown directly into my eyes.

"New bootie?"

"Yeah."

"Poor kid!" The light clunked and creaked up to the far end of the passageway and back again. This same event recurred precisely on the half hour for the rest of the night.

It was well into the early hours of December 2 when I finally dozed off. Later it was not the clunking or creaking that aroused me but rather the lack of it. The thick, black, heavy shoes that had sung me to sleep stopped sharply in the middle of the barracks. Then came a blast of a shrill whistle only to be outdone by the vociferous scream, "REVEILLE! !"

The apprehension that existed during that first night gradually diminished as training progressed. However, the basic pattern of a military regime had been established.

Chronological development supported by precise details.

Concluding sentences make a subjective generalization well supported by the preceding evidence.

The First Appendectomy
WILLIAM A. NOLEN, M.D.

The patient, or better, victim, of my first major surgical venture was a man I'll call Mr. Polansky. He was fat, he weighed one hundred and ninety pounds and was five feet eight inches tall. He spoke only broken English. He had had a sore abdomen with all the classical signs and symptoms of appendicitis for twenty-four hours before he came to Bellevue.

After two months of my internship, though I had yet to do anything that could be decently called an "operation," I had had what I thought was a fair amount of operating time. I'd watched the assistant residents work, I'd tied knots, cut sutures and even, in order to remove a skin lesion, made an occasional incision. Frankly, I didn't think that surgery was going to be too damn difficult. I figured I was ready, and I was chomping at the bit to go, so when Mr. Polansky arrived I greeted him like a long-lost friend. He was overwhelmed at the interest I showed in his case. He probably couldn't understand why any doctor should be so fascinated by a case of appendicitis: wasn't it a common disease? It was just as well that he didn't realize my interest in him was so personal. He might have been frightened, and with good reason.

At any rate, I set some sort of record in preparing Mr. Polansky for surgery. He had arrived on the ward at four o'clock. By six I had examined him, checked his blood and urine, taken his chest x-ray and had him ready for the operating room.

George Walters, the senior resident on call that night, was to "assist" me during the operation. George was older than the rest of us. I was twenty-five at this time and he was thirty-two. He had taken his surgical training in Europe and was spending one year as a senior resident in an American hospital to establish eligibility for the American College of Surgeons. He had had more experience than the other residents and it took a lot to disturb his equanimity in the operating room. As it turned out, this made him the ideal assistant for me.

It was ten o'clock when we wheeled Mr. Polansky to the operating room. At Bellevue, at night, only two operating rooms were kept open—there were six or more going all day—so we had to wait our turn. In the time I had to myself before the operation I had reread the section on appendectomy in the *Atlas of Operative Technique* in our surgical library, and had spent half an hour tying knots on the bedpost in my room. I was, I felt, "ready."

I delivered Mr. Polansky to the operating room and started an intravenous going in his arm. Then I left him to the care of the anesthetist. I had ordered a sedative prior to surgery, so Mr. Polansky was drowsy. The anesthetist, after checking his chart, soon had him sleeping.

Once he was asleep I scrubbed the enormous expanse of Mr. Polansky's abdomen for ten minutes. Then, while George placed the sterile drapes, I scrubbed my own hands for another five, mentally reviewing each step of the operation as I did so. Donning gown and gloves I took my place on the right side of the operating-room table. The nurse handed me the scalpel. I was ready to begin.

Suddenly my entire attitude changed. A split second earlier I had been supremely confident; now, with the knife finally in my hand, I stared down at Mr. Polansky's abdomen and for the life of me could not decide where to make the incision. The "landmarks" had disappeared. There was too much belly.

George waited a few seconds, then looked up at me and said, "Go ahead."

"What?" I asked.

"Make the incision," said George.

"Where?" I asked.

"Where?"

"Yes," I answered, "where?"

"Why, here, of course," said George and drew an imaginary line on the abdomen with his fingers.

I took the scalpel and followed where he had directed. I barely scratched Mr. Polansky.

"Press a little harder," George directed. I did. The blade went through the skin to a depth of perhaps one sixteenth of an inch.

"Deeper," said George.

There are five layers of tissue in the abdominal wall: skin, fat, fascia (a tough membranous tissue), muscle and peritoneum (the smooth, glistening, transparent inner lining of the abdomen). I cut down into the fat. Another sixteenth of an inch.

"Bill," said George, looking up at me, "this patient is big. There's at least three inches of fat to get through before we even reach the fascia. At the rate you're going we won't be into the abdomen for another four hours. For God's sake, will you cut?"

I made up my mind not to be hesitant. I pressed down hard on the knife, and suddenly we were not only through the fat but through the fascia as well.

"Not that hard," George shouted, grabbing my right wrist with his left hand while with his other hand he plunged a gauze pack into the wound to stop the bleeding. "Start clamping," he told me.

The nurse handed us hemostats and we applied them to the numerous vessels I had so hastily opened. "All right," George said, "start tying."

I took the ligature material from the nurse and began to tie off the vessels. Or rather, I tried to tie off the vessels, because suddenly my knot-tying proficiency had melted away. The casual dexterity I had displayed on the bedpost a short hour ago was nowhere in evidence. My fingers, greasy with fat, simply would not perform. My ties slipped off the vessels, the sutures snapped in my fingers, at one point I even managed to tie the end of my rubber glove into the wound. It was, to put it bluntly, a performance in fumbling that would have made Robert Benchley blush.

Here I must give my first paean of praise to George. His patience during the entire performance was nothing short of miraculous. The temptation to pick up the catgut and do the tying himself must have been strong. He could have tied off all the vessels in two minutes. It took me twenty.

Finally we were ready to proceed. "Now," George directed, "split the muscle. But gently, please."

I reverted to my earlier tack. Fiber by fiber I spread the muscle which was the last layer but one that kept us from the inside of the abdomen. Each time I separated the fibers and withdrew my clamp, the fibers rolled together again. After five minutes I was no nearer the appendix than I had been at the start.

George could stand it no longer. But he was apparently afraid to suggest I take a more aggressive approach, fearing I would stick the clamp into, or possibly through, the entire abdomen. Instead he suggested that he help me by spreading the muscle in one direction while I spread it in the other. I made my usual infinitesimal attack on the muscle. In one fell swoop George spread the rest.

"Very well done," he complimented me. "Now let's get in."

We each took a clamp and picked up the tissue-paper-thin peritoneum. After two or three hesitant attacks with the scalpel I finally opened it. We were in the abdomen.

"Now," said George, "put your fingers in, feel the cecum [the portion of the bowel to which the appendix is attached] and bring it into the wound."

I stuck my right hand into the abdomen. I felt around—but what was I feeling? I had no idea.

It had always looked so simple when the senior resident did it. Open the abdomen, reach inside, pull up the appendix. Nothing to it. But apparently there was.

Everything felt the same to me. The small intestine, the large intestine, the cecum—how did one tell them apart without seeing them? I grabbed something and pulled it into the wound. Small intestine. No good. Put it back. I grabbed again. This time it was the sigmoid colon. Put it back. On my third try I had the small intestine again.

"The appendix must be in an abnormal position," I said to George. "I can't seem to find it."

"Mind if I try?" he asked.

"Not at all," I answered. "I wish you would."

Two of his fingers disappeared into the wound. Five seconds later they emerged, cecum between them, with the appendix flopping from it.

"Stuck down a little," he said kindly. "That's probably why you didn't feel it. It's a hot one," he added. "Let's get at it."

The nurse handed me the hemostats, and one by one I applied them to the mesentery of the appendix—the veil of tissue in which the blood vessels run. With George holding the veil between his fingers I had no trouble; I took the ligatures and tied the vessels without a single error. My confidence was coming back.

"Now," George directed, "put in your purse string." (The cecum is a portion of the bowel which has the shape of half a hemisphere. The appendix projects from its surface like a finger. In an appendectomy the routine procedure is to tie the appendix at its base and cut it off a little beyond the tie.

Then the remaining stump is inverted into the cecum and kept there by tying the purse-string stitch. This was the stitch I was now going to sew.)

It went horribly. The wall of the cecum is not very thick—perhaps one eighth of an inch. The suture must be placed deeply enough in the wall so that it won't cut through when tied, but not so deep as to pass all the way through the wall. My sutures were alternately too superficial or too deep, but eventually I got the job done.

"All right," said George, "let's get the appendix out of here. Tie off the base."

I did.

"Now cut off the appendix."

At least in this, the definitive act of the operation, I would be decisive. I took the knife and with one quick slash cut through the appendix—too close to the ligature.

"Oh oh, watch it," said George. "That tie is going to slip."

It did. The appendiceal stump lay there, open. I felt faint.

"Don't panic," said George. "We've still got the purse string. I'll push the stump in—you pull up the stitch and tie. That will take care of it."

I picked up the two ends of the suture and put in the first stitch. George shoved the open stump into the cecum. It disappeared as I snugged my tie. Beautiful.

"Two more knots," said George. "Just to be safe."

I tied the first knot and breathed a sigh of relief. The appendiceal stump remained out of sight. On the third knot—for the sake of security—I pulled a little tighter. The stitch broke; the open stump popped up; the cecum disappeared into the abdomen. I broke out in a cold sweat and my knees started to crumble.

Even George momentarily lost his composure. "For Christ's sake, Bill," he said, grasping desperately for the bowel, "what did you have to do that for?" The low point of the operation had been reached.

By the time we had retrieved the cecum, Mr. Polansky's peritoneal cavity had been contaminated. My self-confidence was shattered. And still George let me continue. True, he all but held my hand as we retied and resutured, but the instruments were in my hand.

The closure was anticlimactic. Once I had the peritoneum sutured, things went reasonably smoothly. Two hours after we began, the operation was over. "Nice job," George said, doing his best to sound sincere.

"Thanks," I answered, lamely.

The scrub nurse laughed.

Mr. Polansky recovered, I am happy to report, though not without a long and complicated convalescence. His bowel refused to function normally for two weeks and he became enormously distended. He was referred to at our nightly conferences as "Dr. Nolen's pregnant man." Each time the reference was made, it elicited a shudder from me.

During his convalescence I spent every spare moment I could at Mr. Polansky's bedside. My feelings of guilt and responsibility were overwhelming. If he had died I think I would have given up surgery for good.

Study Questions

1. Where does the introduction conclude and the chronological sequence of events begin? How important is this fairly long introduction to the events that follow?
2. Nolen is quite graphic in his detailing of the operation procedure. How does he manage to keep the tone light and even humorous despite the seriousness of the event described?
3. How objective is Nolen in retelling the incident he describes? Give examples of objective statements.
4. Does the use of the personal pronoun "I" affect the degree of subjectivity? If so, how?
5. How important is the conclusion of the essay to the reader?

Cockfighting in the Bronx

FREDERICK JOHNSON

Cockfights may be cruel, and in New York they are certainly illegal, but nevertheless every Sunday four or five of them, attended by several hundred people, take place in basements, abandoned buildings and empty halls throughout Spanish sections of the city. The cocks that fight in the barrios today are descendants of the fighting cocks of Latin America—a few are still smuggled into this country every year. For the most part, the birds are carefully bred in basements scattered around Long Island and Brooklyn. The sport has existed for more than 2,000 years, and, especially among Puerto Rican and Latin American immigrants to New York, it represents an enduring tradition, impervious to public disapproval and periodic police raids (a recent raid in the Bronx netted over 60 participants and 28 cocks).

It is no easy matter for an Anglo to see one of these fights, but I got in touch with a Puerto Rican friend who was able to arrange it for me. But first we had to meet a cousin of a friend somewhere in the Bronx who would check me out before I could be admitted to the cockpit.

Juan did not know the exact address, but after driving past some leading contenders for the title of "worst block in the city," he recognized the grubby, blue-enameled storefront social club where we were to meet our contact. The door was open. A couple of men were fixing the wiring on the ceiling lights; others were playing pool. Some older men, with their hats and coats on, were playing dominoes in a corner.

"Where's Pedro?" Juan asked in Spanish. The men nearest the door stared at us blankly. Juan muttered something to me in English about "these suspicious ghetto PRs," but then realized that he was supposed to identify himself before asking any questions. He quickly announced, "I am a friend of Chango's from 103rd Street. He's Pedro's cousin." Their faces relaxed and one of the pool players motioned to a stocky, coffee-colored giant with a Zapata mustache who turned out to be Pedro.

He called over his interpreter but first ventured a question himself: "Why do you want to see the cockfights?"

Since I hadn't said anything about cockfighting, I assumed that Pedro must have heard from 103rd Street.

"I want to write a story about them, but," I emphasized in my limited Spanish, "sin nombres o localidades" (without names or locations).

Pedro said, "Come here tomorrow between two and three. The fight is at another place, but you come here and then we go."

On Sunday I arrived at the club at exactly 2:30 P.M. It looked as it had the night before, but more people were steadily drifting in. The card table was cluttered with dollar bills and a lazy cloud of smoke hung over the group. Pedro nodded to me and I followed him out onto the sidewalk. He pointed to a white building several blocks away and told me to meet him there.

By the time I had parked on a side street and walked to the front of the building, Pedro was waiting for me. I followed him up a flight of stairs, through an empty apartment throbbing with mambo music, down again eight or ten steps, through two more doors, and then into a large back room. There were about 50 men in the room, countless Rheingold beer cans, a thick cloud of cigarette smoke and a great deal of noise. A card game was breaking up and the players were putting away their money. During a lull in the conversation after we entered, Pedro introduced me to the crowd.

Everyone's attention seemed to be loosely fixed on the dozen or so men who were walking slowly about the room. They were the cock handlers, and the lumps in the duffel bags over their shoulders were the fighting roosters. The pacing men were talking to each other, loudly enough for the others to hear. Sometimes their remarks provoked laughter; several times there was a short argument. Much of the talk seemed to be taunting. Pedro explained that the men with the roosters came from all over the city and that their conversation was a standard preliminary to any cockfight. The cock owners were trying to arrange their matches. Pedro translated some of the comments.

"Why won't you fight my Pinto [a cock with reddish-blond feathers]? Is your bird inexperienced?"

"No. That bird weighs too much."

"Are you ready to put your money on Diablo?" (a mean-looking cock with scruffy black feathers).

"If I had cocks like in the old days, I would beat you all in one night."

"Look at this—gallina" (like a hen).

In the middle of this ritual, the proprietor came out of the kitchen with a plate of asopão, a kind of chicken stew, and sat down at the card table to eat.

"Is that last week's loser?" somebody asked him.

"No, he's the winner."

The proprietor poked at a chicken leg with his fork and said, "No, I think this one is fighting tonight."

Pedro is a big gambler on the cockfights and owns several birds himself. He explained that a rooster is usually ready to fight by the time it is one or two years old. One of his best cocks had been in a dozen fights a year for almost three years, but this is an exceptional record. All of his birds received a special diet of raw beef, green bananas, cornmeal and hard-boiled eggs. Pedro, like most of his friends, would never feed a cock chickenfeed.

Pedro's trainer, who breeds, trains and handles his birds at the fights, came in with three roosters in handstitched, initialed bags. Pedro put his hand into one bag and announced, "I am ready to bet $500 on this bird."

A side door was opened onto the outside courtyard and we were ushered down a long fire escape ladder. At ground level we entered a basement door and went into the building's cellar. A string of bare bulbs lit up a long, white-washed room. There were no windows, vents or other exits. In the center of the room there was a grim-looking cockfighting pit, about eight feet square, made of four old apartment doors nailed together. Specks of dried blood and bits of feathers were all over the carpeted floor. On a corner table was a white "Detecto Doctor's Infant Scale" for weighing the cocks to make sure the matches arranged upstairs would be fair. The first two combatants—a red cock and a black one—weighed three pounds, six ounces each.

The birds were brought into the pit by their handlers to give the hundred or so spectators a chance to size them up. Some of the men at ringside reached out to feel the leg muscles; others tested the cocks' reactions by baiting them with their hands. From time to time the handlers waved the cocks at each other and the birds snapped out and pecked violently. Both birds looked lively, but the red-feathered Rubio became an early favorite in the betting.

Before any fight, I learned, the handlers take sharp penknives and scrape and shave down the cocks' thumb claws (the spur located halfway up the leg). Blood is stopped with a styptic *petro duro*. When the stump is about one-half inch long, a vicious-looking curved plastic spur about two inches long is fitted, glued and taped onto each leg. An emery board puts the finishing touches on the point. The feathers behind the cock's neck are then cut away with scissors to allow the cock to move freely and peck rapidly. This is also why a rooster's red fleshy comb is cut down to a stump soon after birth ("when there is a half moon, so it will bleed less," Pedro told me). Some of the body feathers are cut away to streamline the cock. The long reddish-tipped wing and tail feathers are trimmed only slightly because the cock needs them to jump and maneuver.

The referee, who reminded me of a Little League coach, stepped into the pit, set his stop watch and proceeded with the final prefight preparations. Dipping a small sponge into a jar of water, he gently wiped off each cock's head, back and claws. With the cock's beak held open, he squeezed several drops of water into its mouth.

The cleaning process was then repeated with a strong-smelling nail polish remover. All this, it was explained, was to ward off infection and to eliminate the possibility of someone's powdering a cock with a narcotic that would be ingested by a pecking or injected with a slash from a plastic spur.

The referee was handed a wad of bills by each of the owners (about two hundred dollars in all) as the landlord walked through the crowd collecting $3 admission fees from each of the spectators. I tried to pay but my money was refused; I was Pedro's guest.

Seconds before the fight began, a well-dressed man next to me was still frantically trying to get takers for his $30-to-$20 bet on the Rubio. Another man nodded and pointed at him from across the pit, a signal that his bet had been accepted. Everyone was talking, shouting odds or making bets. Wedged into a corner at the front of the pit, I had to stiffen to withstand the pushing from those behind who were straining to see.

The cocks were waved at each other again. They pecked sharply and hooked beaks but were quickly pulled apart. This set off another wave of betting. Then, each of the handlers took a mouthful of water from the jar and blew a noisy spray of water in his rooster's face, then to the underbelly and behind. The purpose, I was told, was to freshen them up.

Wet and furious, the cocks were let go. They jumped up at each other, collided, fell down, jumped up again, their wings making sharp flapping sounds. They went sprawling from one corner to another so fast that I could hardy tell them apart. Apparently the bettors could see signs of a winner, and the betting went wild. The well-dressed guy next to me felt he had picked the wrong rooster and tried to cover his bad money with $20 to $10 on the Diablo. He quickly got three nods.

The birds stopped flying wildly at each other. Then the Rubio rushed the Diablo and pecked rapidly at his head. The Diablo's counterattack was equally ferocious and he drew a barely noticeable spot of blood on the Rubio's head. The Rubio cornered the Diablo, who took some mean pecks. The Diablo supporters seemed to feel the tide was turning again and there was more frantic hedge-betting on the Rubio.

"*Cuidado! Cuidado!*" someone yelled as the pit wall cracked and splintered from the weight of spectators leaning forward to see the action. Finally, the crowd backed off and the wall remained standing.

The Diablo fought his way out of the corner and both cocks again went sprawling, scratching, clawing and pecking wildly all over the pit. Suddenly the rooster and spectator frenzy subsided. The Rubio fought back but more specks of blood and lumps could be seen on his head. Pedro said he thought the Diablo got in a lucky blow to the head. The Rubio moved away. He only pecked back. The Diablo was the aggressor. The action slowed—both roosters were exhausted.

Most cockfights, Pedro said, last about half an hour but this time the referee signaled for the cocks to be picked up after only twenty minutes. The roosters were held facing each other. The Rubio only tried to avoid the Diablo's jabs. It was all over. The fight had gone out of the Rubio, and the Diablo was the winner. Spectators swarmed into the pit. The handlers quietly went off to one side with their birds while about $1,000 in side bets was paid off promptly without the slightest confusion.

While the pit was being cleared and two more cocks freshened for the next fight, the spectators milled around talking with their friends. Some brought beer down from the upstairs back room. There were five fights that Sunday afternoon, all very much like the first. No cocks were killed (although Pedro assures me that it happens all the time), but there were injuries. Cocks are valuable property and referees and handlers do their best to protect their charges. If a cock turns tail and runs from its opponent, the fight is automatically over. The same thing happens if a cock shows its fear by raising its hackles, exposing the white feathers on the vulnerable underside of its neck.

One cock took a terrific beating during the last fight. Its owner scooped it up, called an end to the match, and tended to its wounds. No one expected him to do otherwise. The rooster had a three-inch spur-slash on its back and it seemed to be dying. Its owner stuck the bird's head in his mouth and began to give it artificial respiration.

People were getting into their jackets, collecting and paying off bets and no one seemed at all interested in the wounded bird. A young man standing next to me glanced over toward the handler with the limp rooster dangling from his mouth and said, "Don't worry. They give him penicillin to fight again. He'll be back in three months."

Study Questions

1. How important are the first eight paragraphs? Why doesn't the writer simply start with paragraph 9 ("On Sunday I arrived at the club at exactly 2:30 P.M.")?
2. What does the dialogue contribute to the essay? Does it increase or decrease the objectivity?
3. Irony is a device in which a meaning different from the explicit content of the words is intended. What is the irony of the passage "the referee, who reminded me of a Little League coach"?
4. Why does the author give vivid, specific details but then end with such a condensed statement as "One cock took a terrific beating during the last fight"?
5. Can you tell the writer's feeling about cockfighting? What do you think it is? Identify passages in the essay which led you to your opinion.

Grim Detective Case:
The Search for Vichyssoise

BOYCE RENSBERGER

As Samuel Cochran Jr. drove the seven miles from his home in Bedford, N.Y., to the commuter station in Mount Kisco on a Wednesday morning almost three weeks ago, he noticed an unusual blurring in his vision.

At 61 and nearsighted, he thought his eyes might be getting worse. Riding into Manhattan on the train, however, the problem became noticeably more serious. He was seeing double.

Less than 15 hours later Mr. Cochran was dead, killed by one of the most poisonous substances known to man—botulin toxin. His death touched off a massive international search for more of the toxin before it killed others.

That search, which traced the poison to cans of Bon Vivant vichyssoise soup, is still in progress. As the search unfolded over recent days, it revealed an extraordinary combination of medical and public health detective work that ultimately led to what officials now say could develop into the largest recall ever in an attempt to protect human lives.

As Mr. Cochran got off the train at Grand Central Terminal that morning, the problem seemed hardly more serious than a curious eye malady. About three hours later, in his vice-presidential office in the Bank of New York branch at Fifth Avenue and 43d Street, the problem had worsened to the point that Mr. Cochran decided to consult doctors at the eye institute of Columbia Presbyterian Medical Center, where he has had his eyes checked regularly since 1933.

The doctor there noticed additional symptoms. Mr. Cochran's speech was slightly distorted. Suspecting a stroke, the eye specialist telephoned Mr. Cochran's personal physician in Mount Kisco and all agreed it would be best for him to be treated at Northern Westchester Hospital near his home.

Mrs. Cochran, reached in Bedford, drove into the city to pick up her husband. She took him straight to see Dr. Henry P. Colmore, a 66-year-old internist who has been the couple's doctor since 1947.

"Sam got here around 4 o'clock that afternoon," Dr. Colmore recalled. "By that time he was in pretty bad condition. He had a great deal of difficulty talking. He couldn't make his tongue work."

That meant the 12th cranial nerve, the one by which the brain controls the tongue, had somehow been impaired. Mr. Cochran also found it impossible to swallow. That meant that the ninth cranial nerve had been knocked out.

When the doctor asked Mr. Cochran to turn his eyes to the left and right, he couldn't. Sixth cranial nerve gone. Then Dr. Colmore shone a flashlight into the patient's eyes. The pupils failed to contract. Third cranial nerve.

"I asked him to hold his arms straight out in front," Dr. Colmore said. "His arms were shaking the way mine would if you hung a three-or-four-pound weight from them for a while."

Symptoms Are Puzzling

Curiously, however, the deep tendon reflexes—one of which is the familiar knee-jerk reflex—were unaffected.

"I just couldn't understand this," Dr. Colmore said. "It didn't make any sense. It wasn't a stroke, but there wasn't anything to suggest what it was. Sam hadn't had a fall or anything like that."

Mr. Cocharn, growing weaker and more paralyzed by the minute, was taken to a private room in the Northern Westchester Hospital.

With each passing hour Mr. Cochran's condition deteriorated and still Dr. Colmore, who by now had called in a neurologist and given several diagnostic tests, could not determine what might be the cause, much less prescribe a remedy. One possibility was that an artery supplying the brain was partially blocked, but an anticoagulant drug that would have improved circulation produced no change.

Mrs. Cochran was at her husband's side, unaware that within hours the poison that disabled her husband would attack her nervous system, too. She went home to bed around 10 P.M. Dr. Colmore, deeply troubled by the baffling affliction, also went home.

Shortly after 11 that night a nurse at the hospital called Dr. Colmore. She said Mr. Cochran "just suddenly stopped breathing." Whatever had paralyzed his eyes, tongue, throat and arms had now paralyzed his breathing ability. Death followed in minutes.

Family Is Notified

Dr. Colmore phoned Mrs. Cochran, 64, who immediately called her two sons, Peter and Samuel 3d, in Manhattan. They drove up to Bedford that night.

Shortly before 3 A.M. Dr. Colmore was awakened by a call from the sons. Mrs. Cochran seemed ill. They had heard her speech become slightly impeded and thought the grief was making her delirious.

"I got dressed and went right over," Dr. Colmore said, "and when I heard her talk, it hit me all of a sudden. She was beginning to sound the way Sam did and she was having some of the other symptoms.

"That well-known light bulb came on in my head and I thought: botulism. I hadn't thought about botulism since second-year medical school, but I was sure that's what it was. The only problem was finding the common link—the thing that gave it to both of them.

"Then Mrs. Cochran said: 'I'm doing just like Sam did. You don't suppose it was that soup we had last night? It tasted so bad we couldn't finish it.'

"I didn't answer her question, but I knew that had to be it. That soup was the clincher."

Empty Can Is Found

Privately Dr. Colmore asked the sons to search for the empty soup can. They found it and, taking care not to contaminate themselves, wrapped it in plastic for later analysis.

Dr. Colmore arranged for Mrs. Cochran to go to the hospital. Then, knowing he would have a full day ahead, he went home for breakfast and a shower and to check a standard medical reference work, Beeson and McDermott's "Textbook of Medicine."

He read: "Botulism is a specific and often fatal type of food poisoning that results from ingestion of toxin produced by [the bacterium] Clostridium botulinum . . . severe dryness of mouth . . . blurred vision, diplopia [double vision], dysphonia [difficulty in speaking], dysphagia [difficulty in swallowing], and muscle weakness. Pupils are dilated and fixed . . . but deep tendon reflexes remain intact."

There could be no doubt. Something the Cochrans had eaten, quite possibly the vichyssoise, had given Mr. Cochran a fatal dose of botulin toxin, a substance that, even in minute quantities, can interrupt the ability of nerves to transmit signals.

Hospital Arrangements

Not since 1934 had there been a case of botulism in Westchester County. The disease is rare because commercial canners normally practice good sterilizing techniques. On rare occasions, however, the controls on sterilization machinery break down so that the canned product is not heated enough or long enough.

Something like that, Dr. Colmore reasoned must have happened at the factory where the potato soup was made.

Shortly after 9 A.M. on Thursday—barely 24 hours after Mr. Cochran's symptoms began—Dr. Colmore arranged for Mrs. Cochran to go to Columbia Presbyterian Medical Center in Manhattan. If she developed respiratory failure, botulism's usual fatal effect, the center would be better equipped to help her than the smaller Mount Kisco hospital.

"My main responsibility was the patient," Dr. Colmore said, "but immediately I discharged that, it became a public health case. I was absolutely and totally convinced it was botulism and I knew there could be more of the stuff around."

Fifteen minutes after Mrs. Cochran departed in an ambulance, Dr. Colmore phoned the Westchester County Health Department in White Plains. Health Commissioner Jack Goldman, an intense, fact-finding man, questioned Dr. Colmore closely. Once botulism is confirmed, the only rational course is to get every possible source out of public hands. But, to mount an unfounded publicity and recall campaign against a product is to risk a massive lawsuit.

"Knowing Dr. Colmore, we decided to accept the strong suspicion that the patient had died of botulism," Dr. Goldman said. "We knew we had to initiate a nationwide alert."

The Lid Is Missing

Half an hour after Dr. Colmore's report, Frank Gardner and Charles Gabriel, sanitarians with the health department, rushed to the Cochran home to search for additional evidence. The empty can, which Dr. Colmore had taken to the hospital, lacked the lid embossed with the manufacturer's code number identifying the lot. The number would be needed to trace shipments. With the aid of a Bedford policeman, they broke into the yellow shingled house.

They found the lid in a garbage can and also turned up a discarded shopping list that included vichyssoise. The list indicated it was to have been purchased at a grocery in nearby Katonah. The men drove to the store and found four more cans of Bon Vivant brand vichyssoise, three of which were bulging, a sign of possible gas-producing bacterial activity inside.

All of them bore the same code as the lid: V-141/USA-71, a sequence that, within hours, would be telephoned and telegraphed to scores of public health workers around the country.

While the sanitarians were searching the house, Dr. Goldman phoned state health officials and the United States Food and Drug Administration. By noon, state and Federal officials were in Dr. Goldman's office, turning it into a frenetic command post with three high-priority tasks.

One was to set in motion the machinery that would remove tainted cans from shelves in every grocery in the nation. The second was to warn consumers who might already have purchased the cans. And the third was to do the lab work to make sure they were really dealing with botulism and not something less.

Message Is Relayed

As Mrs. Cochran was being wheeled into Columbia Presbyterian's intensive care unit, an F.D.A. man in Westchester was phoning his boss at the district office in Brooklyn. Joseph Faline, supervising inspector, took the call and, after determining that the Bon Vivant factory was in Newark, relayed the message to John Bogle in the Newark F.D.A. office, which had jurisdiction.

Knowing that Bon Vivant might still be making and shipping deadly soup, Mr. Bogle immediately dispatched a man to the factory with orders to halt operations.

Meanwhile, doctors attending Mrs. Cochran had obtained botulin antitoxin, an antidote that neutralizes the toxin, from the New York City Health Department and administered it to her. Shortly after noon, as Mrs. Cochran lay in bed, her weakened breathing now assisted by a mechanical respirator, Edward Wilkins, head of the Newark F.D.A. office, telephoned Andrew Paretti, president of Bon Vivant, to tell him of the death and ask for the company's distribution records.

Investigation Goes On

Mr. Paretti, who runs the company with his wife as general manager, was shocked to hear of the tragedy. He agreed to cooperate fully, producing the names of the 16 companies to which lot V-141 had been shipped.

Later, as the investigation developed, Mr. Paretti assembled a team of attorneys to counsel him on his every word to F.D.A. investigators.

Even as inspectors examined equipment and performance records at the blue and white one-story cannery topped by an American flag, Mr. Paretti kept the doors locked to all outsiders, refusing to speak to anyone but the F.D.A. The company's only word to the outside world has been a sign over the front door that said, "Bon Vivant, the king of soups."

Inside, Mr. Paretti had delegated several office workers to assist in the investigation, searching for records and explaining canning and sterilization practices, some of which the food and drug inspectors would later deem questionable.

Shortly after the first phone call, both F.D.A. and Bon Vivant had got in touch with all 16 wholesalers, asking that they not resell the soup.

By 2 o'clock Thursday afternoon—just 30 hours after Mr. Cochran's eyes started to bother him and not five hours after Dr. Colmore reported his diagnosis to Westchester public-health officials,—a nationwide team of local, state and Federal health workers and food industry employes was tracking down the 6,444 cans of lot V-141—V for vichyssoise and 141 for May 21st, the 141st day of the year, when Bon Vivant made the soup.

Around 4 P.M. Dr. Goldman held a news conference in his office to announce an embargo on the sale of lot V-141 in Westchester County. At about the same time state health officials announced a similar embargo for the entire state.

As word of the embargo was relayed to news media across the nation, laboratory technicians were still conducting the tests that, late Thursday night, confirmed that they were dealing with botulism.

"It began to look as if there might be thousands of cans out there that could kill people," recalled Kenneth Silver, a spokesman for the F.D.A.'s Brooklyn district office.

Recall Order Enlarged

The official recall, which had already been enlarged to include all Bon Vivant vichyssoise when suspiciously swollen cans from other lots were found, was then further expanded to include all Bon Vivant products.

As inspectors brought thousands of cans of suspect soup to food and drug agency laboratories around the country, technicians worked extended shifts, testing as many cans as possible for the toxin. From each can a solution of filtered soup had to be prepared for injection into mice.

All survived except those injected with extract from four cans found in a Gristede's store in the Bronx. Had those four cans not been found, each almost certainly would have killed at least one person.

As of yesterday, 17 days after the alarm went out, F.D.A. inspectors, aided by scores of local health agency employes, had rounded up 989,724 cans of Bon Vivant products, one of which appears to have been produced as far back as 1948. Of the 6,444 cans of lot V-141, 5,248 are accounted for and 1,196 remain unfound. There is no way of knowing how many of the cans have already been consumed.

Recovery of Mrs. Cochran

Though F.D.A. officials already consider the recall to be one of the most successful ever undertaken, the effort continues. It will go on for some time even though officials are beginning to believe that they have confined the botulism outbreak to one death and one nonfatal case.

The doctors who kept that case nonfatal now say that Mrs. Cochran's body is slowly throwing off the deadly chemical, slowly regaining the functions that were once paralyzed. She is expected to make a full recovery within weeks.

That, however, will not be the end of the matter. Even when the recall is ended, the Bon Vivant company faces the possibility of legal action by the Cochran family and by Federal officials. Flaws uncovered in its canning practices appear to have allowed not only Clostridium botulinum to grow in its products but other organisms as well. Beyond this, F.D.A. officials are saying little about their findings not wanting to influence a possible court action.

Bon Vivant, a company that has been in business for more than a century, had never encountered any serious problems. Until now.

Study Questions

1. Although this essay is an objective report, it incorporates fictional techniques. For example, what personal facts do you know about Mr. Cochran? How does the writer present these facts? Does such a presentation of information make the essay less objective? Why or why not? What other devices commonly used in fiction appear in the essay?
2. This account is taken from *The New York Times.* Are the newspaper rules about telling "who? what? when? where?" observed? If so, where do you find the answers to these questions?
3. The author uses parallel chronology in assembling and recounting the story. What are the two chains of events being reported?
4. How does the author keep the two chronologies separate and clear, and at the same time reveal their interrelationship?

A Day at Manor Nursing Home   STUDENT SAMPLE

On Sunday, August 5, I was awakened by the telephone at 7:10 A.M. Because a girl in housecleaning had been taken ill, my boss wanted me to come in and work. When I arrived at the Manor Nursing Home, I went directly to the time clock and punched in at 8:05.

I then began walking down the corridor toward the janitor's closet. On my way, I heard an old woman's worn voice coming from the direction of the showers. She was screaming at the nurse's aide who was washing her. The aide told her to shut up, and the old woman was silent.

Approaching the closet, I could see that the door was partially opened. Looking in, I saw a short endomorphic figure in a faded pink nightdress bending

Reprinted by permission.

over the box of bathroom tissue. She wanted a roll of the blue color to keep in her night stand. Since she had two other such rolls already, I told her to use up what she had before taking another. She just smiled and walked away.

After she had left, I pulled out my cleaning cart, closed the closet door, and pushed the squeaking cart down the hall. I stopped at room 301 and began to look for a suitable dusting cloth. As I was doing this, a lean old man in a wheel chair demanded that I open the basement door so he could wheel down. Realizing the danger, I refused. He then raised his voice and told me that I hadn't any heart, and that someday someone ought to make a human being out of me! I ignored the scolding and went about my business. From inside the room, I could hear the old man begging passers-by to open the door for him.

For the next few hours, I cleaned patients' rooms and talked with old women who were hung up in their past lives. At 1:35 in the afternoon, I pushed my cart aside and walked down the south corridor, on my way to the water cooler. I heard a raspy scream and almost simultaneously a loud crash. The nurse who was writing at her desk at the end of the hall quickly arose and waddled around the corner and down southeast corridor. Three nurse's aides, one of whom was a young man, ceased passing out trays in the dining room and ran after the nurse.

As I turned the corner, I saw one of the patients, George Faye, lying on the floor in the hall. There was blood dripping from his left temple, where he had hit the floor. The brown-speckled wrinkles on his eyelids held his eyes tightly closed. A tall, dark-haired nurse, who was kneeling by his side, instructed the male nurse to call an ambulance. Perspiration dripping down her cheek, the nurse applied oxygen to Mr. Faye in a frantic effort to revive him.

By this time, a group of about twenty nurse's aides and cleaning girls had gathered. I heard the ambulance siren, and not a minute later two men rolled in a stretcher. They carefully lifted Mr. Faye onto the stretcher and rolled him out the door and into the awaiting ambulance. The ambulance sped away, leaving behind the siren vibrating in our ears.

In an angered tone, my boss asked another cleaning girl and myself what we were doing standing around, and didn't we know we had work to do! We turned and started back down the hall, my fellow worker cursing our boss under her breath. Before turning the corner, I turned back and saw only an empty corridor with the green oxygen tank leaning against the wall.

I walked into one of the rooms and began to mop the floor. A bowlegged old woman, who was sitting in her padded rocking chair, told me that I wouldn't find a speck of dust anywhere in her room but that I could go ahead and clean it anyway. She went on and told me about her late hubby and their mansion-type home. When I finished the room, she was still talking, and continued to do so as I walked out.

At 2:50, I put my cart back in the janitor's closet and got ready to leave for the day. As I was doing so, I could hear Erma Johnson rhythmically groaning in the next room. A month before, Erma had gouged her eye out, and the unconscious groaning was a result of the acute pain.

On my way to the time clock I met a nurse who told me that Mr. Faye was dead upon arrival at the hospital. I punched out at 3:01. As I walked out the door into the blinding sunshine, I could still hear Erma's groans.

Study Questions

1. What is the main-idea sentence of this essay? Does it prepare the reader for the fatal accident which is the most important incident in the day's events? Should the reader be alerted to the accident? If so, how?

2. What in the report is objective, and what reveals the feelings of the writer? What are those feelings?

3. What information has been left out of the report? Is that material necessary or is the reader satisfied with what he knows?

4. In a short paper, the writer attempts to describe the entire day's events. How much of the paper is devoted to particular segments of time? How is the chronological order maintained? How is the reader informed of the passage of time?

5. How is the *selection of material* in this report subjective, even if the language is not?

Nero's Murder of His Mother TACITUS

Cluvius relates that Agrippina in her eagerness to retain her influence went so far that more than once at midday, when Nero, even at that hour, was flushed with wine and feasting, she presented herself attractively attired to her half intoxicated son and offered him her person, and that when kinsfolk observed wanton kisses and caresses, portending infamy, it was Seneca who sought a female's aid against a woman's fascinations, and hurried in Acte, the freed-girl, who alarmed at her own peril and at Nero's disgrace, told him that the incest was notorious, as his mother boasted of it, and that the soldiers would never endure the rule of an impious sovereign. Fabius Rusticus tells us that it was not Agrippina, but Nero, who lusted for the crime, and that it was frustrated by the adroitness of that same freed-girl. Cluvius's account, however, is also that of all other authors, and popular belief inclines to it, whether it was that Agrippina really conceived such a monstrous wickedness in her heart, or perhaps because the thought of a strange passion seemed comparatively credible in a woman, who in her girlish years had allowed herself to be seduced by Lepidus in the hope of winning power, had stooped with a like ambition to the lust of Pallas, and had trained herself for every infamy by her marriage with her uncle.

From *The Complete Works of Tacitus* [*Annals*], translated by Alfred John Church and William Jackson Brodribb. Copyright 1942 by Random House, Inc. Reprinted by permission of the publisher.

Nero accordingly avoided secret interviews with her, and when she withdrew to her gardens or to her estates at Tusculum and Antium, he praised her for courting repose. At last, convinced that she would be too formidable, wherever she might dwell, he resolved to destroy her, merely deliberating whether it was to be accomplished by poison, or by the sword, or by any other violent means. Poison at first seemed best, but, were it to be administered at the imperial table, the result could not be referrred to chance after the recent circumstances of the death of Britannicus. Again, to tamper with the servants of a woman who, from her familiarity with crime, was on her guard against treachery, appeared to be extremely difficult, and then, too, she had fortified her constitution by the use of antidotes. How again the dagger and its work were to be kept secret, no one could suggest, and it was feared too that whoever might be chosen to execute such a crime would spurn the order.

An ingenious suggestion was offered by Anicetus, a freedman, commander of the fleet at Misenum, who had been tutor to Nero in boyhood and had a hatred of Agrippina which she reciprocated. He explained that a vessel could be constructed, from which a part might by a contrivance be detached, when out at sea, so as to plunge her unawares into the water. "Nothing," he said, "allowed of accidents so much as the sea, and should she be overtaken by shipwreck, who would be so unfair as to impute to crime an offence committed by the winds and waves? The emperor would add the honour of a temple and of shrines to the deceased lady, with every other display of filial affection."

Nero liked the device, favoured as it also was by the particular time, for he was celebrating Minerva's five days' festival at Baial. Thither he enticed his mother. . . . And now she was invited to a banquet, that night might serve to conceal the crime. . . . Nero prolonged the banquet with various conversation, passing from a youth's playful familiarity to an air of constraint, which seemed to indicate serious thought, and then, after protracted festivity, escorted her on her departure, clinging with kisses to her eyes and bosom, either to crown his hypocrisy or because the last sight of a mother on the even of destruction caused a lingering even in that brutal heart.

A night of brilliant starlight with the calm of a tranquil sea was granted by heaven, seemingly, to convict the crime. The vessel had not gone far, Agrippina having with her two of her intimate attendants, one of whom, Crepereius Gallus, stood near the helm, while Acerronia, reclining at Agrippina's feet as she reposed herself, spoke joyfully of her son's repentance and of the recovery of the mother's influence, when at a given signal the ceiling of the place, which was loaded with a quantity of lead, fell in, and Crepereius was crushed and instantly killed. Agrippina and Acerronia were protected by the projecting sides of the couch, which happened to be too strong to yield under the weight. But this was not followed by the breaking up of the vessel; for all were bewildered, and those too, who were in the plot, were hindered by the unconscious majority. The crew then thought it best to throw the vessel on one side and so sink it, but they could not themselves promptly unite to face the emergency, and others, by counteracting the attempt, gave an opportunity of a gentler fall into the sea. Acerronia, however, thoughtlessly exclaiming that she was Agrippina, and imploring help for the emperor's mother, was despatched with poles and oars, and such naval implements as chance offered. Agrippina was silent and was thus the less recognized; still, she received a wound in her shoulder. She swam, then met with some small boats which conveyed her to the Lucrine lake, and so entered her house. . . .

Nero, meantime, as he waited for tidings of the consummation of the deed, received information that she had escaped with the injury of a slight wound, after having so far encountered the peril that there could be no question as to its author. Then, paralysed with terror and protesting that she would show herself the next moment eager for vengeance, either arming the slaves or stirring up the soldiery, or hastening to the Senate and the people, to charge him with the wreck, with her wound, and with the destruction of her friends, he asked what resource he had against all this, unless something could be at once devised by Burrus and Seneca. He had instantly summoned both of them, and possibly they were already in the secret. There was a long silence on their part; they feared they might remonstrate in vain, or believed the crisis to be such that Nero must perish, unless Agrippina were at once crushed. Thereupon Seneca was so far the more prompt as to glance back on Burrus, as if to ask him whether the bloody deed must be required of the soldiers. Burrus replied "that the prætorians were attached to the whole family of the Cæsars, and remembering Germanicus would not dare a savage deed on his offspring. It was for Anicetus to accomplish his promise."

Anicetus, without a pause, claimed for himself the consummation of the crime. At those words, Nero declared that that day gave him empire, and that a freedman was the author of this mighty boon. "Go," he said, "with all speed and take with you the men readiest to execute your orders." He himself, when he had heard of the arrival of Agrippina's messenger, Agerinus, contrived a theatrical mode of accusation, and, while the man was repeating his message, threw down a sword at his feet, then ordered him to be put in irons, as a detected criminal, so that he might invent a story how his mother had plotted the emperor's destruction and in the shame of discovered guilt had by her own choice sought death.

Meantime, Agrippina's peril being universally known and taken to be an accidental occurrence, everybody, the moment he heard of it, hurried down to the beach. Some climbed projecting piers; some the nearest vessels; others, as far as their stature allowed, went into the sea; some, again, stood with outstretched arms, while the whole shore rung with wailings, with prayers and cries, as different questions were asked and uncertain answers given. A vast multitude streamed to the spot with torches, and as soon as all knew that she was safe, they at once prepared to wish her joy, till the sight of an armed and threatening force scared them away. Anicetus then surrounded the house with a guard, and having burst open the gates, dragged off the slaves who met him, till he came to the door of her chamber, where a few still stood, after the rest had fled in terror at the attack. A small lamp was in the room, and one slave-girl with Agrippina, who grew more and more anxious, as no messenger came from her son, not even Agerinus, while the appearance of the shore was changed, a solitude one moment, then sudden bustle and tokens of the worst catastrophe. As the girl rose to depart, she exclaimed, "Do you too forsake me?" and looking round saw Anicetus, who had with him the captain of the trireme, Herculeius, and Obaritus, a centurion of marines. "If," said she, "you have come to see me, take back word that I have recovered, but if you are here to do a crime, I believe nothing about my son; he has not ordered his mother's murder."

The assassins closed in round her couch, and the captain of the trireme first struck her head violently with a club. Then, as the centurion bared his sword for the fatal deed, presenting her person, she exclaimed, "Smite my womb," and with many wounds she was slain.

So far our accounts agree. That Nero gazed on his mother after her death and praised her beauty, some have related, while others deny it. Her body was burnt that same night on a dining couch, with a mean funeral; nor, as long as Nero was in power, was the earth raised into a mound, or even decently closed. Subsequently, she received from the solicitude of her domestics, a humble sepulchre on the road to Misenum, near the country house of Cæsar the Dictator, which from a great height commands a view of the bay beneath. As soon as the funeral pile was lighted, one of her freedmen, surnamed Mnester, ran himself through with a sword, either from love of his mistress or from the fear of destruction.

Many years before Agrippina had anticipated this end for herself and had spurned the thought. For when she consulted the astrologers about Nero, they replied that he would be emperor and kill his mother. "Let him kill her," she said, "provided he is emperor."

Study Questions

1. Tacitus' report is not based on direct observation. On what is it based?
2. How does he handle the matter of conflicting sources?
3. How objective is he in reporting from his sources?
4. List the order of events reported by Tacitus. Indicate how he leads the reader from one step to the next.
5. What is the value of the final paragraph? What has the writer achieved by saving this statement for the end? Does his withholding this information until the conclusion detract from the chronological structure of the report?

Arrival at Auschwitz

VIKTOR E. FRANKL

Fifteen hundred persons had been traveling by train for several days and nights: there were eighty people in each coach. All had to lie on top of their luggage, the few remnants of their personal possessions. The carriages were so full that only the top parts of the windows were free to let in the gray of dawn. Everyone expected the train to head for some munitions factory, in which we would be employed as forced labor. We did not know whether we were still in Silesia or already in Poland. The engine's whistle had an uncanny sound, like a cry for help sent out in commiseration for the unhappy load which it was destined to lead into perdition. Then the train shunted, obviously nearing a main station. Suddenly a cry broke from the ranks of the anxious passengers, "There is a sign, Auschwitz!" Everyone's heart missed a beat at that moment. Auschwitz—the very name stood for all that was horrible: gas chambers, crematoriums, massacres. Slowly, almost hesitatingly, the train moved on as if it wanted to spare its passengers the dreadful realization as long as possible: Auschwitz!

With the progressive dawn, the outlines of an immense camp became visible: long stretches of several rows of barbed wire fences; watch towers; search lights; and long columns of ragged human figures, gray in the grayness of dawn, trekking along the straight desolate roads, to what destination we did not know. There were isolated shouts and whistles of command. We did not know their meaning. My imagination led me to see gallows with people dangling on them. I was horrified, but this was just as well, because step by step we had to become accustomed to a terrible and immense horror.

Eventually we moved into the station. The initial silence was interrupted by shouted commands. We were to hear those rough, shrill tones from then on, over and over again in all the camps. Their sound was almost like the last cry of a victim, and yet there was a difference. It had a rasping hoarseness, as if it came from the throat of a man who had to keep shouting like that, a man who was being murdered again and again. The carriage doors were flung open and a small detachment of prisoners stormed inside. They wore striped uniforms, their heads were shaved, but they looked well fed. They spoke in every possible European tongue, and all with a certain amount of humor, which sounded grotesque under the circumstances. Like a drowning man clutching a straw, my inborn optimism (which has often controlled my feelings even in the most desperate situations) clung to this thought: These prisoners look quite well, they seem to be in good spirits and even laugh. Who knows? I might manage to share their favorable position.

In psychiatry there is a certain condition known as "delusion of reprieve." The condemned man, immediately before his execution, gets the illusion that he might be reprieved at the very last moment. We, too, clung to shreds of hope and believed to the last moment that it would not be so bad. Just the sight of the red cheeks and round faces of those prisoners was a great encouragement. Little did we know then that they formed a specially chosen elite, who for years had been the receiving squad for new transports as they rolled into the station day after day. They took charge of the new arrivals and their luggage, including scarce items and smuggled jewelry. Auschwitz must have been a strange spot in this Europe of the last years of the war. There must have been unique treasures of gold and silver, platinum and diamonds, not only in the huge storehouses but also in the hands of the SS.

Fifteen hundred captives were cooped up in a shed built to accommodate probably two hundred at the most. We were cold and hungry and there was not enough room for everyone to squat on the bare ground, let alone to lie down. One five-ounce piece of bread was our only food in four days. Yet I heard the senior prisoners in charge of the shed bargain with one member of the receiving party about a tie-pin made of platinum and diamonds. Most of the profits would eventually be traded for liquor—schnapps. I do not remember any more just how many thousands of marks were needed to purchase the quantity of schnapps required for a "gay evening," but I do know that those long-term prisoners needed schnapps. Under such conditions, who could blame them for trying to dope themselves? There was another group of prisoners who got liquor supplied in almost unlimited quantities by the SS: these were the men who were employed in the gas chambers and crematoriums, and who knew very well that one day they would be relieved by a new shift of men, and that they would have to leave their enforced role of executioner and become victims themselves.

Nearly everyone in our transport lived under the illusion that he would be reprieved, that everything would yet be well. We did not realize the meaning behind the scene that was to follow presently. We were told to leave our luggage in the train and to fall into two lines—women on one side, men on the other—in order to file past a senior SS officer. Surprisingly enough, I had the courage to hide my haversack under my coat. My line filed past the officer, man by man. I realized that it would be dangerous if the officer spotted my bag. He would at least knock me down; I knew that from previous experience. Instinctively, I straightened on approaching the officer, so that he would not notice my heavy load. Then I was face to face with him. He was a tall man who looked slim and fit in his spotless uniform. What a contrast to us, who were untidy and grimy after our long journey! He had assumed an attitude of careless ease, supporting his right elbow with his left hand. His right hand was lifted, and with the forefinger of that hand he pointed very leisurely to the right or to the left. None of us had the slightest idea of the sinister meaning behind that little movement of a man's finger, pointing now to the right and now to the left, but far more frequently to the left.

It was my turn. Somebody whispered to me that to be sent to the right side would mean work, the way to the left being for the sick and those incapable of work, who would be sent to a special camp. I just waited for things to take their course, the first of many such times to come. My haversack weighed me down a bit to the left, but I made an effort to walk upright. The SS man looked

me over, appeared to hesitate, then put both his hands on my shoulders. I tried
very hard to look smart, and he turned my shoulders very slowly until I faced
right, and I moved over to that side.

The significance of the finger game was explained to us in the evening. It
was the first selection, the first verdict made on our existence or non-existence.
For the great majority of our transport, about 90 per cent, it meant death. Their
sentence was carried out within the next few hours. Those who were sent to
the left were marched from the station straight to the crematorium. This
building, as I was told by someone who worked there, had the word "bath"
written over its doors in several European languages. On entering, each prisoner was handed a piece of soap, and then—but mercifully I do not need to
describe the events which followed. Many accounts have been written about
this horror.

We who were saved, the minority of our transport, found out the truth in
the evening. I inquired from prisoners who had been there for some time where
my colleague and friend P—— had been sent.

"Was he sent to the left side?"

"Yes," I replied.

"Then you can see him there," I was told.

"Where?" A hand pointed to the chimney a few hundred yards off, which
was sending a column of flame up into the gray sky of Poland. It dissolved into
a sinister cloud of smoke.

"That's where your friend is, floating up to Heaven," was the answer. But
I still did not understand until the truth was explained to me in plain words.

But I am telling things out of their turn. From a psychological point of
view, we had a long, long way in front of us from the break of that dawn at the
station until our first night's rest at the camp.

Escorted by SS guards with loaded guns, we were made to run from the
station, past electrically charged barbed wire, through the camp, to the cleans-
ing station; for those of us who had passed the first selection, this was a real
bath. Again our illusion of reprieve found confirmation. The SS men seemed
almost charming. Soon we found out their reason. They were nice to us as long
as they saw watches on our wrists and could persuade us in well-meaning tones
to hand them over. Would we not have to hand over all our possessions anyway, and why should not that relatively nice person have the watch? Maybe
one day he would do one a good turn.

We waited in a shed which seemed to be the anteroom to the disinfecting
chamber. SS men appeared and spread out blankets into which we had to throw
all our possessions, all our watches and jewelry. There were still naïve prisoners
among us who asked, to the amusement of the more seasoned ones who were
there as helpers, if they could not keep a wedding ring, a medal or a good-luck
piece. No one could yet grasp the fact that everything would be taken away.

I tried to take one of the old prisoners into my confidence. Approaching
him furtively, I pointed to the roll of paper in the inner pocket of my coat and
said, "Look, this is the manuscript of a scientific book. I know what you will
say; that I should be grateful to escape with my life, that that should be all I

can expect of fate. But I cannot help myself. I must keep this manuscript at all costs; it contains my life's work. Do you understand that?"

Yes, he was beginning to understand. A grin spread slowly over his face, first piteous, then more amused, mocking, insulting, until he bellowed one word at me in answer to my question, a word that was ever present in the vocabulary of the camp inmates: "Shit!" At that moment I saw the plain truth and did what marked the culminating point of the first phase of my psychological reaction: I struck out my whole former life.

Suddenly there was a stir among my fellow travelers, who had been standing about with pale, frightened faces, helplessly debating. Again we heard the hoarsely shouted commands. We were driven with blows into the immediate anteroom of the bath. There we assembled around an SS man who waited until we had all arrived. Then he said, "I will give you two minutes, and I shall time you by my watch. In these two minutes you will get fully undressed and drop everything on the floor where you are standing. You will take nothing with you except your shoes, your belt or suspenders, and possibly a truss. I am starting to count—now!"

With unthinkable haste, people tore off their clothes. As the time grew shorter, they became increasingly nervous and pulled clumsily at their underwear, belts and shoelaces. Then we heard the first sounds of whipping; leather straps beating down on naked bodies.

Next we were herded into another room to be shaved: not only our heads were shorn, but not a hair was left on our entire bodies. Then on to the showers, where we lined up again. We hardly recognized each other; but with great relief some people noted that real water dripped from the sprays.

While we were waiting for the shower, our nakedness was brought home to us: we really had nothing now except our bare bodies—even minus hair; all we possessed, literally, was our naked existence. What else remained for us as a material link with our former lives? For me there were my glasses and my belt; the latter I had to exchange later on for a piece of bread. There was an extra bit of excitement in store for the owners of trusses. In the evening the senior prisoner in charge of our hut welcomed us with a speech in which he gave us his word of honor that he would hang, personally, "from that beam"— he pointed to it—any person who had sewn money or precious stones into his truss. Proudly he explained that as a senior inhabitant the camp laws entitled him to do so.

Where our shoes were concerned, matters were not so simple. Although we were supposed to keep them, those who had fairly decent pairs had to give them up after all and were given in exchange shoes that did not fit. In for real trouble were those prisoners who had followed the apparently well-meant advice (given in the anteroom) of the senior prisoners and had shortened their jackboots by cutting the tops off, then smearing soap on the cut edges to hide the sabotage. The SS men seemed to have waited for just that. All suspected of this crime had to go into a small adjoining room. After a time we again heard the lashings of the strap, and the screams of tortured men. This time it lasted for quite a while.

Thus the illusions some of us still held were destroyed one by one, and then, quite unexpectedly, most of us were overcome by a grim sense of humor. We knew that we had nothing to lose except our so ridiculously naked lives. When the showers started to run, we all tried very hard to make fun, both about ourselves and about each other. After all, real water did flow from the sprays!

Apart from that strange kind of humor, another sensation seized us: curiosity. I have experienced this kind of curiosity before, as a fundamental reaction toward certain strange circumstances. When my life was once endangered by a climbing accident, I felt only one sensation at the critical moment: curiosity, curiosity as to whether I should come out of it alive or with a fractured skull or some other injuries.

Cold curiosity predominated even in Auschwitz, somehow detaching the mind from its surroundings, which came to be regarded with a kind of objectivity. At that time one cultivated this state of mind as a means of protection. We were anxious to know what would happen next; and what would be the consequence, for example, of our standing in the open air, in the chill of late autumn, stark naked, and still wet from the showers. In the next few days our curiosity evolved into surprise; surprise that we did not catch cold.

There were many similar surprises in store for new arrivals. The medical men among us learned first of all: "Textbooks tell lies!" Somewhere it is said that man cannot exist without sleep for more than a stated number of hours. Quite wrong! I had been convinced that there were certain things I just could not do: I could not sleep without this or I could not live with that or the other. The first night in Auschwitz we slept in beds which were constructed in tiers. On each tier (measuring about six-and-a-half to eight feet) slept nine men, directly on the boards. Two blankets were shared by each nine men. We could, of course, lie only on our sides, crowded and huddled against each other, which had some advantages because of the bitter cold. Though it was forbidden to take shoes up to the bunks, some people did use them secretly as pillows in spite of the fact that they were caked with mud. Otherwise one's head had to rest on the crook of an almost dislocated arm. And yet sleep came and brought oblivion and relief from pain for a few hours.

I would like to mention a few similar surprises on how much we could endure: we were unable to clean our teeth, and yet, in spite of that and a severe vitamin deficiency, we had healthier gums than ever before. We had to wear the same shirts for half a year, until they had lost all appearance of being shirts. For days we were unable to wash, even partially, because of frozen water pipes, and yet the sores and abrasions on hands which were dirty from work in the soil did not suppurate (that is, unless there was frostbite). Or for instance, a light sleeper, who used to be disturbed by the slightest noise in the next room, now found himself lying pressed against a comrade who snored loudly a few inches from his ear and yet slept quite soundly through the noise.

If someone now asked of us the truth of Dostoevski's statement that flatly defines man as a being who can get used to anything, we would reply, "Yes, a man can get used to anything, but do not ask us how." But our psychological investigations have not taken us that far yet; neither had we prisoners reached that point. We were still in the first phase of our psychological reactions.

Study Questions

1. Underline examples of subjectivity in the essay. Do these add to or detract from the effect of the total essay? Why?
2. Underline places in the essay where the chronology is broken. Why did the writer choose to disrupt the chronology in each case?
3. Note that the point of view changes frequently from "I" to "you" to "one." When does Frankl use each of these pronouns? Would the essay be improved if only one of these viewpoints was maintained?

A Kidnaped Negro Describes
Slave Trading in New Orleans SOLOMON NORTHRUP

Solomon Northrup, a New York free Negro kidnaped into slavery, labored on Louisiana plantations for a dozen years before his release was effected. He gives a realistic description of transactions in a New Orleans slave pen.

In the first place we were required to wash thoroughly, and those with beards, to shave. We were then furnished with a new suit each, cheap, but clean. The men had hat, coat, shirt, pants and shoes; the women frocks of calico, and handkerchiefs to bind about their heads. We were now conducted into a large room in the front part of the building to which the yard was attached, in order to be properly trained, before the admission of customers. The men were arranged on one side of the room, the women on the other. The tallest was placed at the head of the row, then the next tallest, and so on in the order of their respective heights. Emily was at the foot of the line of women. [Theophilus] Freeman charged us to remember our places, exhorted us to appear smart and lively,—sometimes threatening, and again, holding out various inducements. During the day he exercised us in the art of "looking smart," and of moving to our places with exact precision.

After being fed, in the afternoon, we were again paraded and made to dance. Bob, a colored boy, who had some time belonged to Freeman, played on the violin. Standing near him, I made bold to inquire if he could play the "Virginia Reel." He answered he could not, and asked me if I could play.

From *Basic History of the Old South* by Wendell Holmes Stephenson © 1959 by Wendell Holmes Stephenson. Reprinted by permission of Van Nostrand Reinhold Company.

Replying in the affirmative, he handed me the violin. I struck up a tune, and finished it. Freeman ordered me to continue playing, and seemed well pleased, telling Bob that I far excelled him—a remark that seemed to grieve my musical companion very much.

Next day many customers called to examine Freeman's "new lot." The latter gentleman was very loquacious, dwelling at much length upon our several good points and qualities. He would make us hold up our heads, walk briskly back and forth, while customers would feel of our hands and arms and bodies, turn us about, ask us what we could do, make us open our mouths and show our teeth, precisely as a jockey examines a horse which he is about to barter for or purchase. Sometimes a man or woman was taken back to the small house in the yard, stripped, and inspected more minutely. Scars upon a slave's back were considered evidence of a rebellious or unruly spirit, and hurt his sale.

An old gentleman, who said he wanted a coachman, appeared to take a fancy to me. From his conversation with Freeman, I learned he was a resident in the city. I very much desired that he would buy me, because I conceived it would not be difficult to make my escape from New-Orleans on some northern vessel. Freeman asked him fifteen hundred dollars for me. The old gentleman insisted it was too much as times were very hard. Freeman, however, declared that I was sound and healthy, of a good constitution, and intelligent. He made it a point to enlarge upon my musical attainments. The old gentleman argued quite adroitly that there was nothing extraordinary about the nigger, and finally, to my regret, went out, saying he would call again. During the day, however,

a number of sales were made. David and Caroline were purchased together by a Natchez planter. They left us, grinning broadly, and in the most happy state of mind, caused by the fact of their not being separated. Lethe was sold to a planter of Baton Rouge, her eyes flashing with anger as she was led away.

The same man also purchased Randall. The little fellow was made to jump, and run across the floor, and perform many other feats, exhibiting his activity and condition. All the time the trade was going on, Eliza was crying aloud, and wringing her hands. She besought the man not to buy him, unless he also bought herself and Emily. She promised, in that case, to be the most faithful slave that ever lived. The man answered that he could not afford it, and then Eliza burst into a paroxysm of grief, weeping plaintively. Freeman turned round to her, savagely, with his whip in his uplifted hand, ordering her to stop her noise, or he would flog her. He would not have such work—such snivelling; and unless she ceased that minute, he would take her to the yard and give her a hundred lashes. Yes, he would take the nonsense out of her pretty quick— if he didn't, might he be d——d. Eliza shrunk before him, and tried to wipe away her tears, but it was all in vain. She wanted to be with her children, she said, the little time she had to live. All the frowns and threats of Freeman, could not wholly silence the afflicted mother. She kept on begging and beseeching them, most piteously, not to separate the three. Over and over again she told them how she loved her boy. A great many times she repeated her former promises—how very faithful and obedient she would be; how hard she would labor day and night, to the last moment of her life, if he would only buy them altogether. But it was of no avail; the man could not afford it. The bargain was agreed upon, and Randall must go alone. Then Eliza ran to him; embraced him passionately; kissed him again and again; told him to remember her—all the while her tears falling in the boy's face like rain.

Study Questions

1. Compare this essay with "A Day at Manor Nursing Home." Which is more objective? Point out examples where the less objective essay becomes subjective. Can you suggest why?
2. Does the use of people's names, especially that of the slave dealer and certain of the slaves, increase the effectiveness of the report? Explain.
3. Point out the chronology established in the essay, together with the transitions that make it explicit.
4. What evidence is there to show that this is only part of a longer report?

A Hanging   GEORGE ORWELL

It was in Burma, a sodden morning of the rains. A sickly light, like yellow tinfoil, was slanting over the high walls into the jail yard. We were waiting outside the condemned cells, a row of sheds fronted with double bars, like small animal cages. Each cell measured about ten feet by ten and was quite bare within except for a plank bed and a pot for drinking water. In some of them brown silent men were squatting at the inner bars, with their blankets draped round them. These were the condemned men, due to be hanged within the next week or two.

One prisoner had been brought out of his cell. He was a Hindu, a puny wisp of a man, with a shaven head and vague liquid eyes. He had a thick, sprouting moustache, absurdly too big for his body, rather like the moustache of a comic man on the films. Six tall Indian warders were guarding him and getting him ready for the gallows. Two of them stood by with rifles and fixed bayonets, while the others handcuffed him, passed a chain through his handcuffs and fixed it to their belts, and lashed his arms tight to his sides. They crowded very close about him, with their hands always on him in a careful, caressing grip, as though all the while feeling him to make sure he was there. It was like men handling a fish which is still alive and may jump back into the water. But he stood quite unresisting, yielding his arms limply to the ropes, as though he hardly noticed what was happening.

Eight o'clock struck and a bugle call, desolately thin in the wet air, floated from the distant barracks. The superintendent of the jail, who was standing apart from the rest of us, moodily prodding the gravel with his stick, raised his head at the sound. He was an army doctor, with a grey toothbrush moustache and a gruff voice. "For God's sake hurry up, Francis," he said irritably. "The man ought to have been dead by this time. Aren't you ready yet?"

Francis, the head jailer, a fat Dravidian in a white drill suit and gold spectacles, waved his black hand. "Yes sir, yes sir," he bubbled. "All iss satisfactorily prepared. The hangman iss waiting. We shall proceed."

"Well, quick march, then. The prisoners can't get their breakfast till this job's over."

We set out for the gallows. Two warders marched on either side of the prisoner, with their rifles at the slope; two others marched close against him, gripping him by arm and shoulder, as though at once pushing and supporting him. The rest of us, magistrates and the like, followed behind. Suddenly, when we had gone ten yards, the procession stopped short without any order or warning. A dreadful thing had happened—a dog, come goodness knows whence, had appeared in the yard. It came bounding among us with a loud volley of barks, and leapt round us wagging its whole body, wild with glee at

finding so many human beings together. It was a large woolly dog, half Aire-
dale, half pariah. For a moment it pranced round us, and then, before anyone
could stop it, it had made a dash for the prisoner and, jumping up, tried to lick
his face. Everyone stood aghast, too taken aback even to grab at the dog.

"Who let that bloody brute in here?" said the superintendent angrily.
"Catch it, someone!"

A warder, detached from the escort, charged clumsily after the dog, but it
danced and gambolled just out of his reach, taking everything as part of the
game. A young Eurasian jailer picked up a handful of gravel and tried to stone
the dog away, but it dodged the stones and came after us again. Its yaps echoed
from the jail walls. The prisoner, in the grasp of the two warders, looked on in-
curiously, as though this was another formality of the hanging. It was several
minutes before someone managed to catch the dog. Then we put my handker-
chief through its collar and moved off once more, with the dog still straining
and whimpering.

It was about forty yards to the gallows. I watched the bare brown back of
the prisoner marching in front of me. He walked clumsily with his bound arms,
but quite steadily, with that bobbing gait of the Indian who never straightens
his knees. At each step his muscles slid neatly into place, the lock of hair on his
scalp danced up and down, his feet printed themselves on the wet gravel. And
once, in spite of the men who gripped him by each shoulder, he stepped slightly
aside to avoid a puddle on the path.

It is curious, but till that moment I had never realized what it means to
destroy a healthy, conscious man. When I saw the prisoner step aside to avoid
the puddle I saw the mystery, the unspeakable wrongness, of cutting a life short
when it is in full tide. This man was not dying, he was alive just as we are alive.
All the organs of his body were working—bowels digesting food, skin renewing
itself, nails growing, tissues forming—all toiling away in solemn foolery. His
nails would still be growing when he stood on the drop, when he was falling
through the air with a tenth-of-a-second to live. His eyes saw the yellow gravel
and the grey walls, and his brain still remembered, foresaw, reasoned—reasoned even about puddles. He and we were a party of men walking together,
seeing, hearing, feeling, understanding the same world; and in two minutes,
with a sudden snap, one of us would be gone—one mind less, one world less.

The gallows stood in a small yard, separate from the main grounds of the
prison, and overgrown with tall prickly weeds. It was a brick erection like
three sides of a shed, with planking on top, and above that two beams and a
crossbar with the rope dangling. The hangman, a grey-haired convict in the
white uniform of the prison, was waiting beside his machine. He greeted us
with a servile crouch as we entered. At a word from Francis the two warders,
gripping the prisoner more closely than ever, half led half pushed him to the
gallows and helped him clumsily up the ladder. Then the hangman climbed up
and fixed the rope round the prisoner's neck.

We stood waiting, five yards away. The warders had formed in a rough
circle round the gallows. And then, when the noose was fixed, the prisoner
began to crying out to his god. It was a high, reiterated cry of "Ram! Ram!
Ram! Ram!" not urgent and fearful like a prayer or cry for help, but steady,

rhythmical, almost like the tolling of a bell. The dog answered the sound with a whine. The hangman, still standing on the gallows, produced a small cotton bag like a flour bag and drew it down over the prisoner's face. But the sound, muffled by the cloth, still persisted, over and over again: "Ram! Ram! Ram! Ram! Ram!"

The hangman climbed down and stood ready, holding the lever. Minutes seemed to pass. The steady, muffled crying from the prisoner went on and on, "Ram! Ram! Ram!" never faltering for an instant. The superintendent, his head on his chest, was slowly poking the ground with his stick; perhaps he was counting the cries, allowing the prisoner a fixed number—fifty, perhaps, or a hundred. Everyone had changed color. The Indians had gone grey like bad coffee, and one or two of the bayonets were wavering. We looked at the lashed, hooded man on the drop, and listened to his cries—each cry another second of life; the same thought was in all our minds: oh, kill him quickly, get it over, stop that abominable noise!

Suddenly the superintendent made up his mind. Throwing up his head he made a swift motion with his stick. "Chalo!" he shouted almost fiercely.

There was a clanking noise, and then dead silence. The prisoner had vanished, and the rope was twisting on itself. I let go of the dog, and it galloped immediately to the back of the gallows; but when it got there it stopped short, barked, and then retreated into a corner of the yard, where it stood among the weeds, looking timorously out at us. We went round the gallows to inspect the prisoner's body. He was dangling with his toes pointed straight downwards, very slowly revolving, as dead as a stone.

The superintendent reached out with his stick and poked the bare brown body; it oscillated slightly. "*He's* all right," said the superintendent. He backed out from under the gallows, and blew out a deep breath. The moody look had gone out of his face quite suddenly. He glanced at his wrist-watch. "Eight minutes past eight. Well, that's all for this morning, thank God."

The warders unfixed bayonets and marched away. The dog, sobered and conscious of having misbehaved itself, slipped after them. We walked out of the gallows yard, past the condemned cells with their waiting prisoners, into the big central yard of the prison. The convicts, under the command of warders armed with lathis, were already receiving their breakfast. They squatted in long rows, each man holding a tin panikin, while two warders with buckets marched round ladling out rice; it seemed quite a homely, jolly scene, after the hanging. An enormous relief had come upon us now that the job was done. One felt an impulse to sing, to break into a run, to snigger. All at once everyone began chattering gaily.

The Eurasian boy walking beside me nodded towards the way we had come, with a knowing smile: "Do you know, sir, our friend [he meant the dead man] when he heard his appeal had been dismissed, he pissed on the floor of his cell. From fright. Kindly take one of my cigarettes, sir. Do you not admire my new silver case, sir? From the boxwalah, two rupees eight annas. Classy European style."

Several people laughed—at what, nobody seemed certain.

Francis was walking by the superintendent, talking garrulously: "Well, sir,

all hass passed off with the utmost satisfactoriness. It was all finished—flick!
like that. It iss not always so—oah, no! I have known cases where the doctor
wass obliged to go beneath the gallows and pull the prissoner's legs to ensure
decease. Most disagreeable!"

"Wriggling about, eh? That's bad," said the superintendent.

"Ach, sir, it iss worse when they become refractory! One man, I recall,
clung to the bars of hiss cage when we went to take him out. You will scarcely
credit, sir, that it took six warders to dislodge him, three pulling at each leg. We
reasoned with him. 'My dear fellow, we said, 'think of all the pain and trouble
you are causing to us!' But no, he would not listen! Ach, he wass very troublesome!"

I found that I was laughing quite loudly. Everyone was laughing. Even the
superintendent grinned in a tolerant way. "You'd better all come out and have
a drink," he said quite genially. "I've got a bottle of whisky in the car. We could
do with it."

We went through the big double gates of the prison into the road. "Pulling
at his legs!" exclaimed a Burmese magistrate suddenly, and burst into a loud
chuckling. We all began laughing again. At that moment Francis' anecdote
seemed extraordinarily funny. We all had a drink together, native and European
alike, quite amicably. The dead man was a hundred yards away.

Study Questions

1. Underline each word or phrase in paragraph one which seems subjective. Rewrite the paragraph, omitting these words and phrases. Is the
   paragraph still effective? Why or why not?
2. Reread the paragraph beginning, "It is curious, but till that moment I
   had never realized what it means to destroy a healthy, conscious man."
   Is that paragraph necessary to the essay? If not, what does it add?
3. Underline the transitions Orwell uses. What transitional word does he
   most often use? How else does he establish chronology other than by
   the use of transitions?
4. Orwell continues the essay beyond the death of the convict. What do
   the final paragraphs add to the essay? Do they change the emphasis,
   for example?
5. Orwell writes ". . . the same thought was in all our minds: oh, kill
   him quickly, get it over, stop that abominable noise!" Is his claim that
   all the viewers thought the same thing an example of subjectivity or is
   it authorial license? How proper is such a generalization in a report?

"Out, Out—"

ROBERT FROST

The buzz saw snarled and rattled in the yard
And made dust and dropped stove-length sticks of wood,
Sweet-scented stuff when the breeze drew across it.
And from there those that lifted eyes could count
Five mountain ranges one behind the other   5
Under the sunset far into Vermont.
And the saw snarled and rattled, snarled and rattled,
As it ran light, or had to bear a load.
And nothing happened: day was all but done.
Call it a day, I wish they might have said   10
To please the boy by giving him the half hour
That a boy counts so much when saved from work.
His sister stood beside them in her apron
To tell them "Supper." At the word, the saw,
As if to prove saws knew what supper meant,   15
Leaped out at the boy's hand, or seemed to leap—
He must have given the hand. However it was,
Neither refused the meeting. But the hand!
The boy's first outcry was a rueful laugh,
As he swung toward them holding up the hand,   20
Half in appeal, but half as if to keep
The life from spilling. Then the boy saw all—
Since he was old enough to know, big boy
Doing a man's work, though a child at heart—
He saw all spoiled. "Don't let him cut my hand off—   25
The doctor, when he comes. Don't let him, sister!"
So. But the hand was gone already.
The doctor put him in the dark of ether.
He lay and puffed his lips out with his breath.
And then—the watcher at his pulse took fright.   30
No one believed. They listened at his heart.
Little—less—nothing!—and that ended it.
No more to build on there. And they, since they
Were not the one dead, turned to their affairs.

Study Questions

1. Using the factual information in the poem, compose an obituary notice that might have appeared in the local paper after the boy's death.
2. How does the content of the poem differ from such a newspaper report?
3. What is the apparent purpose of the poem?
4. What kind of subjective details does Frost use in the poem? How are these appropriate to the purpose of the poem?
5. Reading poetry requires an awareness of the complexities of language

beyond that ordinarily required for reading expository prose. An awareness of structure can be helpful, however, in arriving at some understanding of the poem. How?

Late Sunday Morning   JAMES AGEE

They came into the Coffee Shoppe while we were finishing breakfast, and Harmon introduced the other, whose name I forget, but which had a French sound. He was middle-sized and dark, beginning to grizzle, with the knotty, walnut kind of body and a deeply cut, not unkindly monkey's face. He wore dark trousers, a starched freshly laundered white collarless shirt, and a soft yellow straw hat with a band of flowered cloth. His shoes were old, freshly blacked, not polished; his suspenders were nearly new, blue, with gold lines at the edge. He was courteous, casual, and even friendly, without much showing the element of strain: Harmon let him do the talking and watched us from behind the reflecting lenses of his glasses. People in the street slowed as they passed and lingered their eyes upon us. Walker said it would be all right to make pictures, wouldn't it, and he said, Sure, of course, take all the snaps you're a mind to; that is, if you can keep the niggers from running off when they see a camera. When they saw the amount of equipment stowed in the back of our car, they showed that they felt they had been taken advantage of, but said nothing of it.

Harmon drove out with Walker, I with the other, up a loose wide clay road to the northwest of town in the high glittering dusty sunday late morning heat of sunlight. The man I drove with made steady conversation, in part out of nervous courtesy, in part as if to forestall any questions I might ask him. I was glad enough of it; nearly all his tenants were negroes and no use to me, and I needed a rest from asking questions and decided merely to establish myself as even more easygoing, casual, and friendly than he was. It turned out that I had not been mistaken in the French sound of his name; ancestors of his had escaped an insurrection of negroes in Haiti. He himself, however, was entirely localized, a middling well-to-do landowner with a little more of the look of the direct farmer about him than the average. He was driving a several-years-old tan sedan, much the sort of car a factory worker in a northern city drives, and was pointing out to me how mean the cotton was on this man's land, who thought he could skimp by on a low grade of fertilizer, and how good it was along this pocket and high lift, that somehow caught whatever rain ran across this part of the country, though that was no advantage to cotton in a wet year or even an average; it was good in a drowt year like this one, though; his own cotton, except for a stretch of it along the bottom, he couldn't say yet it was going to do either very good or very bad; here we are at it, though.

A quarter of a mile back in a flat field of short cotton a grove of oaks spumed up and a house stood in their shade. Beyond, as we approached, the land sank quietly away toward woods which ran tendrils along it, and was speckled near and far with nearly identical two-room shacks, perhaps a dozen, some in the part shade of chinaberry bushes, others bare to the brightness, all with the color in the sunlight and frail look of the tissue of hornets' nests. This nearest four-room house we were approaching was the foreman's. We drew up in the oak shade as the doors of this house filled. They were negroes. Walker and Harmon drew up behind us. A big iron ring hung by a chain from the low branch of an oak. A heavy strip of iron leaned at the base of the tree. Negroes appeared at the doors of the two nearest tenant houses. From the third house away, two of them were approaching. One was in clean overalls; the other wore black pants, a white shirt, and a black vest unbuttoned.

Here at the foreman's home we had caused an interruption that filled me with regret: relatives were here from a distance, middle-aged and sober people in their sunday clothes, and three or four visiting children, and I realized that they had been quietly enjoying themselves, the men out at the far side of the house, the women getting dinner, as now, by our arrival, they no longer could. The foreman was very courteous, the other men were non-committal, the eyes of the women were quietly and openly hostile; the landlord and the foreman were talking. The foreman's male guests hovered quietly and respectfully in silence on the outskirts of the talk until they were sure what they might properly do, then withdrew to the far side of the house, watching carefully to catch the landowner's eyes, should they be glanced after, so that they might nod, smile, and touch their foreheads, as in fact they did, before they disappeared. The two men from the third house came up; soon three more came, a man of forty and a narrow-skulled pair of sapling boys. They all approached softly and strangely until they stood within the shade of the grove, then stayed their ground as if floated, their eyes shifting upon us sidelong and to the ground and to the distance, speaking together very little, in quieted voices: it was as if they had been under some sort of magnetic obligation to approach just this closely and to show themselves. The landlord began to ask of them through the foreman, How's So-and-So doing, all laid by? Did he do that extra sweeping I told you?—and the foreman would answer, Yes sir, yes sir, he do what you say to do, he doin all right; and So-and-So shifted on his feet and smiled uneasily while, uneasily, one of his companions laughed and the others held their faces in the blank safety of deafness. And you, you ben doin much coltn lately, you horny old bastard?—and the crinkled, old, almost gray-mustached negro who came up tucked his head to one side looking cute, and showed what was left of his teeth, and whined, tittering, Now Mist So-and-So, you know I'm settled down, married-man, you wouldn't—and the brutal negro of forty split his face in a villainous grin and said, He too *ole*, Mist So-and-So, he don't got no sap lef in him; and everyone laughed, and the landowner said, These yer two yere, colts yourn ain't they?—and the old man said they were, and the landowner said, Musta found *them* in the woods, strappin young niggers as that; and the old man said, No sir, he got the both of them lawful married, Mist So-and-So; and the landowner said that eldest on em looks to be ready for a piece himself, and the negroes laughed, and the two boys twisted their beautiful bald gourdlike skulls in a unison of shyness and their faces were illumined with maidenly smiles of shame, delight and fear; and meanwhile the landowner had loosened the top two buttons of his trousers, and he now reached his hand in to the middle of the forearm, and, squatting with bent knees apart, clawed, scratched and rearranged his genitals.

Study Questions

1. In his description of his companions and of the location, Agee is frequently quite general and even vague. List examples of generality and/or vagueness, suggesting for each of these a more specific choice of words. Can you justify Agee's choice of words in each case?
2. On the contrary, Agee is sometimes very specific in his choice of words. Point out examples, especially of nouns and verbs which illustrate precision and suggest more general words which might be substituted.
3. Because Agee's essay is, in fact, an excerpt from a book, there is no main-idea sentence. Which sentence or sentences come closest to being a main-idea sentence? What information is missing which would have aided your understanding of the event?
4. Point out examples of subjective statements.
5. What devices does Agee use in his attempt to remain objective? For example, does his use of dialogue make the essay more or less objective? Why?

PRELIMINARY WORKSHEET

1. Topic   _____

2. Source of information

    a. personal knowledge

        _____

        _____

        _____

b. library resources

_____

_____

_____

_____

_____

_____

_____

3. Purpose of the report _____

_____

_____

_____

_____

4. Complete list of major events in chronological order _____

_____

_____

_____

_____

_____

_____

_____

_____

_____

5. Subjective elements, if any, to be explored within the paper _____

_____

_____

6. Main-idea sentence _____

_____

_____

_____

7. Supplementary information for introduction _____

_____

_____

_____

_____

8. Concluding material _____

_____

_____

_____

_____

EVALUATION GUIDE

Name   _____

Topic   _____

Introduction

    1.   What is the purpose of this report? _____

            _____

            _____

    2.   State the main-idea sentence. _____

            _____

            _____

    3.   How does the main-idea sentence relate to the apparent purpose of the report? _____

_____

_____

_____

Body

1. Is the list of principal details complete? If not, what should be
    added? _____

    _____

    _____

2. Is the list of details in chronological order? If not, which details
    seem out of order, and why? _____

    _____

    _____

3. Which details, if any, seem unrelated to the main point? _____

    _____

    _____

4. What material in the report is subjective in nature? _____

    _____

    _____

5. To what extent is the subjective content of the body appropriate to
    the paper? _____

    _____

    _____

6. Note here any examples of imprecise language. _____

    _____

    _____

7. What information in the report should be made more specific?

_____

_____

_____

Conclusion

1. Do the final sentences round off the report successfully? _____

2. How is the purpose of the paper supported by the conclusion?

_____

_____

_____

_____

_____

Rating

___ This paper should be rewritten completely or in part.

___ This paper is acceptable but needs some minor revisions.

___ This is an outstandingly good paper.

3 Classification/Division: Definition

INTRODUCTORY COMMENTS

A paper which attempts to define contains an explanation of what something *is*. Such a paper should ordinarily begin with an identification of the class to which its topic belongs, followed by an examination of characteristics that distinguish the topic from others. Identification of class and examination of individual differences depend on an awareness of *logical* relationships: they involve a mental sorting and labeling of things *as they are* independent of time relationships, and therefore make use of *logical* rather than *chronological* order.

In the first two chapters, you will remember, you wrote and analyzed compositions that were constructed around a time order determined by the sequence of the events being described. Papers giving directions, describing a process, or presenting a report deal with occurrences which have happened or might be made to happen; their structure is thus largely determined by the chronology of their subjects. A great many topics, however, do not involve a time sequence and therefore cannot be dealt with by means of a purely chronological arrangement. For these you will need to know about logical patterns of order that do not depend on what happens first, next, and so forth.

Classification/division and logical order

Logical order in its broadest sense is an arrangement of objects, individuals, principles, or events into patterns determined by the interrelationships of part to part or part to whole. Two fundamental logical patterns are provided by *classification* and *division*, which provide the basis for a wide variety of structures for writing. In fact, all the remaining chapters in this text are built around various uses of classification and division as logical structures. In this chapter, you will employ both classification and division in their simplest forms, applying them to the *definition* of an object or idea. Chapter Four will require you to apply classification and division in a somewhat more complicated way, as you compare two objects or ideas which belong to the same class. Chapter Five will call for the application of the principles of classification and division to an abstract topic for purposes of persuasion. Then, in the final chapter, as you write another paper designed to argue or persuade, you will make use of sequential logic which is directly based on the concepts of classification and division.

Since classification and division are so important in the rest of this course and indeed in almost all logical activity, it is essential for you to understand them and their uses. *Classification is the process of sorting out individual items and placing them in larger groups according to some logical plan; division is the process of breaking down a larger group into smaller units, again according to some logical plan.* As you can see, the two processes are opposites: classification moves from individuals to a group; division moves from a group to smaller units. However, these two opposite processes often work together logically so that they are almost indistinguishable.

You use classification and division in many of your daily activities. Let us say that you are going through the pockets of your suit before sending it to the cleaners; you *classify* the items you find as either valuable or worthless. If you discover a used kleenex in your pocket, you toss it into the wastebasket. Any money you find, however, you classify as valuable and worth keeping. At the same time, you *divide* money at least into the two subgroups of *coins* and *paper*, putting them into separate compartments in your wallet or purse. Though you hardly think about it, both coins and paper money are further divided into denominations according to the decimal system of our currency, and in handling each individual coin or bill you mentally classify it as a dime, a quarter, a five-dollar bill, etc. If your hobby is coin collecting, you apply classification and division on a much more specialized basis, classifying each new coin according to its country of origin, denomination, date of issue, etc., and dividing your collection as a whole into subclasses such as U.S., European, Asian, etc. Of course a similar logical operation employing classification and division is in use each time you establish or enlarge any kind of collection, whether it be stamps, antique inkwells, books in a library, or silverware in the buffet. In each case, a new item is classified by placing it into a larger group which shares certain common characteristics with it, while the collection as a whole is divided into such subgroups according to some basis of logical arrangement.

Basis for classification and division

As the examples indicate, classification and division involve a process of selection and arrangement that is sometimes based on natural properties. Frequently, however, the basis for both classification and division depends on the purposes or outlook of the person making the arrangement. Animals, for example, divide naturally into male and female according to sex differences. Any arrangement of animals into groups having to do with their attractiveness, however, would be an arbitrary arrangement, largely dependent on the prejudices of the person classifying or dividing. In any case, it is necessary to recognize a basis for classification and division in order that both will be valid. Since you can classify according to almost any system of organization, you must be aware of the basis of your classification, especially if you are going to work with the definition of more than one object. Similarly, successful division requires that you select a principle of organization and make your division both consistent and complete according to that principle. If, for example, you want to divide horses according to speed, "jumpers" would *not* be one of your groups because such a group is not consistent with the basis of division. Similarly, if you divide vertebrates into the families of fish, reptiles, amphibians, birds, and mammals, you would not want to leave out mammals from your list of subgroups because you would not have a complete division if you did.

Working in the other direction but in the same way, an object may belong simultaneously to several different groups or classes. For accurate identification, however, it is important to choose the most fundamental and practical classification as the beginning of the precise determination of identity—which is what definition is. If you wish to explain to a friend what a rose is (to take a trivial example), you should *not* therefore begin by classifying it on the basis of color ("It's a sort of red thing . . ."); nor should you classify it first from the standpoint of odor ("It smells sweet . . ."). Instead, you should start by designating the general family or class to which it belongs: "A rose is a kind of flower. . . ." Such a designation tells what a rose *is* and therefore constitutes the logical starting point for its definition. Information about its size, shape, color, odor, and other distinguishing characteristics would follow the preliminary and primary identification and complete your statement of meaning.

As you can see, then, definition in its purest sense involves two steps: first is the act of classification, or the identification of the group or class to which an object or idea belongs; and second is a division or differentiation of characteristics, a specification of those details which set the object apart from other members of the same class. A paper of definition should therefore begin with a classification of the object or idea being defined, followed by explanatory information organized according to some principle of division.

Generalization and abstraction

Assigning an item to a larger, more general group, the process we call classification, involves a movement from the particular to the general. Classification, then, is the process of *generalization*. The terms "particular" and "general," however, should not be confused with the terms "concrete" and "abstract." That which is *concrete* is capable of being experienced by one or more of the five senses. That which is *abstract* is an idea and therefore cannot be experienced by the senses. While there are degrees of generality, there are no degrees of abstraction. "Silver Lake," for example, is both particular and concrete, since it refers to a specific body of water which can be seen, felt, and tasted, as well as located on a map. The class "lakes" is more general, since it includes a number of specific lakes, yet it is still concrete. "Bodies of water" is an even more general classification, although it, too, is concrete. If we continue to generalize, however, we will eventually classify our general, concrete topic as an abstraction. "Lakes" would ultimately be assigned to the abstract class "nature." Thus the process of generalization can move from the concrete to the abstract when we begin with a concrete topic. If, however, we begin with an abstract topic, like "sorrow," we can assign that topic to more general classes but not to more abstract classes. We might classify "sorrow" as "emotion," thus assigning it to a larger, more general class. "Emotion," however, is no more abstract than "sorrow" since neither can be touched, tasted, smelled, seen, or heard.

Uses of the definition structure

For this assignment you are to write a *one-paragraph* definition of some object. Although definition can be the purpose of a complex essay comprised of a number of paragraphs, more frequently it is developed in a single paragraph and employed as a step in the larger essay. Thus to be able to write a logical and coherent paragraph is a skill which must be mastered before you undertake the task of writing a longer, more complicated essay, where logical sequence is necessary not only within each paragraph but throughout the entire essay. This project, then, will teach you two important skills: first, you will learn the fundamentals of a structural process (classification/division) which you will use over and over again as a way of organizing material; second, you will develop a basic paragraph technique (development by detail) that will be helpful to you in a great many writing assignments. Defining an object or idea by using detail is an essential step in most papers of argument or persuasion, as well as in a great majority of examination topics. Consider how often your other courses call for definitions. In scientific or technical courses, you may be asked to define concrete objects or processes. What is a *sextant?* Define *protoplasm.* Give a definition of a *feedback loop.* In courses dealing with abstract material, similar practices are applied. If you know how to go about defining a concrete object, you are further along the way toward being able to answer such questions as these: What is *feudalism?* Define *personality.* What is meant by the expression *irrational number?*

Defining through the processes of classification and division is a

fundamental step in sorting out your thoughts. It is therefore an important mental skill to master, as well as a basic method of approaching a
solution to your writing problems.

GUIDELINES

1. Choose a topic.

Since the purpose of any definition paper is to inform the reader and give
him a complete idea of some concrete or abstract subject, you should
select a topic about which you are already well informed or choose one
that can be properly researched in the library. Since, however, this assignment is also designed to help you organize factual information, you should
choose a concrete topic to make your explanatory information as specific
as possible. You must be careful, therefore, not to select a subject like
"drugs" that is too broad to allow for detailed consideration. You must
also refrain from writing about a unique object like "my hand-decorated
double-barreled shotgun," since your paper would then be a description
rather than a definition. "Shotguns" would therefore be a more suitable
choice for this assignment, as would a topic like "heroin."

2. Classify the topic.

Assign your topic to the group to which it belongs. Logically speaking,
the class to which you assign your topic should be on the *next* higher
level of generality, its immediate family, in other words. If, for instance,
you were to write about "shotguns," you would upon examination discover that shotguns belong to the family of firearms. Similarly, if you
were to write about "heroin," you would learn that it is first of all a narcotic. "Firearms" and "narcotics" are larger and therefore more general
groupings than either "shotguns" or "heroin." An identification of those
properties common to all members of a group is usually a proper starting
place for the definition of your term. If you were planning to write about
heroin, for instance, you might begin by saying that a narcotic, the class
to which it belongs, is a substance which affects the senses, produces
euphoria (or a "high"), and is habit-forming.

Do not begin, however, by classifying your topic as "something." To
say that a "shotgun" or "heroin" is "something" is to say nothing at all
about either one. The reader still has no information that will help him

identify the subject. You can eliminate the vast universe of "somethings" by beginning, as we have said, with a designation of the group or class to which your topic belongs.

3. Divide the topic.

While classification provides the appropriate beginning of a definition, it does not in itself determine how the rest of the paper should be organized. A suitable arrangement of details, even in a one-paragraph paper, is necessary, however, since a random listing of information will make for a jumbled paragraph which will confuse the reader. The best way to organize is to divide your topic into related or principal groups, categories, characteristics, or kinds. Any division you make, however, must be complete and consistent according to the basis of division you have established. Since some topics can be divided into any number of subtopics, "completeness and consistency" will be determined by the usefulness of your categories to the purpose of your paper. A definition of "hand" might involve a division into such subtopics as: physical constituents, shape, and uses. A topic like "heroin" might be divided into historical background, use and immediate effects, addictive qualities, and lethal possibilities.

4. List details.

Compile lists of details about your topic under each appropriate subgroup or head. If you were compiling data about heroin, you might need to investigate pamphlets or books on drugs to discover the following details for each subtopic:

> *historical background*
> > illegal drug, banned in U.S.
> > no prescriptions available
> > supply imported
> > distributed by pushers
>
> *use and immediate effects*
> > morphine derivative
> > white powder
> > heated with water
> > injected under skin or into veins
> > can be sniffed
> > causes lack of interest in food, sex
>
> *addictive qualities*
> > leads to total dependence
> > addict lives only for heroin
> > addict must get supply with

　　　　ready cash; may commit crime to get money
　　　withdrawal painful
　　lethal possibilities
　　　contamination from needles
　　　possibility of lethal overdose

5. Arrange the subtopics.

For this purpose an *order of climax* is an effective device to use. In such a system of organization, you must first examine your categories or sections and rank them according to their relative importance. Then you should arrange them according to one of the following schemes: either begin with the most important section and work your way in an *order of descending importance* through the others; or start with subordinate material and proceed in an *order of increasing importance* to the most significant portion of your definition. While either order is possible, you should be aware that the order of increasing importance is particularly useful in clarifying emphasis in a definition (usually the "best" is saved for last) and in capturing and holding the interest of the reader by reserving certain key information until the end.

If we look at the division and details compiled and categorized for the definition of heroin, we note that they are grouped under four headings: the drug's historical background, addictive qualities, immediate effects, and lethal possibilities. If we decide that "lethal possibilities" is the most important category, we can arrange the headings as follows:

most important:	*lethal possibilities* because they relate directly to the destructive powers of the drug
second:	*addictive qualities* because they indicate how total dependence on the drug can result in lethal possibilities
third:	*use and immediate effects* because while it is important to know how the drug is administered and what it does, the information does not itself reveal the dangerous consequences of heroin usage
fourth:	*historical background* because these facts offer insight into the subject, but they are not essential to an understanding of what heroin is and does.

If we were to use the *order of increasing importance* in our definition paper, we would begin with the least consequential material (historical background) and work our way upwards through the other categories to the treatment of the drug's lethal possibilities, the last comprising because of its position and size the most significant portion of the essay.

6. Write the main-idea sentence.

This sentence will begin your definition by classifying your topic. It should also state the division of that topic in the order in which the sub-topics will be explored in the paper. A paragraph on heroin might have the following main-idea sentence:

> Heroin is perhaps the most feared narcotic of all because of its history and the dangers that surround its use, including rapid and total addiction as well as certain lethal possibilities.

"Heroin" is the topic; "narcotic" is the class to which heroin belongs; "history," "use," "addiction," and "lethal possibilities" are the groups of distinguishing characteristics which will be examined, the order of their listing in the main-idea sentence paralleling that of their development in the paragraph. Often, of course, it may be necessary or desirable to write two sentences to take the place of a single main-idea sentence.

7. Organize the details within each subtopic.

For this purpose you may use a variety of principles of order:

Chronological Order. This involves, as you have already learned, arrangement according to a time sequence. If part of your topic can best be explained by describing a process or operation, you will of course arrange the details of that process in the chronological order of the steps involved. In explaining the operation of a coffee grinder, for example, you might begin with the part where the coffee beans are put in, the first step in the process. Then you might describe the mechanism for grinding, and finally the spout where the ground coffee emerges from the machine. Thus chronological order may work well for arranging details in a subtopic having to do with process or history.

Spatial Order. Spatial order requires that you arrange details according to the shape or architecture of the object being defined. The appearance of a coffee grinder might well be described in this manner, perhaps beginning at the top of the appliance and working downward. For other objects a more systematic spatial order might be from the bottom up or from left to right. To discuss the use of a refracting telescope, you might begin with the eyepiece and proceed in spatial order through the series of lenses to the object looked at; or you might begin with that object and trace the path of light from it through the lenses to the eye.

Other Types of Order. These are necessary when neither chronology nor a spatial arrangement is appropriate. Some kinds of information may require an order based on construction and/or function (describing a table, for instance). To explore other kinds of material (New England colloquialisms, for instance), you may choose to give a list of examples, perhaps arranged in order of climax. Again, a process of association or a chain of cause-and-effect relationships may provide the basis for arranging details in an order the reader can readily follow. In any event, do not put details into your paper randomly, simply in the order in which they happen to come to mind; keep your own thoughts sorted out and help your reader understand by providing a clear and sensible arrangement.

8. Write the rest of the paragraph.

You have already written a main-idea sentence; to complete your definition and your paper, lead into your subject with introductory or background material. Then expand the details of your list into sentence form, adding transitions and links appropriate to the principles of order you are employing. As in papers employing chronological order, transitions or links are always necessary to show how each section of your paragraph is related to the next, and how each sentence follows from the last. To ensure a continuous movement in your progression of ideas and to facilitate the logical development of your material, you should become familiar with the use of the following devices:

Linking Words or Phrases. The reader is helped to follow your thought if you clearly indicate the relationship between what has gone before and what follows.

1. Relationship of *chronology*, as we have seen in the first two chapters, is shown by terms such as "first," "second," "then," "next," and "finally."

2. Relationship of *space* can be clarified by use of such linking terms as "above," "below," "to the left," "to the right," "nearby," and so on.

3. Relationship of *contrast* can be indicated by words like "however," "moreover," and "instead." *Contrast* means that the second idea is added as something related to, yet different from, the one which precedes it.

4. The relationship of *cause* or *conclusion* can be suggested by expressions like "therefore," "consequently," and "as a result." *Cause* or *conclusion* signifies a dependency, a direct connection between two or more ideas or events.

Key Words. The writer can let the reader know exactly where he is in the sequence of thought by repeating key words or words which stand for them. This kind of repetition links the parts of a sentence or two or more sentences and helps to keep the writer's principal points present in the reader's mind. A variation of this method of supplying transition is the technique of definition itself; that is, a sentence begins or continues with an explanation of a term or an idea.

Sentence Construction Links. Another way of indicating movement from one thought to another is through the use of links made from parts of the sentences themselves. They are of three kinds:

1. The chain link signifies a connection in which the beginning of a sentence makes immediate reference to part or all of the preceding sentences, so that the two sentences become in effect a verbal chain. The second link may be a simple referral, or it may indicate another kind of relationship, such as contrast or cause.

2. Words like "this," "these," "that," "those," and "such" can be used to point back to something that has gone before and thus supply a connection with an immediate reference.

3. Parallel construction or repetition of sentence patterns also facilitates the development of logical sequence.

Supplying the necessary links to ensure a smooth flow of thought from one sentence to another is often a matter of using a combination of these devices. The following sample essay on heroin shows how all of the preceding steps have been followed to produce a well-developed, informative, and interesting single-paragraph essay. The marginal comments accompanying the essay call attention to many of the more important transitions and show how they tie the succession of ideas together.

Linking word showing contrast.	Like other narcotics, heroin is a substance that affects the senses, produces euphoria, and is habit-forming. Heroin is, <u>however</u>, perhaps the most feared narcotic of all because of its history and the dangers that surround its use, including rapid and total addiction as well as certain lethal possibilities. A partly synthetic drug derived from morphine, heroin was <u>first</u> used at the turn of the century to relieve morphine addiction. <u>Unfortunately</u>, heroin addiction soon became more prevalent and more serious than morphine addiction <u>so that</u> the manufacture and sale of heroin were prohibited in the United States. <u>Even though</u> it cannot be obtained from any ethical doctor, it is <u>nevertheless</u> readily available from illegal sources. Obtained <u>from them</u> in powder form, usually adulterated, heroin is sniffed or <u>instead</u> placed in a "cooker" or bottle cap. Water is added and the <u>cooker</u> is held over a flame with tweezers and heated until the mixture dissolves. The liquid is <u>then</u> injected into the skin or a vein. The <u>effects</u> from skin-popping usually take about ten minutes to be felt, <u>but the effects</u> from injecting into
Linking word showing chronology.	
Linking word showing contrast.	
Linking word showing conclusion.	
Linking words showing contrast.	
Chain link referring back to "illegal sources."	
Link to show contrast.	
Chronological link to show time sequence.	

Repetition of key ideas. Linking words to show contrast.	a vein (mainlining) are immediate. These effects include a dreamlike state as well as occasional nausea, itching, constipation, a lack of interest in food or sex, an inability to concentrate and either apathy or excitability, depending on the individual. Even though no one starts out trying to become addicted, total dependence on heroin develops rapidly. In fact, tolerance levels increase after only about
Repetition of key word.	three weeks of daily use, raising the amount necessary to produce a high, the increase in physical dependence corresponding to an increase in intake of the drug. Usually, after an addict has been
Sentence link: refers back to "drug."	taking heroin for years, he no longer gets high or finds any pleasure in taking the drug at all. He keeps on taking it, however, because that is the only way he can prevent the pain of withdrawal. While the symptoms brought on by withdrawal of heroin are rarely fatal, they are extremely painful. The addict abstaining from his required doses of the drug experiences anxiety, itching, watery eyes, runny
Repetition of key ideas.	nose, sweating, chills, cramps, vomiting, diarrhea, and changes in blood pressure, heart rate, and breathing. These symptoms do not come one after the other or grouped in particular ways, and what makes withdrawal so agonizing is the variety of symptoms that
Chronological link.	must be coped with at the same time. Usually, these symptoms begin about a half-day after the addict has taken his last fix, and from start to finish they persist for from one to two weeks, the crisis occurring between thirty-six to seventy hours after the symptoms have begun. Fearful of such suffering, the addict will thus do
Link to show consequence.	anything to get the money to support his habit. He often gets his money by engaging in what are called "drug-related" crimes, including stealing, prostitution, and most frequently becoming a
Repetition of ideas.	pusher or seller of the drug, employed by the underworld which controls drug traffic in this country. In addition to the dangers he faces because he is engaging in crime, the addict's existence is imperilled by drug use itself. Hepatitis and tetanus from unclean needles, infections from oozing sores around the places of injection,
Repetition of key ideas.	and malnutrition are common, as is the danger of overdose, a point reached when the body cannot assimilate a large dose of the drug and death results from malfunction or nonfunction of vital organs. Because of his need for the drug, however, the addict is largely
Contrast links.	unconcerned about these hazards to his safety. Instead, the getting and taking of heroin become his sole reason for living, his physical and psychological need of the narcotic so complete that there is
Parallel construction.	little likelihood of escape except through a program of drug treatment like the use of methadone or through death, which the user may inadvertently bring about.

9. Prepare your final draft.

As you did in the previous assignments, check your paper carefully for clarity, accuracy, and systematic order before you make a final copy to be handed in.

These guidelines have assumed a paper of definition of just one paragraph, on a topic which is a concrete object. However, the same general procedures should be applied either to longer papers or to papers dealing with abstract topics. In a short definition (one paragraph), all the divisions will be brief and linked together with appropriate transitions into a single unit. In a longer paper of definition, each subtopic should be expanded into a paragraph or two, with appropriate links between paragraphs; in addition, the same orderly procedures for structure—classification/division and appropriate arrangement of details—will usually apply to your development of each paragraph within the paper. The substitution of an abstract topic for the concrete one suggested here merely increases the necessity for systematic order and adequate transition to help your reader through more difficult material.

SAMPLE ESSAYS

The Lovely Pig   STUDENT SAMPLE

Introduction is proportionately long for a short paper but interest-catching

Note classification (underlined), which is part of a formal definition.

Details of appearance spatially arranged.

Traditionally, the word "pig" has conjured up an ugly picture of a fat, brainless, filthy animal, but it is definitely a mistake to think of this friendly, obedient creature unfavorably. In fact, if people would just take the time to look more closely at the pig, they would come to see what a remarkable being he is. Although pigs come in different sizes, colors, and breeds, they are all <u>four-legged</u>, <u>cloven-hoofed mammals</u> who are covered with stiff hair similar to (and perhaps eventually identical with) bristles on a hairbrush.

The pig has prominent eyes which, to the observant onlooker, appear intelligent and friendly. Even his mouth, which is part of his long, mobile snout, gives the illusion of a faint smile. His ears are cutely flapped over, like a terrier's. He has such a short neck that he appears to be one solid cuddly chunk. His minuscule tail is curled closely to the body, barely visible. This lovable appearance is truly representative of the pig's gregarious and amiable nature, for pigs are extremely social. They love to be with humans as well as with other pigs. Moreover, learning tricks comes easily to them, and they are faithful, obedient, and docile, all of which makes them wonderful pets.

Details explaining personality, leading to most important information about character.

Reprinted by permission.

Third section of details, explaining habits. Conclusion summarizes main points; last attribute is entirely new and perhaps out of place, but amusing.

Although the misunderstood untidiness of pigs has repelled many people, in actuality pigs are very neat. They cake themselves with mud only to get rid of parasites and protect themselves from insect bites. Far from being an insult, to be called a pig is indeed a compliment. It is to be characterized as cute, agreeable, sociable, neat, intelligent, and, of course, useful to society.

Sea Urchins

RACHEL CARSON

A full-grown black urchin may have a body or test nearly 4 inches in diameter, with spines 12 to 15 inches long. This is one of the comparatively few shore animals that are poisonous to the touch, and the effect of contact with one of the slender, hollow spines is said to be like that of a hornet sting, or may even be more serious for a child or an especially susceptible adult. Apparently the mucous coating of the spines bears the irritant or poison.

This urchin is extraordinary in the degree of its awareness of the surroundings. A hand extended over it will cause all the spines to swivel about on their mountings, pointing menacingly at the intruding object. If the hand is moved from side to side the spines swing about, following it. According to Professor Norman Millott of the University College of the West Indies, nerve receptors scattered widely over the body receive the message conveyed by a change in the intensity of light, responding most sharply to suddenly decreased light as a shadowy portent of danger. To this extent, then, the urchin may actually "see" moving objects passing nearby.

Linked in some mysterious way with one of the great rhythms of nature, this sea urchin spawns at the time of the full moon. The eggs and sperm are shed into the water once in each lunar month during the summer season, on the nights of strongest moonlight. Whatever the stimulus to which all the individuals of the species respond, it assures that prodigal and simultaneous release of reproductive cells that nature often demands for the perpetuation of a species.

Off some of the Keys, in shallow water, lives the so-called slate-pencil urchin, named for its short stout spines. This is an urchin of solitary habit, single individuals sheltering under or among the reef rocks near the low-tide level. It seems a sluggish creature of dull perceptions, unaware of the presence of an intruder, and making no effort to cling by means of its tube feet when it is picked up. It belongs to the only family of modern echinoderms that also

existed in Paleozoic time; the recent members of the group show little change from the form of ancestors that lived hundreds of millions of years ago.

Another urchin with short and slender spines and color variations ranging from deep violet to green, rose, or white, sometimes occurs abundantly on sandy bottoms carpeted with turtle grass, camouflaging itself with bits of grass and shell and coral fragments held in its tube feet. Like many other urchins, it performs a geologic function. Nibbling away at shells and coral rock with its white teeth, it chips off fragments that are then passed through the grinding mill of its digestive tract; these organic fragments, trimmed, ground, and polished within the urchins, contribute to the sands of tropical beaches.

Study Questions

1. Can you discover the method of organization used by the writer of this essay? Is there a pattern of development in the essay?
2. Ms. Carson does not present a formal definition of her term. From material in her description, write a definition of "sea urchins."
3. What division is implicit in the second paragraph?
4. What subgroups does Ms. Carson identify? Do you think that her division is complete? If not, why has she identified these two groups?
5. Since "Sea Urchins" is an excerpt from a longer work, it does not display the unity and tight organization ordinarily expected in an essay. Point out examples of loose organization.

The Ground-hog   WILL CUPPY

February 2

The woodchuck, or ground-hog, is a brownish North American rodent with very peculiar habits. In a wild state he lives on grass, clover, lettuce, and cabbage, but in captivity he prefers bread and milk. He would probably like to have bread and milk all the time but he can't get it. Along in November, after storing some fat under his skin, he crawls into his burrow and goes to sleep until about seven or eight o'clock on the morning of February 2, when he

Title supplied by editors.
From *How to Get from January to December* by Will Cuppy. Copyright 1951 by Fred Fledkamp. Reprinted by permission of Holt, Rinehart and Winston, Inc.

brushes his whiskers and emerges from his home to forecast the weather. If the day is cloudy and cold, he decides that the winter is over, but if the sun is shining brightly and it feels kind of warm he says it's still winter and goes back to sleep for another six weeks, all of which proves that he has no sense whatever. Or it may be that the ground-hog has no such ideas at all, as he is only a lower vertebrate, and lower vertebrates can't think up things like that. Those who can are called higher vertebrates.

Study Questions

1. Define "ground-hog" in formal terms.
2. How objective is Cuppy's definition? Where is it subjective and why?
3. What is the main-idea sentence? Does it fulfill all of the requirements of a main-idea sentence?
4. What is the basis for the division of details in Cuppy's essay?

Personality   STUDENT SAMPLE

Personality is the result of the total pattern of characteristic ways of behaving that comes from the individual's method of adjusting to his environment. A more concrete definition of personality may be arrived at by an examination of three inclusive explanations of personality development, each of which stresses the impact of a different aspect of any person's make-up as the most important and formative part of his personality. One theory, for instance, stresses physiological characteristics as most important, with motivation, drive, and learning as merely secondary formers. Another theory emphasizes primary motives and drives, and a third is based on learned social behavior as the basic foundation of personality. Each of the three explanations incorporates the main points of the other two, but the conflict between them arises as to which factor plays the largest formative part and in essence determines the growth and shape of personality.

The physiological theory is the oldest of the three theories, dating as far back as the ancient Greeks. This theory advocates the importance of heredity and physical characteristics in behavior development. Recent research into this area has led to a classification of individuals according to their physical traits

with an attempt to relate those traits to particular emotions, motives, and drives. Through a series of investigations and interviews, William Sheldon attempted a classification of individuals into endomorphic, mesomorphic, and ectomorphic personalities. Endomorphic refers to those people who are rounded in build with relatively weak bones and muscles and an expanded waistline. Sheldon's studies attributed even temperament, tolerance, complacency, and slow reactions to this group. Mesomorphic personalities are athletic types with strong bones and muscles, who tend to be assertive, energetic, competitive, aggressive, and unrestrained both emotionally and physically. The ectomorphic person, characterized by physical and emotional restraint, self-consciousness, fear of social situations, and overly quick reactions, is of slight stature, with long slender arms and legs and slight muscle development. Sheldon conceded that most people are a combination of two or more of these types, but in most instances there is a dominance of one specific class. Recent investigation tends to negate the strict correlation Sheldon proposed, but many psychologists nevertheless adhere to the theory that characteristics and predispositions that derive from genetic and physical properties are the principal factors from which personality develops.

An interesting though more complex theory of personality development is the psychoanalytical theory, which depicts man at the mercy of his irrational, unconscious thoughts and motives, rather than genetic predispositions. Sigmund Freud, the originator of the psychoanalytical method, conceived the mind as being partly conditioned by heredity or learning, but for the most part controlled by unconscious and primitive motives seldom manifested in overt behavior, but instead repressed. This repression of motives and desires, Freud theorized, leads to the formation of anxieties and defense mechanisms to counteract guilt feelings, which in turn results in observable characteristic ways of behavior defined as personality. To further explain the repression of primary drives and their impact upon the developing personality, Freud divided the mind into three sections, the id, the ego, and the superego. He defined the id as that unconscious section of the mind in which exist all the primitive inborn drives of the individual demanding immediate gratification of any desire. The ego or consciousness, developed with age and learning, is that part which acts as a mediator between the demands of the id and the realities of the environment, subduing the primitive drives of the id to conform to acceptable codes of behavior. The superego is, in the broadest sense, the conscience of the individual. It is the person's sense of right and wrong as it has been formulated and ingrained by the society in which he lives, and it serves as a moral base. Guilt and self-punishment are the superego's effect upon the individual. Man is, then, in Freudian theory, the sum of his adaption to repressions of drives and motives. Modifications of Freud's work have led psychologists to the formulation of concepts that recognize and define inferiority complexes, security needs, extroverted and introverted behaviors. These modifications expand upon Freud's basic premise, however: that drives and motives are the primary bases for the development of personality.

The most recent of the personality theories is the social learning theory which states that all behavior is the result of conditioning. This theory advances the idea that conditioning is responsible for the formation of motives in an individual, rather than those motives influencing learned behavior. Although primitive drives are acknowledged by social learning theories, their importance as formative elements is considered secondary compared to the effects of reward or punishment for a specific act. Much of the foundation of the social learning theory is drawn from the works of B. F. Skinner, who proved through intensive experiments that most of what we consider to be normal behavior is the direct result of reinforcement. If any act is reinforced, the probability of the repetition of that act is increased. Conversely, if an act goes unrewarded or is punished, the probability of recurrence is diminished. This theory of learning can be applied to all behavior, including what we term abnormal or neurotic behavior. Psychologists who adhere to this personality theory may vary somewhat in their conception of how much of one's behavior is a direct result of conditioning, but they all agree that conditioning is the key to the formation of personality.

All three of these theories, then, deal with the problem of defining personality according to what has the most profound effect, initial and subsequent, upon its development. Although there is an almost endless list of personality traits that occur in a myriad of combinations within different individuals, these three approaches to the concept of personality formation attempt to organize varieties of human behavior around some general principle that emphasizes the basic influences from which personality evolves. Although all psychologists concur as to the factors of personality—heredity, drives, motives, emotions, and conditioning—the particular factor upon which they place their emphasis marks the distinction among them.

Study Questions

1. Is there a formal definition of personality given? If so, what is it?
2. What division determines the organization of the essay? What principle of order determines the sequence in which the divisions are treated?
3. Describe the structure of the section dealing with the physiological theory of personality development.
4. State the formal definition and division contained in the explanation of the psychoanalytical theory.
5. The paragraph on conditioning is also an extended definition. What are the key elements of this definition and what principle governs their arrangement?
6. Chart the use of transitions in the introduction and conclusion. How do these transitions help the reader move from one sentence or thought to another?

Students: How to Identify the Species   NORMAN RUNNION

To be a successful teacher—and, later on, to be a successful administrator and college president—you must learn to like students. You do not necessarily have to reach the point where you insist that your daughter marry one, although you shouldn't object either, if she does, because the consequences are her problem, not yours. Your relationships with students should be such that you are not hesitant about inviting them to your house for dinner. Most of your neighbors will not object, particularly if you hold the dinner party at night, when you can draw the curtains. Even if the neighbors do object, the truly liberal professor—which, it is to be hoped, you are—will hold the dinner party anyway. Just bear in mind that segregation of students from the rest of academic society can only lead to deep and unjust divisions which will harm you and the college community.

The danger is that you will be so horrified by your initial encounter with students in the classroom that you will be prejudiced against them for the rest of your career. To help you avoid this, we have prepared brief summaries of various types of students that you will meet. To read about students is to understand them. The journey to the unknown is less fearful if the route is plainly marked.

The Student Revolutionaries

Everyone knows the characteristics of student revolutionaries. If perchance you don't, turn on the nearest television set and wait for the news broadcast. What you see may either frighten or anger you. This is because you haven't met any revolutionaries personally. Once you get to know them, you will discover they are just like other students except that ideas are more firmly fixed in their heads. It is to get these ideas out of their heads that many college presidents call in the police with night sticks. This is not the constructive approach you should take to student revolutionaries.

These young radicals are deeply concerned with the state of the world. Looking about them, they see nothing but violence and false ideals. They feel that the older generation has let them inherit a society that is polluted, crammed with social and racial injustices, and beset by totalitarianism and evil wars. They want to do something about it.

"Well," you tell the chief revolutionary on campus, "that's interesting. I feel exactly the same. You and I think alike."

"You do?" he asks suspiciously.

"Sure I do. That's why I've gone into education. It's where, I think, I can best make a contribution to the betterment of society."

"Yeah?" he pursues. "If that's so, why don't you join us in our demonstrations?"

From *Up the Ivy Ladder*, Copyright © 1969 by Norman Runnion. Reprinted by permission of Doubleday & Company, Inc.

"Because," you say, "I don't think violence is the answer to violence."

"See!" he reports triumphantly to his friends. "I knew he was against us and everything we stand for."

This will mark the end of the dialogue between you and the revolutionaries. You will have been dismissed by them as a knee-jerk liberal, and you never will be able to influence their thinking.

Take this approach instead:

In your conversations with the chief revolutionary, agree that society can be reconstructed only after it has been violently destroyed. Emphasize the need for widespread nuclear warfare. Call for the employment of bacteria and germs. Embrace the thought of a holocaust that will leave nothing but a few men and women living in caves. If you are going to reconstruct society to rid it of its injustices, you must start at the beginning rather than midway through.

The revolutionary will admire your grasp of the realities and consider that your dialectical thinking is surprisingly close to his.

Next, wait until he makes a speech to his followers. Then, as he starts to talk, scream "Fascist!" or "Pig!" Get it going in a good rhythm so that others in the crowd take it up. Combine the two words so that everyone is chanting, "Fascist pig, Fascist pig, Fascist pig!"

After a few minutes, pause and let him get a word in edgewise. This is important. You must let him provide you with an excuse for further interruption. He is certain to say, "So this is your idea of free speech, is it?" Start yelling, "Free speech, free speech, free speech!" so that he can no longer make himself heard. Do this for at least five minutes; then stop again. He will say, "Now, my friends, you know what democracy is really like!" Chant, "Democracy, democracy, democracy!" until he is forced to abandon his speech in disgust.

The revolutionary will be delighted that you believe, as he does, that the Right of Dissent should be both maintained and extended. Because of your actions, he will respect you both as a man and as a teacher. You will have won his confidence by using methods that are far less harmful than police night sticks.

The Intelligentsia

These students, according to most professors, bring joy to teaching. (A professor is likely to say this while enjoying a late-afternoon pipe somewhere on a beach with his family during the three-month-long summer vacation.) The intelligentsia are the ones who understand, who will absorb your wisdom with little effort and preferably with no back talk. This, however, is often the rub. The intelligentsia can rebel as surely as the revolutionaries, but they do it in the classroom, where it can damage your ego. As bright young men and women, they feel the need to assert themselves at the professor's expense.

With an uncanny sense of timing, they can tell when you either have a hangover or are just rereading a lecture—for example, on the political justification of wars—which you had prepared years ago. Then they pounce.

"That's an interesting point, Doctor. But doesn't it conflict with what Hegel said about the American Civil War?"

"Hegel?" you ask. "Did Hegel say anything about the Civil War?"

"Sure he did. It was in the required reading that you gave us last week."

It soon will turn out that Gustavius Hegel was an obscure Union private whose letters to his mother appeared in "Some Personal Tales of the Civil War," a book which you had assigned the class to read if anyone had the inclination, confident that no one would. And Hegel thought the army food was awful, which, you are now told, proves that all wars are hell.

Your immediate temptation might be to ask on the final examination: "Define Hegel's theories of war." The question would be aimed at only one member of the class, and you would blister him for his lack of logic, his weak grasp of the facts, and his bad spelling.

On the other hand you would find it far more productive to take an opposite approach. Open a line of communication with the young man, which needs only consist of walking with him to the student union and offering to buy a cup of coffee. It is quite possible that he will accept the coffee, thank you politely, and disrupt the class even more when he returns to it the next day.

If he does, ignore it and try once more to win him to your side. Buy him a coke instead of coffee. The intelligentsia are vital to your happiness, and efforts spent on getting them to like you are worth while. Bright students can be turned into teaching assistants: they can read and grade freshman themes; freshman themes are the bubonic plague of academic life, and the quicker someone can be found to take them off your hands, the better you will enjoy your teaching career.

The Apathetic

Most of your colleagues will argue that these make up the majority of students at any college or university. Professors usually blame this state of affairs on the admissions office and the president, in that order. (The admissions department reverses this order; for further details, see chapter 6: Admissions.)

The apathetic are easy to spot. They affect a slouch in the chair so sharply angled that the student's rear end rests precariously on the very edge of the seat. His shoulders hang over the top. This is known as the bed position; it permits the student to sleep in relative comfort while at the same time occupying space in the classroom and not being marked absent.

Sometimes, on opening day of classes, you might mistake the apathetic for the intelligentsia. For instance, discussing philosophy, you ask a student in the rear of the room: "Name a philosopher."

"Can't."

"Kant? Excellent."

If you are alert, you will note the sudden suspicion, the attitude of "What's he trying to pull on me?" that flits through the student's eyes, and you will know that he is a lost cause.

The apathetic do have one virtue. Few students are more adept at thinking up excuses for (a) not being in class, (b) not doing the assignment, or (c) missing the final examination. Many a luncheon in the faculty dining room has been enlivened by a barter of the latest excuses, such as, "I heard a new one today: He was skiing, and had to rescue someone, and they were marooned by the blizzard in a cabin overnight."

"Yeah," will come a snarl from the next table. "He was with my daughter."

Undoubtedly your temptation will be to pretend that the apathetic do not exist as human beings in your classroom. You will be encouraged in this attitude by some of your colleagues, who will tell you: "I've got fifty students, and only five of them have any brains I aim all my lectures at those five, and the rest can go to hell."

You will discover that the argument has merit. If you had to teach to the lowest level of the class, you would provide only a mediocre education to those who deserve better. Sometimes, however, you will find that the apathetic are only scared—of both education and you. If you give them a little extra attention outside of class, you may be rewarded by a glimmer of interest in your lectures. In any case, it will not hurt to get the apathetic to like you and to trust you; once you have them firmly in your control, you can tell them that, for their own good and because you are concerned for their happiness, they should transfer out of your course into something less complicated. This way you can both get rid of a hindrance to your teaching and do a disservice to another professor whom you don't like.

The Shaggies

A botanist was known recently to have staggered through the hall of a science building, eyes wide, exclaiming, "I saw a bush today."

"A bush? You always see bushes. Botanists are supposed to see bushes."

"This bush was in my class taking notes."

Beards, particularly those accompanied by pipes, always have been a mark of intellectual distinction. There is something about a neatly trimmed beard which implies that its owner has read a book. The hair and beard of a shaggy, however, implies only lack of a razor and a bath. It is unfortunate for those required to lecture in a small, stuffy classroom that cleanliness has become associated with the Establishment and the over-30s.

If you want to get a choral response from a roomful of shaggies, you can easily do so with certain phrases:

"Kennedy."

—"Beautiful."

"Pot is good for you."

—"Beautiful."

"Your thing."

—"Beautiful."

"Work is slavery."

—"Beautiful."

"Peanut butter is better than pot."

—"Ugly."

The shaggies are the great non-conformists of college and American society. You will discover that this is why they grow huge beards if they are men and long, straggly hair if they are women; dress in identical blue jeans and shawls; wear sandals; and talk alike. This not only sets apart their sharp identities but permits them to spot each other in a crowd.

Yet don't be alarmed by these creatures. Many shaggies are perceptive students and interesting conversationalists. They also flunk examinations and complain about grades as much as anyone. It is a cruel world, you will tell them. They will reply simply. "But it shouldn't be."

The Jocks

Jocks can be among the most interesting students in class, because athletes can be great moralizers. Possibly this is because games signify good fellowship and clean living. Jocks usually do not hesitate to make their views known on many of the great issues of the day. Suppose you are lecturing on the American Black Revolution, and you have emphasized, with feeling, that America has not done what it could for the Negro.

"I think you're wrong," says the jock up in back. "The Blacks get a lot of money."

"Oh?" you ask. "Like for example?"

The jock's face lights up in triumph. "Black basketball players get higher pay than whites. You can look it up in *Sports Illustrated*."

Few students have more academic problems than the jocks, and it is a situation not entirely of their own making. There have been, and are, many academically brilliant athletes on college campuses. But some of them have trouble with their professors simply because they are athletes.

Consider athletes. They are functionaries, as important a part of your college's scene as student unions and fund-raising dinners. If they are good enough, they will provide your college with prestige, money and entertainment, for students and outsiders alike. No Phi Beta Kappa bookworm ever packed 50,000 persons into a football stadium. And if the stadium doesn't hold 50,000 persons, the All-American halfback and his playmates will be able to pay for a new one if they win the conference title enough years in a row.

Who would ever think of holding homecoming in a science laboratory, where straight-A chemistry majors performed on bunsen burners? Returning alumni would not be motivated to part with their annual giving checks. Any normal college, therefore, sets aside money for athletic scholarships knowing that its investment will be repaid in full.

Some of the money the jocks bring into the college may be used to pay for the printing of the academic catalogue. This will describe the virtues of a college education, such as having straight-A chemistry majors performing on bunsen burners. Some professors will believe so firmly in these ideals that they will be willing to flunk out the jock at the first chance they get, since the jock represents a prostituting of the Educational Ideal.

They will do this after spending the previous evening shouting with joy as the jock scores 44 points in a basketball game over the arch-rival. Therefore, take this advice: either don't attend basketball games, or else treat the jock like any another student.

Study Questions

1. This essay, primarily a division, uses other structures you have studied. Point out examples of reporting and giving directions.

2. Despite its humorous overtones, Runnion's essay contains many serious, straightforward statements. Point out examples which are mainly funny, ones which are ironical and ones which mean exactly what they say. Consider how this blend of tones contributes to the overall effect of the essay.
3. Runnion has organized his essay by dividing it into sections which define various types of students. Is the division a random one or does it have some discernible basis?
4. Through his discussion of various types of students does the author aim to define "student" or does he assume the reader's knowledge of what a student is and concentrate on defining "revolutionary," "jock," and so forth.
5. To what audience is Runnion directing his essay? Is interest limited to that group or does Runnion try to appeal to the general reader as well? Give examples to back your points.

Mentally Retarded Children   ORVILLE JOHNSON

A great deal has been written in the professional literature as well as in books, magazines, and newspapers designed for general consumption regarding the care, training, education, and treatment of intellectually retarded persons. This volume of material, unfortunately, has often confused rather than clarified the innumerable problems related to mental retardation. The lack of clarification has been due primarily to the different terminologies used by the various authors in the different professions as well as among those writing within the same discipline. Occasionally authors with a particular bias take advantage of this confusion of terms and present material that while technically accurate leaves the reader with understandings and beliefs that are not in harmony with available information. Students and the general reader of all these materials must, as a result, carefully read and evaluate the characteristics of the children to whom an author is referring in order to relate the material to the appropriate group.

For educational purposes, there are at least three distinct groups of mentally retarded children. . . . Each group has its unique characteristics and problems requiring a distinct educational program. These groups are the *trainable mentally*

From William M. Cruickshank and Orville G. Johnson, Editors, *Education of Exceptional Children and Youth*, Second Edition © 1967. Reprinted by permission of Prentice-Hall, Inc., Englewood Cliffs, New Jersey. Title supplied by editors.

retarded, the educable mentally retarded, and the *slow learners.* A fourth group not considered for educational purposes are those children who are so intellectually deficient that they require constant care and supervision. Many of these persons can never learn to communicate or to provide for their most simple, personal needs such as eating, dressing, and toileting. Others can accomplish these but little more.

The trainable mentally retarded are not usually considered to be educable in the sense that they can learn academic skills to any degree of competency. Further, they require custodial care and supervision for their entire lives. The responsibility for this care has ordinarily been assumed by their parents or by the state through departments of health, welfare, or mental hygiene. Until relatively recently, the trainable retarded have not been considered a responsibility of the public schools. While many can be taught or trained to make limited contributions to their own welfare and the protected environment in which they live, few communities until the last decade or two had made extensive "educational" or training provisions for them.

The educable mentally retarded are defined as those children who are so intellectually retarded that it is impossible for them to be adequately educated in the regular classroom. They are, however, educable in the sense that they can acquire sufficient knowledge and ability in the academic areas that these skills can and will become useful and usable tools. Further, they have a prognosis of social adequacy and occupational or economic self-sufficiency as adults. They will be able to apply the skills learned during the years of their formal education toward maintaining an independent social and economic existence as adults.

The slow learners are the highest intellectual group of retarded children and are largest in number. They form the 15 to 17 per cent of the school population that cannot quite "keep up" and are usually doing the poorest work in the regular classroom. Slow learners are essentially normal in their emotional, social, physical, and motor development. In intellectual development the slow learners are the lower fringe or range of the normal group.

Educators, both general and special, have usually considered the intellectual deviation of the slow learners so slight that they can usually be best accommodated in the regular classroom. In recent years the slow learners have been receiving a great deal of attention from a number of agencies because of their high drop-out rate, low wages, and high incidence of delinquency, truancy, and receipt of public relief. Numerous Federal programs have been instigated and designed to deal directly or indirectly with their problems. Obviously the general curriculum has not provided adequately for their educational needs.

Study Questions

1. The main-idea sentence and a statement of the division appear in the second paragraph. What is the purpose of the first paragraph?
2. What unstated definition is the foundation of the essay?

3. What division governs the organization of the essay? How is each
    section developed?
4. What is the purpose of this essay? How is the purpose made clear in
    the main-idea sentence?
5. This paper has no conclusion. Considering the essay's purpose, write
    a brief closing paragraph.

Of Charity (1 Corinthians 13)   PAUL THE APOSTLE

Though I speak with the tongues of men and of angels, and have not charity,
I am become *as* sounding brass, or a tinkling cymbal.

2. And though I have *the gift of* prophecy, and understand all mysteries,
and all knowledge; and though I have all faith, so that I could remove mountains, and have not charity, I am nothing.

3. And though I bestow all my goods to feed *the poor*, and though I give
my body to be burned, and have not charity, it profiteth me nothing.

4. Charity suffereth long, *and* is kind; charity envieth not; charity vaunteth
not itself, is not puffed up.

5. Doth not behave itself unseemly, seeketh not her own, is not easily provoked, thinketh no evil;

6. Rejoiceth not in iniquity, but rejoiceth in the truth;

7. Beareth all things, believeth all things, hopeth all things, endureth all
things.

8. Charity never faileth: but whether *there be* prophecies, they shall fail;
whether *there be* tongues, they shall cease; whether *there be* knowledge, it shall
vanish away.

9. For we know in part, and we prophesy in part.

10. But when that which is perfect is come, then that which is in part shall
be done away.

11. When I was a child, I spake as a child, I understood as a child, I thought
as a child: but when I became a man, I put away childish things.

12. For now we see through a glass, darkly; but then face to face: now I
know in part; but then shall I know even as also I am known.

13. And now abideth faith, hope, charity, these three; but the greatest of
these *is* charity.

Study Questions

1. What formal definition can be constructed from the description of
    charity given in the passage?
2. Does division play a part in the definition? If so, what part?
3. The author spends as much time saying what charity is *not* as he does
    saying what it is. How is division employed in this aspect of the
    definition?

Song

Love is a sickness full of woes,
  All remedies refusing;
A plant that with most cutting grows,
  Most barren with best using.
      Why so?   5
More we enjoy it, more it dies;
If not enjoyed, it sighing cries,
      Heigh-ho!

Love is a torment of the mind,
  A tempest everlasting;   10
And Jove hath made it of a kind
  Not well, nor full, nor fasting.
      Why so?
More we enjoy it, more it dies;
If not enjoyed, it sighing cries,   15
      Heigh-ho!

Study Questions

1. Like Paul's essay on charity, Daniel's definition of love is a series of assertions about his subject. Which of these assertions, if any, might you find in the dictionary definition of love?

2. Even though these assertions are not of the kind ordinarily found in a dictionary, show how they take the form of a formal definition.

3. How is division used to organize these assertions into a poetic statement about love?

4. Using just one of the poet's assertions about love, construct a classification and division which might serve as the basis for an extended essay.

When Is Death?   LEONARD A. STEVENS

A few years ago, an Englishman named John David Potter was rushed to the Newcastle General Hospital after suffering extensive brain damage in a brawl. Fourteen hours later, he stopped breathing. Ordinarily, the man would have been declared dead, but at that moment a kidney was needed for transplant, and Potter was an obvious donor.

A respirator was applied, and it artificially revived Potter's breathing. This in turn restored his failing heartbeat and circulation, thus preserving the kidneys. These vital organs, now strictly dependent upon the respirator, were kept going 24 hours, even though the doctors knew that Potter had no chance of recovery. Meanwhile, Mrs. Potter had granted permission to remove a kidney for transplant. When this was done, the attending physician ordered the respirator turned off. For the second time, Potter ceased breathing, and his heart stopped forever.

When and from what cause did Potter die? The question was central to the subsequent inquest. The coroner was of the opinion that the kidney had been taken before death. A hospital doctor agreed in part, saying that Potter was *medically* dead when he first stopped breathing, but not *legally* dead until a day later, when the respirator was stopped. A consulting neurosurgeon and government pathologist decided that brain damage had killed Potter before the kidney removal. A jury concluded that the kidney removal had nothing to do with Potter's death, and brought in a verdict of manslaughter against the dead man's assailant in the brawl.

The Potter case is now one of many that emphasize the need for a new definition of death. The problem is essentially medical: in shutting off a respirator, for example, a doctor seems to be opposing the ancient understanding that a medical man should struggle against the onslaught of death down to the last fleeting sign of life. But it prompts great concern in the legal field, too, since courts must often pin down the exact time of death. A doctor, in starting or stopping resuscitative measures, could call into question court decisions which have already fixed the time of death at the point when all vital functions cease. Theologians, also, recognize that they have an interest in how the problem is settled: doctors may appear to be taking into their hands decisions that rightfully belong to God. Indeed, all of us are involved, because the definition of death affects each person's right to meet his end with dignity when the time comes.

Where Is the Boundary?

Until recently, the definition was based on there being a fairly sharp boundary drawn between life and death by the final heartbeat and last breath. But the past 10 or 15 years have brought us many important resuscitative measures, including portable respirators, external heart massage, electrical pacemakers, new drugs, heart-lung machines and improved surgery on the heart. As a result, both the lungs and heart can today be resuscitated after they have completely stopped. The individual's fate then lies in what has happened to the cells of the brain.

When the body's respiratory and circulatory systems cease functioning, vital nerve cells of the brain are denied oxygen and die within three to eight minutes. Even when resuscitative measures successfully maintain these two systems, they in turn may fail to restore or preserve the brain cells. The patient may then have the semblance of being alive when he has really suffered brain damage that permanently denies the experiences that we know as life. Thus, many doctors are moving away from the narrow, traditional focus upon respiration and heartbeat toward a broader definition often referred to as "brain death."

Prolonged loss of consciousness, or coma, undoubtedly comes as close to death as any state of life can be. Coma varies in depth according to the degree of brain damage involved. In time, most victims return to their senses, but if the underlying damage is serious enough, the person suffers "irreversible" coma, and for him, thought and communication have ended. In some instances, the lungs and heart continue spontaneously, and the patient can live in a "vegetative" state for years, providing he is tube-fed and his body needs are cared for. In Montreal, for instance, a 21-year-old woman, Lise Dagenais, died recently after remaining unconscious 12 years as the result of an auto accident.

Natural Course

There are medical leaders who are saying that irreversible coma is a sound reason for declaring a human being dead, even though his heart, lungs and other organs can be maintained with artificial aids. They are not advocating that death should be dealt to such a patient—which would be euthanasia. They are maintaining that resuscitative measures should be removed, allowing death to follow its natural course.

One such leader is Dr. Henry K. Beecher, of the Harvard University Medical School. Dr. Beecher recently headed the 13-member Ad Hoc Committee from the Harvard faculty which examined the problem of defining death and suggested that brain death become the new criterion.* Modern techniques, said the committee, "can now restore 'life' as judged by the ancient standards, even when there is not the remotest possibility of an individual recovering consciousness."

How can coma be diagnosed as irreversible? A number of doctors are devising tests. They generally focus on the electrical activity of the patient's brain, as measured by an electroencephalograph, a machine which records "brain waves." In a live human, an electroencephalogram (EEG) is recorded as a wavy

*Similar recommendations, or at least encouragement, have come from the World Medical Association, the Council for International Organizations of Medical Sciences, the French Academy of Medicine, the American Medical Association and our National Academy of Sciences.

line. But doctors have found that if it flattens out, becomes "isoelectric" (electrically neutral), death soon follows.

Between 1957 and 1967, three doctors at the University of Iowa studied 25 patients with isoelectric EEG's and found that all died (their hearts and breathing ceased) within one to five days after the first "flat" reading. They also studied eight other flat-EEG cases where the patients' breathing was being sustained by mechanical respirators. All of these patients died within one to 38 days after the respirator was applied. The researchers then surveyed the world's medical literature and found no evidence of a patient surviving an EEG that had remained truly isoelectric for a number of hours. The doctors concluded that when brain death is diagnosed, "it is useless and inhuman to maintain the patient on a mechanical respirator."

Additional Yardsticks

To determine whether a patient is truly dead, the Harvard Ad Hoc Committee suggests three other yardsticks in addition to a flat EEG:

1. The patient should be totally unaware and unresponsive, so that "even the most intensely painful stimuli evoke no vocal or other response, not even a groan, withdrawal of a limb or quickening of respiration."

2. The patient should be observed for at least an hour to make certain that there are no muscular movements of spontaneous breathing.

3. Reflexes should be absent. Tendons tapped with a small reflex hammer should not elicit the reflexive muscular responses seen in a living person. Pupils of the eyes should be dilated and unresponsive to a bright light.

All these tests should be repeated at least 24 hours later, and show no change.

Brain death as a criterion for diagnosing life's end has already been employed by a number of doctors. The most publicized instances are found in the recent heart transplants, where the donors have been suffering from irreversible coma. At St. Luke's Episcopal Hospital in Houston, where Dr. Denton Cooley and his surgical team have completed the world's largest number of heart transplants, the following criteria are used to determine a donor's death: He has had an isoelectric EEG for a minimum of 24 hours; he is unable to breathe without a respirator; he shows no signs of reflexes and no spontaneous muscular activity. After an impartial doctor independent of the transplant team has ascertained these facts, the donor is declared dead, and the respirator is turned off.

In cases other than heart transplants, it is difficult to determine how widely accepted the brain-death criterion has become, but it is not unusual to find doctors who have acted upon it in appropriate cases. For example, the unconscious 16-year-old son of a Chicago doctor was recently brought to one of the city's hospitals. The case was accepted by the father's close friend and diagnosed as severe encephalitis which had badly damaged the brain. His breathing ceased, and a respirator was applied, but soon all the signs of brain death were evident. Several times in the next 24 hours the respirator was temporarily turned off; each time the heart and lungs failed to function on their own. Whereupon, after consultation with the family, the attending physician ordered the respirator turned off, and the patient was declared dead.

No Legal Precedent

Doctors who face such grave decisions maintain that the diagnosis of death is strictly a medical matter and must be entrusted to a patient's attending physician. Few people disagree, but of all concerned parties, the legal profession will probably find it hardest to deal with the changing definition. For centuries, courts have defined death as does *Black's Law Dictionary*: ". . . a total stoppage of the circulation of the blood, and a cessation of the animal and vital functions consequent thereupon, such as respiration, pulsation, etc." As of now, there is no legal precedent of a court accepting the brain as the ruling organ in determining death.

Courts often need the precise time and nature of death to settle manslaughter charges, inheritance claims, insurance proceeds, tax problems, and the disposition of jointly held money and property. One often quoted case involves a 1958 auto accident which claimed the lives of an Arkansas couple. The man died instantly, but his wife remained in a deep coma for 17 days before her heart stopped beating. In a legal disagreement over their two wills, an attorney contended that the man and wife had died simultaneously because both lost the power to act in the same instant. The court denied this, and ruled that the woman's beating heart delayed her legal death for the 17 days.

Perspective

Among theologians, the subject of the changing medical definition is widely discussed but not highly controversial. In general, those who have spoken out on the topic agree that responsibility for changing the definition of death belongs to the medical profession. Any discussion of the matter is certain to refer back to a 1957 pronouncement made by Pope Pius XII in response to questions submitted by Dr. Bruno Haid, of the University of Innsbruck, Austria. Dr. Haid asked if he would be bound to use artificial-respiration apparatus in cases of deep unconsciousness judged completely hopeless by a competent doctor. The Pope said no, and went on to declare that when a case becomes hopeless, after everything possible has been done to restore life, the opposition to death should end. The final decision, he added, is up to the patient's family.

For all of us—doctor, lawyer, clergyman or layman—the substantial benefits of modern resuscitation behoove us to seek a new view of death. In the final analysis, a dying person and his family can rely on an ancient pact, unwritten and usually unspoken, between a good doctor and his patient. It is simply that the doctor, backed by his training, experience and the entire history of medicine, has but the single mission of doing what is best for each individual under his care.

This kind of medical perspective was the point of a story told recently at a conference on the subject of death. "A physician friend," said the doctor relating the story, "told me that while he was visiting his elderly, widowed and very lonely father, the father collapsed with an arrested heart. The son began external cardiac massage—then stopped. It seemed to him that it was the right time for his father to die. My friend had the perspective of which I speak."

Study Questions

1. Why does the writer entitle his essay "When Is Death?" rather than "What is Death?"
2. What is the purpose of the example of John Potter?
3. How many definitions of death does Stevens give? Quote them. What definition does he want his readers to accept?
4. This is a long essay, rather than a one-paragraph definition. What method of organization does Stevens use to develop the essay?
5. What is the purpose of the essay? How is it achieved?

The Forms of Marriage   BRONISLAW MALINOWSKI

From the foregoing description it will be clear that there is a considerable range within which the constitution of marriage can vary. For as we have seen there can be many different arrangements in the domestic, legal, economic and ceremonial sides of marriage, and each of their manifold combinations constitutes a distinct form of marriage.

The term "form of marriage" has been as a rule applied to what might be called the *numeric variation* in marriage, i.e., the variation according to the number of consorts united to each other; and the main "forms of marriage" usually listed are monogamy, polygyny, polyandry and group-marriage. To deal with this classification adequately it is necessary to distinguish hypothetical assumptions from actually existing social arrangements. From this point of view we can at once eliminate "group-marriage," since our previous analysis has shown that the *pirrauru* relationship of Australia and similar institutions among the Eskimo and in Siberia can not in their parental, economic, legal or religious functions be regarded as a form of marriage.

Polyandry

This is the name given to a union in which several men are legally bound in marriage to one woman. Polyandry is the rarest of the numeric varieties of marriage, and unfortunately the one on which, in spite of its great theoretical importance, we possess but very meagre and inadequate information. Polyandry is not found among any of the more primitive peoples, and its distribution is almost completely confined to the highlands of S. India and C. Asia, with

From *Sex, Culture and Myth* by Bronislaw Malinowski, © 1962 by A. Valetta Malinowski. Reprinted by permission of Harcourt Brace Jovanovich, Inc.

isolated exceptions, such as one African tribe (Bahima) and some Eskimo, among whom it occurs, but infrequently.

In Tibet and the adjacent countries there exists polyandry of the fraternal type, i.e., several brothers share the wife in common. All the husbands live together with their common wife as members of the same household, and cohabit successively with her. Children born of these marriages are sometimes regarded as the legal descendants of the eldest brother-husband only; in other cases it appears that when a child is born it is attributed to him by whom the mother asserts that she has conceived it.

Among the Nayars of S.W. India there is a so-called form of polyandry which has played an important though rather deceptive part in the theories of marriage. A girl goes through a form of marriage with a man, but then really consorts with a number of men who need not be related to one another. She lives apart from her partners, who cohabit with her successively by agreement among themselves. Owing to the matrilineal institutions of this people, the children of such marriages inherit from their mother's brother, but the social importance of fatherhood is seen in the fact that the woman, when pregnant, always nominates one or other of the men as the father of the child, and he is obliged to provide for it and to educate it.

Another account is that by Dr. Rivers, of the Toda polyandry, which can be taken as the representative of the simpler type of this institution in S. India. Among the Toda, several men, usually two or three brothers, share the wife, but it is the rule that they cohabit with her in succession. Again, the children are not owned in common by the husbands, but each child is allotted individually to one, not with reference to any presumption of physical paternity, but in virtue of a ritual act performed by the man over the child, an act which establishes social paternity and confers legitimate descent on the child.

Polyandry is thus a compound marriage, in which cohabitation is usually successive, and not joint, while children and property are not shared by the husbands.

Polygyny

This is a form of marriage in which several wives are united to one man, each having the status of legal consort, while her offspring are regarded as the legal descendants of the husband. As an institution polygyny exists in all parts of the world. There are very few primitive tribes about whom we are informed that a man is not allowed, if he can, to enter into more than one union. Many peoples have been said to be monogamous, but it is difficult to infer from the data at our disposal whether monogamy is the prevalent practice, the moral ideal, or an institution safeguarded by sanctions. It must be remembered at once that polygyny is never practised throughout the community: there cannot exist a community in which every man would have several wives, since this would entail an enormous surplus of females over males. The second important point with regard to polygyny, which is seldom brought out clearly, is that in reality it is not so much a form of marriage fundamentally distinct from monogamy as rather a multiple monogamy. It is always in fact the repetition of a marriage contract, entered individually with each wife, establishing an individual relationship between the man and each of his consorts. As a rule each relationship is little affected legally or economically by the others.

Where each wife has her separate household and the husband visits them in turn, polygynous marriage resembles very closely a temporarily interrupted monogamy. In such cases there is a series of individual marriages in which domestic arrangements, economics, parenthood as well as legal and religious elements do not as a rule seriously encroach on each other. The polygyny with separate households is more universally prevalent. Among the great majority of the Bantu and Hamitic peoples of Africa, where the number of wives, especially in the case of chiefs, is often considerable, each wife commonly occupies a separate hut with her children, and manages an independent household with well-defined legal and economic rights. Where, on the other hand, as among many N. American tribes, two or more wives share the same household, polygyny affects the institution of matrimonial life much more deeply.

In most cases the motive for polygyny is economic and political. Thus in the Trobriand Islands (Melanesia) the chief's income is due to his wives' annual endowment. In many African communities the chief derives his wealth from the plurality of his wives, who by means of the produce of their agricultural labour enable him to exercise the lavish hospitality upon which so much of his power rests. A multitude of wives, however, may increase not only a man's wealth but also his social importance, reputation and authority, apart from the influence of the number of his children. Hence we find in many Bantu communities of Africa that the desire to have many wives is one of the leading motives in the life of every man; while the fact that in many Melanesian and Polynesian communities polygyny is a prerogative of the chief testifies to the social prestige attaching to it.

Monogamy

Monogamy is not only the most important form of marriage, not only that which predominates in most communities, and which occurs, statistically speaking, in an overwhelming majority of instances, but it is also the pattern and prototype of marriage.

Both polyandry and polygyny are compound marriages consisting of several unions combined into a larger system, but each of them constituted upon the pattern of a monogamous marriage. As a rule polygamous cohabitation is a successive monogamy and not joint domesticity; children and property are divided, and in every other respect the contracts are entered individually between two partners at a time.

Monogamy as the unique and exclusive form of marriage, in the sense that bigamy is regarded as a grave criminal offence and a sin as well as a sacrilege, is very rare indeed. Such an exclusive ideal and such a rigid legal view of marriage is perhaps not to be found outside the modern, relatively recent development of Western Culture. It is not implied in Christian doctrine even. Apart from such isolated phenomena as the recent Church of Latter Day Saints (Mormons) and the heretical sect of Anabaptists (16th century), polygyny was legally practised and accepted by the Church in the middle ages, and it occurs sporadically as a legal institution accepted by Church and State as recently as the middle of the 17th century.

Monogamy as pattern and prototype of human marriage, on the other hand, is universal. The whole institution, in its sexual, parental, economic, legal and religious aspects, is founded on the fact that the real function of marriage—sexual union, production and care of children, and the co-operation which it implies—requires essentially two people, and two people only, and that in the overwhelming majority of cases two people only are united in order to fulfil these facts.

Conjugation necessarily takes place only between two organisms; children are produced by two parents only, and always socially regarded as the offspring of one couple; the economics of the household are never conducted group-wise; the legal contract is never entered upon jointly; the religious sanction is given only to the union of two. A form of marriage based on communism in sex, joint parenthood, domesticity, group-contract and a promiscuous sacrament has never been described. Monogamy is, has been and will remain the only true type of marriage. To place polygyny and polyandry as "forms of marriage" co-ordinate with monogamy is erroneous. To speak about "group-marriage" as another variety shows a complete lack of understanding as to the nature of marriage.

Study Questions

1. Copy the main-idea sentence. Underline the term to be defined, the class to which it is assigned, and the division which governs the organization of the essay.
2. Is the main purpose of the essay to define marriage or to define the various kinds of marriage?
3. How does Malinowski's purpose for writing compare with that of Runnion?
4. To what extent does the author use comparison? Point out examples of sentences which make a clear and direct comparison.

Of the Slavery and Pains Eternal   JEREMY TAYLOR

The slavery of the damned in hell is such, that all their senses, and powers of soul and body, are subject unto eternal pains and torments; with their touch, they are to serve the burning and never-consuming fire; with their taste, hunger and thirst; with their smell, stink; with their sight, those horrid and monstrous shapes which the devils shall assume; with their hearing, scorns and affronts;

with their imagination, horror; with their will, loathsomeness and detestation; with their memory, despair; with their understanding, confusion; with such a multitude of other punishments, as they shall want eyes to weep for them.

Aelian writes of Trizus, the tyrant, that he commanded his subjects not to speak together, and when they used signs, instead of words, he also forbade those; whereupon the afflicted people met in the market-place to at least weep for their misfortunes, but neither was that permitted: greater shall be the rigor in hell, where they shall neither be suffered to speak a word of comfort, nor move hand or foot, nor ease their hearts with weeping. Jeremias the prophet lamented with floods of tears, that Jerusalem, which was the queen of nations, should be made a slave and tributary: what tears are sufficient to lament the damnation of a poor soul who, from an heir and prince of the kingdom of heaven, hath made himself a slave to the devil, and those eternal punishments in hell, unto which he is to pay as many tributes as he hath senses, powers, and members.

As the slaves of the earth are whipped and punished by their masters, so the slaves of hell are tormented by the devils, who have power and dominion over them: children, as slaves, are whipped and chastised by their masters, so the tormentors, making the damned as their slaves, lay upon them a thousand afflictions, griefs, and miseries: every member of their body shall suffer greater pain and torment, than if it were torn from the body. If one cannot tell how to suffer a toothache, headache, or the pain of the cholic, what will it be when there shall not be any joint, or the least part of the body, which shall not cause him an intolerable pain? Not only the head, or teeth, but also the breasts, sides, shoulders, the back, the heart, and all the parts of the body, even to the very bones and marrow. Who can express the number and greatness of their torments, since all their powers and senses, soul and body, are to suffer in a most violent manner? Besides this, every sense from his particular object shall receive a particular punishment.

The eye shall not only be grieved with a scorching heat, but shall be tormented with monstrous and horrible figures: many are affrighted very much, passing through a churchyard, only for fear of seeing a fantasm; in what a fright will be a miserable damned soul, which shall see so many, and of so horrid shapes? Their sight also shall be tormented with beholding the punishment of their friends and kindred. Hegesippus writes, that Alexander, the son of Hyrcannus, resolving to punish certain persons with exemplary rigor, caused eight hundred to be crucified; and whilst they were yet alive, caused their wives and children to be murdered before their eyes; that so they might die not once, but many deaths. This rigor shall not be wanting in hell, where fathers shall see their sons, and brothers their brothers, tormented. The torment of the eyes shall be also very great, in regard that those which have given other scandal, and made others fall into sin, shall see themselves, and those others, in that abyss of torments. To the sight of those dreadful apparitions shall be added the horror and fearful darkness of the place.

The darkness of Egypt was said to be horrible, because there the Egyptians beheld fearful figures and fantasms which terrified them. In the like manner, in that infernal darkness, the eyes shall be tormented with the monstrous figures of the wicked spirits, which shall appear much more dreadful, by reason of the obscurity and sadness of that eternal night.

The hearing shall not only be afflicted by an intolerable pain, caused by that ever burning and penetrating fire, but also with the fearful and amazing noises of thunders, howlings, clamors, groans, curses, and blasphemies. Sylla, being dictator, caused six thousand persons to be enclosed in the circus; and then appointing the senate to meet in a temple close by, where he intended to speak unto them about his own affairs, to strike the greater terror into them, and make them know he was their master, he gave order, that, so soon as he began his oration, the soldiers should kill this multitude of people, which was effected: upon which were heard such lamentations, outcries, groans, clashing of armor, and blows of those merciless homicides, that the senators could not hear a word, but stood amazed with terror of so horrid a fact. What shall be the harmony of hell, where the ears shall be deafened with the cries and complaints of the damned? What confusion and horror shall it breed, to hear all lament, all complain, all curse and blaspheme, through the bitterness of the torments which they suffer?

But the damned shall principally be affrighted, and shall quake to hear the thunderclap of the wrath of God, which shall continually resound in their ears! "Whereas the just," saith the royal prophet, "shall be in the eternal memory of God, and shall not fear the dreadful crack of his wrath."

The smell shall also be tormented with a most pestilential stink. Horrible was that torment used by Mezentius, to tie a living body to a dead, and there to leave them, until the infection and putrefied exhalations of the dead had killed the living. What can be more abominable, than for a living man to have his mouth laid close to that of a dead one, full of grubs and worms, where the living must receive all those pestilential vapors, breathed forth from a corrupt carcass, and suffer such loathsomeness and abominable stink? But what is this in respect of hell, when each body of the damned is more loathsome and unsavory than a million of dead dogs, and all those pressed and crowded together in so strait a compass? Bonaventure goes so far as to say, that if one only of the damned were brought into this world, it were sufficient to infect the whole earth. Neither shall the devils send forth a better smell; for although they are spirits, yet those fiery bodies, unto which they are fastened and confined, shall be of a more pestilential savor.

Hell is the world's sink, and the receptacle of all the filth in this great frame, and withal a deep dungeon, where the air hath no access. How great must the stink and infection needs be of so many corruptions heaped one upon another! and how insufferable the smell of that infernal brimstone, mixed with so many corrupted matters! O gulf of horror! O infernal grave! without vent or breathing place! Eternal grave of such as die continually and cannot die, with what abominable filth art thou not filled!

What shall I then say of the tongue, which is the instrument of so many ways of sinning, flattery, lying, murmuring, and calumniating, gluttony, and drunkenness. Who can express that bitterness, which the damned shall suffer, greater than that of aloes or wormwood? The Scripture tells us, the gall of dragons shall be their wine; and they shall taste the poison of asps for all eternity, unto which shall be joined an intolerable thirst, and doglike hunger: comformable to which David said, "they shall suffer hunger, as dogs." Famine is the most pressing of all necessities, and most deformed of all evils; plagues and wars are happinesses in respect of it. If, then, a famine of eight days be the worst of temporal evils, what shall that famine be which is eternal? Let our epicures hear what the Son of God prophesies: "Wo unto you who are full;" for you shall be a hungered, and with such a hunger as shall be eternal. Hunger in this life doth bring men to such extremity, that not only they come to desire to eat dogs, cats, rats, and mice, but also mothers come to eat their own children, and men the flesh of their own arms, as it fell out to Zeno the emperor. If hunger be so terrible a mischief in this life, how will it afflict the damned in the other! Without all doubt, the damned would rather tear themselves in pieces than suffer it; all the most horrible famines, that Scripture histories propose unto us, are but weak pictures to that which the damned suffer in this unfortunate residence of eternal miseries; neither shall thirst torment them less.

The sense of touching, as it is the most extended sense of all the rest, so it shall be the most tormented in that burning fire; all the torments which the Scripture doth exhibit to us, as prepared for the reprobate, seem to fall upon this only sense: "They shall pass," saith Job, "from extremity of cold to intolerable heats," whole floods of fire and brimstone, which shower down upon those unfortunate wretches; all this belongs unto the sense of touching. We are amazed to think of the inhumanity of Phalaris, who roasted men alive in his brazen bull: this was a joy in respect of that fire of hell, which penetrates the very entrails of the body without consuming them. The burning of a finger only does cause so great a torment, that it is insufferable; but far greater were it to burn the whole arm; and far greater were it, besides the arms, to burn the legs; and far more violent torment would it be to burn the whole body. This torment is so great that it cannot be expressed, since it comprises as many torments as the body of man hath joints, sinews, arteries, etc., especially being caused by that penetrating and real fire, of which this temporal fire is but a painted fire in respect of that in hell.

Amongst all the torments which human justice hath invented for the punishment of crimes, there is none held more rigorous than that of fire, by reason of the great activity of that element. What shall the heat of that fire be, which shall be the executioner of the justice of the God of vengeance! whose zeal shall be inflamed against the wicked, and shall kindle the fire, which shall eternally burn in the extremities of hell! Such are the torments and miseries of hell, that if all the trees in the world were put in one heap, and set on fire, I would rather burn there till the day of judgment, than suffer, only for the space of one hour, that fire of hell. What a miserable unhappiness will it be to burn in those flames of hell, not only for an hour, but till the day of judgment! yea, even for all eternity, and world without end! Who would not esteem it a hideous torment, if he were to be burnt alive a hundred times, and his torment was to last every time for the space of an hour, with what compassionate eyes would all the world look upon such a miserable wretch! Nevertheless, without all doubt, any of the damned in hell would receive this as a great happiness to end his torments with those hundred times burning: for what comparison is there betwixt a hundred hours burning, with some space of time betwixt every hour, and to burn a hundred years of continual torment! And what comparison will there be betwixt burning for a hundred years' space, and to be burning without interruption, as long as God is God!

Who can express the strange and horrible confusion which shall inhabit the appetite of these wretched creatures? If all the disorders of man's life spring from his passions, what disorder must those miserable souls needs feel in that part, what convulsions, what rage, what fury? Alas! that noble passion, love, the queen of all the rest, the sun of life, that passion which might have made them happy for ever, if they had turned it towards God; that amiable object being razed out of them, the perpetual aversion they have to love shall eternally afflict them, the passion of hatred shall be outrageous in the damned, whence shall proceed their continual blasphemies against God, and the perpetual curses and imprecations which they shall make against the creatures; and if they have any desires, they shall be desirous to see all the world partake of their pains; their aversion from all good shall be as much tormenting, as in itself it is execrable: of joy there must no mention be made in that place of dolor; but contrariwise of incredible sadness, which shall oppress them without any consolation. The heat of anger shall redouble the heat of their flames; hope banished from their hearts shall leave the place void to despair, which shall be one of their fiercest tormentors. And though their bodies be within hell's bosom, yet shall they bear about them another hell in their own bosoms.

Consider, now, my soul, whether thou art able to live in this devouring fire, whether thou wilt make choice of thy habitation in eternal flames. This fire is prepared for the devil and his angels; consider whether thou wilt enter in to this cursed crew, and take part of the dregs of their chalice. There is no medium; either thou must forsake thy sins, or else thou must be given up a prey to this eternal torment. I doubt not, thou wilt make a happy choice; and, to escape so dangerous a gulf, cast thy self into the arms of Divine mercy, which only admits the penitent, and say thus: O great God, who art a consuming fire, and makest the fire of thy Divine justice issue from amongst the thorns, to burn the tallest cedars in Lebanon; let the fire, which walks before thee as executioner of justice, never depart from our memory; may it be unto us a pillar of light in the darkness of our errors, a lamp unto our feet, and a lantern to our ways, whereby we may discover this infernal gulf, which is ready to swallow us up. Thou, O Lord, who didst deliver the three children out of the Babylonian furnace, preserve us from those eternal flames, and exempt us from the burning ones of thy wrath; place us in the light and bright one of thy love, where, like Pyratides and sacred Salamanders, we shall live happy, without pain and torment, singing honor, praise, and benediction unto thee, our God, for ever and ever. Amen.

Study Questions

1. Explain why the introductory paragraph of this essay would make an excellent conclusion to the essay.

2. What precisely is being defined in Taylor's essay? List the major details which support and enlarge the definition.
3. What order governs the essay: spatial, chronological, or some other method? Prove your answer by quoting sentences which support it.

PRELIMINARY WORKSHEET

1. Topic _____

2. Source of information

    a. personal knowledge

_____

_____

_____

    b. library resources

_____

_____

_____

_____

_____

_____

_____

3. Classification of topic _____

_____

_____

_____

4. Division of topic into categories/characteristics

    a. _____

    b. _____

    c. _____

    d. _____

    e. _____

      f. _____

      g. _____

5. Main-idea sentence _____

_____

_____

_____

_____

6. Details for each division (arranged spatially, chronologically, or in other ways)

      a. _____

_____

_____

_____

_____

_____

_____

_____

_____

      b. _____

_____

_____

_____

_____

_____

_____

_____

      c. _____

_____

_____

_____

_____

d.

e.

f.

g.

_____

_____

_____

_____

_____

_____

7. Supplementary information for introduction _____

_____

_____

_____

_____

8. Concluding material _____

_____

_____

_____

_____

_____

EVALUATION GUIDE

Name   _____

Topic   _____

Introduction

    1.   State the classification and division that are the basis of this paper.

           _____

           _____

    2.   Is the classification accurate? Does the division provide sufficient information to define the topic? _____

           _____

3. State the main-idea sentence. _____

_____

_____

_____

4. Does the main-idea sentence indicate the division and the order in which the division is later explored? _____

_____

Body

1. Indicate the principle of order that determines the arrangement of details within each section of the body. _____

_____

2. What transitions are used to connect one section to the next?

_____

3. Is the purpose of the paper successfully carried out? If not, what material should be added? _____

_____

_____

_____

_____

_____

Rating

___ This paper should be rewritten completely or in part.

___ This paper is acceptable but needs some minor revisions.

___ This is an outstandingly good paper.

4 Classification/Division: Comparison

INTRODUCTORY COMMENTS

In this chapter you will read and write compositions comparing two objects, building on skills developed in Chapter Three. In that chapter you learned to define a single object or idea by classifying it as a member of some larger group, and then exploring the details which distinguish it from other members of that group.

Comparison also uses classification and division, but its focus involves the systematic analysis of similarities and differences between *two* objects or ideas. Some authorities, it is true, distinguish between comparison (showing similarities) and contrast (showing differences) as forms of composition. However, since you will very rarely have reason to write a paper that consists entirely of either similarities or differences, it seems practical to use the term *comparison* to refer to *any organized exploration of similarities and/or differences between two objects or ideas in the same class or group.*

Classification/division and categorizing

The principles of classification and division are directly applied when the comparisons involve two subjects in the same logical group—for example, snow skiing and water-skiing, or the introvert and the extrovert. Sometimes, however, you may wish to compare two items normally thought of as belonging to widely separate categories—a political contest and a chess game, for example—but even here you will have to classify them in the same group—competitive activities involving strategy—in order to organize your comparison through division.

Purposes of comparison

Nothing exists in and of itself but only in relation to other things or beings. Even in the simple definition you had to begin with a recognition of similarities and proceed to an examination of differences as you assigned an object to a group and then showed how it was different from other members of that group. In the process of defining, however, the discovery of similarities and differences is only secondary to the central purpose of identifying what one object *is*. There are times, on the other hand, when you will wish to concentrate on the similarities and differences themselves in order to compare two objects or illuminate your understanding of one of them.

If you think about your habits of mind, you will very likely discover that many of your actions and most of your choices involve comparison: should you order a hot fudge or strawberry sundae (which do you like better?); should you have a cup of coffee instead of either (which is more important, satisfying your sweet tooth or slimming down your waistline?); will you watch a football game or a comedy on television (which gives you more pleasure?). Obviously, each of these sets of questions involves reviewing alternatives, a process which should lead to some decision. To review the alternatives adequately, you should sort over similarities and differences and arrange them into parallels.

Comparison, however, is not necessarily aimed at making a choice or decision. Its purpose may be simply to clarify: what something *is* can very often be discovered by the recognition of its relationships. You learn something about one object or event by comparing it to or contrasting it with another. You may also, as we have mentioned, compare two items in order to deepen your understanding of some abstract topic to which both are closely related:

> In what way is a lake comparable to a living organism, and what can we learn about how to prevent the "death" of the lake through this comparison?

> How are the learning processes in flatworms and in chimpanzees similar and/or different, and what does the comparison tell us about the nature of learning itself?

As you can see, investigating such questions should lead to a deeper appreciation of the topics involved.

Parallel structure

Clearly, researching such topics will involve you in the exploration of abstract material, and to develop the skill of handling such material you must be able to organize it. One method of doing so is the logical arrangement of similarities and differences necessary for any comparison. Since comparison means a discussion of the likenesses or differences of two or more objects or ideas, it necessitates the use of parallel structure. Parallel structure is a method of organization in which information about two or more objects is presented in a seesaw manner. The central principle of parallel or seesaw structure is that whatever you say in your essay about some aspect of one of your two items should be matched by a remark in similar form about the comparable aspect of the other. The reader will thus be guided by an overall structure that helps him follow and remember what you are saying.

Uses of the comparison structure

Why should you know how to organize a comparison? How can knowledge of this type of writing help you in all your college work? Comparison, like definition, is a structure absolutely basic to most assigned reading and writing, especially essay examinations. Consider such questions as the following: What are the principal differences between acquired and achieved status? Compare the separation of powers in the United States government with that of a typical parliamentary democracy. What are the important differences between classical and operant conditioning? These questions and many others like them clearly call for the use of a comparison structure. Many students go around in circles and write befuddled answers, even though they know a great deal of information. Some knowledge of comparison structures is helpful to such students, for it enables them to sort out their thinking and write more clearly about what they know.

GUIDELINES

1. Choose a topic.

As your topic, select two items (objects or ideas) for comparison, and classify them in terms of the purpose of your comparison. Comparisons may be made for various reasons, as we have noted, such as the choice between two alternatives or the explanation or illumination of a topic by examining the similarities and/or differences between two parts or aspects of it. In effect, then, in this assignment you will be classifying two objects or ideas as members of some larger group which you wish to explore. Consider the following samples:

What are computers and how do they work?—the digital computer and the analog computer

Two approaches to communal living: an American commune and an Israeli kibbutz

Forms of social communication: styles of dress and styles in language

What is intelligence and how may it be measured?—man's world and the dolphin's

In some of these topics there is a *natural* classification of the two items to be compared. The two types of computers are, of course, computers; the kibbutz and the commune are two kinds of communal societies. Wherever the purpose of your comparison is closely related to the category or class in which your two items are naturally classified, you hardly need consider the step of classification. But if your two items for comparison would ordinarily be thought of as members of different classes, you need to construct an artificial but *logical* classification appropriate to your purpose. Thus, styles in dress would not normally be thought of as a form of communication along with styles in language. However, classifying both as forms of communication makes a purposeful and interesting comparison possible. Similarly, both men and dolphins might naturally be labeled as mammals, but any very thorough comparison of them in terms of this classification would be long and tedious, and would hardly have a purpose. On the other hand, classifying them as mammals with intelligence provides a basis for insights into the nature of intelligence and therefore sets up a challenging topic to explore. These last two sample topics, then, involve the use of an artificial but logical classification designed to support the purpose of the comparison. Whether your classification is a natural or purely logical one, you should be aware of it as the basis of your purpose in the paper.

2. Divide the overall topic.

Divide your main topic into subgroups which can be compared. In order to provide an orderly, logical structure within which the details of your comparison can be arranged, it is necessary to begin by establishing categories or groups into which those details can later be classified. Some consideration of the sample topic on human and dolphin intelligence might lead to the following subtopics:

development of intelligence (education)

evidence of intelligence (language)

use of intelligence (social cooperation)

effects of intelligence (relation to environment)

3. List details.

Compile a list of details of similarities and differences under the appropriate categories. You cannot, of course, list all possible details, though you should list enough to provide a solid basis for your paper. Your preliminary list of details for a paper on intelligence in men and dolphins might look something like this:

a. development of intelligence (education)—close similarities

Both men and dolphins:

require a long period of close mothering in infancy

learn in a social setting

fail to learn how to communicate if deprived of close companionship in infancy and childhood

b. evidence of intelligence (language)—similarities with a difference

Men:

produce word-sounds with voice, tongue, teeth, lips

use grammar by which words are joined into sentences

convey feeling through facial expression: smiles, frowns, winks

Dolphins:

produce various sounds with various parts of body: whistles,
squeaks, chirps, jaw-clapping

use sounds as separate signals: no grammar or sentence formation

convey feeling through gross motor activity: nuzzling, nudging

c. use of intelligence (social cooperation)—similarities

Both men and dolphins:

live in groups

depend on communication for sense of well-being

use communication in group projects for mutual assistance

d. effects of intelligence (relation to environment)—differences

Men:

have developed written language and history

measure intelligence in terms of accomplishments

have hands: use tools

are helpless when naked; must alter environment to provide clothing,
shelter for survival

Dolphins:

have no written language; live in the present, without history

do not measure intelligence; simply enjoy it

have flippers: no tools

do not need to alter environment in order to survive

4. Determine the emphasis.

Consider the main emphasis of your paper in relation to your overall
purpose. Your paper will of course include an introduction, a body consisting of a number of separate paragraphs, and a conclusion. Just what
details, however, will be used in each of these parts? To answer this question, you will need to determine the emphasis of your comparison: that
is, you will have to decide whether similarities or differences are more
important for your purpose, or whether both are nearly equal in importance. In other words, you will have to decide whether the body of your
paper will consist primarily of similarities or of differences—or of approxi-

mately equal examples of both. If you are writing about two items generally regarded as very much alike (for example, California sauterne and
French sauterne), you will say very little about similarities, except possibly
in the introduction or conclusion. The emphasis of the body of your paper
will be on differences, which the reader presumably does not know. On
the other hand, you may write about two items usually thought of as
extremely different, such as the faith healer and the patent-medicine sales-
man. Here, while you touch only briefly on the more obvious differences,
probably in your introduction and conclusion, your emphasis will very
likely be on similarities. Many comparison papers properly emphasize
both similarities and differences, usually treated in separate sections, because both relate directly to the purpose of the comparison. Such will
be the case in our sample paper investigating intelligence in men and
dolphins.

5. Compose an introduction which includes a main-idea sentence.

You may build an introductory paragraph for a paper of comparison
around background material on the general class to which the two items
for comparison have been assigned, or around some of the details of similarities and differences from your list. The sample paragraph below begins
with material which leads the reader into the topic, catching his interest
and setting the stage for the comparison. The division which will provide
the structure for that comparison is stated next, and the reader is thus
led to the main-idea sentence at the end of the paragraph. Note that the
main-idea sentence for a paper of comparison should clearly indicate the
purpose of the comparison as well as state the two items that are to be
compared. It (or the accompanying introductory material) should also
state the division which will form the structure of the body and the
emphasis on similarities, or differences, or both.

Man has always prided himself on his ability to think, sometimes
insisting that he alone among the animals possesses the powers of
reasoning. A new popular familiarity with a graceful creature of the
sea called the dolphin, however, suggests that it too is an intelligent
mammal. Anyone who has ever watched dolphins playing "baseball"
in their tanks at Marineland or other seaquariums has been impressed
by behavior that indicates more than simply learned responses, for
not only do dolphins show great enjoyment of the game, they also
demonstrate an ability to evaluate changed situations. The dolphin's
intelligence has also been revealed in scientific examination of his
patterns of behavior and ways of communicating. Part of this research
has included studies comparing the dolphin to man, and what we
learn from these is that while there is a marked similarity in the ways
in which both species develop intelligence, there is a difference in the

ways in which they communicate. Also, though the use of communication skills is similar in both species, there is a profound difference in the effects of their intelligence on their respective environments. This difference, in fact, is so dramatic that it gives us insight into the natural world and offers as well another perspective on the measurement of intelligence besides our traditional human one.

6. Write the body of your paper.

Make use of parallel structure. As noted in the introductory comments, parallel structure is a seesaw method of organization, in which you present similarities or differences through a series of parallels which the reader can easily follow: each item of information about one object of comparison must be balanced by similar or contrasting information about the other. For certain passages of comparison, especially where you are dealing with very close similarities, it may be best *not* to use a parallel structure, but rather to combine or fuse the material about the two items you are comparing into a single unit. Most material for comparison, however, can best be handled in parallel form, using one of the three general methods of seesaw development. The method you choose depends largely on the nature of the material in any given part of your composition. For shorter papers, it might be appropriate to choose only one method and use it throughout; for longer papers it would be better to vary your approach by using some combination of the available methods. In the sample paragraphs below, each of the various methods of development is illustrated by one of the major sections of an essay on intelligence in men and dolphins.

Fusing Similarities. Fused development of very close similarities enables you to avoid awkward repetition of either your key words or your detailed points of comparison. It would be not only awkward but also foolish to say, for example:

> Humans go through a long period of infancy with close maternal care; dolphins also go through a long period of infancy with close maternal care.

The exact detail need be mentioned only once; and if the two topics for comparison have been well established in preceding sentences, the use of such words as "both" or "neither" can prevent monotonous repetition. The sample paragraph below is developed by this method:

> Scientists have discovered that dolphins, like man, require a long period of education within the family and the social group in order to develop their intelligence. This developed intelligence is most

clearly seen in the communications skills by which individuals are able to express their needs, reactions, and perceptions to others in their group. From a close association with parents, especially the mother, and others in their social milieu, both baby dolphins and human children learn appropriate language, how to produce sounds, meanings of sound patterns, and obedience to certain signals. The educational process continues in both species until the infant is weaned and on through adolescence, after which the mature individual is expected to join the adult community. If the young of either species are deprived of such a prolonged period of training and love, they cannot learn to communicate or function normally in their society.

Alternating Differences Sentence by Sentence. Seesaw development, sentence by sentence, requires you to take up similarities or differences one by one, maintaining the comparison consecutively from one sentence to the next. Each comment about one of the items you are comparing is *immediately* balanced by a parallel comment about the other item. This type of organization does not lend itself well to lengthy or involved comparisons, but it is a very natural and economical way to handle a few details.

We humans are of course well aware of the nature of the language we use in communication; the dolphin also uses a language, but it is in many ways different from ours. A visitor to Marineland once asked a dolphin's trainer whether the dolphin could ever learn to talk; the trainer answered that the dolphin *does* talk, but humans aren't intelligent enough to understand him. Because of differences in their capacity to make sounds, the two species use sounds in different ways for communication. Humans have a very flexible tongue and highly developed vocal chords; with these and with the use of their lips and teeth, they have a very large repertory of speech sounds from which to make words. Dolphins, on the other hand, tend to use whistles, grunts, jaw-clapping, chirps, and squeaks for communication. Human languages develop certain rules or patterns of grammar by which words are joined into sentences to express sometimes complicated thoughts. Dolphin language is not yet well understood (by humans), but it appears to consist more of single sound units used as signals than of grammatically formed sentences. In addition to spoken language, human communication depends heavily on nonverbal signals, especially facial expressions such as smiles, frowns, and winks. With his much less mobile face, the dolphin cannot so readily convey emotion, but he appears to express joy and excitement through frisking about in the water or on its surface, and affection through nuzzling and playful nudging. In spite of our difficulty in understanding dolphin language, there can be no doubt that dolphins do communicate with one another in intelligent ways.

Alternating Differences Half-paragraph by Half-paragraph. Seesaw development, half-paragraph by half-paragraph, follows the same principles as the sentence-by-sentence method except that in the first half of the paragraph you deal with a series of details about one of your two items, and in the second half, with the other idea, making sure to maintain parallel order. The half-paragraph–by–half-paragraph method, suitably balanced, is less cumbersome and confining than the sentence-by-sentence approach, though it is especially important to call the reader's attention to the comparison through a transitional sentence (underlined in the sample below) placed midway in the paragraph.

> While it is not always easy to determine the purposes, if any, behind communication among dolphins, their use of communication during cooperative endeavors for mutual assistance suggests another similarity to human intelligence. We like to think that humans are operating at their highest level of development when they are mutually cooperative. In spite of the glorification of violence and conflict in much of man's history, all the great religions have held up the ideals of peace, self-sacrifice, and love as his noblest aims. And certainly men spend much time and effort on learning language and perfecting devices for communication, all signs of mutuality and interdependence. Perhaps even more obviously than humans, dolphins show an admirable social concern and act upon it. John C. Lilly in his book *Man and Dolphin* tells of a dolphin being accidentally struck on the side of his head as he was being delivered to an oceanarium: "He was knocked unconscious and dropped to the bottom. The other dolphins pushed him to the surface and held him there until he began to breathe again." This was really a life-saving act, for a dolphin cannot remain unconscious or under water long without drowning. Like humans, then, dolphins appear to behave in ways that indicate a complex level of interdependence, maintained by means of communication.

Alternating Differences Paragraph by Paragraph. Seesaw development, paragraph by paragraph, demands that you explore in detail one of your two items for comparison before turning to the other. Again, the details you enumerate should not be haphazardly arranged, for the paragraph on the first item should set the pattern for the paragraph on the second. In this way, the paragraphs will be parallel in structure and will thus help the reader remember the details of the actual comparison. Of course, each paragraph will be developed according to the principles of order and transition outlined in the guidelines for Chapter Three. Note that in the sample essay on dolphin and human intelligence, only one division of the comparison is carried out in a paragraph-by-paragraph seesaw. It would be possible, of course, to develop an entire comparison essay by this general method. In that case, there would be two overall patterns possible:

1. You might begin with all your material on dolphins, devoting a paragraph to each division of the topic, before turning to a parallel series of paragraphs about humans.

2. You might balance your paragraph on the evidence of intelligence in dolphins directly with a paragraph on the evidence of intelligence in humans, before going on to the next division, uses of intelligence in social cooperation, and so on.

In either plan, the total structure of the paper will necessarily involve a number of paragraphs, and will be determined by *both* the division of your material *and* the importance of balanced parallels.

While there are some striking similarities between human and dolphin intelligence, the most important one concerns the achievements of intelligence, a difference which is directly related to differences in physical characteristics. Man has become what he is largely through the tools he has been able to develop because of his hands. Rather a helpless specimen in his naked, natural state, he has managed to build shelters, make clothes, and provide himself not only with all the necessities of life but often with many luxuries. His inventive use of tools ultimately produced a written language and the means of mass communication, with the result that his history and store of knowledge could be recorded and built upon in a cumulative way. He has affected his environment drastically—some might say catastrophically—and has been inclined to measure intelligence by the extent of achievements: a skyscraper, a church, a highway, a book, a theory of relativity. He has given himself a history and constructed a time scheme. But somewhere along the line he has cut himself off from the laws of instinctual behavior and therefore become separated from all the other creatures who still obey the authority of nature.

By contrast, the dolphin's flippers have no power to make or use tools and so to alter his environment. And as far as researchers can determine, he has no way to record the past except what might be passed down in direct communication from one generation to another. The dolphin may swim thousands of miles, but he is confined to observing the world rather than changing it. He seems to live in the instinctive present, navigating with a kind of built-in radar, and has no need to measure intelligence or time; he simply appears to enjoy the present moment for what it is.

7. Use linking words.

Link your paragraphs together through the use of logical transitions.
Parallel structure throughout your paper will of course help to tie together
the details within each paragraph as well as the larger ideas which form
the paragraph topics. However, you should make sure to use the transitional devices discussed in earlier guidelines to help the reader understand
how each part of your material relates to the rest. As you reread the
sample paragraphs on men and dolphins above, note especially the first
and last sentences of each to see how the repetition of key words and
ideas, expressions of logical relatedness and contrast, and reminders of
the nature of the comparison itself help you to follow the overall plan of
the paper.

8. Write your conclusion.

Your conclusion should restate the purpose of your comparison. As before, your conclusion should bring things to a close and should not introduce totally new material. However, remember that your comparison was
directed toward a purpose, perhaps that of choosing between two alternatives, but more likely that of discovering a deeper insight into some idea.
If the body of the paper has been successful, you should be able in your
conclusion to carry your reasoning a little farther than before. The sample
conclusion below is a direct expansion of the main-idea sentence, building
on materials from the body of the paper. Yet it gives the reader the feeling
not only that the paper has been completed but also that an enriching idea
has been developed.

Man's alienation from other natural creatures is a lonely state,
which leads him to try to understand the natural world by studying
other species. The dolphin, an ocean mammal which has evolved
along different paths from man's, is a likely subject for study, for
his development seems at about the same stage as man's in terms of
brain size and certain patterns of social behavior. But in his journeys
through watery currents the dolphin leaves no buildings and prints no
records of his existence. Human civilization as we know it depends
upon the tool-using and record-keeping capacities of human intelligence. Although these capacities are precisely the ones that enable
man to alter the environment, sometimes to his own detriment, society
invariably rewards them, and our educational system is largely
geared toward developing them. Human intelligence, in fact, is generally measured in ways that depend almost entirely upon the ability
to handle written communication. Our study of the dolphin, however,
shows that there is at least one other kind of intelligence man might
well value and incorporate into his systems of measurements: it is
the ability to have fun, to communicate directly, and to join in co-

operative endeavors for mutual assistance—without damaging the environment in the process.

9. Prepare your final draft.

After you have completed your rough draft, you should polish and revise it, paying careful attention to the purpose and emphasis of your comparison, parallel structure, precision of language, and use of transitions. When you have revised your paper carefully, you should prepare a final copy, taking time to proofread it thoroughly before handing it in.

SAMPLE ESSAYS

Das Abendessen   STUDENT SAMPLE

Introductory comments, establishing the writer's familiarity with the topic of the comparison.

During the five weeks I spent in Germany last spring, I found the differences between being entertained German style and being entertained American style quite marked. My brother Bill and his German wife Bärbel had warned me that I would be surprised at the formality of German social life, but I was hardly prepared for the very great difference between that formality and the typically casual dinner (or more likely "cook-out") of American life. One important reason for the difference is the fact that European meat is generally less tender than ours and so requires long, slow cooking and service at table with a sauce or gravy: to broil a piece of German beef for an outdoor, informal meal is to invite disaster. Another reason, of course, is simply the long history of maintaining social formalities in Europe, as opposed to our free-and-easy frontier tradition. But whatever the reasons, an evening with friends in Germany is fundamentally a very different affair from its American counterpart, and the differences begin with the invitation itself and continue on through the hostess gift, the contents and style of the meal, and the customs relating to staying after for a visit.

Reasons for differences, briefly examined.

Main-idea sentence giving topic and division of details of comparison to be discussed in the body of the paper.

A dinner invitation in the United States is invariably casual. Why not? A meal is only food to our countrymen. An American invitation is rendered quite offhandedly. We are a casual nation

Topic sentence for first division of details.

Reprinted by permission.

Half-paragraph on
American casual
invitations.

Half-paragraph on
German formal
invitations.

Half-paragraph on
German hostess gifts.

Half-paragraph on
American hostess gifts.

Half-paragraph on
German dinner menu.

Transitional sentence
leading to second half of
paragraph.

Half-paragraph on
American dinner menu.

Sentence on American
after-dinner visit.

Sentence on German
after-dinner visit.

and invite new friends to break bread with us with no hesitation.
An American hostess feels no embarrassment at all in telling people
on her guest list that the meal will include others who are asked
only to repay a past due social obligation or to solidify a business
deal. I've done it myself with no qualms. Not so the German invitation. Only friends of long standing are invited to meals. In Germany
the host—not the hostess—delivers the invitation. He does this
face to face, with a bit of ceremony, or with a carefully worded,
almost stilted, hand-written note.

In Germany, one very courtly custom is *always* observed. The
dinner guest takes flowers to the hostess. If a German hostess has
six sets of guests, she will have six bouquets of flowers on the
buffet. This is a relatively inexpensive custom because fresh flowers
are sold in marketplaces and on street corners in even the tiniest of
villages all over Europe. A large bunch of lovely flowers can be
bought for the equivalent of seventy-five cents in American money.
Here in the States, the so-called "hostess gift" is traditionally sent
to the home of the hostess the day after one is entertained. Although Americans do sometimes send flowers, they are prohibi-
tively expensive, and wine or candy is more usual.

German meals are heavy. The style of cooking tends toward
thick gravies, starchy dumplings, and many creamed vegetables. At
a typical meal which I ate at the home of Herr and Frau Ludwig
Engelbert in Würzburg, I was served two goulash dishes, one made
with pork and one with venison. The other guests and I also enjoyed heavy-textured but simply delicious home-made potato dumplings, sweet-sour red cabbage, three kinds of home-made bread, lots
of gravy, sour cream, rich creamery butter, and an unusual dish I
learned later was cooked cucumbers. The dessert was a huge Torte
or cake made with fresh strawberries and served with a big bowl of
whipped cream. Although I enjoyed the meal very much and over-
ate blissfully, I had to contrast it in my mind to the more spartan
American meal. We are more likely to serve a cup of light soup, a
salad, and meat, usually broiled, to get rid of the fat in our heavier
American beef. Our bread will be hot and delicious, but if we eat
both bread and potato at the same meal we usually feel we must
offer an apology, don't we? We always serve a hot vegetable, but
most of us admit quite casually that it came from the freezer by
way of a three-minute boil in salted water. A fruit dessert, prettily
arranged, to be sure, or a simple cake with a low-calorie topping is
quite normal and most acceptable here in America.

It is considered a compliment to one's hosts to linger on for a
few hours after an American meal to watch TV, play cards, or listen
to stereo. Not so in Germany. It is poor manners not to stay for at
least an hour after the meal, but it is worse manners to stay more
than an hour and a half. This custom is dictated by the early-to-
work hours of the average German.

Conclusion summarizing
writer's reactions to the
two types of
dinners.

I enjoyed my introduction to German style living and reveled in the fine cooking of my European hostesses. Although I am looking forward to returning to Würzburg in the future, I must admit that it was also a welcome relief to come home to the balanced American cuisine with its careful attention to such American worries as calories, carbohydrates, and cholesterol counts.

The Politics of Skiing   JOHN KENNETH GALBRAITH

Early this year I was writing and skiing in Switzerland. Back home, people were electioneering—New Hampshire, Florida, looking forward to Wisconsin, Nebraska. The many who were then seeking office were reaching out to persuade the few who were not.

My friends were calling to ask how I could bear to be absent. Senator Kennedy, Senator Tunney, Pierre Salinger stopped by for a few brief runs down the slopes or, in the case of Salinger, a quick glance in that direction. I thought them a bit reproachful. Clearly I was neglecting my civic duty. Skiing, yes, but not in an election year.

Eventually I yielded and came back to campaign. I slightly doubt that in an election speech I have ever persuaded anyone who wasn't previously persuaded or who wouldn't have come around anyway. People have often informed me, following one of my more impassioned efforts, and often with some vehemence, that I had confirmed them in their previous view. But I spoke and voted and even voted for myself, for I was a candidate for the Democratic delegation in Massachusetts.

As the year has passed and the election has approached, I've wondered about my decision. Maybe the best way to learn about politics is to go skiing. The two are alike in all particulars, but in skiing things are clearer on the whole.

Both politics and skiing are afflicted by professionals—the professional politician and the expert skier. The beginning of wisdom about both is to know that everything they tell you about their profession is wrong.

Given a choice between a smooth, straight path to his goal and a difficult and devious way of getting what he wants, the politician never hesitates. He instinctively embraces the difficult and devious.

In skiing, none but an idiot would choose a tortuous, steep and bumpy trail in preference to a flat slope. But the professional does and, like the politician, he thinks it is better. There is merit, he believes, in making things hard for himself.

Reprinted by permission from *Travel and Leisure*, Autumn 1972, p. 38.

In both politics and skiing, form and style count for much, performance for
almost nothing. The professional politician delights in rhetoric, rejoices in the
deathless phrase. What his oratory accomplishes is something else. More often
than not it is ignored.

The professional skier tells you to keep your legs close together and lean
forward and downhill. Any lunk knows that for getting safely to the bottom
it's better to have your legs far apart to protect your balance. And elementary
instinct tells you to keep your uphill shoulder right against the slope to protect
your body from the forces of gravity. All skiing is a triumph of awkwardness
over the law of gravity.

Both skiers and politicians attract an especially colorful train of nonfunc-
tional hangers-on. Gstaad, where I go in the winter, rejoices each February in
a brilliant—and, I believe, expanding—constellation of expensive tarts, minor
and major deadbeats, major tax evaders, cosmopolitan rumpots, backgammon
players, refugees from alimony, members of encounter groups, one devotee of
statutory rape, one super annuated spy, and one man who is variously suspected of being an informer for the IRS and a member of the CIA.

None ski. Any candidate for public office, unless he is of uniquely austere demeanor and surpassing diligence, can count on attracting a similar, although possibly less interesting, range of talent.

Both politicians and skiers divide naturally as between liberals and conservatives. This is true for amateurs and professionals alike. The division needs no comment in the case of pols. But no less in skiing you have men (I think of myself as one) who ski circumspectly with a view to the enjoyment of the masses, who stop to assist the fallen, who fill in the cavities when they themselves take a fall as they often do, who sacrifice performance to the social conscience of the true liberal.

And you have men who go barreling down the mountain, scattering the population in terror before them and (one assumes) muttering phrases about the survival of the fittest and the public be damned. Since concentration is on self, the performance, though socially depraved, is technically superior. I think of my frequent skiing companion, Mr. William F. Buckley, Jr.

There is another resemblance between skiing and politics that has nothing to do with ideology. I mentioned at the outset that I was skiing last winter. I did so until one bright Sunday when I went out in the company of another professor of mature years. It was a day of brilliant sun; the snow was good except for occasional bare patches. Precisely when I was least expecting it— when my feeling of confidence and my sense of mastery were greatest—I fell on a rock and broke my behind. Exactly the same happens in politics. And to a lot of men in an election year.

Study Questions

1. Galbraith's introduction takes up four paragraphs, nearly one-third of the entire essay. Is this much background necessary? Why or why not?
2. The main-idea sentence (last sentence of paragraph 4) asserts an obvious untruth. What is the effect of this sentence on the tone and emphasis of the essay as a whole?
3. The detailed similarities in the body of the essay are divided into four groups or classes, each identified by a topic sentence with the key word "both." What are those classes? Is the division consistent and clear?
4. Write a new main-idea sentence for the essay, including a clear statement of the division and subtopics.
5. Is the final paragraph, actually a discussion of an additional similarity, a satisfactory conclusion to the essay? Why or why not?

Tumors: Benign and Malignant

W. D. SNIVELY, JR.
DONNA R. BESHEAR

During the course of normal wear and tear, cells continuously proliferate to replace the worn-out tissue. Following injury or disease, cell proliferation increases to repair and regenerate the damaged tissue, then slows to normal when it has served its purpose. Sometimes, however, cell proliferation begins and continues indefinitely at a rate faster than normal. Such accelerated activity, which has no apparent relationship to growth and maintenance of body tissues, leads to development of a tumor mass. This process is *neoplasia* (new growth).

Classification of Neoplasms

. . .

Because neoplasms vary so greatly in their characteristics, particularly their potential for change, some sort of classification is needed. Classifying tumors is not always a simple matter, but it is important to do so since the tumor type has a bearing on treatment and prognosis.

Tumors are first divided into two main groups, *benign* and *malignant*. Some tumors cannot readily be placed in either category, and occasionally a tumor is transformed from benign to malignant over a period of time. Next, they are classified histogenically, that is, according to the tissue where the lesion originated. In some cases it may be impossible to determine the histogenesis. Generally, tumors are named according to their probable histogenesis, their anatomical site, and, of course, whether they are benign or malignant; e.g., a fibrosarcoma is a malignant tumor arising in fibrous tissue, and a leiomyoma is a benign tumor arising in smooth muscle.

Benign and Malignant Tumors

The essential feature of all malignant and, to a lesser extent, benign tumors is failure of the mechanism that controls the cell mass and lack of functional contribution of this tissue. With a few exceptions, benign and malignant tumors differ in several specific respects, including clinical effects, structure, growth, metastasis, and recurrence.

Clinical effects. The benign, or simple, tumor is significant clinically chiefly because of the pressure it exerts on other tissues as it increases in size. These growths cause death only infrequently, usually by accident of position. For example, a tumor growing within the cranial cavity, however slowly, sooner or later will cause death. A benign tumor may indirectly cause serious damage or death by producing a secondary disease, as may occur when a functionally active benign tumor of glandular tissue causes secondary disease by overproduction of hormones; this is the case in adrenal adenomas.

No matter where the malignant tumor, or cancer, grows, if neglected, it

Reprinted by permission from *Textbook of Pathophysiology* (Philadelphia: J. B. Lippincott, 1972), pp. 109–114. Title supplied by editors.

usually kills by destroying tissues, interfering with physiological functions, causing hemorrhage or ulceration in infected areas, and producing secondary starvation.

Structure. Benign tumors are well *differentiated* (specialized in form, character, or function) and may perfectly reproduce the structure of their tissue of origin, whereas malignant cells tend to *dedifferentiate* (lose specialization and revert to a more primitive form), sometimes to such a degree that the parent structure cannot be determined. Cells may be *pleomorphic,* varying in size and shape. The faster the cell growth, the more primitive are the cells. Some tumors totally lack structural and cellular differentiation; they are described as *anaplastic.* On the other hand, some malignant tumors are so well differentiated as to be almost indistinguishable from normal tissue. The nucleus of a malignant cell is likely to be enlarged, and the nucleolus is large in proportion to the nucleus.

Growth. Benign tumors grow by expansion and frequently are surrounded by a capsule of compressed tissue—a reassuring finding since tumors with capsules are always benign. Although malignant tumors *never* have capsules, the absence of a capsule does not necessarily mean that the tumor is malignant, as many benign tumors, particularly those arising in connective tissue, do not have capsules.

Malignant tumors grow by invasion. They compress and penetrate surrounding tissues, crowding into spaces between tissue cells, and eventually destroying and replacing normal cells. Usually they grow rapidly, whereas benign tumors are relatively slow growing. Sudden rapid growth of a benign tumor may indicate malignant change. Sometimes, however, a benign tumor will greatly increase in size over a period of a few days because of hemorrhage into the tumor, but this is not actual tumor growth. The growth rate of a neoplasm may be assessed by the histologic appearance, particularly by the number of mitotic figures present. In benign neoplasms, mitotic figures are absent or scanty, whereas in malignant neoplasms they are usually numerous. The faster the growth, the more numerous the mitotic figures.

Metastasis. When a malignant neoplasm invades lymphatic or blood vessels, neoplastic cells are carried to other parts of the body. Secondary tumors may grow from these cells in a process called *metastasis.* Metastatic growth *always* indicates malignancy. Benign tumors do not metastasize. Once a tumor has metastasized, surgical removal of the primary tumor is usually useless. Life expectancy is short, since eventually, vital structures will be damaged or destroyed by malignant neoplasms growing in or near them.

Recurrence. Sometimes a malignant tumor reappears following its removal by surgery or treatment by radiotherapy. This means that some of the neoplastic cells escaped destruction and subsequently multiplied, forming another mass. Such cells may lie dormant for a long time, perhaps years, before they cause a recurrence. Similarly, cells in metastatic sites may remain dormant for years before their presence becomes clinically obvious. . . .

Study Questions

1. On the basis of the information in the introductory paragraphs, write a one-sentence formal definition of *tumor*.
2. Copy the main-idea sentence. How does this sentence relate to the structure of the essay?
3. Some writers, especially when writing for technical magazines or textbooks, use interior headings. Do the headings in this essay clarify the text? Why are they necessary?
4. In the paragraphs discussing the differences between benign and malignant tumors, details about each are exactly balanced. How does the parallel structure help the reader understand the technical language?
5. Is the objectivity of the language a help or a hindrance to the reader? If you were to write about the difference between benign and malignant (cancerous) tumors, how would you approach your subject?

A Potent Poison   JOHN CROMPTON

How it came about that snakes manufactured poison is a mystery. Over the periods their saliva, a mild digestive juice like our own, was converted into a poison that defies analysis even today. It was not forced upon them by the survival competition; they could have caught and lived on prey without using poison just as the thousands of non-poisonous snakes still do. Poison to a snake is merely a luxury; it enables it to get its food with very little effort, no more effort than one bite. And why only snakes? Cats, for instance, would be greatly helped; no running fights with large, fierce rats or tussles with grown rabbits —just a bite and no more effort needed. In fact, it would be an assistance to all the carnivorae—though it would be a two-edged weapon when they fought each other. But, of the vertebrates, unpredictable Nature selected only snakes (and one lizard). One wonders also why Nature, with some snakes, concocted poison of such extreme potency.

In the conversion of saliva into poison one might suppose that a fixed process took place. It did not; some snakes manufactured a poison different in every respect from that of the others, as different as arsenic is from strychnine, and having different effects. One poison acts on the nerves, the other on the blood.

The makers of the nerve poison include the mambas and the cobras and their venom is called neurotoxic. Vipers (adders) and rattlesnakes manufacture the blood poison, which is known as haemolytic. Both poisons are unpleasant, but by far the more unpleasant is the blood poison. It is said that the nerve poison is the more primitive of the two, that the blood poison is, so to speak, a newer product from an improved formula. Be that as it may, the nerve poison does its business with man far more quickly than the blood poison. This, however, means nothing. Snakes did not acquire their poison for use against man but for use against prey such as rats and mice, and the effect on these of viperine poison is almost immediate.

As a slight complication it so happens that the two poisons are rarely quite pure. So the nerve poison of the cobras, etc. usually possesses a trace of the blood poison of the vipers, and vice versa. But it is legitimate, as well as convenient, to class the two poisons as two different concoctions. . . .

On being bitten by a snake possessing neurotoxic poison, such as a cobra, the usual symptoms are a searing pain from the wound itself, then a weakness in the legs, gradually developing into incapability of making any movement at all. Saliva dribbles from the mouth owing to the paralysis of the muscles of the mouth. The tongue, too, becomes paralysed and the victim, though able to hear, is unable to speak. He begins to vomit, and has difficulty in breathing. This difficulty increases until he is suffocating, and finally breathing stops altogether. Meanwhile the heart has been racing on, and it continues to beat for a considerable time after breathing has stopped.

What happens is this: when the poison is injected it is distributed by the blood and attacks the nerve cells and nerve centres. It also attacks the central nervous system. Finally it paralyses the nerve centres that control breathing, and the lungs collapse. It has, however, a stimulating effect on the heart and only after the lungs have collapsed does the heart, owing to the accumulation of carbon dioxide, cease to operate. But if the poison is injected direct into a vein its transit is so rapid that the heart stops almost immediately. (Experimental animals, such as dogs, have died while the injection was actually being made, death thus occurring almost as quickly as if they had been shot through the brain.)

It is not easy to obtain data of the symptoms of poisoning by the deadlier snakes. Snakes can be made to bite unfortunate experimental animals, but these animals, whether they live or die, cannot tell us their symptoms, and post-mortems get us little further. Not a few men have been bitten by the bad types of snakes and recovered, and here, one would think, would be an ideal source of knowledge. Not a bit; the majority remember next to nothing. Besides other sufferings, the subject is in a state of terror, and terrified men are not in a state of mind to note and memorize symptoms.

And one can hardly experiment on human beings. Volunteers for, say, mamba poisoning would be hard to come by. Nevertheless one brave soul *did* undergo such a test. Some time ago, a Dr. Eizenberger decided to experiment on himself. He did not propose, however, to kill himself, and used such a small dose that he thought the effect would be negligible—he could always use a larger dose if this one proved to have no effect. He took one drop of the venom of the green mamba of West Africa (*Dendraspis viridis*). This drop he diluted with ten times the quantity of water, and of this very weak solution he only injected 0.2 cc. into his forearm.

A burning sensation was felt immediately, and five minutes later there was a swelling over the puncture, accompanied by itching. Soon he knew that his nerves were affected. Ordinary everyday noises became deafening. His car seemed to make such a din, bumping and banging, and he thought a tyre must be punctured and got out to look. Saliva flowed copiously in his mouth and he felt as if he were intoxicated. Soon (about fifteen minutes after the injection) he was seized with nausea and weakness and decided the time had come to put an end to this experiment and do what he could to stop any further absorption of the venom. It was far too late, but he applied a tourniquet, cut open the swelling and soused the bleeding cut with a hot solution of permanganate.

His chin, lips and the tip of his tongue became numb. This numbness spread over his face and down his throat. His eyes and the base of his tongue became painful, and he lost all feeling in his fingers and toes. His ears started to drum and the pain and stiffness of his tongue travelled down his throat, which became acutely sore. It became difficult to talk or swallow, and difficult and painful to breathe.

Alarmed and fearing collapse, Doctor Eizenberger gave himself an injection of strychnine, which had a good effect and improved his circulation.

Then his hand and forearm swelled up and the parts that had been numb became painful. After five hours a touch on any part of his body was painful, and swallowing was very difficult. But the worst was over. He went to bed and passed the night in a feverish state. In the morning his tongue and throat still pained, but these discomforts gradually passed off.

He made a complete recovery, and this is the case with all who are bitten by neurotoxic snakes and escape death. However severe the complications, if they do recover, recovery is complete—which can by no means be said of bites received from vipers.

And now to the blood or haemolytic poison, the poison of the vipers. There are many vipers, including the American rattlesnakes. All are venomous to a certain extent, but only a few are really deadly. Of these the puff adder and Russell's viper probably head the list.

Although the effects are more unpleasant, in these days of serum treatment a man has more chance with viperine poison than with neurotoxic (cobra, mamba, etc.) simply because the former takes longer to act and he has more time to get to a place where he can be given a shot of antivenine.

This haemolytic poison breaks down the blood and destroys its ability to coagulate. The blood-vessels, particularly the capillaries, are also broken down, and the changed blood oozes through the surrounding tissues, generally to a considerable extent. This occurs first at the site of puncture which becomes discoloured, swells and bleeds. As the poison spreads through the body large black or purple patches appear in various parts and blood issues from the mouth and nose. In fact, the subject appears to be the victim, not of poison but of a merciless "beating up." For instance, a Mr. Wertzer in South Africa, bitten in the forearm by a haemolytic snake became a hideous sight with large black patches down both arms, down the thighs and over the stomach. He had a "black eye" the size of a plate and blood streamed from mouth and nose.

Internal bleeding also occurs in the stomach, bladder and bowels; the skin becomes cold and clammy, the subject vomits continually and has no control over his bowels. Unlike the neurotoxic poison the haemolytic poison slows down the heart and death may occur in a few hours or after several days.

There is indirect danger attached to viperine poisoning; when the danger seems passed, the large blood-suffused areas of muscle may begin to mortify, causing death weeks later. And if this secondary poisoning is not fatal, pieces of flesh may slough off and come away. In Africa one occasionally meets natives with no calves, or very little, the flesh having sloughed off following the bite of an adder.

Study Questions

1. As the title and the opening paragraph suggest, this excerpt is from a larger piece of writing in which comparison is *not* the principal structure. The passage given here, however, does make a balanced and parallel comparison between the two types of snake poison. On the other hand, the passage lacks any conclusion at all. How serious is this lack? Try writing a brief paragraph to conclude the comparison which has been made.
2. Prepare a list in parallel columns of the differences stressed in this comparison. Why did the author choose to discuss certain differences in sentence-by-sentence "see-saw" structure, but devote separate passages of several paragraphs each to a discussion of symptoms and long-run results? Would a different structure have made the passage clearer and easier to follow?
3. Locate the transitional expression that joins the major section on neurotoxic venom to the discussion of viperine or haemolytic poison. Is this very direct and somewhat abrupt transition satisfactory? Try writing a smoother connection between these two parts of the essay.
4. How is chronology made an important structural device throughout the selection?

Sound and Light   STUDENT SAMPLE

If the person across the hall from you is playing his stereo at sufficient volume in a lighted room, you may hear the sound but not see the light; at the same time, someone across the street may see the light but not hear the sound. Just

Reprinted by permission.

as there are dog whistles that people cannot hear, there are forms of light we cannot see. A man who is shot and instantly killed may see a flash of light but never hear the report of the gun. These examples illustrate some of the most interesting similarities and differences between sound and light, two forms of vibration that have a direct impact on our senses. The first concerns their ability to pass through various media; the second has to do with the frequency of their vibration in relation to pitch or color; and the third reflects the very dramatic difference in the speed at which they travel.

Sound and light are basically different types of wave motion, and thus they travel through various media in different ways. Sound waves vibrate in the direction in which they travel. Though air is the most usual medium for sound, these waves may also be carried by water and through certain solid materials such as the wood of a guitar or violin. Still other materials—fiberglass insulation, for example—tend to absorb sound; and others, such as concrete and stone, reflect it. On the other hand, light waves, which are pulsations of electromagnetic energy, vibrate in all directions. While they travel well through air, they do not cause the air itself to vibrate, as sound waves do, but instead pass through it almost as if the air were not there. They travel best, however, in a total vacuum. Certain materials such as water or clear glass also allow light to pass through, though slightly slowed down. Other materials—anything we call opaque—absorb light and prevent it from passing through; and still others, such as the silvered backing of a mirror, reflect it almost completely. Because sound and light travel in different ways in relation to the media they pass through, there is a great difference in the distances they cover. Sound waves are gradually absorbed by the air through which they move, and so they cannot travel much more than twenty miles; but light waves cross unimaginable distances intact in the near-perfect vacuum of interstellar space.

Neither form of vibration, however, consists of only a single frequency or rate of pulsation; both sound and light exist in a spectrum or range, and how a sound or light ray is perceived by our senses depends partly on its particular rate of vibration. Sounds of low pitch are the slower vibrations; if the frequency is less than 27 vibrations per second, it becomes an indistinct rumble which many people cannot hear at all. On the other hand, although some musical instruments, like the piano, have pulsation rates of over 4,186 cycles per second and can still be heard by the human ear, sounds of even faster vibrations and thus very high pitch can not be discerned by man. Similar limitations hold for record players and tape equipment; small and inexpensive sets are not capable of reproducing very low or very high frequencies. Greater "presence" and the full range of sound are made possible by better stereos with various speakers specifically designed to carry the extreme ranges of pitch as well as the middle range.

In a parallel but different way, the spectrum of visible light consists of a range of frequencies, with the slower vibrations corresponding to red light and the higher frequencies perceived as violet, and the other colors of the rainbow in between. Light vibrates at a frequency enormously faster than that of sound: the figure one followed by fourteen zeros approximates the number of cycles per second for red light. Energy vibrating at a slightly slower rate is not visible to the eye, but these *infrared* rays can be felt as heat and recorded on photographic film. At the other end of the spectrum, violet light has a frequency about five times that of red, and the still faster vibrations are those of *ultraviolet* light, which is beneficial in small amounts but which can be harmful, especially to the eyes, even though it is invisible. By passing white light through a prism, it is possible to separate the various colors of light into a continuous series or spectrum, but no one has succeeded in reproducing the full glory of a natural rainbow.

Because both sound and light are perceived by our senses, the difference in their speed of travel leads to the oddities of perception already mentioned; the sounds of steam whistles, baseball bats, and guns, if far enough away, seem to do strange things. The difference in speed between sound and light is, in fact, tremendous. Sound waves travel in air at a speed of roughly 750 miles an hour, or about 1,100 feet a second. Light waves in a vacuum travel at more than 186,000 miles a second, the fastest speed known. If a light wave could be reflected around the world, it would return to its starting point in less than one-seventh of a second, whereas a sound wave would take 36 hours for the trip.

It is possible to hear an echo precisely because of the slow speed at which sound travels; a shout from your voice takes a perceptible amount of time to travel to a distant building or cliff and be reflected back to your ears. Light is also reflected back by certain objects, but its speed is so great that there is no noticeable delay between the time you glance at a mirror and the time your image is returned to your eyes—a kind of instantaneous echo. This very great speed of light makes possible the measurement of the enormous distances in space. If the sun were suddenly to stop giving light, we would continue to see it for more than eight minutes, for it takes about 500 seconds for light to reach the earth from the sun. On the other hand, the distances of space are so great that if the North Star suddenly exploded, we would not see the explosion for about 460 years. In spite of the speed of light, then, we are observing a distant past when we look at the stars. An observer on the star Rigel, training a very powerful telescope on the earth, might today see the ships of Columbus reaching America for the first time.

Whenever a thunderstorm occurs, the difference in the speeds of light and sound is apparent, for although the flash of lightning and the crash of thunder occur simultaneously, the sound of the thunder does not reach us until after we have seen the lightning. In fact, the sound of thunder will be delayed by one second for every one-fifth mile it travels before it is heard. Thus, if a person sees lightning flash, he can estimate its distance from himself by counting the seconds until he hears the thunder.

Light and sound, then, are different in a number of important ways. In fact, even in the degree of their importance to man they are different. Although sound helps to make the world pleasant and safe, it is not essential to man; without light and the energy it provides, however, life itself could not exist.

Study Questions

1. The writer gives the appearance of defining both "sound" and "light," but in fact does not do so. From information in the paper, and adding any necessary material from other sources, construct the missing definitions.
2. Outline the division employed in the essay and the details given in support of each subtopic.
3. The essay makes use of relatively few transitions between paragraphs and almost no sentence transitions. To what extent does the carefully worked-out parallel structure take the place of explicit transitions? Where does the reader feel the lack of transitions?
4. How does the writer use examples in order to make the technical material of the essay accessible to the average reader? Is he completely successful in all parts of the essay?
5. Is the conclusion an adequate summation of the essay as a whole and the comparison it develops?

Women, Sex, and Sin
MARGARET MEAD

The Manus didn't know what to do with women twenty-five years ago, and they know almost as little today. The whole ethos is an essentially masculine one, in which the protective capacities of the male rather than the specifically maternal capacities of the female are the ones woven into the idea of parenthood. The ideal of personality is active, assertive, demanding, with great emphasis upon freedom of movement. There is likewise a very low interest in biological parenthood, in the breast-feeding tie between mother and child, or in any softness of feminine sex responsiveness which would yield too easily to evoke a measure of masculine anger.

Twenty-five years ago, the most valued women in the village were dominating women, even those who dominated their husbands, women who had strong clear minds, and who, as mediums, controlled a good part of the public affairs of the village. The woman who was regarded as the most dangerous woman in the village was a good-natured, easily responsive, slightly stupid widow, who was said to have been responsible for the deaths of six good men. Young women who were recalcitrant at marriage could be disciplined into shape, if necessary, as had been done in the case of one Peri wife who was finally shaped into compliancy on one of the smaller islands by a week end of rape in which her husband and a group of his age mates participated. The pliant, the warm, the responsive were simply so many danger spots—girls who might be persuaded into running away or simply yielding to seduction. As daughters, as sisters, as wives, and as widows they were regarded as both dangerous and essentially unattractive.

In the long years between betrothal as a little girl of eight or ten and marriage, the girl of Old Peri was not being "good" in the sense that she was expected to be pure in heart and mind and never let her thoughts wander into areas of lust or even of desire, like the traditional expectation for unmarried Catholic girls in southern Europe. She was, it is true, expected to be circumspect, to obey the rules and avoidances, expected not to say her future husband's name, not to let herself get into any situation where property that had already been expended in her name would be jeopardized. Her virginity and reputation were rather like a sack of money which she was left to guard alone in the house, and out of loyalty to her relatives, fear of their anger and of the penalties which their Sir Ghosts would exact, she guarded them. A theft, or even a slight defection which turned her head away from the main task for a moment would bring ruin on many people—perhaps death to one of her closest kin. Nor did her kin trust to her conscience; she was watched and chaperoned very severely; the slightest indiscretion brought down torrents of abuse and recrimination.

The young men were in a slightly different position. If one of them had an affair, it would bring about an awful row between the Sir Ghost of their own household and that of the girl's kin; there would be expiations and payments, and perhaps someone would die in the end, but the attitude toward the young men was more that of indulgence toward a successful bandit. Failure to guard in the case of the girl was far more serious than success in breaking in on the part of the boy. Virginity was merely important as it affected the marriage arrangements. If the girl's lapse or the boy's lapse could be glossed over, expiatory payments made, ghosts and Sir Ghosts appeased, the mere technical matter of physical virginity did not matter very much.

To the young girl growing up in the village, the one person on whom her mind could not dwell, the one person about whom she could not daydream, give a sly, quick look or a provocative nudge in a crowd, was her fiancé. Toward him her relatives focused all the feeling they had shown earlier toward any failure of the girl to control her sphincters; his name, his appearance, everything about him was considered shame-evoking. The young girl's mother and all her older female relatives shared in this attitude toward him. Where she had been freer with her father than her mother could be, once betrothed she was again bound in with her mother because her father could no longer take her with him, and because of the taboos which she and her mother shared. Her materials for fantasy were the shame-arousing, unmentionable future marriage relationship, possibilities of seduction and rape which would only bring disaster in their train, and a conscious focus on the outward and visible forms of her present and future position—how many dog's teeth, how much shell money had been and would be given away in her name, how many strings of ornaments, how many money aprons would she wear as a bride, with how many canoe loads of sago would she be fetched back home after the birth of her child.

Thus, all through girlhood the way was paved for married women to shrink from their husbands' advances and still conform to the moral code, avoiding out of sheer fear and not out of any compliancy the anger of their husbands' ghosts as they had avoided the anger of their own. They ran then, as they do today, the risk of being violently attracted by an extra-marital adventure, which presented the contrast between the appeal of danger and the inhibitions of shame. Just as in the men's lives there was an overlay of careful, continuous industriousness supported by ghostly sanctions, while underneath there was a far easier, more reckless self-confidence which was given very little scope, so also among the women a heavily sanctioned demand for circumspection and diligence screened a vigorous, reckless wilfulness, which only very, very heavy sanctions could prevent from coming into play. Meanwhile, at no point was there a chance to develop any gentleness associated with sex behaviour in marriage itself.

Into this background of active, demanding babyhood and early childhood, inhibited and chaperoned girlhood set against the ever-present possibility of seduction and rape, and finally marriage—which was only made tolerable by emphasis upon the role of the economically successful woman who kept her husband's house and provided beadwork for her brother—came the first teaching of the Mission. Here one of the special aspects of Catholic as compared with

Protestant missions came into play. When the Manus saw Catholic women, they saw nuns, not wives. For the little girls who went away to mission schools (there were two such women in Peri), sisters did not present an ideal to which they could ever aspire, but were rather earthly representatives of heavenly powers, intent, like the ghosts of old, upon making the girls quiet, obedient, and well-disciplined. They learned standards of personal neatness, learned to read and write, learned to sing, but they had no models of Christian marriage which seriously challenged the models which they had learned in their youth.

Then, in 1946, came the emancipation of women by the New Way, the removal of all taboos, the disappearance of the old name avoidances, the pro-hibition of child betrothals, the permission for women to consent to their own seductions, the prohibition against fathers or brothers becoming angered by the behaviour of daughters and sisters. There was the exhortation to young couples to behave in a way which was a mixture of work boys' memories of the marriages of Australian officials—in which husbands were protective of their wives, helped them on and off with their evening wraps, and hired servants to work for them, talked to them at meals, and kissed them on arrival and depar-ture—and a model derived from American films—in which free choice of a mate and conspicuous, demonstrative public affection were felt to be the key to American marriage.

It was Manus men, and not Manus women, who had been work boys in Australian households, who had seen American films. The emancipation of the women was presented to them by fiat; no more taboos—if you have a husband, speak his name. Explore freely if you are unmarried, and, once married, by choice, of course, publicly demonstrate your affection for your husband, and have as many children as possible so as to make the Manus, now so few, into many. As monarchs in Europe once ordered their people to follow them into baptism and membership in the Christian Church, so Manus men laid down the rules by which women in the New Way were to become emancipated and affectionate. There were to be no more taboos, girls and boys were to go to school together, young people to experiment in the choice of a mate. Having once been ordered to be compliant, to hide behind their avoidance mats and cloaks, to sit quietly and do beadwork, women were now ordered to be spon-taneous, responsive, actively loving. And the men, modelling themselves on Australians, who had not expected their wives to care for children and do all the housework, having no servants, took over part of the care of even the very young babies.

The present results of this emancipation of women are both astonishing and depressing. Twenty-five years ago, the most conspicuous thing about Manus women was that they were deprived in those areas of affectionate domesticity which most societies permit to women and driven into continuous public economic participation. Today, the most conspicuous point is the extent to which they have been driven into a public display of a new form of personal relations, with little or no understanding or preparation for the new role. Manus women, twenty-five years ago, were singularly unattractive, angular, assertive, walking without any sense of the appeal of their own femininity, muting and constricting their femininity, emphasizing, with strident voice and sharp, unappealing gestures, that it might be possible to rape them, it might even be possible to seduce them—if enough risk attached—but what love and tenderness they had were already bespoken in formal terms by brothers. Manus women today are almost equally unattractive, but they look and act very differently. Where their contours were once sharp and angular, they are now softer, a little blurred. Where before, if one laid one's hands on a girl's shoulder, the muscles quivered like a taut bowstring, unused to gestures which were not menacing, stylized, and brittle, today they are heavier and slower, their bodies give a little beneath one's hand. The tense restiveness is gone, but no responsiveness has come to take its place. It is easy to see how husbands who once would have beaten them—as opponents in an unresolved contest—now beat them to get any response out of them at all. Whereas twenty-five years ago a husband's main complaints were about acts—a wife gossiped about him with her relatives or his brother's wife, a wife got up at night without her grass skirt when there were strangers sleeping in the house or was careless in feeding the baby—today the overwhelmingly most frequent complaint is that she "fastens her mouth." Some phrase, some slight act, will set her to brooding, and brooding she grows silent until her husband in a rage beats her, a beating which typically ends either in her running away or in a sexual reunion which has the elements of successful rape.

In the past, sex was something to be avoided by women in marriage, and in general; for men it was a reckless, brief adventure, usually accompanied by some kind of trouble. Women had grudged their husbands the brief encounters with captured prostituted stranger women, and did their best to spoil their husbands' pleasure by screeching taunts from a distance as they swung on bamboo swings far out over the lagoon, their laughter designed to echo into the men's house and make the men impotent. Today there are constant complaints both of sexual rejection and of wives who insist upon their husbands sleeping with them just to prove they haven't been with other women. "The one time you must have intercourse with your wife," say Peri men, "is if you have already been with another woman. Otherwise she is sure to find out and be angry." Counterpointed to this is the ideal extra-marital affair which emphasizes choice—"She paid her half of the fine; she said she had chosen me," "This is really from the desire of both." But, even more important, the wonderful thing about lovers is that you don't have to sleep with them. If either man or woman feels tired and disinclined toward love-making, the couple can simply sit and talk, and they need not have sex relations.

So, in spite of the apparent great change from a system in which women were the helpless pawns of complicated marriage exchanges, completely controlled by fathers, brothers, and husbands, to a system of marriage by choice and freedom of consent, the crucial position of sex has not changed very much. Sex is still associated with anger, with rights, with expression of or response to various sorts of resistance, and love is defined as a relationship in which sex can be ignored in favour of affection. As women once screamed their anger and jealousy because a man took a fish from his catch to his sister's house and sat quietly beside her fire, so they now rage over comparable incidents such as a husband bringing home a piece of cloth for his mistress, or his mother cooking him a meal. Quarrels in the village hinge not on the number of actual adulteries, but on the glances, tokens, and hints of adulteries long past, or perhaps never to come. The coincidence of two people who have had an affair turning up in a distant village the same day, even though they hardly exchange a word there, gives the pair enormous pleasure and is guaranteed, if it is discovered, to throw their offended spouses into a rage.

In fact, there is a correspondence between the present chief requirement of a wife, that she should protect her husband's mind-soul from the sin of anger, and the chief enjoyment of illicit love, which is to tease and tantalize one's rivals. This teasing may go so far as, for example, Benedikta taking delight in getting her husband to buy her, with her own money, some conspicuous object, like a knife with a red handle, which she exhibited conspicuously, walking about, certain that her lover's wife would fall into the trap of thinking her lover had given it to her. Or two women whose lovers were friends would put on skirts of the same material, thus emphasizing the relationships and setting echoes going in the heads of the two wives who were their rivals. It is a game played by those who do not in any case expect satisfaction from sex, in whatever form it comes, and who get what satisfaction they can out of playing with dissatisfaction.

Appropriately enough, illicit love affairs and gambling were associated together. Men enjoyed giving women, their own or their friends' mistresses, money to gamble with; women enjoyed borrowing money from their lovers and lovers' friends, and gambling games were watched closely by hawk-eyed spouses alert for trouble. Among the occasional couples where both gambled, the style of the game was upset and inexplicable rows developed, as when Maria had a temper tantrum in "court" because her husband paid back his share of a debt to her with money she had lent a friend of his not knowing that part of it was for her own husband.

So women and sex remain associated with sin; where once they were associated with the punitive anger of ghosts, now they are associated with the jealous anger of men and women. Where once women were unwillingly circumspect and men grudgingly prudent, in order to prevent the ghost from visiting illness and death on them or their relatives because they had violated property rights or upset important economic affairs, today virtue consists in men and women leading quiet lives. Husbands and wives should reject overtures and opportunities so that there will be no anger between them, which might endanger the lives of their children, or anger concealed in the heart of the spouse, or in their own hearts because of the anger of the spouse. The responsiveness of men to resistance, either active or passive, the insistent demand of the jealous woman for sex expression, of her husband, keep this edge between sex and anger keen and sharp. From Christian teaching the Manus learned that sex was evil—a matter on which they were well convinced already—at least as far as women were concerned, but that sexual sins could be confessed and forgiven. From observation of Australian life, lightly reinforced by American films, they came to the conclusion that somehow Western white men seemed to manage their sex lives better, for there was so much less quarrelling, and that this better management came from giving women more consideration, not beating them, helping them with their work, and giving them freedom of choice, and being mildly demonstrative in public. But the type of deeply responsible, tender marriage, which stands as the ideal of Catholic teaching, they never have had a chance to see.

For the woman who is intelligent, ambitious, and active, the New Way, in spite of its nominal emancipation of women, offers no roles comparable to the part that women could play as mediums and entrepreneurs in the old system. The most that the wife of a member of the new bureaucracy is expected to do is to be a model for the rest of the community, keep her house and children in a modern way, and never embarrass her husband by being old-fashioned. This was the role played by the wife of Samol in Bunai; her baby received the most perfect infant care, her clothes were the most carefully chosen. Not until the Manus are introduced to the sort of women's clubs which have grown up around Port Moresby and in modern Samoa will the women have any glimpse of any sort of responsible public role again.

Meanwhile, there remains with them the remembrance of gentleness received from old women, not mothers but grandmothers or aunts, who, freed from the tempestuousness of active sex lives, freed from quarrelling with their husbands, were gentle and indulgent to small children. In the memories of the middle-aged men who are still dissatisfied with their marriages, who quarrel with their wives and beat them, the nostalgia for these kind old women can be heard, with its echo that some day their marriages, if they live long enough, will have in them women who are as kind and gentle as Pomat's Tchalolo grandmother or Kilipak's aunt, Isali. Something of the tenderness of these contacts used to survive in the relationship between brother and sister, and appeared again in the marriages of many years' standing, when the shame of speaking together and eating together had worn off. When husband and wife had co-operated in many enterprises, after she had borne him many children, as they came to the point of being grandparents, a gentleness could settle between them.

At present when people are still young, public opinion will side strongly with the wife who is asked to do more than her share in supporting the household, but as they grow older, the case of the sickening husband with a wife who neglects him focuses the rage of the community, as it did when Christof, his arm shrunken and helpless, his legs mere sticks, was cut by his wife. When I arrived on this scene a few people were gathered around Christof. His wife, who had done the slashing, was sitting at a distance unconcernedly working on thatch. Suddenly their grown son, a great, husky creature, hurled himself through the room and began kicking his mother violently. People rushed to restrain him, and the councillor pontificated, "Don't add one trouble to another." His mother put on a dramatic, hysterical act to get attention from the bystanders, and even with this she received no sympathy. One of the gentlest of bystanders commented, "I am like that also, Piyap. If my mother didn't give food to my father, I'd fight her." And when I asked, "If your father would have fought your mother, would you have helped her?" I received an astonished, "Indeed, no!" One of the very young men summed it up: "I heard what it was about. They weren't giving Christof anything to eat. Yesterday he was angry, and he did not eat. Today they all went to the bush, and then they cooked food and gave him none. And he, is he a strong man? His arm and his leg are useless. He's just like a child [a great exaggeration]. Why don't they care for him? Now, Sepa [the daughter] wanted to give food to her father, and her mother was angry and cut her husband with a knife. Tomas heard this and he quarrelled with his mother. His mother said, 'All right, beat me if you wish. This food, was it something you produced, so you have a right to talk?' Then Tomas said, 'Every day I bring sago, fish, and other things to you all, and I think you don't give any to my father.' Then Tomas was angry, and he attacked his mother."

The councillor's comment was that if the family decided to bring the matter to "court," Tomas would be in particular trouble because he had broken an important law of the New Way, the law that forbade one to get involved in one's relatives' quarrels.

When the case came to "court," the weight of disapproval was directed against the wife. This was a familiar pattern. If the blame could be firmly affixed to a woman, then any failure of the New Way among men need not be faced so directly. Women after all were still uneducated, illiterate, and undependable. For their part, the women felt many of the new procedures as traps. When they gave evidence it was written down and if, on being asked to repeat it, they gave a slightly different version, the whole weight of the "court" would come down upon them. The disapproval of indirect evidence also weighed heavily upon them, for when they would protest that they "knew" something was going on, the men would doggedly confront them with a "Did you see it with your eyes? Did you touch it with your hands?" So, in spite of their nominal emancipation, they still live in a world which in repudiating sex also repudiates women, and which in exalting fatherhood leaves less room for motherhood, except as a sort of delegated fatherhood.

Study Questions

1. Make an outline showing the various sets of comparisons made in this essay. How is parallel structure employed in the overall essay? Are some paragraphs balanced comparisons? If so, what is balanced in each?
2. Besides the major comparison (Manus girls 25 years ago and today), what other comparisons does the writer make?
3. How does the Manus woman of today compare with Lawrence's concept of the modern woman?
4. How much of the final paragraph is "conclusion"?

Cocksure Women and Hensure Men   D. H. LAWRENCE

It seems to me there are two aspects to women. There is the demure and the dauntless. Men have loved to dwell, in fiction at least, on the demure maiden whose inevitable reply is: Oh, yes, if you please, kind sir! The demure maiden, the demure spouse, the demure mother—this is still the ideal. A few maidens, mistresses and mothers *are* demure. A few pretend to be. But the vast majority are not. And they don't pretend to be. We don't expect a girl skilfully driving her car to be demure, we expect her to be dauntless. What good would demure and maidenly Members of Parliament be, inevitably responding: Oh, yes, if you please, kind sir!—Though of course there are masculine members of that kidney.—And a demure telephone girl? Or even a demure stenographer? Demureness, to be sure, is outwardly becoming, it is an outward mark of femininity, like bobbed hair. But it goes with inward dauntlessness. The girl who has got to make her way in life has got to be dauntless, and if she has a pretty, demure manner with it, then lucky girl. She kills two birds with two stones.

With the two kinds of femininity go two kinds of confidence: there are the women who are cocksure, and the women who are hensure. A really up-to-date woman is a cocksure woman. She doesn't have a doubt nor a qualm. She is the modern type. Whereas the old-fashioned demure woman was sure as a hen is sure, that is, without knowing anything about it. She went quietly and busily clucking around, laying the eggs and mothering the chickens in a kind of anxious dream that still was full of sureness. But not mental sureness. Her sureness was a physical condition, very soothing, but a condition out of which she could easily be startled or frightened.

It is quite amusing to see the two kinds of sureness in chickens. The cockerel is, naturally, cocksure. He crows because he is *certain* it is day. Then the hen peeps out from under her wing. He marches to the door of the hen-house and pokes out his head assertively: *Ah ha! daylight, of course, just as I said!*—and he majestically steps down the chicken ladder towards *terra firma*, knowing that the hens will step cautiously after him, drawn by his confidence. So after him, cautiously, step the hens. He crows again: *Ha-ha! here we are!*—It is indisputable, and the hens accept it entirely. He marches towards the house. From the house a person ought to appear, scattering corn. Why does the person not appear? The cock will see to it. He is cocksure. He gives a loud crow in the doorway, and the person appears. The hens are suitably impressed, but immediately devote all their henny consciousness to the scattered corn, pecking absorbedly, while the cock runs and fusses, cocksure that he is responsible for it all.

So the day goes on. The cock finds a tit-bit, and loudly calls the hens. They scuffle up in henny surety, and gobble the tit-bit. But when they find a juicy morsel for themselves, they devour it in silence, hensure. Unless, of course, there are little chicks, when they most anxiously call the brood. But in her own dim surety, the hen is really much surer than the cock, in a different way. She marches off to lay her egg, she secures obstinately the nest she wants, she lays her egg at last, then steps forth again with prancing confidence, and gives that most assured of all sounds, the hensure cackle of a bird who has laid her egg. The cock, who is never so sure about anything as the hen is about the egg she has laid, immediately starts to cackle like the female of his species. He is pining to be hensure, for hensure is so much surer than cocksure.

Nevertheless, cocksure is boss. When the chicken-hawk appears in the sky, loud are the cockerel's calls of alarm. Then the hens scuffle under the verandah, the cock ruffles his feathers on guard. The hens are numb with fear, they say: Alas, there is no health in us! How wonderful to be a cock so bold!—And they huddle, numbed. But their very numbness is hensurety.

Just as the cock can cackle, however, as if he had laid the egg, so can the hen bird crow. She can more or less assume his cocksureness. And yet she is never so easy, cocksure, as she used to be when she was hensure. Cocksure, she is cocksure, but uneasy. Hensure, she trembles, but is easy.

It seems to me just the same in the vast human farmyard. Only nowadays all the cocks are cackling and pretending to lay eggs, and all the hens are crowing and pretending to call the sun out of bed. If women to-day are cocksure, men are hensure. Men are timid, tremulous, rather soft and submissive, easy in their very henlike tremulousness. They only want to be spoken to gently. So the women step forth with a good loud *cock-a-doodle-do!*

The tragedy about cocksure women is that they are more cocky, in their assurance, than the cock himself. They never realise that when the cock gives his loud crow in the morning, he listens acutely afterwards, to hear if some other wretch of a cock dare crow defiance, challenge. To the cock, there is always defiance, challenge, danger and death on the clear air; or the possibility thereof.

But alas, when the hen crows, she listens for no defiance or challenge. When she says *cock-a-doodle-do!* then it is unanswerable. The cock listens for an answer, alert. But the hen knows she is unanswerable. *Cock-a-doodle-do!* and there it is, take it or leave it!

And it is this that makes the cocksureness of women so dangerous, so devastating. It is really out of scheme, it is not in relation to the rest of things. So we have the tragedy of cocksure women. They find, so often, that instead of having laid an egg, they have laid a vote, or an empty ink-bottle, or some other absolutely unhatchable object, which means nothing to them.

It is the tragedy of the modern woman. She becomes cocksure, she puts all her passion and energy and years of her life into some effort or assertion, without ever listening for the denial which she ought to take into count. She is cocksure, but she is a hen all the time. Frightened of her own henny self, she rushes to mad lengths about votes, or welfare, or sports, or business: she is marvellous, out-manning the man. But alas, it is all fundamentally disconnected. It is all an attitude, and one day the attitude will become a weird cramp, a pain, and then it will collapse. And when it has collapsed, and she looks at the eggs she has laid, votes, or miles of typewriting, years of business efficiency—suddenly, because she is a hen and not a cock, all she has done will turn into pure nothingness to her. Suddenly it all falls out of relation to her basic henny self, and she realizes she has lost her life. The lovely henny surety, the hensureness which is the real bliss of every female, has been denied her: she had never had it. Having lived her life with such utmost strenuousness and cocksureness, she has missed her life altogether. Nothingness!

Study Questions

1. Can you tell in the first paragraph what the comparison is?
2. State briefly the comparison and Lawrence's attitude toward it.
3. Outline the roles of the cocksure male and the hensure female as far as the kinds of jobs they do.
4. State Lawrence's definition of "cocksureness" and "hensureness." You may find that you will have to derive your own definition from a careful study of the complete essay.
5. The whole essay is based on an analogy—equating men with cocks and women with hens. Do you think the analogy is a sound one? State your reasons for believing that it is or for believing that it is not.
6. Does the purpose of the comparison reveal itself in the conclusion? State this purpose briefly.

Merged or Submerged   ELIZABETH VAN GUILDER

A funny thing happened on the way to our twenty-fifth anniversary. My husband and I stopped fighting the battle of the sexes and began to think of each other as people. Just when this began we can't pinpoint, but we know exactly when we noticed that it had happened.

It was the morning my husband turned to me and asked if I would possibly have time to make his lunch for him (he brown bags it to work) because he hadn't had time to do it the night before. I looked at him, and a funny kind of smile came over his face as he caught my thought.

Twenty-five years ago the dialogue would have gone like this:

"Where the hell is my lunch? Did you forget it again? If I ran my office the way you run this house—"

"I'm so sorry, dear; I'll get it right away."

That night we reminisced about the people we were twenty-five years ago and the people we are today. We are so very different, in our attitudes toward ourselves and toward each other, and particularly in our interpretations of our roles as partners in marriage. In the early days of our marriage, I saw myself as the inheritor of a tradition which made the male unquestioned "head of the house," in every possible connotation of the word. This submission involved all aspects of our living together but was most particularly apparent in the management of money and in the way we divided all the chores involved in the keeping of the house and the rearing of our family. These traditional roles seem to be almost nonexistent today, so changed are our concepts of the man–woman relationship in the light of the attitudes now common in American society.

I did not think twenty-five years ago that I was a particularly submissive wife. We had solemnly agreed before our wedding day that *our* marriage would be different—more modern, more "equal." We defined this, percentagewise, as 51–49, a distinct improvement over the 60–40 marriages we saw around us. What was not then apparent to me was that, if a simple majority vote is taken, 2 percent is as final as 20. If someone always has two points on you, you don't often get to win! Not that I wasn't consulted—and, because my husband is an essentially kind and fair person, I was often allowed to prevail. But it was always clearly understood by each of us that the concession was *his* to make. In the event of an impasse he was without question the decision maker. I can remember saying, quite seriously, "Somebody has to be the captain or the ship sinks."

Well, the ship isn't sinking, and we long ago forgot to worry about who was issuing the orders. In fact, there have been times when the only way the boat floated at all was for both of us to bail, bail, bail. Together. No, today we seem to function without any clear definition of just who is boss over what. And my husband finds this, he says, a pleasant relief from the awesome responsibility of *always* having to decide. Because, brother, if it goes wrong, you've got only yourself to blame! This decision making by the male may once have been essential, but for a modern woman to concede this prerogative is almost a cop-out on her part, an admission that she doesn't really want to bear her share of the burden or assume her role as a responsible partner.

Female irresponsibility and male dominance were nowhere more evident than in the management of money. He was the breadwinner, the keeper of the purse, the dispenser of all goodies. I, like my mother-in-law before me, had my "housekeeping money" which I could dispense as I chose. Everything else—for clothing, furniture, curtains, an occasional frivolity—had to be requested, teased, cajoled or bargained for, explained. I practically had to submit a technical brief outlining the recommendation for expenditure. And yet, I enjoyed and encouraged this; it was pleasant to continue the childish habit of dependence.

Today I have my own checking account, my own job, my own money. We don't think of money as "his" and "hers," but as "ours." Each has the right to use what he earns as he sees fit; each of us assumes responsibility for the mutual obligations involved in running a home and raising a family. There is no question of dominance and submission: a committee of equals determines priorities, and the money is dispensed or saved in accordance with the decision.

The second area, housekeeping, twenty-five years ago was a scene you wouldn't believe. We were the products of a time gone by, of an age when women regarded themselves as adjuncts to the male, not really functioning except when they functioned as wives, mothers, and companions in ways acceptable to the husband and father. Our prototypes were our own mothers and the mothers of most of our friends.

Women, having little outside the home to interest and motivate them, had to channel all their intelligence and ingenuity into making that home. I patterned myself after my mother-in-law. Because Mom was a bright person with a lot of energy, she had to make her role into something important or it would have been intolerable. So she became Superhousewife. Everything was starched, ironed, cleaned, waxed, scrubbed, shined, slipcovered, doilied, and *kept*. Her house was the most *kept* house I had ever seen. It was beautiful. It smelled good; it looked good; it ran like a clock; and everybody in it was miserable. When you sat down on the couch, Mom hovered nearby, ready to plump up the down cushions as soon as you got up.

I, too, believed that dust bunnies were a no-no, a smudged window a blot on my personal worth. You won't believe this, but I even ironed my husband's socks. Not without protest, at first, but—well, here's the dialog as George and I recall it, from the day I first performed the ritual of doing the laundry:

"Honey, my socks aren't ironed."
A peal of laughter. "You funny thing—who irons socks?"
Dead silence. Then a growl: "My mother does. . . . I like 'em that way."
"Oh."

Of course, this was before wash-and-wear, and in defense of George and his mother, socks did get a little lumpy. Nor was my Superhousewife mother-in-law by any means unique in this: her friends ironed socks, too. I blush to confess—forgive me, Gloria Steinem—that I dutifully ironed those socks. What's important is not whether I did or didn't—but the simple truth that I never questioned his right to ask (demand?) nor mine to comply (obey?).

Now, with housekeeping removed from the male-dominant/female-submissive syndrome, I am happy to report that the housework still gets done, by whoever is best able (and willing) to do it. If no one can, things wait their turn. Sometimes it's a whole family project, with everybody pitching in to get it done in order to get on to something more interesting. We've streamlined the process in order to achieve the most comfortable home with the least possible effort. Superhousewife, Jr., doesn't live here any more. We're two people living in a reasonably clean and orderly home, with chores divided according to desire and capability—but almost all are interchangeable. He can do dishes or make pancakes without wondering where his masculinity went; I have learned to put away the frivolous pseudo-feminine rites of being a little stupid about money, a little frightened of everything crawly, a little dependent in every situation. I can balance my own checkbook, kill my own spiders, and mix a very fine extra dry martini.

Looking back to those earlier years, I can remember so clearly how we also divided up the chores of child care. His to love, provide for, play with, teach, or discipline the children; but mine involved all the traditionally female tasks, particularly those connected with the alimentary canal. From feeding to diapering, it was mine. How differently we saw things with the advent of our last child fifteen years after the first! Father was as capable and willing to do any and all of the pleasant or unpleasant tasks, as able to get up at 2:00 A.M., as

Mother, and so our third child was in a sense his first; he came to know and enjoy him in a way never open to him before.

As you can see, it's been a long time since anyone quibbled about which job was whose. We're more analogous now to a well-coordinated team pulling our wagonload of responsibilities. If memory serves me, the best team is the one which together exerts equal effort, at precisely the same time, thus drawing the load with the minimum of friction.

This change in us is a reflection, I think, of what has been going on in the world in the past few decades. When Betty Friedan wrote *The Feminine Mystique*, it was not so much the call to revolution she supposed it to be as a response to something already in progress. A newer tradition is being born to supplant the old concepts of Man and Woman. These two mythic beings have been recreated as People, who have to decide that the great experience of life is to be shared—not partitioned off into segments labeled "his" and "hers."

I think there's a warning in this somewhere for the more militant feminists among us. I suspect they should take a good look at life as we experience it today and compare it with what their mothers and grandmothers knew. Except in a few areas where change necessarily comes slowly, the event has already taken place or is moving inexorably in that direction. To become raucous and demanding, denigrating the male instead of loving him, could be a terrible mistake. It could lead even to a reversal of the beautiful trend which, all unaware, has come upon us.

Study Questions

1. Is the comparison of the essay stated in the first paragraph?
2. How many paragraphs are devoted to introductory material?
3. What specific illustrations does the author use to develop her comparison?
4. Compare the specific illustrations or examples of "Cocksure Women and Hensure Men" with the examples of "Merged or Submerged?" Do the specific examples show any basic difference in attitude toward sex roles?
5. Do you find any agreement in the conclusion of the two essays? If so, state your ideas about the agreement. If not, explain how they differ in their conclusions.
6. The author reaches a generalization in her conclusion, a generalization based upon personal experience. Do you know people for whom the author's experience would not be true? Do you think the generalization is true enough for large numbers of people to make it a valid one?

Fashions in Love

ALDOUS HUXLEY

Human nature does not change, or, at any rate, history is too short for any changes to be perceptible. The earliest known specimens of art and literature are still comprehensible. The fact that we can understand them all and can recognize in some of them an unsurpassed artistic excellence is proof enough that not only men's feelings and instincts, but also their intellectual and imaginative powers, were in the remotest times precisely what they are now. In the fine arts it is only the convention, the form, the incidentals that change: the fundamentals of passion, of intellect and imagination remain unaltered.

It is the same with the arts of life as with the fine arts. Conventions and traditions, prejudices and ideals and religious beliefs, moral systems and codes of good manners, varying according to the geographical and historical circumstances, mold into different forms the unchanging material of human instinct, passion, and desire. It is a stiff, intractable material—Egyptian granite, rather than Hindu bronze. The artists who carved the colossal statues of Rameses II may have wished to represent the Pharaoh standing on one leg and waving two or three pairs of arms over his head, as the Indians still represent the dancing Krishna. But with the best will in the world they could not have imposed such a form upon the granite. Similarly, those artists in social life whom we call statesmen, moralists, founders of religions, have often wished to mold human nature into forms of superhuman elegance; but the material has proved too stubborn for them, and they have had to be content with only a relatively small alteration in the form which their predecessors had given it. At any given historical moment human behavior is a compromise (enforced from without by law and custom, from within by belief in religious or philosophical myths) between the raw instinct on the one hand and the unattainable ideal on the other—a compromise, in our sculptural metaphor, between the unshaped block of stone and the many-armed dancing Krishna.

Like all the other great human activities, love is the product of unchanging passions, instincts, and desires (unchanging, that is to say, in the mass of humanity; for, of course, they vary greatly in quantity and quality from individual to individual), and of laws and conventions, beliefs and ideals, which the circumstances of time and place, or the arbitrary fiats of great personalities, have imposed on a more or less willing society. The history of love, if it were ever written (and doubtless some learned German, unread, alas, by me, *has* written it, and in several volumes), would be like the current histories of art—a record of succeeding "styles" and "schools," of "influences," "revolutions," "technical discoveries." Love's psychological and physiological material remains the same; but every epoch treats it in a different manner, just as every epoch cuts its unvarying cloth and silk and linen into garments of the most diverse fashion. By way of illustration, I may mention that vogue of homosexuality which seems, from all accounts, to have been universal in the Hellenic world. Plutarch attributes the inception of this mode to the custom (novel in the fifth century, according to Thucydides) of exercising naked in the palestra.[1] But whatever may have been its origin, there can be no doubt that this particular fashion in love spread widely among people who were not in the least congenitally disposed to homosexuality. Convention and public opinion molded the material of love into forms which a later age has chosen to call "unnatural." A recrudescence of this amorous mode was very noticeable in Europe during the years immediately following the War. Among the determining causes of this recrudescence a future Plutarch will undoubtedly number the writings of Proust and André Gide.

The present fashions in love are not so definite and universal as those in clothes. It is as though our age were dubiously hesitating between crinolines and hobble skirts, trunk hose and Oxford trousers. Two distinct and hostile conceptions of love coexist in the minds of men and women, two sets of ideals, of conventions, of public opinions, struggle for the right to mold the psychological and physiological material of love. One is the conception evolved by the nineteenth century out of the ideals of Christianity on the one hand and romanticism on the other. The other is that still rather inchoate and negative conception which contemporary youth is in process of forming out of the materials provided by modern psychology. The public opinion, the conventions, ideals, and prejudices which gave active force to the first convention and enabled it, to some extent at least, to modify the actual practice of love, had already lost much of their strength when they were rudely shattered, at any rate in the minds of the young, by the shock of the War. As usually happens, practice preceded theory, and the new conception of love was called in to justify existing post-War manners. Having gained a footing, the new conception is now a cause of new behavior among the youngest adolescent generation, instead of being, as it was for the generation of the War, an explanation of war-time behavior made after the fact.

Let us try to analyze these two coexisting and conflicting conceptions of love. The older conception was, as I have said, the product of Christianity and romanticism—a curious mixture of contradictions, of the ascetic dread of passion and the romantic worship of passion. Its ideal was a strict monogamy, such as St. Paul grudgingly conceded to amorous humanity, sanctified and made eternal by one of those terrific exclusive passions which are the favorite theme of poetry and drama. It is an ideal which finds its most characteristic expression in the poetry of that infinitely respectable rebel, that profoundly anglican worshiper of passion, Robert Browning. It was Rousseau who first started the cult of passion for passion's sake. Before his time the great passions, such as that of Paris for Helen, of Dido for Æneas, of Paolo and Francesca for one another, had been regarded rather as disastrous maladies than as enviable

[1]Plutarch, who wrote some five hundred years after the event, is by no means an unquestionable authority. The habit of which he and Thucydides speak may have facilitated the spread of the homosexual fashion. But that the fashion existed before the fifth century is made sufficiently clear by Homer, not to mention Sappho. Like many modern oriental peoples, the ancient Greeks were evidently, in Sir Richard Burton's expressive phrase, "omnifutuent."

states of soul. Rousseau, followed by all the romantic poets of France and England, transformed the grand passion from what it had been in the Middle Ages—a demoniac possession—into a divine ecstasy, and promoted it from the rank of a disease to that of the only true and natural form of love. The nineteenth-century conception of love was thus doubly mystical, with the mysticism of Christian asceticism and sacramentalism, and with the romantic mysticism of Nature. It claimed an absolute rightness on the grounds of its divinity and of its naturalness.

Now, if there is one thing that the study of history and psychology makes abundantly clear, it is that there are no such things as either "divine" or "natural" forms of love. Innumerable gods have sanctioned and forbidden innumerable kinds of sexual behavior, and innumerable philosophers and poets have advocated the return to the most diverse kinds of "nature." Every form of amorous behavior, from chastity and monogamy to promiscuity and the most fantastic "perversions," is found both among animals and men. In any given human society, at any given moment, love, as we have seen, is the result of the interaction of the unchanging instinctive and physiological material of sex with the local conventions of morality and religion, the local laws, prejudices, and ideals. The degree of permanence of these conventions, religious myths, and ideals is proportional to their social utility in the given circumstances of time and place.

The new twentieth-century conception of love is realistic. It recognizes the diversity of love, not merely in the social mass from age to age, but from individual to contemporary individual, according to the dosage of the different instincts with which each is born, and the upbringing he has received. The new generation knows that there is no such thing as Love with a large L, and that what the Christian romantics of the last century regarded as the uniquely natural form of love is, in fact, only one of the indefinite number of possible amorous fashions, produced by specific circumstances at that particular time. Psychoanalysis has taught it that all the forms of sexual behavior previously regarded as wicked, perverse, unnatural, are statistically normal (and normality is solely a question of statistics), and that what is commonly called amorous normality is far from being a spontaneous, instinctive form of behavior, but must be acquired by a process of education. Having contracted the habit of talking freely and more or less scientifically about sexual matters, the young no longer regard love with that feeling of rather guilty excitement and thrilling shame which was for an earlier generation the normal reaction to the subject. Moreover, the practice of birth-control has robbed amorous indulgence of most of the sinfulness traditionally supposed to be inherent in it by robbing it of its socially disastrous effects. The tree shall be known by its fruits: where there are no fruits, there is obviously no tree. Love has ceased to be the rather fearful, mysterious thing it was, and become a perfectly normal, almost commonplace, activity—an activity, for many young people, especially in America, of the same nature as dancing or tennis, a sport, a recreation, a pastime. For those who hold this conception of love, liberty and toleration are prime necessities. A strenuous offensive against the old taboos and repressions is everywhere in progress.

Such, then, are the two conceptions of love which oppose one another today.

Which is the better? Without presuming to pass judgment, I will content my-self with pointing out the defects of each. The older conception was bad, in so far as it inflicted unnecessary and undeserved sufferings on the many human beings whose congenital and acquired modes of lovemaking did not conform to the fashionable Christian-romantic pattern which was regarded as being uniquely entitled to call itself Love. The new conception is bad, it seems to me, in so far as it takes love too easily and lightly. On love regarded as an amuse-ment the last word is surely this of Robert Burns:

> I waive the quantum of the sin,
>   The hazard of concealing;
> But oh! it hardens all within
>   And petrifies the feeling.

Nothing is more dreadful than a cold, unimpassioned indulgence. And love infallibly becomes cold and unimpassioned when it is too lightly made. It is not good, as Pascal remarked, to have too much liberty. Love is the product of two opposed forces—of an instinctive impulsion and a social resistance acting on the individual by means of ethical imperatives justified by philosophical or religious myths. When, with the destruction of the myths, resistance is re-moved, the impulse wastes itself on emptiness; and love, which is only the product of conflicting forces, is not born. The twentieth century is reproducing in a new form the error of the early nineteenth-century romantics. Following Rousseau, the romantics imagined that exclusive passion was the "natural" mode of love, just as virtue and reasonableness were the "natural" forms of men's social behavior. Get rid of priests and kings, and men will be for ever good and happy; poor Shelley's faith in this palpable nonsense remained un-shaken to the end. He believed also in the complementary paralogism that you had only to get rid of social restraints and erroneous mythology to make the Grand Passion universally chronic. Like the Mussets and Sands, he failed to see that the Grand Passion was produced by the restraints that opposed them-selves to the sexual impulse, just as the deep lake is produced by the dam that bars the passage of the stream, and the flight of the aeroplane by the air which resists the impulsion given to it by the motor. There would be no air-resistance in a vacuum; but precisely for that reason the machine would not leave the ground, or even move at all. Where there are no psychological or external re-straints, the Grand Passion does not come into existence and must be artificially cultivated, as George Sand and Musset cultivated it—with what painful and grotesque results the episode of Venice made only too ludicrously manifest.

"J'aime et je veux pâlir; j'aime et je veux souffrir," says Musset, with his usual hysterically masochistic emphasis. Our young contemporaries do not wish to suffer or grow pale; on the contrary, they have a most determined desire to grow pink and enjoy themselves. But too much enjoyment "blunts the fine point of seldom pleasure." Unrestrained indulgence kills not merely passion, but, in the end, even amusement. Too much liberty is as life-destroying as too much restraint. The present fashion in lovemaking is likely to be short, because love that is psychologically too easy is not interesting. Such, at any rate, was evidently the opinion of the French, who, bored by the sexual license produced by the Napoleonic upheavals, reverted (so far, at any rate, as the upper and middle classes were concerned) to an almost anglican strictness under Louis-Philippe. We may anticipate an analogous reaction in the not distant future. What new or what revived mythology will serve to create those internal restraints without which sexual impulse cannot be transformed into love? Christian morality and ascetic ideals will doubtless continue to play their part, but there will no less certainly be other moralities and ideals. For example, Mr. D. H. Lawrence's new mythology of nature (new in its expression, but reassuringly old in substance) is a doctrine that seems to me fruitful in possibilities. The "natural love" which he sets up as a norm is a passion less self-conscious and high-falutin, less obviously and precariously artificial, than that "natural love" of the romantics, in which Platonic and Christian notions were essential ingredients. The restraints which Mr. Lawrence would impose on sexual impulse, so as to transform it into love, are not the restraints of religious spirituality. They are restraints of a more fundamental, less artificial nature— emotional, not intellectual. The impulse is to be restrained from promiscuous manifestations because, if it were not, promiscuity would "harden all within and petrify the feeling." The restraint is of the same personal nature as the impulse. The conflict is between a part of the personality and the personality as an organized whole. It does not pretend, as the romantic and Christian conflict pretends, to be a battle between a diabolical Lower Self and certain transcendental Absolutes, of which the only thing that philosophy can tell us is that they are absolutely unknowable, and therefore, for our purposes, nonexistent. It only claims to be, what in fact it is, a psychological conflict taking place in the more or less known and finite world of human interests. This doctrine has several great advantages over previous systems of inward restraint. It does not postulate the existence of any transcendental, non-human entity. This is a merit which will be increasingly appreciated as the significance of Kant's and Nietzsche's destructive criticism is more widely realized. People will cease to be interested in unknowable absolutes; but they will never lose interest in their own personalities. True, that "personality as a whole," in whose interests the sexual impulse is to be restrained and turned into love, is, strictly speaking, a mythological figure. Consisting, as we do, of a vast colony of souls —souls of individual cells, of organs, of groups of organs, hunger-souls, sex-souls, power-souls, herd-souls, of whose multifarious activities our consciousness (the Soul with a large S) is only very imperfectly and indirectly aware—we are not in a position to know the real nature of our personality as a whole. The only thing we can do is to hazard a hypothesis, to create a mythological figure, call it Human Personality, and hope that circumstances will not, by destroying us, prove our imaginative guesswork too hopelessly wrong. But myth for myth, Human Personality is preferable to God. We do at least know something of Human Personality, whereas of God we know nothing and, knowing nothing, are at liberty to invent as freely as we like. If men had always tried to deal with the problem of love in terms of known human rather than of grotesquely imagined divine interests, there would have been less "making of eunuchs for the kingdom of heaven's sake," less persecution of "sinners," less burning and imprisoning of the heretics of "unnatural" love, less Grundyism, less Comstockery, and, at the same time, less dirty Don-Juanism, less of that curiously malignant and vengeful lovemaking so characteristic of the debauchee under a Christian dispensation. Reacting against the absurdities of the old mythology, the young have run into absurdities no less inordinate at the other end of the scale. A sordid and ignoble realism offers no resistance to the sexual impulse, which now spends itself purposelessly, without producing love, or even, in the long-run, amusement, without enhancing vitality or quickening and deepening the rhythms of living. Only a new mythology of nature, such as, in modern times, Blake, Robert Burns, and Lawrence have defined it, an untranscendental and (relatively speaking) realistic mythology of Energy, Life, and Human Personality, will provide, it seems to me, the inward resistances necessary to turn sexual impulse into love, and provide them in a form which the critical intelligence of Post-Nietzschean youth can respect. By means of such a conception a new fashion in love may be created, a mode more beautiful and convenient, more healthful and elegant, than any seen among men since the days of remote and pagan antiquity.

Study Questions

1. There are several comparisons made in the course of the essay. What is the comparison in the introductory paragraphs?
2. What do you think is the main comparison as far as the purpose of the essay?
3. How does Huxley use his introductory comparison to define love—its basic materials and its changing fashions?
4. What two influences played a part in the nineteenth century's conception of love?
5. Do you think Huxley's comparisons and explanations have served to illuminate his idea of the newest concept of love? Can *you* define his concept from this essay? If so, try to state it in one or two sentences.

The Flea   JOHN DONNE

Mark but this flea, and mark in this
How little that which thou deny'st me is;
It sucked me first, and now sucks thee,
And in this flea our two bloods mingled be;
Thou know'st that this cannot be said

A sin, nor shame, nor loss of maidenhead;
  Yet this enjoys before it woo,
  And pampered swells with one blood made of two,
  And this, alas, is more than we would do.

Oh stay, three lives in one flea spare,   10
Where we almost, yea, more than married are.
This flea is you and I, and this
Our marriage bed, and marriage temple is;
Though parents grudge, and you, we are met
And cloistered in these living walls of jet.   15
  Though use make you apt to kill me,
  Let not to that, self-murder added be,
  And sacrilege, three sins in killing three.

Cruel and sudden, hast thou since
Purpled thy nail in blood of innocence?   20
Wherein could this flea guilty be,
Except in that drop which it sucked from thee?
Yet thou triumph'st and say'st that thou
Find'st not thyself, nor me the weaker now.
  'Tis true. Then learn how false fears be: 25
  Just so much honor, when thou yield'st to me,
  Will waste, as this flea's death took life from thee.

The Fly   WILLIAM BLAKE

Little Fly,
Thy summer's play
My thoughtless hand
Has brush'd away.

Am not I   5
A fly like thee?
Or art not thou
A man like me?

For I dance,
And drink, and sing,   10
Till some blind hand
Shall brush my wing.

If thought is life
And strength and breath,
And the want   15
Of thought is death;

Then am I
A happy fly,
If I live
Or if I die.   20

Study Questions

1.   What similarities does Blake find in the man and the fly?
2.   What conclusion does Blake's comparison lead him to?
3.   Although Donne titles his poem "The Flea," he is not comparing the
     flea itself to man (note, for example, the line "we are met/And
     cloistered in these living walls of jet"). What is the basis of the
     comparison?
4.   Donne is using the flea as an argument for something he wants. What
     exactly is the purpose of the comparison?
5.   In the final five lines of the poem, Donne makes a further comparison.
     What is being compared there?

Love of Death and Love of Life   ERICH FROMM

... There is no more fundamental distinction between men, psychologically
and morally, than the one between those who love death and those who love
life, between the *necrophilous* and the *biophilous*. This is not meant to convey
that a person is necessarily either entirely necrophilous or entirely biophilous.
There are some who are totally devoted to death, and these are insane. There
are others who are entirely devoted to life, and these strike us as having accomplished the highest aim of which man is capable. In many, both the
biophilous and the necrophilous trends are present, but in various blends. What
matters here, as always in living phenomena, is which trend is the stronger,

Abridged from pp. 38–48 in *The Heart of Man* by Erich Fromm. Volume Twelve of
Religious Perspectives Series, planned and edited by Ruth Nanda Anshen. Copyright
© 1964 by Erich Fromm. By permission of Harper & Row, Publishers, Inc.

so that it determines man's behavior—not the complete absence or presence of one of the two orientations.

Literally, "necrophilia" means "love of the dead" (as "biophilia" means "love of life"). The term is customarily used to denote a sexual perversion, namely the desire to possess the dead body (of a woman) for purposes of sexual intercourse, or a morbid desire to be in the presence of a dead body. But, as is often the case, a sexual perversion presents only the more overt and clear picture of an orientation which is to be found without sexual admixture in many people. . . .

The person with the necrophilous orientation is one who is attracted to and fascinated by all that is not alive, all that is dead; corpses, decay, feces, dirt. Necrophiles are those people who love to talk about sickness, about burials, about death. They come to life precisely when they can talk about death. A clear example of the pure necrophilous type is Hitler. He was fascinated by destruction, and the smell of death was sweet to him. While in the years of his success it may have appeared that he wanted to destroy only those whom he considered his enemies, the days of the *Götterdämmerung* at the end showed that his deepest satisfaction lay in witnessing total and absolute *destruction*: that of the German people, of those around him, and of himself. A report from the First World War, while not proved, makes good sense: a soldier saw Hitler standing in a trancelike mood, gazing at a decayed corpse and unwilling to move away.

The necrophilous dwell in the past, never in the future. Their feelings are essentially sentimental, that is, they nurse the memory of feelings which they had yesterday—or believe that they had. They are cold, distant devotees of "law and order." Their values are precisely the reverse of the values we connect with normal life: not life, but death excites and satisfies them.

Characteristic for the necrophile is his attitude toward force. Force is, to quote Simone Weil's definition, the capacity to transform a man into a corpse. Just as sexuality can create life, force can destroy it. All force is, in the last analysis, based on the power to kill. I may not kill a person but only deprive him of his freedom; I may want only to humiliate him or to take away his possessions—but whatever I do, behind all these actions stands my capacity to kill and my willingness to kill. The lover of death necessarily loves force. For him the greatest achievement of man is not to give life, but to destroy it; the use of force is not a transitory action forced upon him by circumstances—it is a way of life.

This explains why the necrophile is truly enamored of force. Just as for the lover of life the fundamental polarity in man is that between male and female, for the necrophile there exists another and very different polarity: that between those who have the power to kill and those who lack this power. For him there are only two "sexes": the powerful and the powerless; the killers and the killed. He is in love with the killers and despises those who are killed. Not rarely this "being in love with the killers" is to be taken literally; they are his objects of sexual attraction and fantasies, only less drastically so than in the perversion mentioned above or in the perversion of necrophagia (the desire to eat a corpse) a desire which can be found not rarely in the dreams of necrophilous persons. I know of a number of dreams of necrophilous persons in which they have sexual intercourse with an old woman or man by whom they are in no way physically attracted, but whom they fear and admire for their power and destructiveness.

The influence of men like Hitler or Stalin lies precisely in their unlimited capacity and willingness to kill. For this they were loved by the necrophiles. Of the rest, many were afraid of them, and preferred to admire, rather than to be aware of their fear; many others did not sense the necrophilous quality of these leaders, and saw in them the builders, saviors, good fathers. If the necrophilous leaders had not pretended that they were builders and protectors, the number of people attracted to them would hardly have been sufficient to help them to seize power, and the number of those repelled by them would probably soon have led to their downfall.

While life is characterized by growth in a structured, functional manner, the necrophilous person loves all that does not grow, all that is mechanical. The necrophilous person is driven by the desire to transform the organic into the inorganic, to approach life mechanically, as if all living persons were things. All living processes, feelings, and thoughts are transformed into things. Memory, rather than experience; having, rather than being, is what counts. The necrophilous person can relate to an object—a flower or a person—only if he possesses it; hence a threat to his possession is a threat to himself; if he loses possession he loses contact with the world. That is why we find the paradoxical reaction that he would rather lose life than possession, even though by losing life he who possesses has ceased to exist. He loves control, and in the act of controlling he kills life. He is deeply afraid of life, because it is disorderly and uncontrollable by its very nature. The woman who wrongly claims to be the mother of the child in the story of Solomon's judgment is typical for this tendency; she would rather have a properly divided dead child than lose a living one. To the necrophilous person justice means correct division, and they are willing to kill or die for the sake of what they call justice. "Law and order" for them are idols—everything that threatens law and order is felt as a satanic attack against their supreme values.

The necrophilous person is attracted to darkness and night. In mythology and poetry he is attracted to caves, or to the depth of the ocean, or depicted as being blind. (The trolls in Ibsen's *Peer Gynt* are a good example; they are blind, they live in caves, their only value is the narcissistic one of something "home brewed" or home made.) All that is away from or directed against life attracts him. He wants to return to the darkness of the womb, and to the past of inorganic or animal existence. He is essentially oriented to the past, not to the future which he hates and is afraid of. Related to this is his craving for certainty. But life is never certain, never predictable, never controllable; in order to make life controllable it must be transformed into death; death, indeed, is the only certainty in life.

The necrophilous tendencies are usually most clearly exhibited in a person's dreams. These deal with murder, blood, corpses, skulls, feces; sometimes also with men transformed into machines or acting like machines. An occasional dream of this type may occur in many people without indicating necrophilia.

In the necrophilous person dreams of this type are frequent and sometimes repetitive.

The highly necrophilous person can often be recognized by his appearance and his gestures. He is cold, his skin looks dead, and often he has an expression on his face as though he were smelling a bad odor. (This expression could be clearly seen in Hitler's face.) He is orderly, obsessive, pedantic. This aspect of the necrophilous person has been demonstrated to the world in the figure of Eichmann. Eichmann was fascinated by bureaucratic order and death. His supreme values were obedience and the proper functioning of the organization. He transported Jews as he would have transported coal. That they were human beings was hardly within the field of his vision, hence even the problem of whether he hated or did not hate his victims is irrelevant.

But examples of the necrophilous character are by no means to be found only among the inquisitors, the Hitlers, and the Eichmanns. There are any number of individuals who do not have the opportunity and the power to kill, yet whose necrophilia expresses itself in other and, superficially seen, more harmless ways. An example is the mother who will always be interested in her child's sicknesses, in his failures, in dark prognoses for the future; at the same time she will not be impressed by a favorable change; she will not respond to the child's joy; she will not notice anything new that is growing within him. We might find that her dreams deal with sickness, death, corpses, blood. She does not harm the child in any obvious way, yet she may slowly strangle his joy of life, his faith in growth, and eventually she will infect him with her own necrophilous orientation.

In this description of the necrophilous orientation I may have given the impression that *all* the features described here are necessarily found in the necrophilous person. It is true that such divergent features as the wish to kill, the worship of force, the attraction to death and dirt, sadism, the wish to transform the organic into the inorganic through "order," are all part of the same basic orientation. Yet as far as individuals are concerned, there are considerable differences with regard to the strength of these respective trends. Any one of the features mentioned here may be more pronounced in one person than in another; furthermore, the degree to which a person is necrophilous in comparison with his biophilous aspects, and finally the degree to which a person is aware of the necrophilous tendencies or rationalizes them, varies considerably from person to person. Yet the concept of the necrophilous type is by no means an abstraction or a summary of various disparate behavior trends. Necrophilia constitutes a fundamental orientation; it is the one answer to life which is in complete opposition to life; it is the most morbid and the most dangerous among the orientations to life of which man is capable. It is the true perversion: while being alive, not life but death is loved; not growth but destruction. The necrophilous person, if he dares to be aware of what he feels, expresses the motto of his life when he says, "Long live death!"

The opposite of the necrophilous orientation is the *biophilous*; its essence is love of life in contrast to love of death. Like necrophilia, biophilia is not constituted by a single trait, but represents a total orientation, an entire way of being. It is manifested in a person's bodily processes, in his emotions, in his thoughts, in his gestures; the biophilous orientation expresses itself in the whole man. The most elementary form of this orientation is expressed in the tendency of all living organisms to live. In contrast to Freud's assumption concerning the "death instinct," I agree with the assumption made by many biologists and philosophers that it is an inherent quality of all living substance to live, to preserve its existence; as Spinoza expressed it: "Everything insofar as it is itself, endeavors to persist in its own being." He called this endeavor the very essence of the thing in question.

We observe this tendency to live in all living substance around us; in the grass that breaks through the stones to get light and to live; in the animal that will fight to the last in order to escape death; in man who will do almost anything to preserve his life.

The tendency to preserve life and to fight against death is the most elementary form of the biophilous orientation, and is common to all living substance. Inasmuch as it is a tendency to *preserve* life, and to *fight* death, it represents only *one* aspect of the drive toward life. The other aspect is a more positive one: living substance has the tendency to integrate and to unite; it tends to fuse with different and opposite entities, and to grow in a structural way. Unification and integrated growth are characteristic of all life processes, not only as far as cells are concerned, but also with regard to feeling and thinking.

The most elementary expression of this tendency is the fusion between cells and organisms, from nonsexual cell fusion to sexual union among animals and man. In the latter, sexual union is based on the attraction between the male and the female poles. The male-female polarity constitutes the core of that need for fusion on which the life of the human species depends. It seems that for this very reason nature has provided man with the most intense pleasure in the fusion of the two poles. Biologically, the result of this fusion is normally the creation of a new being. The cycle of life is that of union, birth, and growth—just as the cycle of death is that of cessation of growth, disintegration, decay.

However, even the sexual instinct, while *biologically* serving life, is not necessarily one which *psychologically* expresses biophilia. It seems that there is hardly any intense emotion which cannot be attracted to and blended with the sexual instinct. Vanity, the desire for wealth, for adventure, and even the attraction to death can, as it were, commission the sexual instinct into their service. Why this should be so is a matter for speculation. One is tempted to think that it is the cunning of nature to make the sexual instinct so pliable that it will be mobilized by any kind of intense desire, even by those which are in contradiction to life. But whatever the reason, the fact of the blending between sexual desire and destructiveness can hardly be doubted. (Freud pointed to this mixture, especially in his discussion of the blending of the death instinct with the life instinct, as occurring in sadism and masochism.) Sadism, masochism, necrophagia and coprophagia are perversions, not because they deviate from the customary standards of sexual behavior, but precisely because they signify the one fundamental perversion: the blending between life and death.

The full unfolding of biophilia is to be found in the productive orientation. The person who fully loves life is attracted by the process of life and growth in all spheres. He prefers to construct rather than to retain. He is capable of wondering, and he prefers to see something new to the security of finding confirmation of the old. He loves the adventure of living more than he does certainty. His approach to life is functional rather than mechanical. He sees the whole rather than only the parts, structures rather than summations. He wants to mold and to influence by love, reason, by his example; not by force, by cutting things apart, by the bureaucratic manner of administering people as if they were things. He enjoys life and all its manifestations rather than mere excitement.

Biophilic ethics have their own principle of good and evil. Good is all that serves life; evil is all that serves death. Good is reverence for life, all that enhances life, growth, unfolding. Evil is all that stifles life, narrows it down, cuts it into pieces. Joy is virtuous and sadness is sinful. Thus it is from the standpoint of biophilic ethics that the Bible mentions as the central sin of the Hebrews: "Because thou didst not serve thy Lord with joy and gladness of heart in the abundance of all things" (Deut. 28:47). The conscience of the biophilous person is not one of forcing oneself to refrain from evil and to do good. It is not the superego described by Freud, which is a strict taskmaster, employing sadism against oneself for the sake of virtue. The biophilous conscience is motivated by its attraction to life and joy; the moral effort consists in strengthening the life-loving side in oneself. For this reason the biophile does not dwell in remorse and guilt which are, after all, only aspects of self-loathing and sadness. He turns quickly to life and attempts to do good. Spinoza's *Ethic* is a striking example of biophilic morality. "Pleasure," he says, "in itself is not bad but good; contrariwise, pain in itself is bad." And in the same spirit: "A free man thinks of death least of all things; and his wisdom is a meditation not of death but of life." Love of life underlies the various versions of humanistic philosophy. In various conceptual forms these philosophies are in the same vein as Spinoza's; they express the principle that the sane man loves life, that sadness is sin and joy is virtue, that man's aim in life is to be attracted by all that is alive and to separate himself from all that is dead and mechanical.

I have tried to give a picture of the necrophilic and the biophilic orientations in their pure forms. These pure forms are, of course, rare. The pure necrophile is insane; the pure biophile is saintly. Most people are a particular blend of the necrophilous and the biophilous orientations, and what matters is which of the two trends is dominant. Those in whom the necrophilous orientation gains dominance will slowly kill the biophilic side in themselves; usually they are not aware of their death-loving orientation; they will harden their hearts; they will act in such a way that their love of death seems to be the logical and rational response to what they experience. On the other hand, those in whom love for life still dominates, will be shocked when they discover how close they are to the "valley of the shadow of death," and this shock might awaken them to life. Hence it is very important to understand not only how strong the necrophilic tendency is in a person, but also how aware he is of it. If he believes that he dwells in the land of life when in reality he lives in the land of death, he is lost to life since he has no chance to return.

Study Questions

1. What is the purpose of Fromm's essay? Is its aim to encourage choice, to clarify or to increase understanding?
2. Fromm's essay is primarily a half-essay by half-essay comparison. There are places in the essay, however, where the comparison is half-sentence by half-sentence or sentence by sentence. Point out examples of these.
3. How important is definition in this essay? To what extent does Fromm define? What words are not defined which might have been because of their obscurity?
4. Within the half-essay by half-essay structure of the comparison, how parallel are the points of comparison?

PRELIMINARY WORKSHEET

1. Topic _____

2. Source of information

    a. personal knowledge

_____

_____

_____

    b. library resources

_____

_____

_____

_____

_____

_____

3. Purpose of comparison _____

_____

_____

_____

_____

4. Classification of subjects of comparison _____

_____

_____

_____

5. Division of subjects into categories/characteristics

    a. _____

    b. _____

    c. _____

    d. _____

    e. _____

    f. _____

    g. _____

6. Main-idea sentence _____

_____

_____

_____

7. Details for each division (arranged spatially, chronologically, or in other ways)

    a. _____

_____

_____

_____

    b. _____

_____

_____

_____

c. _____

_____

_____

_____

_____

d. _____

_____

_____

_____

_____

e. _____

_____

_____

_____

_____

f. _____

_____

_____

_____

_____

g. _____

_____

_____

_____

8. Supplementary information for introduction _____

_____

_____

_____

_____

9. Concluding material _____

_____

_____

_____

_____

_____

EVALUATION GUIDE

Name   _____

Topic   _____

Introduction

    1.   What is the purpose of the comparison? _____

_____

_____

_____

    2.   State the main-idea sentence. _____

_____

_____

_____

    3.   Does the main-idea sentence indicate purpose and specify division in the order followed in the paper? _____

_____

_____

_____

Body

    1.   What principle of order determines the arrangement of the details within each section of the comparison?

       section a. _____

section b.   _____

section c.   _____

section d.   _____

section e.   _____

section f.   _____

section g.   _____

2. What type of parallel structure is used in each section?   _____

_____

_____

_____

3. List the major transitions joining the sections of the comparison to each other.   _____

_____

4. How does the emphasis of the paper (similarities or differences or both) support the purpose of the comparison?   _____

_____

_____

_____

_____

_____

Conclusion

1. Does the conclusion restate and support the purpose of the comparison?   _____

_____

Rating

___ This paper should be rewritten completely or in part.

___ This paper is acceptable but needs some minor revisions.

___ This is an outstandingly good paper.

5   Persuasion: Division of Reasons

INTRODUCTORY COMMENTS

In your previous writing assignments you have been concerned with collecting and organizing information in order to describe a process, report an event, define an object or idea, or compare two objects. In all of these papers you had to be concerned with completeness, specificity, and accuracy, but the mental process involved in their composition was primarily one of collecting and reporting information, organized according to a pattern appropriate to the topic. Writing an essay meant to persuade or to argue a point involves a more complex mental operation called *reasoning*, the process of *drawing conclusions* from known or presumed facts. When you argue or persuade, you employ this process as you lead your reader to accept your argument by presenting him with information which supports the conclusion you are trying to establish.

In the final two chapters you will study papers which attempt to argue or persuade. As you do, you will see that the principles of classification and division are directly applied to the two major structures around which an argument can be developed. In the final chapter, you will make use of a logical structure in which a connected series of classifications and divisions forms the basis of the sequential argument. In this chapter, you will use classification and division directly, as you organize your material around a division of reasons. In both chapters, the purpose of your paper will be to persuade your reader that your argument is sound.

Properly, to persuade is to attempt to influence the opinions or behavior of others; to argue is to state dispassionately and in an organized manner the reasons or facts in support of a position. However, the two rhetorical terms are closely related, and similar structures for organization will serve for either. Therefore, *persuasion* and *argument* will be treated as equivalent terms and used interchangeably in this and the following chapter.

Purposes of persuasion

But why should you attempt to persuade? For that matter, is it really possible to convince anyone of anything? Many students despair of persuasion through reasoning. They feel that they never win arguments, that their opponents don't listen, and that nobody ever convinces anybody of anything he doesn't already want to believe.

Admittedly, argument can be difficult and sometimes fruitless, for a variety of reasons. First of all, everyone is unique; people do not think exactly alike, nor should they be expected to do so. Then there are those who have settled so deeply into their choices and beliefs that they tend not to allow the possibility of dispute. Finally, one problem with argument has to do with the ability of those who argue to remain calm during debate; many people become so emotional when arguing that they can't think straight and end up saying something they don't really mean or nothing at all.

Even though you may be among those who feel that argument can seem to lack purpose or value, there will be times when you will want or need to state your position and defend it. You may wish to justify your own position in the minority, or simply to argue for the freedom to be yourself. At other times you may actually hope to accomplish something —to effect a change in the rules of your college, to protect an endangered part of the environment, or to help elect a candidate. In any of these cases you will hardly expect to persuade *all* your readers, but you may nevertheless hope to have an effect on some of them. Readers who already agree with you may be moved to action. Readers who have previously made up their minds to disagree may be brought to acknowledge that there are at least possible alternate positions. Readers who have no position on the issue may be led to study the question, to agree, or even to respond in a more positive fashion.

Current events demonstrate that argument can be effective. Consider the gains that have been made, slowly and painfully to be sure, by the movement for women's rights; or, more recently, by the movement for student participation in campus government. Consider the extraordinary reversal in American attitudes toward mainland China in recent years. All these changes show the possibility of altering attitudes through reasoning. They also demonstrate what can be done if persuasion is relatively objective and carefully planned, however violent the controversies occasioned, which sometimes led to or accompanied the presentation of the arguments themselves.

Argument structured by division of reasons

One of the most persuasive ways to organize an argument is around a division of reasons. This structure is particularly helpful in three ways. First, it provides a simple and accessible method for planning the overall order in which to present your evidence: listing your major reasons in support of your argument will provide a clear basis for dividing your topic into parts so that you can determine a paragraph structure for your paper. Second, a division of reasons will help to give you confidence in your material so that you can maintain an objective attitude, relying on facts rather than emotive language to convince your reader. Finally, such a division naturally helps you move from the abstract concepts ordinarily involved in argumentative topics to concrete examples and illustrations.

If, for instance, you wish to argue that your college should adopt a pass-fail grading system, you might discover reasons like the following:

1.   Grades as we know them are punitive: they tend to penalize a student for the mistakes he has made in the process of learning.

2.   Grades cannot be completely objective and accurate, and the difference between A and B or B and C is largely a matter of subjective judgment.

3.   People change; yet transfer and graduate applications, as well as many job applications, may be judged on the basis of grades earned long ago.

The breakdown of the topic into such a division obviously provides a ready framework for a paper, since each of these reasons should be explored in a separate section of the body. In addition, because you in effect will be developing three separate arguments, each of which may be directly substantiated by evidence, it will be easier to argue objectively. Furthermore, the evidence will necessarily include specific information which will make your argument concrete rather than abstract. Note, however, that while the division allows for a separation of the topic into units or paragraphs, the actual order in which you take up the paragraphs and give details within them will have to be determined on some other basis. The guidelines which follow present detailed suggestions for both arrangements.

Cause-and-effect relationships

There are some important considerations connected with the persuasion paper structured around a division of reasons, for reasons imply a cause-and-effect relationship. Whenever you give a reason for taking a particular action, you state or at least imply that the action will cause certain desirable effects, or that a contrary action will cause certain undesirable effects. Your success with this assignment therefore depends on your understanding of cause and effect.

In their most basic sense, *cause* is an agent or force, producing an effect; and *effect* is that which is brought about by some cause or agency, a consequence, a result of some determining force or operation. Some philosophers distinguish among a variety of causes, but all you have to know is, first of all, that cause and effect imply a relationship of determination or production, and second, that cause can be of two major kinds: one answers the question, "Who or what brought it about?" and the other, "Why was it done?"

Arguments built around a list of reasons can focus on either cause or effect. In the example given above concerning grading systems, one major cause (grades) was seen to produce a series of effects. A paper arguing against the grading system would therefore examine these effects in sequence and, by showing that they are undesirable, argue for the replacement of the system with an alternative.

Similarly, an essay may be planned around a single effect resulting from a combination of causes. Such would be the case with an argument for a complex, multifaceted attack on the problems of poverty: poverty results from many causes acting in combination, and it can be eradicated only by attacking all the major causes simultaneously.

One word of warning: since any event may have several causes or effects, you must be aware of *all* the cause-and-effect relationships involved and assess their relative importance. For example, if a group of students sets fire to a campus building, there are at least three distinct causes of the fire: the equipment that started it, the students who set it, and the reasons behind their action. Both the equipment used (a match) and the agents (the students) are causes, but the one which should probably be investigated most thoroughly involves the reasons for the students' action. Dealing with these motives is a much more complicated matter than simply making a rule against the possession of matches or dismissing the students from college.

Since causes and effects are numerous and varied, in writing an essay based on cause-and-effect relationships, you must be very careful to avoid fallacies like the following.

Oversimplification. "I'm sure Chuck will be a better basketball player than Tom: he's an inch and a half taller." Extra height is certainly one reason why some basketball players are better than others—but you oversimplify if you make it the only reason. Some shorter players may be just as good because they have extra speed or better ball-handling skills or better judgment. When you organize an argument around a list of reasons, make sure you avoid oversimplification; consider all of the major relevant causes.

Non Sequitur. You should also be sure that there is a connection where you state that there is one. "I'm voting for Williams for senator: he has such a good, honest face on television." This is an example of the non sequitur ("it does not follow") fallacy. The fact that Williams looks honest does not guarantee that he is honest. And while honesty is a desirable quality in senators, they need other qualities as well: intelligence, for example, and energy.

Post Hoc Fallacy. Closely related to non sequitur is the post hoc ("after this") fallacy. The assumption here is that because one event follows another in time, the two also have a cause-and-effect relationship. "A black cat crossed my path this morning, and it's been a terrible day: I lost my wallet, I flunked a geology quiz, and I just know something else bad is going to happen." This person's anxieties about possible bad luck may have been a partial cause of his problems—but few of us would believe that the cat was in any way a direct cause, though it did cross his path before unfortunate things began to happen.

Thus the writer of a persuasion paper based on reasons must make sure that the cause-and-effect relationships he is talking about actually exist and that they are indeed relevant to the topic he is examining.

Emotive language

Specific proofs are persuasive when carefully and appropriately used. However, you must be aware that no speaker or writer explicitly states all that he conveys to his hearer or reader. His choice of words conveys not only information, but also attitudes and feelings. For example, if a politician refers to his opponent as a "Red," he tells us more about his prejudices than about his opponent. A word with many connotations is "emotive"—it expresses feelings of strong approval or disapproval and is likely to generate a strong reaction.

The use of emotive language is a typical technique of advertisers, political speechmakers, and others who often think they are being honest and logical. As you prepare your arguments, you should be careful to avoid the following misuses of language:

Appeal to General Prejudice. Using loaded words or relying on negative connotations:

1.   In striking down the censorship law, the court paved new and important ground in defending the rights and dignity of the individual.

2.   The court's decision was actually a vote in favor of smut and filth [same court, same case, same decision].

Transfer. Associating your product or idea with some generally accepted or approved idea which is not necessarily relevant:

1.   The mothers of American soldiers cry out for a change in Washington.

2.   Joe Namath gets the closest shaves ever with new Gillette blades.

Transfer can also work in reverse (sometimes this is known as "name calling"):

3.   Mayor Daley and his staff faced the difficult task of managing and controlling a mob infiltrated by Marxists, acid-heads, and other perverts.

4.   The young idealists remained brave under the vicious assaults of the bloodthirsty mayor and his Fascist henchmen [same demonstrators, same police force].

Bandwagon. The "everybody's doing it" approach:

1.   Every day more and more drivers are using STP oil treatment.

2.   Don't waste your vote!! Go with the winner: vote Smith.

Argumentum ad Hominem. Attacking the man's personality instead of his ideas:

My opponent keeps talking about beautifying America—but just look at how he wears his hair!!

Gobbledygook and Jargon. Using professional or trade terms or fancy polysyllabic words to hide bad thinking or no thinking:

Sinistrality is a partial determinant of undesirable speech problems.

Translated, this means, "Left-handedness is a partial cause of stuttering." Once translated, the statement becomes suspect. Can left-handedness, of itself, *cause* stuttering, or is it possible that both stuttering and left-handedness share some other cause?

It is your responsibility as a reader to reject arguments which merely rely on propaganda devices instead of discussing the real issues involved. It is your responsibility as a writer to give facts together with reasons when you try to persuade, rather than relying on emotional language.

Arguments of the opposition

What should you do about opposing arguments? It is certainly your responsibility to be aware of what is being said on the other side of the question. But how much attention you pay to your opponents varies with the topic and the approach. You may decide that your paper does not require any direct mention of opposing arguments if your strongest points are actually specific refutations of such arguments. Or you may decide that part of your paper must be given to the opposing argument and your reasons why it is unsound. Perhaps an entire paper might be written in this way (for example, you might write a paper on "Five Basic Reasons for Disagreeing with the Anti-Vivisectionists"). But you cannot afford simply to pretend that your opponents' arguments do not exist. If you ignore some opposing views, do so in the conviction that your own material actually meets their position head-on.

Uses of arguments developed by division of reasons

When you write to the editor of a paper or make a political speech or talk to voters, you will very often find a list of reasons a good framework around which to build. Similar principles apply when you are engaged in a sort of political action at home: for example, explaining why you want an apartment of your own instead of staying with your family; or persuading your brother to lend you his new shirt. You will use the list of reasons often in your course work, too: examination questions in history and sociology, for example, often call for a discussion of causes or results. But this structure has a more fundamental value: it will help you to clarify your own thinking, enabling you to know and say why you believe as you do and giving you the skill to read and listen more critically when others attempt to persuade you that they are right.

GUIDELINES

1. Choose a topic.

The topic may be from one of your courses, but it must be something about which there is some disagreement; otherwise, why write a persuasive paper about it? It should also be a topic that lends itself well to development by means of a division of reasons. Note how each of the following topics might be argued from the opposite point of view and how each might be structured around a list of reasons:

Everyone should experience an encounter group.

Biology is important to the art major.

TV is important in language study.

Fiction provides the best history textbook.

E.S.P. (extrasensory perception) does exist.

2. Divide your argument into reasons.

The best way to do this is to examine your topic and ask: *why* do you believe your conclusion should be accepted? As you develop a list of reasons, you will note that while the process of division is the same as that used in defining or comparing, in that both involve a separation into component parts, there is this difference: it is impossible to construct a complete division of reasons. Since you cannot attempt an exhaustive list, your argument will be somewhat open-ended. To ensure the success of your argument, first write down those reasons which are most important and most convincing. As your next step, select the reasons you wish to develop in detail in your paper, and jot down ideas for the specific examples and factual evidence which will support each. A preliminary list for a paper giving evidence for the existence of E.S.P. might look something like this:

a. Scientific experiments show that thoughts can be transferred without using communication by any of the five ordinary senses. (J. B. Rhine; hypnotist in Koestler article)

b. New breakthroughs in physics suggest there may be a "mind stuff" —a substance which has neither weight nor density. (Neutrino: cannot be sensed by five regular senses; can pass through matter—even through a brain—without effect; yet is real)

c. Creative genius seems to involve contact with sources of inspiration that are outside the mind and are not explained by any sensory communication. (Mozart, Yeats, Nietzsche, Bobby Fischer)

3. Arrange your list of reasons.

For some topics a chronological order of reasons may be appropriate. For others you should use logical order, such as order of climax or anticlimax. These logical plans involve arranging your list of reasons according to their relative importance. To develop an order of climax, you should as before save your most important or most convincing reason for the end. With some arguments, however, you may prefer to begin with your most convincing reason and then let the others follow in a descending order of importance; this method is known as the order of anticlimax. Of course, with either climactic or anticlimactic order, you will wish to make sure that none of your reasons are weak. All your reasons and the evidence supporting them should be strong enough to have an effect on the reader; at the same time, differences in their relative strength provide a basis for arranging them in an order that will help the reader follow your argument and be convinced by it.

In the sample material on E.S.P., the reason related to recent breakthroughs in physics is in part tentative; it suggests that a hitherto unknown substance might be the mechanism through which E.S.P. operates. The reason related to creative genius, on the other hand, is historically valid as well as dramatically interesting since it deals with real people and their important achievements. To organize these reasons in an order of climax we should arrange them as follows:

a. breakthroughs in physics and a possible "mind stuff."

b. scientific experiments with thought transference.

c. creative genius and the sources of inspiration.

4. Compose an introduction which includes a main-idea sentence.

Material for your introductory paragraph might include background on the history of your topic, definitions of key terms, or a criticism of the position of those who disagree with you. Whatever you include in your introduction, however, you should state explicitly in a main-idea sentence just what it is you are arguing. Such a sentence will also help your reader follow your line of thought if it includes, or is followed by, a statement of your reasons in the order in which they are to be examined in the body of the paper. The sample introduction below begins with background material designed to catch the reader's interest and to define the essential topic of the argument. Then comes the main-idea sentence stating the argument itself, after which the reasons advanced as evidence are stated in order.

"Doubting Thomas," according to the Biblical account, did not trust his sense of sight alone and had to touch the wounds left from the Crucifixion before he could believe that he was in the presence of Christ. While most people today do not demand the evidence of *two* senses, many still doubt the reality of knowledge gained in any way other than by at least *one* of the traditional five senses. They feel that extrasensory perception is a kind of hocus-pocus which is all right for games or TV entertainment but not anything to be taken seriously in the real world. In recent years, however, several reasons have combined to suggest that E.S.P. should indeed be taken seriously. Science itself, which builds its theories on evidence gained through the senses, provides two of these reasons, first in the recent breakthroughs in quantum physics and the resulting possibilities, and second in the investigations of the phenomena of thought transference. A third reason can be discovered in the mystery of creative genius—not a new phenomenon, but one which cannot yet be explained in terms of ordinary sensory perception.

5. Write the body of your paper.

Develop one paragraph or a group of paragraphs for each reason. Arrange the detailed evidence in support of each reason in order, perhaps chronologically, perhaps in order of climax or anticlimax. Within each paragraph, too, make use of appropriate transitions that show the reader the connections between one piece of evidence and the next. There should also be transitional material, which should lead smoothly from one paragraph to the next while at the same time reminding the reader of the overall structure of the paper. In the sample body below the major transitions from one paragraph to the next are underlined:

The first reason mentioned derives from new breakthroughs in physics and allows for at least the possibility of a rational explanation of E.S.P. Although apparently no one has yet been able to grasp the full meaning of the discoveries, they have excited the minds of scientists and nonscientists alike. A report issued recently by a committee of leading physicists argues that their research is important—and therefore deserving of funds—because it has "a direct bearing on a question that has engaged human thought for 2,000 years—the ultimate nature of substance." The discovery of the neutrino, a particle of matter lacking the usual properties of weight or density, is difficult to comprehend for people who have been conditioned in the materialism of the past hundred years. Nevertheless, the neutrino seems to be able to pass through the brain or anything else without displacement and without detection by any of the senses. Matter may not be the whole truth after all. There may be a kind of "mind stuff" as well. And if there is "mind stuff," there could certainly be extra-sensory perception, for the five senses perceive only matter which can be seen, touched, tasted, smelled, or heard either directly or by devices which are extensions of these senses.

While discoveries in physics suggest that the world may contain possibilities beyond our sensory reactions to matter, these discoveries are beyond the understanding of most of us. Easier to understand, at least on their practical level, are careful experiments that have been conducted by reputable people in order to show thought transference, a second reason for believing in E.S.P. Dr. J. B. Rhine of Duke University set up experiments where a person "guessed" a series of cards turned up by another person who was not seen by the one "guessing." The number of correct responses was far greater than simple laws of chance would allow. There was no logical explanation except for some kind of thought transference. Other well-documented experiments in telepathy are described in Arthur Koestler's essay "Echoes of the Mind," *Esquire*, August, 1972. Included are such accounts as that of a person under hypnosis carrying out suggestions with no words spoken.

Experimental science, then, provides reasons for believing in the existence of thought transference without ordinary sensory communication, as well as for suspecting a possible "mind stuff" by means of which extrasensory perception may take place. The most convincing evidence for E.S.P., however, has so far defied scientific proof: this is the creative output of certain geniuses. Mozart described his compositions as something that "came" to him. He said, "Whence and how they come I know not—my subject enlarges itself, becomes methodized and defined, and the whole, though it be long, stands almost complete and finished in my mind. . . ." Poets have often described a "flash" of insight, which they then struggle to put into the right form. W. B. Yeats had a long, complicated system worked out for his conception of the universe, including his ideas about extrasensory perception. Nietzsche said of his inspiration for *Thus Spoke Zarathustra:* "Provided one has the slightest remnant of superstition left, one can hardly reject completely the idea that one is the mere incarnation, or mouthpiece, or medium of some almighty power." Even in the game of chess some players' ability seems almost supernatural. "There is some strange magnetic influence in Bobby that spiritually wrecks his opponents," says Soviet Grand Master Yuri Iverbakh of Bobby Fischer. Whether artists call their times of greatest creation "intense concentration," "a kind of madness," or "divine power," many indicate a feeling of being in the grip of a compulsive and mysterious form of energy.

6. Write the conclusion.

Summarize your position and state your final argument. Suitable material for your conclusion might include brief mention of additional reasons in support of your main idea, together with a restatement in new terms of the principal reasons you have already discussed. The concluding paragraph of the sample paper on E.S.P. first reinforces the reason having to do with the insights of genius and then indirectly reminds the reader of the first two reasons treated by introducing additional material on scientific investigations, all of which give further support to the paper's main argument.

Over the years there have been countless anecdotes of unexplainable coincidence, mysterious messages, and hunches. These insights, often experienced by people of average intelligence, may well be supposed to be similar to the flashes of creative inspiration reported by geniuses. Somehow we obtain knowledge or understanding in ways that do not depend on ordinary matter and its impact on the five senses, and science itself seems to be recognizing this fact. Such groups as the Royal Astronomical Society of Great Britain and space research scientists in Russia are exploring physics and/or parapsychology in studies which seem to point to the end of the arbitrary division between mind and matter, spirit and body, which prevailed in the nineteenth and early twentieth centuries. "The Age of Aquarius" admits the reality of E.S.P.

7. Prepare your final draft.

Before writing a final draft for submission, recheck your paper to make sure that it is accurate and clear. Check also to make certain that you have avoided the most common fallacies in cause-and-effect reasoning (oversimplification, post hoc, and non sequitur) and that your language and tone are appropriate to an intelligent discussion of the topic, not to the "hard-sell" techniques of propaganda.

SAMPLE ESSAYS

Ban Shakespeare   BERNARD A. DRABECK

"Full of sound and fury, signifying nothing"—that's about all I remember of Shakespeare's *Macbeth* from high school, and that is about what I thought of the play at the time. My class spent three months reading that play with Miss Brown, who seemed to prefer Spelling and Vocabulary Drill. Well, maybe "reading" is the wrong word. Agonizing, dissecting, destroying, or maybe even worrying, the way a dog does a bone, those might be more accurate ways of describing what went on. A lot of "toil and trouble," and it wasn't just with *Macbeth* my senior year. It was the same with *Julius Caesar* and *Hamlet* when I was a sophomore and junior, too. "To be or not to be," "Friends, Romans, countrymen, lend me your ears," and "the noblest Roman of them all"—and all the time picking the text apart, memorizing bits and pieces, and answering foolish questions like "Who was Yorick?" and "Did Caesar have epilepsy?" and "Who was the third murderer?" Who knew? Who cared? At least I am sure I neither knew nor cared, just as I am sure the whole class felt that Shakespeare was a bore, an overrated writer from another age who lived only to write mysterious plays that made high school students miserable.

Fortunately, my ideas about Shakespeare have changed since those unhappy days, but I often wonder what might have happened if I hadn't had another exposure, when I was older and hopefully wiser, to the works we had so uncheerfully annihilated

First paragraph of introduction consists of personal examples in the form of a report.

Second paragraph of
introduction analyzes
experiences of first
paragraph.

Statement of the
argument.

List of reasons, in order
of their treatment in
the body.

First reason, itself divided
into *kinds* of difficult
vocabulary.

Unfamiliar words.

Obsolete words.

Changed meanings.

Invented words.

Allusions.

Full statement of first
reason Shakespeare is so
inaccessible: difficult
vocabulary. Link to
argument.

under the absolutely uninspired leadership of Miss Brown. I also wonder, just as frequently, why it was necessary for us to be exposed to Shakespeare at all at that stage of our education. Or in fairness, why Shakespeare had to be exposed to us. After all, an initial encounter of this kind was a great disservice to him, too, since most of my fellow sufferers were left with a distaste which they never had a chance to get rid of. Well, after thinking about justice to us and to Shakespeare, it came to me that the best way to treat Shakespeare at an early age is not to treat him at all—to ban him, in other words, from the high school curriculum. I feel this is an educationally desirable move, because there is so much in Shakespeare that makes him alien to the high school experience. First of all, his vocabulary is extremely difficult, if not occasionally incomprehensible. Secondly, there is the whole matter of poetry and the problems young students have with it. And last, I think Shakespeare is beyond high school students: their lack of experience and maturity prevents any proper appreciation of his revelations about life.

I don't think there is much argument about the difficulty of Shakespeare's language. Statistics alone reveal that he uses more (and more unfamiliar) words than almost any other writer in the English language. But the plays themselves provide the best evidence of perplexities secondary school students face when they try to read *Hamlet, Julius Caesar,* or *Macbeth.* Sometimes the words are merely strange, like "mountebank," "calumny," "bodkin," and "obsequies." But sometimes the words have gone out of use entirely, like "charactery," "rheumy," "wafture," "chopine," "splenetive," and "impartment." Occasionally passages are confusing because words meant different things to the Elizabethans than they do to us: "let" signifying "prevent"; "fond" meaning "foolish"; "bestowed" referring to "housed." Often Shakespeare seems to have made up words to suit his poetic purposes, and his most common method of doing this was to anglicize foreign (particularly Latin) words: "incarnadine" for "make red," "speculation" meaning "sight." And then there are all those references to names and places —references editors have spent so much time and space explaining, but which the high school student doesn't comprehend anyway. How can the story of Niobe be told in a brief note? How can the inexperienced reader be given the Biblical, historical, mythological, and social background he needs to understand about Jephthah, Hyperion, Mars, legal practices, Troy, Pelion, and Olympus? And if he doesn't understand all these, how can he arrive at any intelligent reading of the words? And if he can't read the words intelligently, that is to say, with some grasp of their significance, why spend the time reading at all? Or at least, why read Shakespeare before there is some awareness that the time spent in deciphering words is worth it, that what Shakespeare says is so true and so right that the end is worth the means? And this kind of awareness, I maintain, the high school student does not yet possess.

Similarly, Shakespeare's plays are poetry, not prose. Poetry is not, as many people suppose, hearts and flowers. Poetry is instead distilled language, with everyday sentence structure changed or shortened to make the words fit the pattern of the line. Look at passages like

Definition of poetry.

> There lives within the very flame of love
> A kind of wick or snuff that will abate it.
> And nothing is at a like goodness still,
> For goodness, growing to a pleurisy,
> Dies in his own too much.
> (*Hamlet*, IV, vii, 115–119)

> Come, seeling night,
> Scarf up the tender eye of pitiful day,
> And with thy bloody and invisible hand
> Cancel and tear to pieces that great bond
> Which keeps me pale!
> (*Macbeth*, III, ii, 46–50)

Examples of poetic language.

> And Caesar's spirit ranging for revenge,
> With Ate by his side come hot from Hell,
> Shall in these confines with a monarch's voice
> Cry "Havoc," and let slip the dogs of war . . .
> (*Julius Caesar*, III, i, 270–273)

Does it really help the high school student to talk about metaphor in the first selection, or personification in the second, or alliteration and hyperbole in the third? Miss Brown, I remember, talked about them a lot, but I never could really sort out which was which; nor did being able to pick out the figures of speech or thought make much difference, because it never really made the passage any clearer if I was able to recognize the name for a technique I couldn't appreciate anyway. I certainly didn't see what Shakespeare was driving at in any of these places, and the rest of the lines were equally out of my reach. Part of it was the words, but part of it was also the fact that the text was too rich for me to digest or absorb. I couldn't possibly begin to cope with the complex imagery, irony, paradox, involuted structure, hard-to-follow reasoning, and rhetorical flourishes that are the substance of Shakespeare's poetry, and I do not believe that any of my contemporaries were any more successful with that aspect of Shakespeare than I was.

Full statement of second reason: difficulties inherent in poetry.

Transitional sentence leading to consideration of third reason.

Beyond the puzzle of the words and the intricate obscurity of the poetry, there is another factor which makes the plays impenetrable enigmas to students in that age bracket. In *Hamlet*, *Macbeth*, and *Julius Caesar*, Shakespeare expresses sophisticated insights into matters of love, loyalty, idealism, the essence of kingship, ambition, and life itself; and these insights are usually foreign to the sympathies or experience of high schoolers. In *Hamlet*, for instance, a central theme of the play is revenge, and there are at least three quests for revenge in the play—Fortinbras is out to retrieve the lands lost by the death of his father in a duel with Hamlet Senior; Laertes is hot to retaliate against the perpetrator of the deaths of his father and sister, and of course Hamlet himself is charged to avenge his father's "foul and unnatural murder." Part of the subtlety and part of the greatness of the play lies in the carefully delineated differences among these three avengers, but part of the difficulty of the text lies in an investigation of revenge itself. What is revenge? What are the obligations of honor as they involve members of a family? Just what are the duties of family members to one another? Isn't revenge simply another name for murder? And what happens if a person is bound to revenge but is held back because his sensibilities will not allow him to take another's life, no matter how strong the call to vengeance is? How are the ties of blood connected with the blood bath that revenge brings about? And what about the dilemma that faces those who find duty too unpleasant to endure? Is suicide a desirable way of escaping from this dilemma? Questions such as these must be considered, if not answered, if there is to be any understanding of what *Hamlet* is about, and questions such as these are simply too profound for the high school student to comprehend.

Since his language, his poetry, and his subjects are entirely beyond the abilities of secondary school students, I think it is a mistake to force a premature exposure of Shakespeare on those who are in no way ready to appreciate him. It is true that the greatest scholars cannot finally agree on the substance or the significance of the tragedies I have been discussing, but their disagreements arise from knowledge, not from ignorance. Besides, if critics cannot hope to solve the textual and interpretative puzzles in the plays, how can high school students presume to deal with them? And finally, if the dramas remain a textbook mystery, what will the outcome of this high school experience be? It will be, I am convinced, just what mine was—a dull and musty tribulation to be endured rather than a living experience to be cherished.

I have heard, I must admit, that there are some gifted, inspiring teachers who bring Shakespeare to life even for high school students, but they are the exception while the Miss Browns remain the rule. Therefore, I think *Hamlet*, *Macbeth*, and *Julius Caesar* should be eliminated from the high school curriculum. If this is done, the student can more profitably and more enjoyably spend his time on material that is less obtuse and oblique. In this way, he will not be taxed beyond his strength, patience, or ability, and in this way, Shakespeare himself will be saved from a fate and judgment he does not deserve.

I Hate Horses

BIL GILBERT

During the course of a misspent life as a naturalist, I have, without regret, lavished time, money and affection on raccoons, foxes, ferrets, llamas, cheetahs, bears, hawks, crows, snakes, turtles, dogs, cats and certain even more improbable beasts. I have also, either voluntarily or involuntarily, been burdened with horses off and on since childhood, invariably to my deep regret. To be perfectly frank, I find horses about as personable as crows, more delicate than hummingbirds, less efficient than bicycles, and more expensive than floozies.

A horse is an animal who, left in front of an oat bin, will eat himself to death. A hot horse will drink water until his hoofs fall off. Horses are very good at poisoning themselves; they have a fine instinct for finding, and an insatiable appetite for eating, toxic herbs that brighter animals avoid.

Horses also have weak nerves; they are the most hysterical of all domestic animals. They will not only stay in a burning barn, but if led out will break away and go back to be broiled alive. Mice, bits of paper blowing about, a flapping leather strap, oddly shaped rocks, wheelbarrows, beer cans or simply reflected light will give a horse the screaming meemies. However, the same enormous, cowering beastie that rears at a gun wrapper will, in a savage fit of paranoia, turn on a man and bite or stomp on him.

Besides the afflictions that they bring on themselves out of sheer stupidity or cowardice, horses are prone to a really spectacular number of diseases. A few of these troubles are: Ringbone, Spavin, Corns, Seedy Toe, Thrush, Colic, Constipation, Azotemia, Heaves, Coughs, Colds, Hives, Fever, Wolf Teeth, Sleeping Sickness, Boils, Poll Evil, Capped Hocks—and, neither last nor least, Fistula of the Withers. I have designated some of these afflictions in horsey parlance. If you get a horse, any veterinarian can translate them into common English and a common $25 medical bill.

So far as I know, horses also are the only animals who catch madness the way other creatures catch cold. For example, there are "weavers"—animals who sway from side to side in their stall, hour after hour, day after day. Weavers, because they are weavers, have prodigious appetites but are seldom fit for riding—their energy having been expended in pursuit of their mania. And weaving is contagious. If one horse in a barn is a weaver, soon every other horse will pick up the habit, and the stable will resemble the rehearsal hall of the Bolshoi Ballet.

There also are "cribbers"—horses who suck, chew and mouth endlessly on the edges of stall doors, mangers or other pieces of wood. Cribbers grind down their teeth and fill up their stomachs with slivers. And there are "wind suckers." They repeatedly throw back their foolish heads and swallow great gulps of air, which gives them colic and ulcers.

Finally, there are a great many horses whose difficulties are individual and

Condensation from *The Reader's Digest*, March 1969. Reprinted with permission from *The Saturday Evening Post*, © 1968, Indianapolis, Indiana.

bizarre. Some will fly into a tantrum if, when being curried, the right side is not brushed before the left. There are horses who detest women. There is a horse I know who *must* have a duck in his stable, another who will drink only if the handle of the bucket is turned toward him. Krafft-Ebing would have had a lot more fun with horses than with people.

In view of what can and usually does go wrong with a horse, it is not surprising that the first consideration in buying one is to find a "sound" animal. This is not easy because (1) horses are, as indicated above, naturally unsound, and (2) horse sellers have as many ways of camouflaging horse defects as horses have defects. The tricks of the horse-selling trade are many. Some are new, as, for example, the use of tranquilizers to improve, temporarily, the manners of manic horses. Some are old. One quack remedy says that heaves—equine emphysema—can be suppressed for a day or two by pouring coal oil into a horse's left ear. Some horse peddlers can still be identified by the telltale whiff of kerosene about them, while alert horse buyers can be spotted by their habit of sniffing in a nag's left ear.

Of the three nags with which I now share my property, income and time, one is a little white-faced gelding of vaguely Morgan antecedents, called Governor. He will, of course, as almost all horses will, blow up his stomach when being saddled, the better to be able later to slip his girth. However, he never kicks, seldom bites, and if the person riding him has strong arms and strong will, Governor moves along very nicely for an hour or so.

We also have a pair of Tennessee Walker mares, a mother-and-daughter combo. When we bought them, the only obvious blemish was on the older mare, Rosie—a long scar on the inside of one leg. The scar was the result of an old injury, a common, run-of-the-mill horse accident. Rosie had stuck her foot through a barbed-wire fence. Being a horse rather than something smarter, she had, instead of withdrawing her leg, tried to pull the fence down—in the process, cutting through an artery.

Both mares, like Governor, were said to be "broke the best," which means that with some caution, persistence and guile, the animal can be ridden with fair safety and comfort. This proved to be the case. It is true, too, that Rosie, unless cross-tied, will bite hell out of you while you are trying to saddle her. Becky, the daughter, is a little difficult to catch in the field, and she is inclined to lounge around, eating clover and sniffing the breeze. Also, she is terrified of snowdrifts, gas meters, spotted dogs and *one* nearby yellow highway sign marked CURVE.

But we're satisfied. When we think what horses *can* be, these failings seem hardly worth mentioning.

Study Questions

1. In the last sentence of paragraph 1, Gilbert sums up his reasons for hating horses. They are lacking in personality, and are delicate, inefficient, and expensive. Do the following paragraphs develop these

reasons in the same order? If not, is there an order, or does the list of reasons seem random?

2. Construct a formal definition of *horse* from material in the introduction. Does this definition represent what you think a horse is?

3. The third reason given for hating horses contains a division and several definitions. What is the term being divided? What definitions are given? Are they adequate representations of a true condition or part of Gilbert's made-up case against horses?

4. How is most of the paragraph dealing with a "sound" animal organized?

5. How do the reasons given in support of Gilbert's argument relate to the horses he owns?

The Burning Heart   ROBERT FARRAR CAPON

There are, of course, plenty of people who stand ready to give you advice about what to do for simple indigestion: Most of them are no help at all. They have a blind and unshakable faith that logic will take the full measure of life under any and all circumstances, and they counsel you, with pitiless rectitude, that the best way to avoid difficulty is to keep away from the things that cause it. Accordingly, they will advise you to stop eating greatly, or to quit fasting, or to give up tobacco, whiskey, and hot sausages. In other words, they tell you to abandon all those extremes and counterpoisings by which you have so far kept your balance on the high wire of existence, and sit down quietly on the ground where you won't get hurt. They invite you to join them in a condition of philosophical indifference—in a state of *ataraxia*, where you will never-again give an emphatic damn about anything, nor ever, under any circumstances, allow yourself to get worked up.

Such remedies are fanatical. They have about them the monomaniacal logic of schemes to eliminate inconvenient thoughts by chopping off the heads that think them. The world is a tissue of involvements inseparably interwoven with bothers. It is no solution to get rid of the second by abolishing the first. If the only way around distress is to stop loving, well, then, let us be men about it and settle for distress.

Furthermore, when my gorge rises violently, I thank no man for self-righteous lectures on preventive medicine. I do not want to be told what will help me next time; what I need is something that will work this time—something that will meet me where I am, here in the thick of my inconvenient loves, and not in some cautious never-never land of pure thoughts and wheat germ bread.

Accordingly, as far as I am concerned, the only sane answer to the lower heartburn is a remedy that can be taken after the fact to bring the fire under control. Fortunately, there are literally hundreds of them. Indeed, standing in front of the usual drugstore counter display, it is hard to make up one's mind just which of the little wonder-working rolls of pills to settle on. At that level, therefore, I leave you to your own devices. My real purpose here is to persuade you of the merits of a better remedy than all the pills in the world: baking soda.

Well! you say. I thought *that* went out with gas lights. Why should I forsake my laboratory-tested, ultra-scientific array of pills for something my wife keeps in the kitchen closet with the detergents?

I shall tell you why. To begin with, you want two kinds of relief from heartburn. The first is the extinguishing of the fire by the simple device of neutralizing the acid that threatens to burn its way straight out of the front of your chest. Any alkalizing agent, of course, will cut the acid in your stomach; but only one that is swallowed *in solution* will be effective in the esophagus. Pills will prevent further heartburn; but half a teaspoon of bicarbonate of soda in half a glass of water is present help all the way down: It deals with the heartburn you have. Furthermore, as everyone should know, baking soda is one of the greatest sweetening and deodorizing agents in the world. It renders the added service of killing odor as well as flame. Almost instantly it makes a man bearable again, not only to himself, but to others.

The second kind of relief for which heartburn cries out is the restoration of the ability to belch satisfactorily. As a matter of fact, the most characteristic torment of the whole situation lies in the tension between a growing certainty that one good belch would set things right and a gnawing suspicion that you may never in this world belch again at all. A pill sent down to remedy *that* distress is worse than useless. It goes quietly, as an undercover agent; it does its work and is never heard from again. All that you, as its principal, know is that at some unspecified point, things imperceptibly begin to get better. You are denied the satisfaction of dramatic changes joyfully proclaimed.

With baking soda, however, a mere one minute's wait rewards you with a glowing, not to say resounding *report*. The relief, so long awaited, comes in force: not little by little like spies in the night, but all at once, like an army with banners and shouting. Add to that the fact that bicarbonate of soda has no particular flavor other than a bland saltiness—and that it is cheaper than any pill you can buy—and you have more than enough reasons for preferring it to pills right now. It has no delicious mintiness to stick in the back of your throat for hours and remind you of indigestion the next time you eat candy. It just works *fortiter suaviterque*, mightily and sweetly, like the Wisdom of God; and like the same Wisdom, it courteously lets us get about our business without backward looks or second thoughts. It is hard to ask for more.

Nevertheless, you get it without asking. Baking soda is so much more than a digestive that the mind boggles. Your roll of pills will do one thing and one only; your box of sodium bicarbonate will do a hundred and still have talents left to spare. Since this book is above all a celebration of the material and the common, I would like at this point to enter baking soda as a candidate for the title of Most Extraordinary Ordinary Thing in the World. Firmly convinced that it will win hands down over all comers, I take the liberty of composing the citation to be read in the ceremony at which the title is bestowed.

Sodium Bicarbonate, NAHCO₃, Baking Soda, Bicarbonate of Soda:

Longtime and steadfast retainer of the human race, your many names betokening not only varied talents, but also innumerable kindnesses for which men hold you dear: Friend of the flatulent, Soother of the savage, scotch-soaked breast, and blessed Bestower of peaceful sleep after four beers, two heroes, and a sausage pizza;

Sweetener of life in general and of organic disagreeabilities in particular: Cleanser of vile coffeepots and putrid refrigerators, Tamer of gamy bones, Purifier of school lunch vacuum bottles whose milk has turned to cheese, Polisher of teeth, Gracer of breath, Remover of smells from diapers, nursing bottles, smoking pipes and old hair brushes, Deodorizer of floors made foul by messing cats, Sweetener of urine-soaked mattresses, and Restorer of freshness to automotive interiors rendered uninhabitable by retching children;

Leavener, and nearly omnicompetent Lifter of the otherwise forlorn flatness of our lives: Raiser of biscuits, muffins, cookies, cake, and bread, and faithful member, in this capacity, of many committees—notably of Baking Powder- and Self-Rising Cake Flour;

Last, but far from least, sovereign Extinguisher of conflagrations of all sorts, from the metaphorical burning in the stomach to the literal flaming of the fat that falls in the fire: Soother of sore throats and bee stings, Cooler of prickly heat and sunburn, Smotherer of grease fires, Protector of the home and Very Present Help in all our troubles;

We who stand so deep in your debt praise your generosity; we who play not more than two instruments, who understand only four languages and can hardly express ourselves in any of them, salute the range of your abilities; we who require praise and publicity for what little we do stand in awe of your humility;

ACCEPT, THEREFORE, at our hands, this ORDER OF MERIT which we, though unworthy, bestow: If we were half as faithful as you have been, we would be twice as good as we are. May God hasten the day.

One more word of counsel on the subject of the lower heartburn before we move on to higher things: Eat lightly and simply the day after your great feast. Your stomach, so lately and sorely tried, needs time to recover its cast-iron properties.

Study Questions

1. Many doctors would disagree with the author's remedy, saying that overuse of bicarbonate of soda may produce irritation of the gastro-intestinal tract and promote an alkaline imbalance. What would be the author's response to such medical logic?
2. Father Capon, the author, begins by recommending baking soda for heartburn. He goes on to praise it for many other reasons. In a sense this is a digression. Do you feel it adds or detracts from the writing? Why? (You might consider tone and intention.)
3. What are some of the words or phrases which might indicate that the author is connected with the clergy?
4. What are the three paragraphs which actually explain why baking soda is good for heartburn?
5. What are the reasons given in these three paragraphs?

FROM *Medieval Court Records:*
The Case of a Woman Doctor in Paris, 1322

Witnesses were brought before us . . . in the inquisition made at the instance of the masters in medicine at Paris against Jacoba Felicie and others practising the art of medicine and surgery in Paris and the suburbs without the knowledge and authority of the said masters, to the end that they be punished, and that this practice be forbidden them. . . .

The dean and the regent masters of the faculty of medicine at Paris intend to prove against the accused, Mistress Jacoba Felicie, (1) that the said Jacoba visited, in Paris and in the suburbs, many sick persons afflicted with grave illness, inspecting their urine both in common and individually, and touching, feeling, and holding their pulses, body, and limbs. Also (2) that after this inspection of urine and this touching, she said and has said to those sick persons: "I shall make you well, God willing, if you will have faith in me," making an agreement concerning the cure with them, and receiving money for it. Also (3) that after an agreement had been made between the said defendant and the sick persons

Translated by Mary Martin McLaughlin from *Chartulary of the University of Paris,* H. Denifle and E. Chatelain, eds. (Paris: Delalain, 1891). From *The Portable Medieval Reader* ed. by James Bruce Ross & Mary Martin McLaughlin. Copyright 1949 by The Viking Press, Inc. Reprinted by permission of The Viking Press, Inc.

or their friends, concerning curing them of their internal illness, or from a wound or ulcer appearing on the outside of the bodies of the said sick persons, the said defendant visited and visits the sick persons very often, inspecting their urine carefully and continually, after the manner of physicians and doctors, and feeling their pulse, and their body, and touching and holding their limbs. Also (4) that after these actions, she gave and gives to the sick persons syrups to drink, comforting, laxative, digestive, both liquid and nonliquid, and aromatic, and other drinks, which they take and drink and have drunk very often in the presence of the said defendant, she prescribing and giving them. Also (5) that she has exercised and exercises, in the aforesaid matters, this function of practising medicine in Paris and in the suburbs, that she has practised and practises from day to day although she has not been approved in any official *studium* at Paris or elsewhere. . . .

These are the arguments which Jacoba said and set forth in her trial. . . .

The said Jacoba said that if the statute, decree, admonition, prohibition, and excommunication which the said dean and masters are trying to use against her, Jacoba, had ever been made, this had been only once, on account of and against ignorant women and inexperienced fools, who, untrained in the medical art and totally ignorant of its precepts, usurped the office of practising it. From their number the said Jacoba is excepted, being expert in the art of medicine and instructed in the precepts of said art. For these reasons, the statute, decree, admonition, prohibition, and excommunication aforesaid are not binding and cannot be binding on her, since when the cause ceases, the effect ceases. . . .

Also the said statute and decree, etc., had been made on account of and against ignorant women and foolish usurpers who were then exercising the office of practice in Paris, and who are either dead or so ancient and decrepit that they are not able to exercise the said office, as it appears from the tenor of the said statute and decree, etc., which were made a hundred and two years ago, at which time the said Jacoba was not, nor was she for sixty years afterwards, in the nature of things; indeed, she is young, thirty or thereabouts, as it appears from her aspect. . . .

Also it is better and more becoming that a woman clever and expert in the art should visit a sick woman, and should see and look into the secrets of nature and her private parts, than a man, to whom it is not permitted to see and investigate the aforesaid, nor to feel the hands, breasts, belly and feet, etc., of women. Indeed a man ought to avoid and to shun the secrets of women and their intimate associations as much as he can. And a woman would allow herself to die before she would reveal the secrets of her illness to a man, because of the virtue of the female sex and because of the shame which she would endure by revealing them. And from these causes many women and also men have perished in their illnesses, not wishing to have doctors, lest they see their secret parts. . . .

Also, supposing without prejudice that it is bad that a woman should visit, care for, and investigate, as has been said, it is, however, less bad that a woman wise, discreet, and expert in the aforesaid matters has done and does these things, since the sick persons of both sexes, who have not dared to reveal the aforesaid secrets to a man, would not have wished to die. Thus it is that the laws say that lesser evils should be permitted, so that greater ones may be avoided. For this reason, since the said Jacoba is expert in the art of medicine, it is, therefore, better that she be permitted to make visits, in order to exercise the office of practice, than that the sick should die, especially since she has cured and healed all those. . . .

Also, it has been ascertained and thus proved, that some sick persons of both sexes, seized by many severe illnesses and enduring the care of very many expert masters in the art of medicine, have not been able to recover at all from their illnesses, although the masters applied as much care and diligence to these as they were able. And the said Jacoba, called afterwards, has cured these sick persons in a short time, by an art which is suitable for accomplishing this.

Study Questions

1. What structural principle governs the arrangement of charges against the woman doctor?
2. After giving the charges made against Jacoba, the author presents

Jacoba's response: the reasons she is innocent of the crimes charged against her. Is there a logical sequence in their order of presentation? Explain.

3. What is the first reason she gives for being innocent of the charges against her? How is this reason developed?

4. What is the second reason given for her innocence?

5. The third and fourth reasons are related. What are these reasons, and how is evidence to support them organized?

6. On the basis of the evidence, would you judge Jacoba guilty or not guilty of the charge made against her?

Legalizing Cohabitation   STUDENT SAMPLE

Cohabitation of unmarried college students is not only frowned upon by society but also illegal. There are three major reasons why the laws forbidding such unions should be changed. Cohabitation during college years can be economically advantageous to the students concerned. Secondly, in the event of a future marriage with the same partner, cohabitation allows the relationship to grow under real conditions and thus would ensure a compatible marriage. In fact, even if the future marriage is with a different partner, the experience of cohabitation can be worthwhile. Finally, cohabiting with a person of the opposite sex allows a person time and opportunity to grow from a self-centered individual with only personal concerns to one who realizes the needs of both himself and his mate.

Although most colleges require freshmen to live on campus, older students are usually allowed to take apartments. In many cases, by the time a student is in his later college years, he has developed a love relationship with another person and the possibility of marriage has arisen. Both the cost of living and the cost of college, however, have become more and more expensive, thus making marriage (itself an expensive institution) out of the question for the time being, at least. Sharing an apartment, however, without the burden of matrimony or issue, can cut down on living expenses and, if two persons choose to live together for this reason, no law should prevent them.

Moreover, since most persons plan to enter marriage at some time in the future, it is important for them to experience a parallel relationship in a true-to-life way. Statistics reveal, in fact, that many marriages have been broken up because of fantasies of marital bliss. If a couple has a trial "marriage," not

Reprinted by permission.

bound under law, the legal marriage, with that person or with another, will have a better chance of working out because both persons will see each other as they are, not in an artificial dating situation. Of course, an important factor that should be considered in setting up a household that is a matter of choice, not legality, is the chance that one partner may walk out, leaving the other person alone and perhaps scarred by a bad emotional experience. This problem would be greatly intensified if a child had resulted from the relationship. If both persons are aware of the possibility of a breakup and the harm such a separation may cause, however, they should be free to enter such a union without concern for civil sanction.

Finally, as a single person, a student centers his life around his own needs

and wants. Entering into marriage with no experience of having shared his life
with another causes a difficult, sometimes impossible, adjustment. By experi-
encing cohabitation, a person can learn how much of himself he must give to
sustain a relationship and how he can manage to do so. He also learns how
much he can possess his mate and what freedom he must allow. Individuality
must not suffer, but each must learn to accommodate the needs of the other, in
this way making both persons other rather than self-concerned. Because such
a growth experience is necessary in the development of individual maturity, it
should not be concerned with nor restricted by law.

Cohabitation, then, can provide many benefits to those who experience it.
Not only can it be of economic value to a student, but it can also prepare him
for a legal marriage which will not end in divorce. Even more important, cohabitation can aid in developing a more mature, considerate human being. All
in all, if people can enter into a cohabitative relationship with an open and
understanding mind, they will profit greatly from the experience.

Study Questions

1. In what way could the introduction have been expanded to include a
   broader statement of the argument?
2. What pertinent material has been omitted from the paragraph exploring economic reasons?
3. What significant and true problem about marriage is incorporated
   into the second reason? Is the author's solution to the problem the
   only one? Is it convincing?
4. To what extent might specific examples clarify the third reason?
5. Does the argument as the author presents it suggest that difficulties
   of adjustment doom any initial relationship?

Servants or Oppressors?   RAMSEY CLARK

If too many Americans believe the police do not follow the law; that they do
not really warn the ignorant of their rights and question unfairly and relent-
lessly; that they arrest and hold without significant evidence and bring an
exhausted, confused, injured and frightened victim to witness a line-up and

then urge an immediate identification of a suspect; that they stop and frisk on bare suspicion or to intimidate; that they tap phones and bug rooms and perhaps worse; that they care more for order than justice; that a pay-off is possible and the rich will never have serious problems with police; and if Americans harboring these beliefs live in mass urban society where police are always present and must be; where you see them every day; where you feel powerless against them and do not trust them—then there is trouble. Then we have become a nation in which the breakdown between the public and the police is complete, in which we govern by force and fear while denying freedom.

The police relationship with the community served is the most important and difficult law enforcement problem of the 1970's. Effective law enforcement depends not only on the respect and confidence of the public but on a close, direct and continuous communication between the police and every segment of the population. Indeed, one is not possible without the other. Strong community ties provide the base for police prevention, deterrence, detection and control.

Only where such ties exist do police have the chance to work effectively. School authorities can then learn how to watch for, identify and report the presence of narcotics peddlers and student addicts. Students are more likely to understand the risks of LSD and refuse to joy-ride with friends in a stolen car. Slum dwellers who know police can complain of consumer fraud in the hope that action may result. Addicts, alcoholics and the mentally ill may find treatment through police who are in contact with friends, family or those in need themselves. The thief and the dangerously violent, frequently unrestrained in the ghetto, will be identified and apprehended when the people trust the police.

Strong police ties with residents in every block of densely populated slum areas are the only opportunity for law enforcement to measure the dimension and the nature of our vast unreported ghetto crime. Police presence can cool rather than heat angry street crowds where officers are known and respected. On campus, police can placate rather than provoke. Organized crime cannot reap the profits of gambling, narcotics traffic, loansharking and prostitution, which account for most of its income, where police-community relations are strong and there is law enforcement commitment to eliminate such activity. Extortion, blackmail and strong-arm tactics cannot then be safely used.

Runners, peddlers, pimps and their sources are readily known within the community. There is no more effective, efficient, dependable or inexpensive way to curb dangerous drugs than through community contacts. In truth, there is no other way. The people of a neighborhood know the addicts and they know the suppliers. A consensual crime in which the victim will not willingly reveal the seller, narcotics traffic poses perhaps the most difficult of all investigative challenges. The people who live where criminal activity flourishes risk most from its presence. They see what is visible, suffer most of the crime that occurs, and are the sources of leads and evidence of criminal activity.

A police department with strong community contacts has the best chance of anticipating incipient riot conditions. Measurement of tension can be made accurately only from within a community. People there, concerned for their own safety and welfare and that of their neighbors, anxious to avoid a riot, to control narcotics traffic or to alert police to a fight, are the foundation for effective police action.

"Police-community relations" is a facile phrase that is difficult to define. A cryptic term, it conjures so many different meanings that we often miss the real one.

Police-community relations are not public relations. They are the farthest thing from mere appearance or "image," as we have come to call it. Police-community relations measure the substance of the most significant quality of police service—the total bundle of all the communications and contacts, of all the attitudes and points of view that run between the police and the entire community they serve; what every element of the city knows and thinks of police service—and most important, what is done in the light of that knowledge and opinion.

If police are alienated from the public, they have mistaken their very purpose and lost their chance to succeed. Is the relationship between police and community one of confidence, of respect, of understanding of the importance of the mission, of full support and free interchange? Or is it a relationship of fear and mistrust? Or perhaps there is no relationship at all, but rather a void, an absence of communication or simply a community's awareness of a foreign force characterized by a specially painted automobile with an unknown person behind the wheel.

Police-community relations cannot be analyzed in a vacuum. The policeman is not a scientist working in a quiet and isolated laboratory. His laboratory is a whole city with all of its people and all of their needs. Relations between police and the community mirror the social structure and the quality of the lives of the people within a city. If there is poor communication between police and public, then that is not the only inadequate communication within that city. It merely reflects other isolations, other alienations and other estrangements. But when segments of the city cannot communicate with the police, the problem becomes critical; for the police, who must serve every part of the city, cannot perform effectively unless they have full and reliable information concerning crime. The police bear most of the pressures, tensions and strains that result from a general lack of communication. It is important, therefore, that they recognize this problem.

Study Questions

1. Clark opens his essay with a long series of "if" clauses, followed by "then there is trouble." Is his single sentence more effective than a series of sentences, each concluding with "then there is trouble," would be? Explain.

2. What is Clark's main-idea sentence? What division is given in it? Is this division carried out in the essay?

3. Beginning in paragraph 3 and continuing through paragraph 6, the author gives reasons in support of his position, which take the form of a list of causes or effects. Select one paragraph (from 3 to 6) and examine the cause-and-effect relationships it contains.

4. The conclusion, which begins in paragraph 7, has two functions. What are they?

5. In the conclusion, the author constructs an elaborate definition of police–community ties. What is this definition, and how is it used in the final paragraphs of the essay?

Why Should a Colored Man Enlist?

FREDERICK DOUGLASS

This question has been repeatedly put to us while raising men for the 54th Massachusetts regiment during the past five weeks, and perhaps we cannot at present do a better service to the cause of our people or to the cause of the country than by giving a few of the many reasons why a colored man should enlist.

First. You are a man, although a colored man. If you were only a horse or an ox, incapable of deciding whether the rebels are right or wrong, you would have no responsibility, and might like the horse or the ox go on eating your corn or grass, in total indifference, as to which side is victorious or vanquished in this conflict. You are however no horse, and no ox, but a man, and whatever concerns man should interest you. He who looks upon a conflict between right and wrong, and does not help the right against the wrong, despises and insults his own nature, and invites the contempt of mankind. As between the North and South, the North is clearly in the right and the South is flagrantly in the wrong. You should therefore, simply as a matter of right and wrong, give your utmost aid to the North. In presence of such a contest there is no neutrality for any man. You are either for the Government or against the Government. Manhood requires you to take sides, and you are mean or noble according to how you choose between action and inaction.—If you are sound in body and mind, there is nothing in your *color* to excuse you from enlisting in the service of the republic against its enemies. If *color* should not be a criterion of rights, neither should it be a standard of duty. The whole duty of a man, belongs alike to white and black.

"A man's a man for a' that"

Second. You are however, not only a man, but an American citizen, so declared by the highest legal adviser of the Government, and you have hitherto expressed in various ways, not only your willingness but your earnest desire to fulfill any and every obligation which the relation of citizenship imposes. Indeed, you have hitherto felt wronged and slighted, because while white men of all other nations have been freely enrolled to serve the country, you a native born citizen have been coldly denied the honor of aiding in defense of the land of your birth. The injustice thus done you is now repented of by the Government and you are welcomed to a place in the army of the nation. Should you refuse to enlist *now*, you will justify the past contempt of the Government towards you and lead it to regret having honored you with a call to take up arms in its defense. You cannot but see that here is a good reason why you should promptly enlist.

Third. A third reason why a colored man should enlist is found in the fact that every Negro-hater and slavery-lover in the land regards the arming of Negroes as a calamity and is doing his best to prevent it. Even now all the weapons of malice, in the shape of slander and ridicule, are used to defeat the filling up of the 54th Massachusetts (colored) regiment. In nine cases out of ten, you will find it safe to do just what your enemy would gladly have you leave undone. What helps you hurts him. Find out what he does not want and give him a plenty of it.

Fourth. You should enlist to learn the use of arms, to become familiar with the means of securing, protecting and defending your own liberty. A day may come when men shall learn war no more, when justice shall be so clearly appre-hended, so universally practiced, and humanity shall be so profoundly loved and respected, that war and bloodshed shall be confined only to beasts of prey. Manifestly however, that time has not yet come, and while all men should labor to hasten its coming, by the cultivation of all the elements conducive to peace, it is plain that for the present no race of men can depend wholly upon moral means for the maintenance of their rights. Men must either be governed by love or by fear. They must love to do right or fear to do wrong. The only way open to any race to make their rights respected is to learn how to defend them. When it is seen that black men no more than white men can be enslaved with impunity, men will be less inclined to enslave and oppress them. Enlist there-fore, that you may learn the art and assert the ability to defend yourself and your race.

Fifth. You are a member of a long enslaved and despised race. Men have set down your submission to Slavery and insult, to a lack of manly courage. They point to this fact as demonstrating your fitness only to be a servile class. You should enlist and disprove the slander, and wipe out the reproach. When you shall be seen nobly defending the liberties of your own country against rebels and traitors—brass itself will blush to use such arguments imputing cowardice against you.

Sixth. Whether you are or are not, entitled to all the rights of citizenship in this country has long been a matter of dispute to your prejudice. By enlisting in the service of your country at this trial hour, and upholding the National Flag, you stop the mouths of traducers and win applause even from the iron lips of ingratitude. Enlist and you make this your country in common with all other men born in the country or out of it.

Seventh. Enlist for your own sake. Decried and derided as you have been and still are, you need an act of this kind by which to recover your own self-respect. You have to some extent rated your value by the estimate of your enemies and hence have counted yourself less than you are. You owe it to yourself and your race to rise from your social debasement and take your place among the soldiers of your country, a man among men. Depend upon it, the subjective effect of this one act of enlisting will be immense and highly bene-ficial. You will stand more erect, walk more assured, feel more at ease, and be less liable to insult than you ever were before. He who fights the battles of

America may claim America as his country—and have that claim respected. Thus in defending your country now against rebels and traitors you are defending your own liberty, honor, manhood and self-respect.

Eighth. You should enlist because your doing so will be one of the most certain means of preventing the country from drifting back into the whirlpool of Pro-Slavery Compromise at the end of the war, which is now our greatest danger. He who shall witness another Compromise with Slavery in this country will see the free colored man of the North more than ever a victim of the pride, lust, scorn and violence of all classes of white men. The whole North will be but another Detroit, where every white fiend may with impunity revel in unrestrained beastliness towards people of color; they may burn their houses, insult their wives and daughters, and kill indiscriminately. If you mean to live in this country now is the time for you to do your full share in making it a country where you and your children after you can live in comparative safety. Prevent a compromise with the traitors, compel them to come back to the Union whipped and humbled into obedience and all will be well. But let them come back as masters and all their hate and hellish ingenuity will be exerted to stir up the ignorant masses of the North to hate, hinder and persecute the free colored people of the North. That most inhuman of all modern enactments, with its bribed judges, and summary process, the Fugitive Slave Law, with all its infernal train of canting divines, preaching the gospel of kidnapping, as twelve years ago, will be revived against the free colored people of the North. One or two black brigades will do much to prevent all this.

Ninth. You should enlist because the war for the Union, whether men so call it or not, is a war for Emancipation. The salvation of the country, by the inexorable relation of cause and effect, can be secured only by the complete abolition of Slavery. The President has already proclaimed emancipation to the Slaves in the rebel States which is tantamount to declaring Emancipation in all the States, for Slavery must exist everywhere in the South in order to exist anywhere in the South. Can you ask for a more inviting, ennobling and soul enlarging work, than that of making one of the glorious Band who shall carry Liberty to your enslaved people? Remember that identified with the Slave in color, you will have a power that white soldiers have not, to attract them to your lines and induce them to take up arms in a common cause. One black Brigade will, for this work, be worth more than two white ones. Enlist, therefore, enlist without delay, enlist now, and forever put an end to the human barter and butchery which have stained the whole South with the warm blood of your people, and loaded its air with their groans. Enlist, and deserve not only well of your country, and win for yourselves, a name and a place among men, but secure to yourself what is infinitely more precious, the fast dropping tears of gratitude of your kith and kin marked out for destruction, and who are but now ready to perish.

When time's ample curtain shall fall upon our national tragedy, and our hillsides and valleys shall neither redden with the blood nor whiten with the bones of kinsmen and countrymen who have fallen in the sanguinary and wicked strife; when grim visaged war has smoothed his wrinkled front and our country shall have regained its normal condition as a leader of nations in the occupation and blessings of peace—and history shall record the names of heroes and martyrs—who bravely answered the call of patriotism and Liberty —against traitors, thieves and assassins—let it not be said that in the long list of glory, composed of men of all nations—there appears the name of no colored man.

Study Questions

1. When did Douglass write this essay? How important is the time of the writing to the content of the essay?
2. Is Douglass a black or a white writer? How important is his color to the persuasiveness of his argument?
3. Sum up each of Douglass' arguments in one sentence. Is each a convincing and valid argument?
4. What *order* seems to control the list of reasons—climactic, anti-climactic, or what?
5. Is Douglass guilty of any fallacies, such as Bandwagon, Ad Hominem or Hasty Generalization? If so, where?

The Case Against Women   JAMES THURBER

A bright-eyed woman, whose sparkle was rather more of eagerness than of intelligence, approached me at a party one afternoon and said, "Why do you hate women, Mr. Thurberg?" I quickly adjusted my fixed grin and denied that I hated women; I said I did not hate women at all. But the question remained with me, and I discovered when I went to bed that night that I had been sub-consciously listing a number of reasons I do hate women. It might be interest-ing—at least it will help pass the time—to set down these reasons, just as they came up out of my subconscious.

In the first place, I hate women because they always know where things are. At first blush, you might think that a perverse and merely churlish reason for hating women, but it is not. Naturally, every man enjoys having a woman around the house who knows where his shirt studs and his briefcase are, and things like that, but he detests having a woman around who knows where *everything* is, even things that are of no importance at all, such as, say, the snapshots her husband took three years ago at Elbow Beach. The husband has never known where these snapshots were since the day they were developed and printed; he hopes, in a vague way, if he thinks about them at all, that after three years they have been thrown out. But his wife knows where they are, and so do his mother, his grandmother, his great-grandmother, his daughter, and the maid. They could put their fingers on them in a moment, with that quiet air of superior knowledge which makes a man feel that he is out of touch with all the things that count in life.

A man's interest in old snapshots, unless they are snapshots of himself in action with a gun, a fishing rod, or a tennis racquet, languishes in about two hours. A woman's interest in old snapshots, particularly of groups of people, never languishes; it is always there, as the years roll on, as strong and vivid as it was right at the start. She remembers the snapshots when people come to call, and just as the husband, having mixed drinks for everybody, sits down to sip his own, she will say, "George, I wish you would go and get those snapshots we took at Elbow Beach and show them to the Murphys." The husband, as I have said, doesn't know where the snapshots are; all he knows is that Harry Murphy doesn't want to see them; Harry Murphy wants to talk, just as he himself wants to talk. But Grace Murphy says that she wants to see the pictures; she is crazy to see the pictures; for one thing, the wife, who has brought the subject up, wants Mrs. Murphy to see the photo of a certain costume that the wife wore at Elbow Beach in 1933. The husband finally puts down his drink and snarls, "Well, where are they, then?" The wife, depending on her mood, gives him either the look she reserves for spoiled children or the one she reserves for drunken workmen, and tells him he knows perfectly well where they are. It turns out, after a lot of give and take, the slightly bitter edge of which is covered by forced laughs, that the snapshots are in the upper right-hand drawer of a certain desk, and the husband goes out of the room to get them. He comes back in three minutes with the news that the snapshots are not in the upper right-hand drawer of the certain desk. Without stirring from her chair, the wife favors her husband with a faint smile (the one that annoys him most of all her smiles) and reiterates that the snapshots *are* in the upper right-hand drawer of the desk. He simply didn't look, that's all. The husband knows that he looked; he knows that he prodded and dug and excavated in that drawer and that the snapshots simply are not there. The wife tells him to go look again and he will find them. The husband goes back and looks again— the guests can hear him growling and cursing and rattling papers. Then he shouts out from the next room. "They are *not* in this *drawer*, just as I told you, Ruth!" The wife quietly excuses herself and leaves the guests and goes into the room where her husband stands, hot, miserable, and defiant—and with a certain nameless fear in his heart. He has pulled the desk drawer out so far that it is about to fall on the floor, and he points at the disarray of the drawer with bitter triumph (still mixed with that nameless fear). "Look for yourself!" he snarls. The wife does not look. She says with quiet coldness, "What is that you have in your hand?" What he has in his hand turns out to be an insurance policy

and an old bankbook—and the snapshots. The wife gets off the old line about
what it would have done if it had been a snake, and the husband is upset for
the rest of the evening; in some cases he cannot keep anything on his stomach
for twenty-four hours.

Another reason I hate women (and I am speaking, I believe, for the American male generally) is that in almost every case where there is a sign reading
"Please have exact change ready," a woman never has anything smaller than a
ten-dollar bill. She gives ten-dollar bills to bus conductors and change men in
subways and other such persons who deal in nickels and dimes and quarters.
Recently, in Bermuda, I saw a woman hand the conductor on the little railway
there a bill of such huge denomination that I was utterly unfamiliar with it. I
was sitting too far away to see exactly what it was, but I had the feeling that
it was a five-hundred-dollar bill. The conductor merely ignored it and stood
there waiting—the fare was just one shilling. Eventually, scrabbling around
in her handbag, the woman found a shilling. All the men on the train who
witnessed the transaction tightened up inside; that's what a woman with a ten-
dollar bill or a twenty or a five-hundred does to a man in such situations—she
tightens him up inside. The episode gives him the feeling that some monstrous
triviality is threatening the whole structure of civilization. It is difficult to analyze this feeling, but there it is.

Another spectacle that depresses the male and makes him fear women, and
therefore hate them, is that of a woman looking another woman up and down,
to see what she is wearing. The cold, flat look that comes into a woman's eyes
when she does this, the swift coarsening of her countenance, and the immediate
evaporation from it of all humane quality make the male shudder. He is likely
to go to his stateroom or his den or his private office and lock himself in for
hours. I know one man who surprised that look in his wife's eyes and never
afterward would let her come near him. If she started toward him, he would
dodge behind a table or a sofa, as if he were engaging in some unholy game of
tag. That look, I believe, is one reason men disappear, and turn up in Tahiti or
the Arctic or the United States Navy.

I (to quit hiding behind the generalization of "the male") hate women because they almost never get anything exactly right. They say, "I have been
faithful to thee, Cynara, after my fashion" instead of "in my fashion." They
will bet you that Alfred Smith's middle name is Aloysius, instead of Emanuel.
They will tell you to take the 2:57 train, on a day that the 2:57 does not run,
or, if it does run, does not stop at the station where you are supposed to get
off. Many men, separated from a woman by this particular form of imprecision,
have never showed up in her life again. Nothing so embitters a man as to end
up in Bridgeport when he was supposed to get off at Westport.

I hate women because they have brought into the currency of our language
such expressions as "all righty" and "yes indeedy" and hundreds of others. I
hate women because they throw baseballs (or plates or vases) with the wrong
foot advanced. I marvel that more of them have not broken their backs. I
marvel that women, who coordinate so well in languorous motion, look uglier
and sillier than a goose-stepper when they attempt any form of violent activity.

I had a lot of other notes jotted down about why I hate women, but I seem to have lost them all, except one. That one is to the effect that I hate women because, while they never lose old snapshots or anything of that sort, they invariably lose one glove. I believe that I have never gone anywhere with any woman in my whole life who did not lose one glove. I have searched for single gloves under tables in crowded restaurants and under the feet of people in darkened movie theatres. I have spent some part of every day or night hunting for a woman's glove. If there were no other reason in the world for hating women, that one would be enough. In fact, you can leave all the others out.

Study Questions

1. Thurber, the famous American humorist, does not prove that he hates women. Rather, he lists reasons he has for hating them. He says that he has listed them "just as they came out of [his] subconscious." Is the arrangement of the reasons arbitrary as he suggests or do you find an order in their presentation? Explain.
2. What is the first reason Thurber gives for hating women? How much of the essay is devoted to this reason? Why is so much space necessary? How does he organize his explanatory material?
3. Some of the reasons Thurber gives for hating women are trivial. Do these weaken the overall argument?
4. Which of the reasons indicate that Thurber might be somewhat serious in his argument?
5. Construct either a refutation of Thurber's position or suggest the principal points in a paper called "The Case Against Men."

The Invisible Poor   MICHAEL HARRINGTON

The millions who are poor in the United States tend to become increasingly invisible. Here is a great mass of people, yet it takes an effort of the intellect and will even to see them.

I discovered this personally in a curious way. After I wrote my first article on poverty in America, I had all the statistics down on paper. I had proved to my satisfaction that there were around 50,000,000 poor in this country. Yet, I

realized I did not believe my own figures. The poor existed in the Government reports; they were percentages and numbers in long, close columns, but they were not part of my experience. I could prove that the other America existed, but I had never been there.

My response was not accidental. It was typical of what is happening to an entire society, and it reflects profound social changes in this nation. The other America, the America of poverty, is hidden today in a way that it never was before. Its millions are socially invisible to the rest of us. No wonder that so many misinterpreted Galbraith's title and assumed that "the affluent society" meant that everyone had a decent standard of life. The misinterpretation was true as far as the actual day-to-day lives of two-thirds of the nation were concerned. Thus, one must begin a description of the other America by understanding why we do not see it.

There are perennial reasons that make the other America an invisible land.

Poverty is often off the beaten track. It always has been. The ordinary tourist never left the main highway, and today he rides interstate turnpikes. He does not go into the valleys of Pennsylvania where the towns look like movie sets of Wales in the thirties. He does not see the company houses in rows, the rutted roads (the poor always have bad roads whether they live in the city, in towns, or on farms), and everything is black and dirty. And even if he were to pass through such a place by accident, the tourist would not meet the unemployed men in the bar or the women coming home from a runaway sweatshop.

Then, too, beauty and myths are perennial masks of poverty. The traveler comes to the Appalachians in the lovely season. He sees the hills, the streams, the foliage—but not the poor. Or perhaps he looks at a run-down mountain house and, remembering Rousseau rather than seeing with his eyes, decides that "those people" are truly fortunate to be living the way they are and that they are lucky to be exempt from the strains and tensions of the middle class. The only problem is that "those people," the quaint inhabitants of those hills, are undereducated, underprivileged, lack medical care, and are in the process of being forced from the land into a life in the cities, where they are misfits.

These are normal and obvious causes of the invisibility of the poor. They operated a generation ago; they will be functioning a generation hence. It is more important to understand that the very development of American society is creating a new kind of blindness about poverty. The poor are increasingly slipping out of the very experience and consciousness of the nation.

If the middle class never did like ugliness and poverty, it was at least aware of them. "Across the tracks" was not a very long way to go. There were forays into the slums at Christmas time; there were charitable organizations that brought contact with the poor. Occasionally, almost everyone passed through the Negro ghetto or the blocks of tenements, if only to get downtown to work or to entertainment.

Now the American city has been transformed. The poor still inhabit the miserable housing in the central area, but they are increasingly isolated from contact with, or sight of, anybody else. Middle-class women coming in from Suburbia on a rare trip may catch the merest glimpse of the other America on the way to an evening at the theater, but their children are segregated in suburban schools. The business or professional man may drive along the fringes of slums in a car or bus, but it is not an important experience to him. The failures, the unskilled, the disabled, the aged, and the minorities are right there, across the tracks, where they have always been. But hardly anyone else is.

In short, the very development of the American city has removed poverty from the living, emotional experience of millions upon millions of middle-class Americans. Living out in the suburbs, it is easy to assume that ours is, indeed, an affluent society.

This new segregation of poverty is compounded by a well-meaning ignorance. A good many concerned and sympathetic Americans are aware that there is much discussion of urban renewal. Suddenly, driving through the city, they notice that a familiar slum has been torn down and that there are towering, modern buildings where once there had been tenements or hovels. There is a warm feeling of satisfaction, of pride in the way things are working out: the poor, it is obvious, are being taken care of.

The irony in this . . . is that the truth is nearly the exact opposite to the impression. The total impact of the various housing programs in postwar America has been to squeeze more and more people into existing slums. More often than not, the modern apartment in a towering building rents at $40 a room or more. For, during the past decade and a half, there has been more subsidization of middle- and upper-income housing than there has been of housing for the poor.

Clothes make the poor invisible too: America has the best-dressed poverty the world has ever known. For a variety of reasons, the benefits of mass production have been spread much more evenly in this area than in many others. It is much easier in the United States to be decently dressed than it is to be decently housed, fed, or doctored. Even people with terribly depressed incomes can look prosperous.

This is an extremely important factor in defining our emotional and existential ignorance of poverty. In Detroit the existence of social classes became much more difficult to discern the day the companies put lockers in the plants. From that moment on, one did not see men in work clothes on the way to the factory, but citizens in slacks and white shirts. This process has been magnified with the poor throughout the country. There are tens of thousands of Americans in the big cities who are wearing shoes, perhaps even a stylishly cut suit or dress, and yet are hungry. It is not a matter of planning, though it almost seems as if the affluent society had given out costumes to the poor so that they would not offend the rest of society with the sight of rags.

Then, many of the poor are the wrong age to be seen. A good number of them (over 8,000,000) are sixty-five years of age or better; an even larger number are under eighteen. The aged members of the other America are often sick, and they cannot move. Another group of them live out their lives in loneliness and frustration: they sit in rented rooms, or else they stay close to a house in a neighborhood that has completely changed from the old days. Indeed, one of the worst aspects of poverty among the aged is that these people are out of sight and out of mind, and alone.

The young are somewhat more visible, yet they too stay close to their neighborhoods. Sometimes they advertise their poverty through a lurid tabloid story about a gang killing. But generally they do not disturb the quiet streets of the middle class.

And finally, the poor are politically invisible. It is one of the cruelest ironies of social life in advanced countries that the dispossessed at the bottom of society are unable to speak for themselves. The people of the other America do not, by far and large, belong to unions, to fraternal organizations, or to political parties. They are without lobbies of their own; they put forward no legislative program. As a group, they are atomized. They have no face; they have no voice.

Thus, there is not even a cynical political motive for caring about the poor, as in the old days. Because the slums are no longer centers of powerful political organizations, the politicians need not really care about their inhabitants. The slums are no longer visible to the middle class, so much of the idealistic urge to fight for those who need help is gone. Only the social agencies have a really direct involvement with the other America, and they are without any great political power.

To the extent that the poor have a spokesman in American life, that role is played by the labor movement. The unions have their own particular idealism, an ideology of concern. More than that, they realize that the existence of a reservoir of cheap, unorganized labor is a menace to wages and working conditions throughout the entire economy. Thus, many union legislative proposals—to extend the coverage of minimum wage and social security, to organize migrant farm laborers—articulate the needs of the poor.

Study Questions

1. What is the purpose of the introduction? How is it accomplished?
2. Construct an appropriate main-idea sentence for the essay.
3. Harrington gives a series of reasons why the poor are invisible in America and why they "tend to become increasingly invisible." How are these reasons related to the causes and effects which he also discusses?
4. A chronological arrangement divides the reasons into two sections. Why?
5. Choose the reason you think is most effective. Why do you think it is? Indicate how it is developed into a section of Harrington's argument.
6. From the information given, develop a definition of "the invisible poor."
7. What is the purpose of the essay? How is it accomplished?

The Tryal of G. B. at a court of Oyer and Terminer, Held in Salem, 1692

COTTON MATHER

Glad should I have been, if I had never known the Name of this Man; or never had this occasion to mention so much as the first Letters of his Name. But the Government requiring some Account of his Trial to be inserted in this Book, it becomes me with all Obedience to submit unto the Order.

I. This G. B. was Indicted for Witch-craft, and in the prosecution of the Charge against him, he was Accused by five or six of the Bewitched, as the Author of their Miseries; he was Accused by Eight of the Confessing Witches, as being an head Actor at some of their Hellish Randezvouzes, and one who had the promise of being a King in Satan's Kingdom, now going to be Erected: He was accused by Nine Persons for extraordinary Lifting, and such feats of Strength, as could not be done without a Diabolical Assistance. And for other such things he was Accused, until about thirty Testimonies were brought in against him; nor were these judg'd the half of what might have been considered for his Conviction: However they were enough to fix the Character of a Witch upon him according to the Rules of Reasoning, by the Judicious *Gaule*, in that Case directed.

II. The Court being sensible, that the Testimonies of the Parties Bewitched, use to have a Room among the *Suspicions* or *Presumptions*, brought in against one Indicted for Witchcraft; there were now heard the Testimonies of several Persons, who were most notoriously Bewitched, and every day Tortured by Invisible Hands, and these now all charged the Spectres of G. B. to have a share in their Torments. At the Examination of this G. B. the Bewitched People were grievously harassed with Preternatural Mischiefs, which could not possibly be dissembled; and they still ascribed it unto the endeavors of G. B. to Kill them. And now upon his Tryal of one of the Bewitched Persons, testified, that in her Agonies, a little black Hair'd Man came to her, saying his Name was B. and bidding her set her hand unto a Book which he shewed unto her; and bragging that he was a *Conjurer*, above the ordinary Rank of Witches; That he often Persecuted her with the offer of that Book, saying, *She should be well, and need fear nobody, if she would but Sign it*; But he inflicted cruel Pains and Hurts upon her, because of her denying so to do. The Testimonies of the other Sufferers concurred with these; and it was remarkable, that whereas *Biting* was one of the ways which the Witches used for the vexing of the Sufferers; when they cry'd out of G. B. Biting them, the print of the Teeth would be seen on the Flesh of the Complainers, and just such a Set of Teeth as G. B's would then appear upon them, which could be distinguished from those of some other Mens. Others of them testified, That in their Torments, G. B. tempted them to go unto a Sacrament, unto which they perceived him with a Sound of Trumpet, Summoning of other Witches, who quickly after the Sound, would come from all Quarters unto the Rendezvouz. One of them falling into a kind of Trance, afterwards affirmed, that G. B. had carried her into a very high Mountain, where he shewed her mighty and glorious Kingdoms, and said, *He would give them all to her, if she would write in his Book;* but she told him, *They were none of his to give;* and refused the Motions; enduring of much Misery for that refusal.

It cost the Court a wonderful deal of Trouble, to hear the Testimonies of the Sufferers; for when they were going to give in their Depositions, they would for a long time be taken with Fits, that made them uncapable of saying anything. The Chief Judg asked the Prisoner, who he thought hindred these Witnesses from giving their *Testimonies?* And he answered, *He supposed it was the Devil.* That Honourable Person, then repli'd, *How comes the Devil so loathe to have any Testimony born against you?* Which cast him into very great Confusion.

III. It has been a frequent thing for the Bewitched People to be entertained with Apparitions of *Ghosts* of Murdered People, at the same time that the *Spectres* of the Witches trouble them. These Ghosts do always affright the Beholders more than all the other spectral Representations; and when they exhibit themselves, they cry out, of being Murdered by the Witchcrafts or other Violences of the Persons who are then in Spectre present. It is further considerable, that once or twice, these *Apparitions* have been seen by others, at the very same time that they have shewn themselves to the Bewitched; and seldom have there been these *Apparitions,* but when something unusual or suspected, have attended the Death of the Party thus Appearing. Some that have been accused by these *Apparitions* accosting of the Bewitched People, who had never heard a word of any such Persons ever being in the World, have upon a fair Examination, freely and fully confessed the Murthers of those very Persons, altho these also did not know how the Apparitions had complained of them. Accordingly several of the Bewitched, had given in their Testimony, that they had been troubled with the Apparitions of two Women, who said, that they were G. B's two Wives, and that he had been the Death of them; and that the Magistrates must be told of it, before whom if B. upon his Tryal denied it, they did not know but that they should appear again in the Court. Now, G. B. had been Infamous for the Barbarous usage of his two late Wifes, all the Country over. Moreover, it was testified, the Spectre of G. B. threatning of the Sufferers, told them, he had Killed (besides others) Mrs. *Lawson* and her Daughter *Ann.* And it was noted, that these were the Vertuous Wife and Daughter of one at whom this G. B. might have a prejudice for his being serviceable at *Salem Village,* from whence himself had in ill Terms removed some Years before: And that when they dy'd, which was long since, there were some odd Circumstances about them, which made some of the Attendents there suspect something of Witchcraft, tho none Imagined from what Quarter it should come.

Well, G. B. being now upon his Tryal, one of the Bewitched Persons was cast into Horror at the Ghost of B's two Deceased Wives then appearing before him, and crying for *Vengeance* against him. Hereupon several of the Bewitched Persons were successively called in, who all not knowing what the former had seen and said, concurred in their Horror of the Apparition, which they affirmed that he had before him. But he, tho much appalled, utterly deny'd that he discerned any thing of it; nor was it any part of his *Conviction.*

IV. Iudicious Writers have assigned it a great place in the Conviction of *Witches, when Persons are Impeached by other notorious Witches, to be as ill as themselves; especially, if the Persons have been much noted for neglecting the Worship of God.* Now, as there might have been Testimonies enough of G. B's Antipathy to *Prayer,* and the other Ordinances of God, tho by his Profession, singularly Obliged thereunto; so, there now came in against the Prisoner, the Testimonies of several Persons, who confessed their own having been horrible *Witches,* and ever since their Confessions, had been themselves terribly Tortured by the Devils and other Witches, even like the other Sufferers; and therein undergone the Pains of many *Deaths* for their Confessions.

These now testified, that G. B. had been at Witch-meetings with them; and that he was the Person who had Seduc'd, and Compell'd them into the snares of Witchcraft: That he promised them *Fine Cloaths,* for doing it; that he brought Poppets to them, and Thorns to stick into those Poppets, for the Afflicting of other People; and that he exhorted them with the rest of the Crew, to Bewitch all *Salem Village,* but besure to do it Gradually, if they would prevail in what they did.

When the *Lancashire Witches* were Condemn'd I don't remember that there was any considerable further Evidence, than that of the Bewitched, and than that of some that confessed. We see so much already against G. B. But this being indeed not enough, there were other things to render what had already been produced *credible.*

V. A famous Divine recites this among the Convictions of a Witch; *The Testimony of the party Bewitched, whether Pining or Dying; together with the joint Oaths of sufficient Persons that have seen certain Prodigious Pranks or Feats wrought by the Party Accused.* Now, God had been pleased so to leave this G. B. that he had ensnared himself by several Instances, which he had formerly given of a Preternatural Strength, and which were now produced against him. He was a very Puny Man, yet he had often done things beyond the strength of a Giant. A Gun of about seven foot Barrel, and so heavy that strong Men could not steadily hold it out with both hands; there were several Testimonies, given in by Persons of Credit and Honor, that he made nothing of taking up such a Gun behind the Lock, with but one hand, and holding it out like a Pistol, at Arms-end. G. B. in his Vindication, was so foolish as to say, That *an* Indian *was there, and held it out at the same time:* Whereas none of the Spectators ever saw any such *Indian;* but they supposed the *Black Man,* (as the Witches call the Devil; and they generally say he resembles an *Indian*) might give him that Assistance. There was Evidence likewise brought in, that he made nothing of taking up whole Barrels fill'd with *Malasses* or *Cider,* in very disadvantageous Postures, and Carrying of them through the difficultest Places out of a Canoo to the Shore.

[Yea, there were two Testimonies that G. B. with only putting the Fore Finger of his Right hand into the Muzzle of an heavy Gun, a Fowling-piece of about six or seven foot Barrel, did lift up the Gun, and hold it out at Arms-end; a Gun which the Deponents though strong Men could not with both hands lift up, and hold out at the But-end, as is usual. Indeed, one of these Witnesses was over-perswaded by some Persons to be out of the way upon G. B's Tryal; but he came afterwards with Sorrow for his withdraw, and gave in his Testimony: Nor were either of these Witnesses made use of as Evidences in the Trial.]

VI. There came in several Testimonies relating to the Domestick Affairs of *G. B.* which had a very hard Aspect upon him; and not only prov'd him a very ill Man; but also confirmed the belief of the Character, which had been already fastened on him.

'Twas testified, that keeping his two Successive Wives in a strange kind of Slavery, he would when he came home from abroad, pretend to tell the Talk which any had with them; That he has brought them to the point of Death, by his harsh Dealings with his Wives, and then made the People about him, to promise that in case Death should happen, they would say nothing of it; That he used all means to make his Wives Write, Sign, Seal, and Swear a Covenant, never to reveal any of his Secrets; That his Wives had privately complained unto the Neighbours about frightful Apparitions of Evil Spirits, with which their House was sometimes infested; and that many such things have been whispered among the Neighbourhood. There were also some other Testimonies relating to the Death of People whereby the Consciences of an Impartial Jury were convinced that *G. B.* had Bewitched the Persons mentioned in the Complaints. But I am forced to omit several passages, in this, as well as in all the succeeding Tryals, because the Scribes who took notice of them, have not supplyed me.

VII. One Mr. *Ruck,* Brother-in-Law to this *G. B.* testified, that *G. B.* and he himself, and his Sister, who was *G. B's* Wife, going out for two or three Miles to gather Straw-berries, *Ruck* with his Sister, the Wife of *G. B.* Rode home very Softly, with *G. B.* on Foot in their Company, *G. B.* stept aside a little into the Bushes; whereupon they halted and Halloo'd for him. He not answering, they went away homewards, with a quickened pace, without expectation of seeing him in a considerable while; and yet when they were got near home, to their Astonishment, they found him on foot with them, having a Basket of Straw-berries. *G. B.* immediately then fell to Chiding his Wife, on the account of what she had been speaking to her Brother, of him, on the Road: which when they wondred at, he said, *He knew their thoughts. Ruck* being startled at that, made some Reply, intimating, that the Devil himself did not know so far; but *G. B.* answered, *My God makes known your Thoughts unto me.* The Prisoner now at the Bar had nothing to answer, unto what was thus witnessed against him, that was worth considering. Only he said, *Ruck, and his Wife left a Man with him, when they left him.* Which *Ruck* now affirm'd to be false; and when the Court asked *G. B. What the Man's Name was?* his Countenance was much altered; nor could he say, who 'twas. But the Court began to think, that he then step'd aside, only that by the assistance of the *Black Man,* he might put on his *Invisibility,* and in that *Fascinating Mist,* gratifie his own Jealous Humour, to hear what they said of him. Which trick of rendring themselves *Invisible,* our Witches do in their Confessions pretend, that they sometimes are Masters of; and it is the more credible, because there is Demonstration, that they often render many other things utterly *Invisible.*

VIII. *Faltring, faulty, unconstant, and contrary Answers upon judicial and deliberate Examination,* are counted some unlucky Symptoms of Guilt, in all

Crimes, especially in Witchcrafts. Now there never was a Prisoner more eminent for them, than *G. B.* both at his Examination and on his Trial. His *Tergiversations, Contradictions,* and *Falsehoods,* were very sensible: he had little to say, but that he had heard some things that he could not prove, Reflecting upon the Reputation of some of the Witnesses. Only he gave in a Paper to the Jury; wherein, altho' he had many times before, granted, not only that there are *Witches,* but also, that the present Sufferings of the Country are the effects of *horrible Witchcrafts,* yet he now goes to evince it, *That there neither are, nor ever were Witches, that having made a Compact with the Devil, can send a Devil to Torment other people at a distance.* This Paper was Transcribed out of *Ady;* which the Court presently knew, as soon as they heard it. But he said, he had taken none of it out of any Book; for which, his Evasion afterwards, was, That a Gentleman gave him the Discourse in a Manuscript, from whence he Transcribed it.

IX. The Jury brought him in *Guilty:* But when he came to Dy, he utterly deni'd the Fact, whereof he had been thus convicted.

Study Questions

1. At the end of the second paragraph, Mather mentions "Rules of Reasoning, by the Judicious *Gaule*" and says they were applied in the case of G. B. What are those rules? How do they serve as the basis for the structure of the report?

2. What is the relationship between the rules as they are cited and the second paragraph of the essay?

3. What methods of organization are used in the presentation of evidence for each "Rule of Reasoning"?

4. How is each rule related to cause-and-effect reasoning? What fallacy is common to all of them?

5. What is the author's attitude toward the defendant? What sections of the report reveal this attitude? Does the author's attitude affect your opinion of the defendant? His guilt? The author himself?

6. How would you dispute the charges or the evidence against G. B.? What explanation could you offer for the unusual incidents described?

PRELIMINARY WORKSHEET

1. Topic _____

2. Source of information

      a.   personal knowledge

         _____

         _____

         _____

      b.   library resources

         _____

         _____

         _____

         _____

         _____

         _____

3. Statement of argument _____

         _____

         _____

         _____

4. Reasons for basis of proof   a. _____

         _____

         b. _____

         _____

         c. _____

         _____

5. Main-idea sentence _____

         _____

         _____

6. Development of argument with details and examples

    a.   topic sentence

         _____

         _____

         _____

       1 _____

       2 _____

       3 _____

       4 _____

    b.   topic sentence

         _____

         _____

         _____

       1 _____

       2 _____

       3 _____

       4 _____

    c.   topic sentence

         _____

         _____

         _____

       1 _____

       2 _____

       3 _____

       4 _____

7. Supplementary information for conclusion

         _____

         _____

         _____

         _____

EVALUATION GUIDE

Name

Topic

Introduction

1. State the main-idea sentence.

    _____

    _____

    _____

2. From the sentence determine the author's position on the argument.

    _____

    _____

    _____

3. Does this sentence contain a statement of division in order of treatment?

    _____

4. List the topics of the division

    a. _____

    b. _____

    c. _____

    d. _____

Body

1. Does the body explore all of the listed subtopics, with a paragraph for each?

    _____

2. How is each subtopic developed?

    _____

    _____

    _____

3. Is sufficient evidence given in support of each reason?

Conclusion

1. Does the concluding paragraph restate the argument?

2. Are you convinced by the argument? If so, why? If not, why not?

Rating

__ This paper should be rewritten completely or in part.

__ This paper is acceptable but needs some minor revisions.

__ This is an outstandingly good paper.

6 Persuasion: The Sequential Argument

INTRODUCTORY COMMENTS

A sequential argument proceeds through a series of connected statements to a conclusion. It is therefore a more rigid form of argument than one based on a division of reasons. The latter might be thought of as an open-ended argument: you cannot possibly include all possible reasons or causes in favor of your conclusion, and you may in fact omit or ignore reasons or causes which go counter to your conclusion. Hence such an argument leaves a great deal of room for disagreement and is not likely to persuade completely. Often your reader or listener will say, "Yes, that may be true—at least I can understand why you believe as you do—but don't forget these reasons on the other side."

A sequential argument, by contrast, is logically complete; that is, when successful, it is convincing and unanswerable. There are, however, two problems involved in the construction of such an argument. First of all, you must persuade your reader that the steps within it are *true*. Second, you must show that the logical connections between the steps of your argument and your conclusion are *valid*. If you can do both, if you can demonstrate the truth and validity of your argument, then your reader *must* accept your conclusion as sound.

In a sense this final paper is a culmination of various aspects of this course, since parts of your argument will be structured around various types of writing you have already learned—chronology, definition, comparison, division, even a list of reasons. Beyond these, however, and binding them together into a cohesive unit, will be the overall structure determined by the logic of the argument itself. You will be able to handle such a structure only if you have some clear awareness of the whole process of reasoning, especially as it involves inductive and deductive procedures.

Inductive reasoning

Reasoning normally proceeds in either of two directions: inductively or deductively. Induction is the process of bringing together separate facts as evidence in support of a general statement; it is reasoning which compiles particular instances and moves from them to a general principle. Much learning takes place by induction. The infant who repeatedly receives attention when he cries but is ignored when quiet soon concludes that tantrums are a useful form of behavior. A psychologist might object at this point that the spoiled child has merely developed a conditioned response and not reasoned to an induction. The processes, however, are closely analogous. Induction occurs when you consciously formulate a general conclusion based on a series of particular experiences or observations.

One further example may help to make this process clear: you doubtless know someone who firmly believes that all flavors of ice cream are pleasant-tasting. This ice-cream glutton—let us call him Jack—may never have said, "All flavors of ice cream are pleasant-tasting," yet this is a proposition he has more or less consciously arrived at over the years through a succession of specific experiences, perhaps as follows:

> When he was four, Jack's parents gave him some vanilla ice cream; he loved it because he found it cool and delicious. After that first experience Jack was always eager to have more vanilla.
>
> When he was five, Jack was offered some chocolate ice cream. At first he was hesitant to taste it because it looked so different from vanilla. Nevertheless, he was persuaded to try some and found the new flavor just as delightful as vanilla.
>
> When he was eight, Jack was given some strawberry ice cream. This time, though his hesitancy about a new flavor was not so strong as before, he was still uncertain about the outcome until he tried the strawberry. Then he learned that he liked strawberry ice cream just as well as vanilla and chocolate.

And so it went for Jack, encountering new flavors of ice cream, trying them, and finding that he liked them. Eventually he came inductively to the conclusion "All flavors of ice cream are pleasant-tasting." He reviewed all his past specific experiences with various flavors of ice cream and *generalized* them into a universal statement.

Deductive reasoning

Reasoning that proceeds in the opposite direction, from a general statement to a particular conclusion, is called deduction. It is the process of applying a generalization to one new specific instance.

Jack, our ice-cream-eating friend, may some day come upon a new flavor of ice cream which sounds at first so strange that even he is reluctant to try it. Perhaps pumpkin ice cream is the new special at the Dairy Bar. If Jack is a reasoning, logical person, he may say to himself:

All flavors of ice cream are pleasant-tasting.

Pumpkin is a flavor of ice cream.

Therefore, pumpkin ice cream is pleasant-tasting.

At this point, Jack will try the pumpkin and, very probably, discover that he does indeed like it. His deductive reasoning—moving from the previously arrived-at generalization about ice cream flavors through the deductive process to a conclusion about a new flavor—will have persuaded him to believe that he should try the pumpkin flavor, in every expectation of liking it.

Deductive reasoning applies a generalization to some new specific. In Jack's case the generalization is one he had previously arrived at inductively. Sometimes the generalization is one that other observers have developed through the inductive process. But whatever the origin of the general statement, deduction is simply the process of applying it to a particular instance to reach a new conclusion.

Of course, Jack will probably never go through the formal steps in reasoning we have outlined. He is more likely, when he encounters pumpkin ice cream for the first time, to say, "Well, I've liked every new flavor I've tried so far, so why not try this one?" This too follows a deductive line of reasoning, even though some of the steps of the argument are not explicitly stated. Most of the time you will reach your conclusions by just such an abbreviated process; and when simple and concrete matters are involved, this process is sufficient. When you attempt to deal with abstract material, however, shortcuts might lead you into difficulty, but you can avoid or detect faulty logic if you list all the steps of the argument in order.

Structure of the sequential argument

Perhaps the basic and most useful shape for a logical argument is that of the *syllogism,* a formal statement of the deductive process itself, beginning with a broad generalization and applying it to a particular instance. Jack's deductive argument about pumpkin ice cream, above, is a clear example of that process. Let us analyze an even simpler example to show how a sequential argument, or syllogism, may be constructed.

1. All lions are carnivores.
2. Elsa is a lion.
3. Therefore, Elsa is a carnivore.

Notice first of all that we have three statements, each of which asserts a *classification.* Secondly, note that the three statements share only three key terms, and these three terms represent three distinct levels of generality. Furthermore, note that a proper assertion in a syllogism uses a

linking verb, like "is" or "are." For convenience in discussing the syllogism, the first two assertions are known as *premises*; they establish the
logical basis for the third assertion, known as the *conclusion*. In the conclusion two of the three terms are linked together in a classification, which
is logically justified because these two terms are each appropriately linked
to the third, or *middle* term, in the two premises.

The logical connections among the three terms and the three assertions may be made clear through a set of diagrams which will also show
why "lions" in the sample is called the *middle term*. The first premise
asserts that *all* lions are included in the set or class of carnivores:

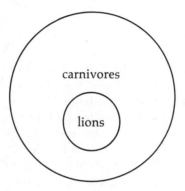

There may well be other carnivores in addition to lions, but the assertion
tells us nothing about them; it simply affirms that all lions are carnivores.
Here, "carnivores" is the most general, the most inclusive, category.

"Lions," however, is also a set or class, as a further diagram will
show. The second assertion or premise tells us that the specific individual
named Elsa belongs in the class of "lions." Using an "x" to represent Elsa,
we may diagram the second premise as follows:

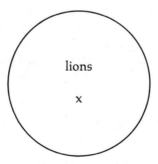

Now, superimposing one diagram on the other, we can see the reason
for the "Therefore" of statement three, the conclusion of the sequential
argument:

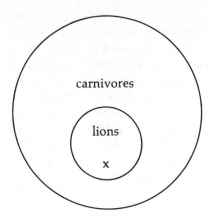

If all lions belong to the set or class of carnivores, and if Elsa belongs to the set or class of lions, then Elsa must necessarily also belong to the larger set or class of carnivores.

It is important to note at this point that there are many other possible ways of stating logically connected arguments; however, the kind of sequence we have examined in detail is the simplest and clearest form of logic and is therefore the one you should try to use as the basis of your reasoning in this assignment. This particular method of reasoning can be used reliably and with little difficulty as the basic structure of an argument, providing you take care to demonstrate both the *truth* of your first two assertions and the *validity* of their connection with your *conclusion*.

Validity and truth

As we have implied, if the first two steps in an argument are true, and if the logical connections among the three steps are valid, then the conclusion must also be true. Of course, when you deal with a controversial topic, you cannot hope to guarantee the truth of your assertions, but only try to persuade your readers to believe them. But if your assertions are obviously false, then your conclusion will also be false, no matter how valid the logical connections may be.

All creatures that live in the sea are fish.

Whales are creatures that live in the sea.

Therefore, whales are fish.

This sequential argument is logically valid—that is, it might be diagramed in just the same way as the Elsa-lion-carnivore example above to show that the connections among the statements work. There is just one difficulty, however: the first premise is false; hence the conclusion is also false. To assess the effectiveness of a sequential argument, then, you must be concerned with both the validity of the logical connections and the truth of the assertions made. As you write your paper for this assignment, and also as you read materials organized around sequential arguments, you must be alert for problems of both validity and truth. You can make your own arguments more convincing, and you can recognize weaknesses in the arguments of others, if you know how to identify certain *fallacies* in reasoning or assertion.

Fallacies

Certain common mistakes in reasoning or assertion are known as fallacies, or false arguments. Fallacies may be divided into two classes, those which relate to the structure (or validity) of an argument and those which pertain to its truth. To test the *validity* of a sequential argument, check its three statements against a few simple rules, or draw a diagram of the assertions. In this way you can clearly demonstrate certain fallacies in reasoning.

1. *The middle or intermediate term* (the one which connects the other two but does not itself appear in the conclusion) *should be preceded by "all" or "every" in the first premise.*

Some blue-eyed men are thieves.

John is a blue-eyed man.

Therefore, John is a thief.

In this example the middle term, "blue-eyed men," is labeled "some" rather than "all." The sequential argument is quite clearly false, as a diagram will show:

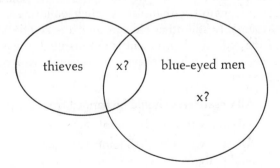

The overlapping circles represent the first assertion in the sequence: *some* blue-eyed men are thieves—but presumably, also, some are *not*. The information given in the second assertion, then, does not tell us where to place the "x" to represent John. Whether he is or is not a thief cannot be determined on the basis of the statements given.

2. *The use of "all" or "every" in the conclusion must be supported by the same use of "all" or "every" in the premise.*

All unsafe cars should be banned from public highways.

Some old cars are unsafe to drive.

Therefore, all old cars should be banned from public highways.

Here the middle term, "unsafe cars," is properly introduced by "all." The term "old cars," however, is introduced by "all" in the conclusion but only "some" in the second premise. A diagram will readily show the fallacy in this sequence:

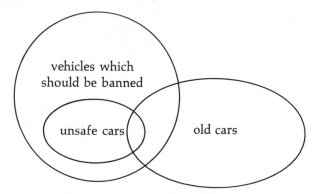

The first assertion diagrams well, with *all* unsafe cars included within the set or class of vehicles which should be banned. However, the circle representing "old cars" can overlap the others only partially, since our second assertion specifies *some* old cars. As the diagram shows, there may be some old cars which are safe but should nevertheless be banned for reasons other than safety (their polluting effect, perhaps). There are presumably still other old cars which *need not* be banned. The conclusion of the sequential argument is not justified: the argument is invalid. However, a very minor change in wording will produce a perfectly valid sequence:

All unsafe cars should be banned from the public highways.

All cars with worn ball joints are unsafe.

All cars with worn ball joints should be banned from
public highways.

Here the use of "all" in *both* the second premise and the conclusion leads to a diagram (p. 261) clearly supporting the validity of the conclusion.

3. *Avoid the use of negative assertions wherever possible.* Quite valid sequential arguments can be constructed using negative statements, but such arguments can be confusing, and the rules applying to negative

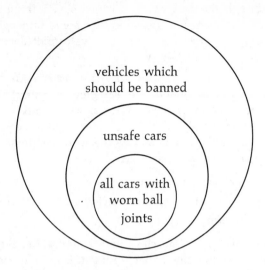

statements are both complex and subtle. Therefore, you will do well to convert negative statements into affirmative ones in order to check the validity of a sequence.

Ginny is not a freshman.
No freshmen attended class today.
Therefore, Ginny was present today.

You can very likely see the fallacy here: the first two assertions simply do not justify the conclusion—in fact, on the basis of the first two assertions no conclusion is possible about Ginny's presence. However, the fallacy is much more clearly shown if we convert all statements into affirmative terms and then diagram the result:

All freshmen were absent today.
Ginny is an upperclassman.
Therefore . . .

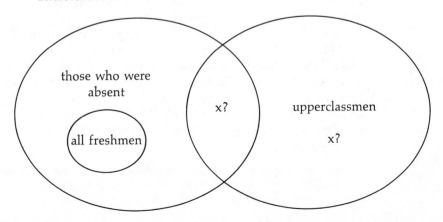

Although the first two assertions say nothing about the attendance of upperclassmen, it is possible that some upperclassmen were absent and others were present today. And we cannot determine where to place the "x" representing Ginny.

4. *If there are more than three terms among three assertions, no conclusion can be drawn.* The sample concerning Ginny also illustrates this fourth way in which sequential arguments can slip into fallacies. By definition the simplest and clearest type of sequential argument contains only three terms and asserts the relationship of two of these to a middle term, and hence to each other.

> All clams are mussels.
>
> But weight lifting is a muscle-building activity.
>
> Therefore, all clams are weight lifters.

"Mussels" and "muscles" may sound alike, but they are not the same thing, and this sequential argument is quite obviously invalid.

To check a sequential argument for validity, then, look for the proper use of "all" or "every" (see Rules 1 and 2, above); convert negative assertions into affirmative ones (Rule 3); and make sure the sequence of three statements contains only three terms (Rule 4). If you are still in doubt, draw a diagram of the assertions to see whether the conclusion is really justified.

Fallacies concerning the *truth* of an argument are sometimes readily discovered, especially if one or another of the premises is obviously false. More often, however, a fallacious argument is stated in condensed or misleading form (not necessarily with any deliberate intent). It is often helpful to restate an argument in the simplest possible sequential terms to discover possible fallacies, such as the following:

False Analogy. A false analogy occurs when a comparison is faulty or inadequate. Many arguments proceed on the basis that one thing is *like* another in *many respects* and therefore may be presumed to be like it in *all ways.* While an analogy is not a very strong argument, it is sometimes a reasonable way of making your point. You must be sure, however, that you do not push your analogy too far and break it down in the process.

Adolf Hitler, in an essay on "Man and Race," once argued that because different species in nature do not interbreed successfully (with the exception of such sterile hybrids as the mule, the result of a mating between a horse and an ass), races should not be allowed to mix. The analogy may at first sound plausible, but its weakness immediately becomes apparent when we state the argument in the form of a sequence of assertions:

> Different species of animals, by definition, do not successfully interbreed.

The races of men are exactly comparable to different species of animals.

Therefore, races of men should not interbreed.

The second premise, which Hitler conveniently omitted from his essay, is obviously false. All men are of the same species, and whatever "race" may mean, it is not the same thing. Therefore, the whole argument advanced by Hitler rests on a false analogy.

Begging the Question. Such an assertion is often called arguing in a circle. We assert the truth of a conclusion which merely makes the same assertion as the first two statements:

The Scripture is the inspired word of God. I know this because the Scripture says so, and the Scripture is of course true, being the inspired word of God.

Similarly,

Classical music is the best because the experts who like classical music say so.

False Dilemma. A whole range of alternatives between two extreme positions is ignored:

We must honor our commitment in Southeast Asia. Only a complete military victory will suffice. (Would every conceivable negotiated peace be dishonorable?)

The Either-Or Fallacy. This variation of the false dilemma assumes there are only two sides to a complex problem:

We should win the war or get out. (There may be other alternatives, such as partial withdrawal, losing the war, etc.)

Faulty Statistics. Statistics are used in a misleading way:

The average salary in this factory is $10,000 per year. (But five workers earn $5,000, three $6,000, one $7,000, and one $50,000. The average is therefore $10,000, but most people assume average to mean typical and would therefore be deceived by the generalization.)

Faulty Sampling. This occurs when evidence is too selective or too random:

After polling the members of the police department for their opinions, the selectmen of the town refused to allow the sale of the magazine that the police had termed "obscene." (But policemen are not necessarily qualified to determine a matter so complex as obscenity in literature.)

You should be alert for fallacies such as these when you argue and when you study the arguments of others. A fallacious argument may sometimes seem persuasive, but a truly effective one is properly logical —that is, both valid and true.

Uses of the sequential argument

Thinking that is structured around a series of logically connected steps will be of use to you in the same kinds of situations as thinking that is structured around the division of reasons you studied in the preceding chapter. If you are familiar with the procedure involved in organizing a paper around the formal statement of a deductive argument, you have learned a structural device that can be employed in a great variety of reading and writing assignments, as you attempt to persuade others, and as you analyze what others are saying when they try to persuade you. The value of knowing the sequential argument goes beyond its usefulness as a tool for organization, however, for your ability to handle the deductive argument should enable you to reason more effectively as you construct your own arguments or examine those of others. What you should discover as you work on your own writing and study the sample essays is that the correct use of logically connected sequences is the foundation for all clear thinking. Of course, as we have noted, the sequential argument does make use of skills and structures developed earlier in the course; but this final exercise brings them all together within a larger logical framework. Understanding that logical framework should help you grapple directly and purposefully with the real problems, the serious problems, of your life.

GUIDELINES

1. Choose a topic.

Your topic should be controversial but arguable. Perhaps one of your other courses will supply material for a topic; perhaps you will wish to write on some current controversy in your college, your community, or the world at large. Whatever your choice, however, the topic you select should meet the following requirements:

a. It must be broad or pertinent enough to interest other people.

Although you might like to defend your belief that chewing gum is good for the soul, most persons would not share your enthusiasm and would be unwilling to spend time reading what you have to say.
b.   It must be narrow enough, on the other hand, to be dealt with in a single essay. Books have been written about man's moral or immoral nature, so how could you hope to deal with the subject in one short paper?
c.   Your position must be debatable. There is no point in writing an argument if everyone already agrees with you.
d.   You must believe in your argument. If you don't, chances are that what you write will not convince anyone else.

Good topics for this assignment might be the following:

Legalizing abortion
The American consumer—victim of planned obsolescence
The value of smoking
Suicides are psychotic
Training the mentally retarded
Standardizing state license laws

2. Construct the sequential argument.

The easiest way to begin is to state your topic in a simple proposition which might be the conclusion of a sequential argument. Then work backward to state the premises for that argument.

Let us suppose, for example, that we wish to argue that suicides are psychotic. The conclusion of a syllogism making this assertion might be:

A person who attempts suicide is at the moment of the gesture psychotic.

Since any conclusion contains two of the three terms necessary for a sequential argument, we have only to discover a middle term, one to which "suicide" and "psychotic" can be related, to construct an appropriate syllogism. Such a term can be found by considering what a psychotic condition is—an inability to distinguish between reality and unreality. Using this information, we can arrive at the sequential argument that will provide the overall framework for our paper:

Major premise: All persons who are unable to distinguish between reality and unreality are psychotic.
Minor premise: A person who attempts suicide is at the moment of the gesture unable to distinguish between reality and unreality.
Conclusion: Therefore, a person who attempts suicide is at the moment of the gesture psychotic.

3. Accumulate and organize information.

After you check to see that your syllogism does not contain any of the fallacies we have discussed, you can then proceed to acquire and arrange the material you need to support your position. Since the body of the paper will develop first the major premise and then the minor, you must decide what the focus of the argument will be for each section. This decision will then determine the structure of each part and will serve as the basis for organizing the list of details you must compile. As is true with essays built around other structures, additional information can be included in the introduction or conclusion, both of which are necessary to make the argument effective and complete. A preliminary list, suitably arranged, for our paper about suicides might be as follows:

Introduction
    Examples to catch reader's interest: girl swallowing glass, boy hanging himself
    Definition of suicide
    Discussion of various methods used
    Statement of sequential argument
Body
    Material for major premise: All persons unable to distinguish between reality and unreality are psychotic.
        Point of argument: What is a psychotic? (Definition)
        Example: Hospitalized patient thinking nurses were Cleopatra
        Comparison: Difference between psychotic and "normal" fantasizing
    Material for minor premise: A person who attempts suicide is at the moment of the gesture unable to distinguish between reality and unreality.
        Point of argument: A suicide violates reality in ignoring generally accepted reasons for living.
        Division of reasons: Moral, logical, altruistic, instinctive
            Moral reasons: regarding life as worthless; example, automobile suicide
            Logical reasons: inability to recognize alternatives; example, diabetic woman
            Altruistic reasons: overlooking pain caused to others; example, middle-aged novelist
            Instinctive reasons: suppressing instinct for survival; example, Marilyn Monroe
Conclusion:
    Restatement of sequential argument, showing logical connections between premises and conclusion

4. Compose an introduction which includes a main-idea sentence.

As before, the introduction tells the reader something about the subject and excites his interest and attention. In addition, the introduction must include a main-idea sentence which clearly states the conclusion of your argument. Around the main-idea sentence, and perhaps leading up to it, you should give information that enlarges the reader's understanding of the key issues in your argument. Such information might include a brief history of the problem, some definitions, or illustrative anecdotes.

could therefore begin with a paragraph giving reports of suicide attempts
   An introduction to our paper arguing that suicides are psychotic
which had different results, each one, of course, chronologically arranged
and with a transition calling attention to the contrast connecting the two. In a second introductory paragraph, the difference between them can be a link to the previous paragraph and a lead-in to a consideration of the common element in both cases—the deliberate attempt at self-destruction. After a definition of suicide and a consideration of methods used, this section can conclude with an explicit statement of the sequential argument (the main-idea sentence), which will serve as the basis of organization for the rest of the paper.

One day last year Mary K., a girl in her early twenties, rushed into the emergency room of a Baltimore hospital and announced that she had just swallowed a handful of fragments from a broken mirror. She was immediately given several "cotton sandwiches," consisting of swatches of cotton batting placed between two slices of bread. For three days she was kept in a state of absolute rest and quiet while physicians watched for signs of hemorrhaging. Since none appeared, it was clear that the cotton had, as it was hoped, wrapped itself around the glass, allowing it to pass through the digestive system without the internal cutting and bleeding which would otherwise have resulted. After the cotton-wrapped glass had been eliminated from her body, the girl recovered without any apparent physical aftereffects. Not as fortunate was Harold M., a small-town teenager who was found hanging in a closet in his home. When his mother discovered him he was already dead, and emergency lifesaving efforts were of no avail.

Although the results were different in each case, both of these persons were among several thousands who each year attempt suicide; that is, they tried to take their own lives. Young and old, male and female—statistics on suicides include them all, as well as the variety of methods used. These methods can be uncommon, like the ingesting of broken glass described above, or the more familiar methods of hanging, slashing wrists or throat, taking poisons, shooting, or drinking and driving. Whatever the method, it seems to me that in seeking death as the only way out of a predicament, the person who deliberately tries to kill himself has severely distorted his vision to the point where he actually becomes blinded to the possibilities of life. Because of this distortion the suicide has in effect lost his ability to distinguish between that which is real and that which is unreal. He therefore is, at the moment of the gesture at least, engaging in behavior that can properly be termed psychotic.

5. Prove the first step of your sequential argument.

Write a series of paragraphs developing support for your major premise. Sometimes (as in "Apartheid," p. 272) the major premise is so generally accepted that no proof is necessary. In other cases you must demonstrate that your assertion is true. Often this demonstration can be handled by a series of particular examples (the inductive method). At other times only a clear and complete definition of terms is suitable. As we have already indicated in our preliminary list, such a method is appropriate for our paper on suicides. Thus we should first define *psychotic* and then give an example of psychotic behavior. Next, on the basis of this example and making use of a comparison structure, we can show how the psychotic's loss of contact with reality differs from the "normal" person's daydreams or fantasies. This first section of the body of our paper will then consist of two paragraphs:

> A psychotic condition refers to a state of mind in which there is confusion between reality and unreality. The person suffering from a severe psychosis experiences delusions and fantasies so extreme that he cannot function normally in society and must consequently be hospitalized. Such a person might, for instance, say and believe that he is Napoleon or Jack the Ripper, or he might confuse the identities of those around him. In one clinic a patient insisted that all black-haired nurses were Cleopatra, and since he disliked Cleopatra, he attacked those nurses both verbally and physically. Once, for instance, he acted out his hostility by flinging the contents of his bedpan at a nurse after she had administered an enema.
>
> Of course this patient, like other institutionalized psychotics, was able to recognize some elements of his environment. He could tell time; he knew what clothes were for and how to get into them. Sometimes he knew who some people were or at least could perceive their functions in relation to himself. But even though he was able to acknowledge some of the realities around him, he nevertheless lived in a dream world and acted as if it were real. In this way he differed from the so-called "normal" person, who also engages in daydreaming, but is able to recognize his fantasies for what they are. Such a

person may momentarily confuse fact and fiction, but he nevertheless can, if he must, separate the real from the unreal in his life.

6. Develop the second step of your argument.

Write a series of paragraphs to support your minor premise. Usually this section will constitute the heart of your argument, because it is here that you must convince your reader to accept an assertion that makes your conclusion valid and true.

In our paper on suicides this section would be devoted to proving the following:

A person who attempts suicide is at the moment of the gesture unable to distinguish between reality and unreality.

Obviously, this contention is a controversial one, and while most people would not disagree with the assertions and definitions in our first step, many would dispute the claim in our minor premise.

In our preliminary planning we discovered that there are four principal motivations for continuing existence: moral (it is wrong to take life); logical (alternative solutions); altruistic (responsibility to others); and instinctive (the impulse to survive). Using this division, we can construct a series of paragraphs, one devoted to each motivation, showing by examples and explanation why a person who overrides any or all of these motivations has in fact lost contact with reality. The accumulation of this evidence, suitably tied together by transitions and links, will lead to the demonstration of the minor premise itself. In the five sample paragraphs below, certain key transitional devices are underlined and commented on in the marginal notes. There are, as you will notice, many other transitions and links than those called to your attention. If you are in doubt about how to make use of transitions in your own sequential argument, refer back to the guidelines in Chapters One and Three for more examples and explanations.

Linking word and repetition of key ideas to remind the reader of the previous paragraph and show its connection to this one.

Such a separation of the real from the unreal is not possible for the would-be suicide, for while he is in most ways what can be called "normal," he has entered a period of anxiety depression so severe that he can no longer be objective about life or death. Sometimes this depression arises from feelings of inadequacy or fear.

Parallel structure to show a connected list of examples.

Sometimes it is caused by a desire to achieve importance or express hostility. Sometimes anxiety arises from the conviction that life is so terrible that it is not worth living. In any case, however, if the anxiety depression is total, it controls all thought and blinds the person involved to the moral, logical, altruistic, and instinctive reasons for living that are found in most other people.

List of key ideas forming the topics of the next paragraphs.

Repetition of key word.

It is an almost universal moral belief that life is precious and that we have no right to take our own lives or the lives of others. If the suicide ever held this conviction, he forgets it in his desire for self-destruction; he no longer believes that his own life has any value. This attitude can include not only a negative self-image but also a powerful hostility toward others who should have recognized the suicide's importance. Thus the gesture of self-destruction in this instance is prompted by the controlling fantasy, "I'll show them. I'm not worth anything, but they'll be sorry after I'm gone." Sometimes the desire to hurt is so strong that a person actively seeks to take others with him when he goes. When a driver bent on killing himself smashes into another car, causing multiple fatalities, he has committed both murder and suicide, his moral regard for other life as well as for his own buried beneath his all-consuming passion for annihilation and revenge.

Reminder of the key idea of the major premise (the middle term of the syllogism). Repetition of key word.

Just as far removed from reality is a person so depressed that he convinces himself there is no logical reason for living. Trapped in a situation he is sure he cannot control or change except by suicide, he refuses to review, consider, or accept alternatives. Such a person was Louise N., a diabetic, who was told her leg would have to be amputated because of a gangrenous ulcer. Her doctors said that the ulcer could not be cured and that without amputation the gangrene was certain to spread until it killed her. She refused to undergo surgery, however, even when her family begged her to give consent, because she said she could not face life as a cripple. She therefore chose to die needlessly because she was unable or unwilling to live with the medical solution available to her. In this case the suicide's anxiety depression was so severe that her fantasies about "the only way out" prevented her from analyzing her situation logically.

Reference again to the middle term. Repetition of key word.

Similarly absorbed in his fantasy is the suicide who has become so self-centered in his thinking that he loses sight of the altruistic reasons for living. As we have already said, the suicide often wishes to hurt those he leaves behind; but even if this hostility is not present, he may simply forget what his death by suicide will do to those who survive him. When a middle-aged athlete and novelist, proud of his physical and mental prowess, stabbed himself not too long ago, he did so out of the conviction that his death was necessary to prevent the debilitating effects of approaching old age: he wanted to die at the height of his powers. His preoccupation with approaching age and what he felt he must do to forestall it was so intense that he forgot completely about the impact his suicide would have on his wife and children. That impact was even more tragic than the simple fact of his death, for he not only left them deprived of his presence as a husband and father but also caused them extreme anxiety and torment because of his lack of concern and their conviction that they had failed him. He had been worried, it is clear, only about himself; and so he closed his mind to the responsibilities he had to others, making his gesture a symptom of psychotic imbalance.

Repeated reminder of the
connection between the
middle term and the
conclusion.
Repetition of key word.

Equally symptomatic of such an imbalance is the suicide's will-
ful suppression of what is considered to be the strongest instinct
in all men, that of self-preservation. Most behavior is not self-
destructive and in fact is generated by the will to survive. True,
many of us engage in foolhardy or downright dangerous pursuits,
like smoking or eating improper foods or drinking excessively or
taking unnecessary chances. When we do, it may be that we are
being somewhat psychotic ourselves, allowing our view of reality
to be overruled by whim. The suicide, however, seeks total annihilation, not whimsical gratification; his action is a deliberate betrayal
of the universal impulse to continue living. When a movie star like
Marilyn Monroe swallows an overdose of sleeping pills because she
is depressed about her loss of youth, she is not only the victim of a

Reminder of entire list
of reasons.

fantasy which is morally, logically, and altruistically crippled. She is
also allowing her notions about the desirability of death to overcome
her primal instincts to hold on to life.

7. Write the conclusion.

Show why your central idea must follow from the chain of argument you
have presented. In this section, in addition to restating your position, you
may also wish to add information about the subject that will further en-
lighten the reader. In addition, you may wish to recognize or refute some
of the opposing arguments. Finally, you can, if appropriate, use the conclusion to tell the reader about changes that can or should be made in law,
society, education, etc., to activate the position for which you are arguing.

In our sample paper about suicides, the conclusion does not allow for
refutation of contradictory premises, since the arguments against the developed sequence are so extensive that they cannot possibly be handled in
a paragraph or two. Neither does the paper call for an enactment of legis-
lation or public policy. In this instance, therefore, the paper may conclude
with a further attempt to convince readers that our position is sound and
tenable. It might be best to begin with fresh material about the treatment
of persons who attempt suicide, and in the final paragraph tie that treatment in with the paper's chief assertion.

Suicide attempts often fail. Sometimes a person is talked out of it,
sometimes he makes the attempt and then changes his mind, and
sometimes he is found by others who can administer or obtain medical
assistance. Of course, not all emergency treatment is effective, and
the suicide may find that he has succeeded in his original purpose,
even if afterward he might have changed his mind. Those who are
saved, however, are usually given psychiatric as well as medical aid,
since the gesture is interpreted as a desire for help and a means of
calling for attention.

Whether or not the would-be suicide is successful, at the time of his attempt he has surrendered to a total self-concern that prompts him to take the final step towards self-inflicted death. In making this decision he has blinded himself to the moral, logical, altruistic, and instinctive reasons for life that operate in others. Therefore, by surrendering to a desire that shuts out reality as it applies to himself and others, he is engaging in psychotic behavior. That is, he is suffering from a mental disorder so extreme that he loses contact with the world and is no longer reacting in a "normal" way.

8. Check your first draft.

a. Does your sequential argument provide the framework for the entire paper?

b. Have you committed any of the fallacies you were warned against in this and the preceding chapters?

c. Have you used transitions between sentences and paragraphs to ensure a smooth flow of thought?

9. Prepare your final draft.

Polish and perfect your paper, and as before, be sure to proofread before submitting your final copy.

SAMPLE ESSAYS

Apartheid   STUDENT SAMPLE

Examples to shock the reader and stir his interest and sympathy.

A black man who sits on a park bench which is reserved for white men is subject to a fine of up to $840, jail for up to three years, whipping, or any combination of these three punishments. Similarly, a boy who continues to live with his parents after he is eighteen must have a special permit or he is guilty of a crime. Again, every African (black person) is required to carry a reference book at all times. If he can not produce this book or it is not in proper order, he is guilty of a crime and may be fined or imprisoned. These are examples of the regulations which govern black men under apartheid.

Reprinted by permission.

Definition of key term,
apartheid.
Further information
concerning key term,
included to show basis
for the system.

As the name indicates, apartheid refers to a system of government which treats the blacks as a completely separate political entity. This system was instituted by Dutch settlers in South Africa who, fearful of rebellion or miscegenation, eventually gained complete control of the country and formed a republic completely excluding the black population. Ideally, any system of government is organized by and for all the people it presumes to serve. Obviously, in practice any political system is bound to include if not encourage some inequalities and injustices. However, any system of government which flagrantly ignores its responsibilities to a major portion of the population, while it is anxious to protect only a few, fails to serve its proper purpose and therefore should be abolished. The system of apartheid, in fact, is such a government, for apartheid is a dehumanizing political practice which severely represses the blacks in every aspect of their existence, from work, education, home life, and religion to personal freedom and dignity.

Major premise.

Main-idea sentence,
stating the minor
premise and showing the
structure of the essay.

In South Africa, the blacks have been so dehumanized by the treatment they suffer from the whites that they have been reduced to the position of animals. There is a standard joke among the blacks which says that it is better to be treated like a dog than an underdog. As a dog, one gets the scraps from the master's table; as the underdog, all one gets is "boys' meat," a term used for the worst cuts of meat (not even good enough for a dog) which the

Example to prove the
minor premise.

"boss" buys for his black help. "Boy" is the denigrating term used to refer to any African male, be he six or sixty.

General proofs that apartheid "represses the blacks in every aspect of their existence."

Apartheid is deeply ingrained in every sphere of every South African's life. It is the personification of the white man's fear of blackness. Because he is so vastly outnumbered, the South African white "boss" severely limits the freedoms of the blacks, lest they rise up in number against him. In addition, the white government spends a great deal of time, money, and energy keeping the races apart. Blacks must ride on separate buses and trains, sit on separate benches in the park, use separate toilets, go to separate schools, churches, hospitals, and theaters. Ninety percent of the labor force of South Africa consists of blacks. They are employed extensively in the mines, in industry, and as domestic servants, but they are not allowed to hold any type of skilled job. They earn next to nothing for wages.

Proof of educational repression.

The education system for black South African children is appalling. Black schools receive very little government funding because most of the funds allocated for blacks are spent in enforcing apartheid. As a result, there are very few schools and even fewer teachers. It is ironic that the government requires the African children to go to school, but it does not even provide them with books or educational materials, much less schools and teachers. Moreover, the curriculum is very rigidly controlled by the government. The children learn only what the government wants them to know.

Blacks are forbidden to live in urban areas. Instead they are herded into small government-built townships outside the cities, in order to keep them separate from the whites. The townships consist of rows upon rows of little one-room houses, for which the Africans have to pay rent. Some of these townships are so far away from urban areas that it takes a commuter two hours or more to go to work, as there isn't even a decent commuting system. There

Proof of repression of home life.

are some ancient buses (African-owned, because Africans aren't allowed to ride "European" or "white" buses) that run into the cities. The trains for blacks are a hazardous nightmare. If the government doubled the size of the trains and ran them twice as often as it does, there still wouldn't be enough of them, and as a result they would still not be safe. People have gotten trampled to death trying to get on a train. Often those people who can't fit inside the train just hang on to the outside, or perhaps they are lucky enough to find a small space between cars.

Proof of religious repression.

One would think that all men, as God's children, could worship Him together. But the black South Africans have to worship in separate churches. Many rural Africans adhere to their old tribal religions; but in the more urbanized areas, due to the missionary influence, they are Christians. The white missionaries stripped the Africans of their own religion, yet these same white people prohibit them from praying in white churches.

Some of the larger cities have special hospitals for the "non-whites" (a government term), but because there is a very limited number of black doctors and nurses and because very few white doctors want to work in black hospitals, these hospitals are inadequately staffed. Their equipment and supplies are minimal. It sometimes takes a week for a black man to get admitted to a hospital; to get treatment takes much longer. Many, many Africans die in hospitals while waiting for medical attention. It is understandable why the witch doctors are still popular.

Proof of further repression through poor medical care.

Although black South Africans have, for the most part, reconciled themselves to this sort of life, one thing they will never accept is the "pass laws." The government requires every adult from the age of sixteen to carry a passbook, or what could be called a passport to life. Without his pass, an African is as good as dead. These passbooks restrict the area where he can live and work, where he can travel, whom he can visit and when. They contain information about his entire life—criminal record, job status, tax-payment record. They contain his photograph and his fingerprints. At all times he is required to have this pass on his person, for he can be stopped and asked to produce it at any time. He even needs it to pick up a package at the post office. To be found without it or to have it not in order constitutes a crime which is punishable by imprisonment or exile to a remote part of the country. Moreover, the passbook can be revoked at any time for no specific reason.

Proof of repression of "personal dignity and freedom."

How much more severely could a government repress the human rights of the governed, or at least a segment of the governed? The rights to "life, liberty, and the pursuit of happiness," guaranteed to Americans by our government, are denied black South Africans by theirs. No government should have such power. Apartheid is inhumane; it must be abolished.

Restatement of major and minor premises. (Reference to American rights acts as support for the major premise.) Explicit statement of the conclusion of the syllogism.

The Language of Love   MAX WEATHERLY

"Before they lead me into that little square room tomorrow, Miss Tittywopp, I gotta tell ya something."

"Yes, Monroe?" It was the grillwork between teacher and student that made it possible to hold back tears: it represented a certain pattern of action beyond which she felt she shouldn't go; it was necessary dignity.

"My last thoughts'll be of you." He searched her face for the expected, the needed, tears. "I've always loved you, Miss Tittywopp."

Inundation. The grillwork liquefied and disappeared. "Why didn't you tell me," sobbing, "Monroe?"

"I reckon it was that old nonverbal syndrome." Sigh. "Hayakawa says we think one way, act another way, and talk yet another way. Semantic gap, maybe. I reckon holding up that filling station and knocking that guy off was a realization growing out of early erotic frustrations. I didn't actually *want to*, you see. I wanted to insert my male member in its erected state into your sweet little vaginal canal and tell you that way. I—"

"Oh, Monroe, I wanted to cook for you and make you happy. You could have stuck your—your finger in my eye if you'd wanted to. Oh, oh, oh . . ." All floodgates now open.

"Inadequacies of language, I reckon." He sighed.

Monroe was right. He was right indeed—and the trouble begins, ironically enough, with the word *love*. The ancient Greeks, monuments of sensibility that they were, had three words for love: *eros*, representing the feelings that existed so tragically and vainly between Monroe and his schoolteacher; *filios*, representing the feelings Monroe harbored for his close kin; and *agape*, naming the kind of love he held for his fellow man—the feelings that broke down under some deep-seated strain and opened the way for him to commit the ultimate act of hate.

We modern Americans, monuments of insensibility that we are, tend to simplify *ad absurdum* for what we insanely call "convenience." We have "all-purpose" cleaners, automobiles, foods, vacations and clothing, to mention only a few current simplifiers. We also have far too many all-purpose words—and one of them is *love*, which names an emotion of such infinite variety that it demands the deepest delineation. Due to its myriad uses in all three areas defined by the Greeks, *love*, the modern word, has collected denotations, connotations, and semantic furbelows to such an extent that to my mind it now resembles a swarm of bees "protecting" the queen. And I wonder (when I'm not making love) what we're afraid of? What are we *really* doing in the name of "linguistic convenience"?

In the realm of erotica plain old instinct will get you a long way without a word. In addition there is man's most honest organ, the eye. When I lived in Arabia I learned that Arabs, who take the greatest delight in "outwitting" each other (I'm avoiding the phrase *lying to* out of love for my Arab friends who lie to each other in the Western, or acceptable, manner), depend heavily on what they read in each other's eyes. Over the centuries they have become so adept at this that we Americans, having witnessed breathtaking demonstrations of that ability (and probably having been caught in a couple of breathtaking lies ourselves) either adopted a handful of the devious expressions which Arabs themselves used or stopped, if you can believe it, lying to them. The eye is rather honest and it works as well in love as it does in business. Laying hands on your beloved, for example, you can with only a modicum of perceptiveness tell right away whether or not your attentions are welcomed.

But what do we do for words? I know a man who is so emotionally stimulated by (read "in love with") a woman of our mutual acquaintance that his knees, poor devil, turn to glue the moment he sees her. He becomes so hung-up for appropriate words that he stands slack-shouldered in her presence with the most pained expression upon his face and with his palms nearly dripping. I never know whether to laugh, cry, or just kiss them both and walk away when we meet in the corridors of the university where we teach. She could probably rummage around in her mind and find some make-do words, for she is equally enamored of him. But she is female, as you've already guessed, and is therefore culturally denied the right (read "pleasure") of initiative. So the years go by and they stand gazing at each other like a pair of virgin iguanas.

And the problem isn't merely his shyness: he would be far less shy if there were words at hand which weren't either asinine or "obscene." He has, my friend, too much integrity, too much essential dignity (if you can believe it) to say, "Will you join me for a cup of coffee?" He doesn't want to drink coffee, he wants to make joyous, raunchy, glorious, and patently physical love. He wants to wallow in the Elysian Fields of erotica with his lady love. But there isn't any word for what he wants. Well, there is, but it would alienate her.

Let's suppose he suffers through the cup-of-coffee insanity and they have indeed achieved the threshold of one of their bedrooms by some miracle of communication. What then? She can't (so how does he?) say, "Let's undress and climb on the rack," in an appropriate manner. Of course most people "know." But suppose she doesn't? And, since "knowing" suggests prior experience, is she, culturally shackled hand and foot, apt to demonstrate it? Then what should they say? And, for that matter, how many words should they use? (Who among us has not at one awful time or another talked something to death?) I myself have been in situations where the pantomime became downright ludicrous.

I want to suggest nonpsychological origins of shyness. I say there is no dumbshow dumber than a man and a woman about to enjoy each other's bodies for the first time! I say the language of erotica is, by dismal default, silence.

Filially, our language doesn't stand up much better. Monroe's primary relationship to Miss Tittywopp was, after all, filial. As his schoolteacher she was a parent symbol: That she became anything more was, even if a reason for rejoicing, secondary. Was it, then, any easier for him to stay after school and say, "You are so good to me, Miss Tittywopp. You seem to have my best interests at heart and you seem to want to help me become a better person. I love you"? Indeed it was not! For in classless and sexless America, Miss Tittywopp would in all likelihood have assumed (feared) that her young male charge was making advances.

Poor Monroe might have been able to go home and say to his mother, "I love you." But, depending on the spectrum of her various neuroses, he might also have got his ears boxed. Such a declaration to his father would have been met with indignation or, at best, a hurried visit to the psychiatrist; and, said to his brother, the words would have got him snickered at.

Until they began voting for all the wrong candidates, I very much loved my two older brothers. I'm sure there was a fairly usual amount of erotic love in my feelings, but it was mostly a wish to be like them physically and psychologically—identification, hero worship. But I couldn't even say to my brother Pete, "I hero-worship you." I couldn't even say, "I love you," to my two sisters, whom I indeed loved, each in different ways. Yet I felt love, a certain kind of love, and wanted very much to express it.

There is one beam of light in the filial darkness: one can, reduced by default as I have shown to wordlessness, act out one's love. Why? Because there is time. For better or for worse, we humans spend more time, in the aggregate, with our *filials* than we do with our *eroses* or our *agapes*. And I must say I think there is some validity in acting out one's love as opposed to verbalizing it. My father could not, for his own special reasons, even *like* me. He spent the first twenty-five years of my life acting out that painful fact. Then he arrived at two points in his own life: (1) his last years, and (2) the realization that he had made a tragic mistake. He spent, therefore, his final four years acting out an apology to me; and I spent them trying to act out my forgiveness. I hope we both succeeded, but the fact will never be established. And therein lies the greatest objection to acting out.

The fact remains that we English-speaking peoples need words badly, appropriate words. I think I'll tack a sign on the front of my house, "words wanted."

Erotica and filiality are names of important and beloved emotions. But when I compare them to the high, wide and deep inferences of *agape* they recede slightly toward the trivial. Surely there is more human happiness because of, and more human suffering for the lack of, *agape*. If Monroe's *agape* had held up, for instance, he would not have killed the filling-station attendant: the poor man would still be alive, for which at least his wife would be grateful (not to mention his known children) and poor old Monroe would be free to find some way however stumblingly to tell Miss Tittywopp that he loved her.

But we English-speakers (or so we can technically call ourselves) can't go around saying, "I *agape* you," to Tom, Dick, and Jane no matter how close we might happen to be. I once tried such an experiment: I went to my favorite professor one gorgeous spring afternoon determined to speak to him of my gratitude, my devotion and, in short, my *agape*. "Professor Doggyball," I said manfully, "I think you're a great man—I guess I sort of love you." He searched my face in a panic. "Well. Thanks, Weatherly." He managed a most patronizing chuckle. "I'm not sure what my wife'd say about that, but thanks." I departed, my rapport with him in shambles and my ego in shreds. One time a young lawyer my own age did me a legal favor free of charge. When I wrote my thanks I signed the letter (where you would ordinarily put *sincerely* or *cordially*) *agape*. I thought surely my gesture would be understood in view of his youth, but I never heard from him again.

Flower people are doing their dead level best to pound the square word *love* into the round hole *agape*. The word is, joyfully, coming into wider use nowadays—even between men friends in eroticaless situations. As a result of a recent television program, I got a fan letter from a teenager in Connecticut signed, "Love and flowers, Gail Smith." And I thought that was a pretty nifty way of putting it. So maybe there is some hope.

You see, it's *agape* and not *eros* that makes the world go round. That's one thing we Madison Avenue-oriented Americans can't seem to get through the semantic fog emanating from that benighted area. It's *agape* that has made the men of this earth give up cannibalism and slavery, however slowly they have done it. *Agape* has produced great works of art and enriched men's lives. It can even be said to feed on itself and propagate itself in just that way. It could eliminate war, I think, given a fair chance by heavily verbal Greed (e.g., avarice, craving, covetousness, rapacity, voraciousness, gluttony, cupidity, insatiability, and their myriad cousins like mania and rage). But it will never get that chance until there are ways of saying it!

I think I'll tack another sign up on the front of my house, "WANTED: WAYS OF SAYING IT."

I maintain that each of us is being separated from everyone else with the reverse speed of love. It's like the expansion of the solar system but it's more immediate because instead of planets it's people! If we could just say, "Love!" or, "I Love You!" it would seem that perhaps the process could be reversed. The awful outward-going would suddenly become an inward-going and soon we'd be together again and could touch each other and take each other in our arms like *The Catcher in the Rye* and be real human beings again.

And I further say that anything else, any other course, leads to a graveyard, a corporeal and linguistic graveyard. The silly dialogue with which I began writing could be my funeral oration in that linguistic graveyard. Oh, we aren't dead yet, I would have to admit. But if something isn't done our demise isn't very far off, as civilizations are born and killed. And if we are really headed for that great lexicon in the sky, I have a feeling we won't have left behind nearly as interesting a language as did our forebears, the ancient Greeks.

Study Questions

1. What does the fictional situation of Monroe and Miss Tittywopp contribute to the essay?
2. What is the central concern of the essay? State that concern in the syllogism around which Weatherly's argument actually is developed.
3. What division does the author use? How does this division help him prove his minor premise?
4. What kinds of detail are used to illustrate each section of the division? How are these arranged?
5. Does Weatherly keep his major concern hidden until the end of the essay? If not, point out sentences that reveal that concern earlier.
6. How convincing is Weatherly's argument? How do division and details contribute to its effectiveness?

Does Anyone Have Time to Think?   NORMAN COUSINS

We in America have been concerned for some years with the lot of under-privileged peoples throughout the world. But we have yet to do anything for one of the most underprivileged peoples of all. Ourselves.

We have more food than we can eat. We have more money per person than anywhere else in the world; with 6 percent of the population we hold 80 percent of the wealth. We have bigger homes, bigger television sets, bigger cars, bigger theaters, bigger schools. We have everything we need, in fact, except the most important thing of all—time to think and the habit of thought. We lack time for the one indispensable for safety of an individual or a nation.

Thought is the basic energy in human history. Civilization is put together not by machines but by thought. Similarly, man's uniqueness is represented not by his ability to make objects but to sort them and relate them. Other animals practice communication; only man has the capacity for comprehension. Displace or eliminate thought, and the species itself has as little claim on survival as the dinosaurs with the four-foot skulls and the pea-sized brains. The impotence of the brute alongside the power of the sage is represented by thought.

Consider where we in America stand today. We have been told and we have told ourselves that we have the responsibility to lead. We are asked to keep freedom alive; we are asked to find some way to prevent a war that would incinerate one billion or more human beings and twist and deform the rest. It is not a simple task. Leadership today requires not so much a determination to smash the other fellow as an understanding of the lessons of human experience. It requires a profound knowledge of the diseases of civilizations. It requires ability to anticipate the effects of actions. In short, it requires thought. But who is doing the thinking? Who is giving sustained and incisive thought to the most complicated and dangerous problem in the age of man?

Next question: Does anyone have time to think? Does the President have time to think? The daily calendar of an American President, with its endless appointments and gladhanding chores, not only excludes sustained thought but creates the kind of staccato, jangling pattern of mental activity that leads to a demand for surcease rather than study. A day on the golf links thus becomes a useful cathartic for eliminating congested impressions and helping a man to retain his sanity, but it doesn't necessarily provide the occasion for concentrated and consecutive thought.

If the President has no time to think, then who? Almost everyone in Washington is spending so much time being strategical that almost no one is being historical. There are so many movers and shakers that there is hardly any room for thinkers.

This is not a political party matter; the churning and flailing easily cross

Norman Cousins, "Does Anyone Have Time to Think?" *Present Tense: An American Editor's Odyssey* (New York: McGraw-Hill, 1967), pp. 222–224. Originally published as an editorial in *Saturday Review*, March 26, 1955. By permission of the author.

party lines. Washington does not exist in terrible isolation. Washington can be only a reflection and a projection of the national character and temperament. If officeholders are too busy to think, do they differ from the business executive, college president, teacher, man on the assembly line, or housewife?

The paradox, of course, is that we are busy doing nothing. Never before has so much leisure time been available to so many. Leisure hours now exceed working hours. But we have a genius for cluttering. We have somehow managed to persuade ourselves that we are too busy to think, too busy to read, too busy to look back, too busy to look ahead, too busy to understand that all our wealth and all our power are not enough to safeguard our future unless there is also a real understanding of the danger that threatens us and how to meet it. Thus, being busy is more than merely a national passion; it is a national excuse.

The real question, however, concerns not the time or lack of it we provide for thought, but the value we place on thought. What standing does thoughtfulness enjoy in the community at large? What great works of contemporary literature assign importance to thought or make heroes of thoughtful men? Action, accumulation, diversion—these seem to be the great imperatives. We are so busy entertaining ourselves and increasing the size and ornamentations of our personal kingdoms that we have hardly considered that no age in history has had as many loose props under it as our own.

Everyone seems to agree, from the President down, that we have to find some way other than war to protect ourselves, support the cause of freedom in the world, and serve the cause of man. But who is giving any consecutive thought to an "other way"? We ask the world's peoples to spurn the idea of communism, and we back up this advice with the offer of guns, but what revolutionary idea do we ourselves espouse? War in Asia seems all too imminent but we talk about it as though it is some unpleasant little business at a distance instead of the curtain raiser for a war in which the big bombs will be dropped on America just as surely as they will be dropped on the enemy. Meanwhile, we are told by government that there is no real defense against atomic attack, after all. Surely all this requires some thought.

This nation of ours will not reproduce itself automatically. The meaning and the wonder of it will not be sustained by momentum alone. If we have something worth saving, as we have, somewhere in our national culture or economy we shall have to find a proper place for thought.

There is no point in passing the buck or looking for guilty parties. We got where we are because of the busy man in the mirror.

Study Questions

1. Cousins' major premise could be worded: "Time to think is absolutely necessary to ensure survival of our culture and economy." What are his minor premise and conclusion? To which of the three parts of the syllogism does he devote most words to proving?

2. What effect on the reader is Cousins trying to achieve in the first paragraph? What effect does he strive for in his second paragraph? Does he achieve his intended effects?

3. Although this essay develops one main syllogism, there are a number of lesser syllogisms that help to support the main one. For example, in paragraph 4, the writer makes the statement that leadership "requires thought," which serves as a major premise for a sequential argument. The next paragraph proves the minor premise of that syllogism. What is that premise? From these two premises, what conclusion must be stated? How does this conclusion help support the main syllogism?

4. Underline the logical transitions in the essay. How does the writer make questions serve as transitions?

5. This essay was written in 1955 and speaks of "imminent" war in Asia. Given present circumstances, does Cousins seem to have been a prophet? Does his argument still seem valid?

The Classified Minds

ARCHIBALD MacLEISH

... When the Attorney General brings a suit to kill a newspaper story every-thing is at stake: not only worth and competence but the future of the Republic itself. For the Republic is a self-governing society, and no society can govern itself if the apparatus of government, the bureaucracy temporarily in power, can cut it off from the source of all government, the facts.

Mr. Lincoln put the proposition in iron words a century and more ago. What we have in this country, Mr. Lincoln said—what must not be allowed to vanish from the earth—is government of the people, by the people and for the people. Which means that the government we do not have is government against the people. But what act of government could be more obviously an act against the people than the Attorney General's? It is not *The Times* which will suffer if publication of this material is enjoined: *The Times* has other stories to fill its columns. The sufferers will be the people in their grave and difficult task of governing themselves.

And they will suffer not at the periphery of their responsibility but at the center of it, for the question with which the challenged articles deal is the ques-tion of peace or war, meaning in the most literal sense the question of life and death—the life and death not only of armies but of nations also—including very possibly our own.

What we as a self-governing people need to know at this particular moment of our bewildering time—what we need to know more than anything else in the dark around us—is whether our Asian war is a war we should have fought and must now go on fighting, or whether the whole thing was, from its origins in the minds of men now dead, a calamitous mistake, a ruinous disaster. And it is precisely to this need that the material, if we may judge by the installments already printed, is addressed.

We have here, in their own words, the changing and developing opinions of some of the best informed and most respected men of the generation. Nothing could better instruct a self-governing people caught in an ambiguous and mysti-fying war than precisely these troubled voices.

But these voices, the Attorney General protests, are Top Secret voices, not available to the public ear, meaning not available to the people. They have been tagged and stamped Top Secret, and only the duly certified may listen to them. But who is to certify the listeners to a colloquy as grim as this? Mr. Hoover? And who is to stamp a thought Top Secret in a self-governing state? Who is to say for the people, "This shall be secret from us and this shall be Top Secret?"

The people accept Top Secret in "Superspy" and "Mission Impossible" but in real life they laugh at it, and with reason. There is hardly a man in the top levels of Government who hasn't lost his respect for the rubric—usually on the day when his incoming box contained a Top Secret document, the gist of which he had read in *The Washington Post* the week before.

The fact is that except in actual war, when troop movements and weapon developments and strategic planning must necessarily be confidential, there are no Government secrets. There are merely things said and done which officers of government would find it convenient to keep in a locked drawer. There is merely, that is to say, official convenience, the opposite of official embarrassment.

But in a society in which the people are responsible for governing themselves, official convenience cannot take precedence over the public need to know. And the public need to know is a strength, not a weakness. Back at the beginning of the Hitler war there were faint-hearted Americans who said a free society could never defeat a police state because the police state would keep its secrets. As it turned out the open societies drove the keepers of the secret out of Normandy and over the Rhine and discovered at Buchenwald what the secret really was.

What worries me about all this is not the classified documents. It is the classified minds. The Attorney General obviously thinks at one level only, the level of what he would call security. Having claimed the right to defend the security of the nation against the people by listening in on their telephone conversations and by building up secret police files for use against them he now, quite logically, insists on his duty to suppress facts they need to know.

It is all of a piece, but not of a piece Mr. Lincoln would have admired. To the Attorney General the Government comes first and the people after. To Mr. Lincoln the people are the Government. Even the "silent majority" may come to grasp that difference.

Study Questions

1. Construct the syllogism MacLeish presents in paragraph 1.
2. Which part of the syllogism does MacLeish attempt to prove? How does he support his argument?
3. What elements of the *ad hominem* fallacy are present in this essay? What persons does MacLeish openly refer to? How does he use these references to gain support for his position?
4. Compare the use of questions in this essay and Cousins'. In which essay is there more variety in the questions and how they are used? Point out examples in each of the questions that seem to have the same purpose.
5. How does MacLeish define "top secret," "government secrets," and "classified minds"? How are these definitions worked into the argument itself?

Social Attitudes and the Obese

JEAN MAYER

Wherever fat people have existed and whenever a literature has reflected aspects of the lives and values of the period, a record has been left of the low regard usually held for the obese by the thinner and clearly more virtuous observer.

Saint Jerome contended that "a fat paunch never breeds fine thoughts." Chesterfield declared that "obesity and stupidity are such companions that they are considered synonymous." In one of his journals Arnold Bennet referred to an acquaintance, Jimmy Glover, as a "fat man." It was as if he, having said that, need say no more.

There is a most respectable precedent for the terseness of Bennet's comment. The Old Testament (Judges 4:17) informs us that "Eglon, King of Moab, was a very fat man." It is as if the peculiar and unattractive qualities of fat people legitimize their employment as scapegoats, as licensed figures of fun, and as fit objects of contempt, abuse, and moral instruction.

Back in the days of the two-line joke, audiences were permitted to be delighted by such wheezes as these: "You should be ashamed, laughing at that fat man." "I'm just having fun at his expanse." or "Why is it you fat fellows are always good-natured?" "Because we can't either fight or run." A very thin man met a very fat man in a hotel lobby. "From the looks of you," said the fat man, "there might have been a famine." "From the looks of you," replied the thin man, "you might have caused it." Obesity has been laboriously defined as a "surplus gone to waist." And we've been told of the woman who was so fat that when she fell down, she rocked herself to sleep trying to get up.

There has always been something so fascinating about the mere fact of fatness that men of all nations and of many degrees of wisdom or lack of it have formulated opinions on the state, its origins, and its correction. Shakespeare's characters are at their most eloquent when the topic is obesity. "Make less thy body hence and more thy grace. Leave gormandizing. Know the grave doth gape for thee thrice wider than for other men." And, of course, to Julius Caesar, the Bard attributed the notion of the harmlessness of fat companions in warning against "the lean and hungry look" of "Yon Cassius."

In *Coming Up for Air*, George Orwell has the narrator, himself a fat man, sum it up: "They all think a fat man doesn't have any feelings. A man who's been fat from birth isn't quite like other men. He goes through life on a light-comedy plane . . . as low farce." Sometimes the situation is just as sad and much less tolerable. When W. D. Howells was consul at Venice, he was told by a tall lanky man, "If I were as fat as you, I would hang myself." And Osborn in his otherwise lightly satirical picture-essay, *The Vulgarians*, pontificates, "The fat and the fatuous are interchangeable."

There are, most certainly, rationalizations galore to supply seeming justification for the frequent rudeness and the occasional brutality which fat people en-

Jean Mayer, *Overweight: Causes, Cost, and Control* © 1968. Reprinted by permission of Prentice-Hall, Inc., Englewood Cliffs, New Jersey.

counter in person and in print. Obesity, as we have already noted, is usually taken to be a self-induced condition which can be easily remedied by a modest exercise of will. It is attributed to one of the easiest forms of self-indulgence in a prosperous culture. Further, over-eating where food is in abundance requires neither courage nor skill, neither learning nor guile. Gluttony demands less energy than lust, less industry than avarice. The fat human being, accordingly, is taken to be both physically and morally absurd, and to constitute a living testimony to the reality and the vapidity of his sins.

In his first popular success, *The Bridge of San Luis Rey*, Thornton Wilder says this of the obese Archbishop of Lima: "Some days he regarded his bulk ruefully; but the distress of remorse was less poignant than the distress of fasting, and he was presently found deliberating over the secret messages that a certain roast sends to a certain salad that will follow it."

Occasionally an author permits himself to be distressed at the presence of obesity and to be kindly toward its victims, to the degree of suggesting that they have little choice. Giuseppe di Lampedusa in *The Leopard* has Prince Fabrizio express his distaste for the plump young ladies of Palermo: "Incredibly short, improbably dark, unbearably giggly." He charges their condition to, among other factors, the dearth of proteins and the overabundance of starch in their food. But William Barrett, writing in *Partisan Review* of American tourists in Europe, labels them: "Eaters of soft white doughy bread, ice cream, pie and doughnuts." And Maugham reminds us: "Tolstoi made the plump Pierre Bezukjov in *War and Peace* a moral weakling.

One Michael Argyle, described as a lecturer in social psychology, informed an Oxford audience a few years ago (and the *New York Times* duly reported it) that "thin people have higher moral standards than fat people." (*New York Times*, August 2, 1961) Graham Greene, in describing the glib journalist Parkinson in the novel *The Burned-out Case* said, "Virtue had died long ago within that mountain of flesh for lack of air." Alberto Moravia went so far as to give one of his stories the title "Appetite." In it, Faustina denounces Carlo, who weighs 210 pounds, "I'm angry at you for what you are—a great fat glutton." And in *Lord of the Flies*, a book which threatened for a while to be confused with revelation, the character Piggy loomed as a flabby symbol of moral debility and ethical ineffectiveness.

All this business of devouring more food than one needs takes place and is noted in a world where for most of mankind getting enough food has always been and continues to be the difficult, even the impossible thing. On successive days in 1962, two significant stories were in the news. From Jakarta it was said that residents, described as foreigners and wealthy Indonesians, were driving 72 miles to get a loaf of bread at almost 50 cents. Then from Erzerum came word of

> a small bowl containing a little flour meal and a lot of boiled water. Its contents will serve as breakfast, lunch and dinner for several of the victims of the severe famine that grips Turkey's eastern provinces. (*New York Times*, January 19, 1962; January 20, 1962)

All wealth has been impolitely defined as theft. Is it possible that among those who are openly hostile to fat people there are some who equate the over-nourishment of one particular individual with the undernourishment, even the starvation of another?

Is there a case for such a contention, or is a cause-and-effect relationship completely absent? It would be well for the obese to know. In January of 1966 Dr. Albert Szent-Gyorgyi, Nobel Laureate in Physiology and Medicine, predicted that if the world's present rate of population growth continues, "human beings ultimately will have to kill and eat one another." It is not difficult to guess which group, the obese or the nonobese, would be likely to be the first candidates for the kitchens. In any event, fat people are fortunate that their enemies in civilized countries usually employ against them only the weapon of verbal aggression. For in certain institutions built around the command-obedience syndrome fat people have often had a painful time.

A Providence, Rhode Island judge (July 27, 1953) once ordered a woman to reduce from 225 pounds to 190 in ten weeks. A Cincinnati patrolman was fired (*New York Herald Tribune*, January 12, 1960) because he had gained 13 pounds. A Connecticut State Police commissioner embarked on a program intended to "trim his troopers." They were warned if they wanted promotions they'd better start tightening their belts. (*Boston Globe*, July 16, 1959) Much attention (*Boston Globe*, February 9, 1963) was given to the plight of an airman first class. He was five feet nine, and weighed 225 pounds, an amount held by his superiors to be 37 pounds too much. It was said that he was told to "reduce or be discharged without pension rights." In the *Saturday Evening Post* (September 25, 1965) James Phelan stated, "There are no fat FBI agents." About eight years before, all agents had been instructed to bring themselves within the limits set by an insurance chart. And from Denmark there came in September 1965 (*Boston Globe*, September 19, 1965) a new political group, the "Reform Party," which included in its program a plan to tax fat people. "For every two pounds of overweight, citizens would hand over one hour's pay every month."

Fat people do reduce. At least, some of them do. Some of these even remain reduced. When a newsmaking person embarks on or completes a weight-losing program, either the man himself or the press gives us the word. Alfred Hitchcock (*Saturday Evening Post*, August 1957) revealed that when younger he'd weighed 365 pounds, but he'd brought his weight down to 200 by eating only steak and cutting out liquor. The *New York Times* disclosed that rigid dieting had lowered the weight of Maria Callas from 215 to 135 (October 30, 1956). The *Herald Tribune* (August 25, 1958) announced that Jackie Gleason had cut down from 280 to 220. From the *Boston Globe* we learned (November 5, 1961) that Bernard Goldfine had lost 40 pounds after six months in jail. Walter Winchell (December 19, 1957) proclaimed that "Count Basie took off 50 pounds 'Off liquor, on steaks'" and that Joe Louis shed 45 pounds on the same regimen. Leonard Lyons was our source of information (*Boston Herald*, January 11, 1961) that the then Vice-President Lyndon Baines Johnson had "dieted away 31 pounds" in less than ten weeks since being elected to that post. Clearly the press believes the reducing prowess of the notable to be a matter of public interest.

The potential for this interest must have existed for a long time. And it extended to the eating habits of the celebrated, their attitudes toward their own obesity and to that of others, and their programs, if any, for defeating it. For much information of this character is available to us.

We're told that Abbot Mendel was too fat to travel comfortably, that Gibbon was so obese he could not rise, that Emperor Charles V of the Holy Roman Empire ate himself to death. Frank Harris, who had so much to say about his own behavior, said also this: "I've bought myself a stomach pump and one half hour after dinner I pump myself out." Accounts have reached us of the extreme obesity of Swift, Gautier, Balzac, Dryden (Swift's cousin), and Boccaccio, and of Lord Byron's invention of a reducing diet . . . cold boiled potatoes and wine. Axel Munthe, however, happily recalled that Maupassant "did not fancy thin women and that his Yvonne drank bottles of cod liver oil by the dozen in an unsuccessful effort to get fat."

A. T. Banker tells us that Dylan Thomas said of himself, "I am fat and slothful." O. Henry sounds almost personal in his "The Skylight Room" when he writes of "the tragedy of tallow, the bane of bulk, the calamity of corpulence." Samuel Chotzinoff has said (*Holiday*, June 1963) that Gian-Carlo Menotti "shuns fat people like the plague." And Norman Douglas cautioned, "Beware of the fat Neapolitan." Back in the 1920's there was an American popular song called "O Katerina" one of the lines of which maintained that "to win my love you must be leaner." It is rare that a writer of fiction thinks of a fat person as conceivably lovable. In *Some Came Running* James Jones has his hero Dave Hirsch say to Gwen French, "Is the truth, the reason you won't go out with me, won't have an affair with me, is it because I'm fat?" In his earlier novel, *From Here to Eternity*, Jones devised a character of pathologic brutality, whose associates gave him a nickname that he deeply hated, "Fatso." In *Summertime Ends*, a half-tract, half-novel, its author John Hargrave tells of "Trimnal the parson, a tub of lard." In a James Michener story, a character states that "the warden was fat, cowardly." And John Osborne's self-pitying Jimmy Porter in *Look Back in Anger* declaims "I'm not a pig. I just like food. That's all."

Whole novels have been written on one or another aspect of getting fat, being fat, or attempting to become less fat. Gerda Rhoads (Ballantine, 1957) wrote one called *The Lonely Women*, held to be "a frank and biting novel about the slimming industry." Another novel, *The Man Who Ate the World* (Ballantine, 1960), by Frederick Pohl dealt with Sonnie Trumie, a compulsive eater who "ate until eating was pain and then he sat there sobbing until he could eat no more." James M. Cain in *The Butterfly* wrote largely about a woman's heroic efforts to reduce. And back in 1922 Henri Beraud won the Prix Goncourt with his *The Martyrdom of the Obese*.

The obese, let it be noted, are not completely without friends. The *New York Times* (December 9, 1962) in its 1962 appeal for help for the "One Hundred Neediest Cases" included two fat girls. Case 2 was Etta, nine years old and "seriously overweight—may require extensive therapy, since doctors can find no physical cause for her obesity." Case 8 was Fanny. She was "fifteen, weighs 180 pounds and is so ridiculed by her schoolmates she often refuses to go to school." Aldous Huxley (*Ends and Means*) asserts that "people have a right to be plump." The 230-pound president of the Club Sympathique des Femmes

Fortes (*Boston Traveler*, March 14, 1957) exulted, "The fat woman is a Rubens who doesn't know it." Edward Weeks (*Atlantic Monthly*, October 1965) confided: "There is something about a fat man that invites confidence." And the New York columnist Jimmy Breslin (*Boston Globe*, September 24, 1963) found in Queens (or in his heart) a six-foot-five saloon-keeper named Gibby. Gibby, Breslin alleged, weighed 611½ pounds and his wife, Eileen, was said to insist there were "acres and acres of him and they're all mine."

These are a few shining exceptions in a world that looks at fat people and likes them not and sometimes seems to wish them ill. Even those servants moving toward mastery, the machines, may have received and welcomed the message. For the *New York Times* of January 26, 1962 had an ominous Associated Press account from London. In busy Victoria Station there was an "I-speak-your-weight machine." "One night recently . . . an unusually obese man stepped on the scales." The machine's voice reported the man's weight as 18-stone-7 (259 pounds). And then, "it went on chanting '18-stone-7, 18-stone-7, 18-stone-7' for the next ten minutes until a repair man finally muzzled it."

The anthropologist, Dr. Ashley Montagu, supplies an explanation for the occurrence of instances of public approval of obesity. "Obesity in some cultures," he says, "constitutes a validation of both success of the male and of his obese female. In some African, Polynesian and Middle Eastern cultures, women and sometimes men (particularly those of high caste) were especially fattened as a form of both conspicuous consumption and social desirability." Montagu continues,

> . . . being well-padded came to stand not only for affluence but also for the ability to survive. Thus, to this day in regions where food is abundant, many mothers in the Western world do not consider that their young children are prospering unless they approximate a globe. Such a globular view of the ability to survive probably harks back to the time when food was less abundant and the focus of attention was on keeping children adequately nourished.

The time "when food was less abundant" for millions of people in the United States was not so long ago. In his book, *Eat, Drink, and Be Wary*, published in 1935, I. G. Schlink declared that "only about 10 per cent of the population received an income which permits them to eat good, well-selected foods in adequate amounts." A year later Paul de Kruif, in *Why Keep Them Alive*, stated, "Malnourished wretchedness among children is widespread, notorious, too terrible for any luckier, well-fed human being to face and go on living." In the *Atlantic Monthly* of January 1937, Maxine Davis in an article called "Hungry Children" wrote that the Children's Bureau, examining households in Atlanta, Memphis, Racine, Terre Haute, . . . found "one-fifth of the families' diet consisted of bread, beans, and potatoes." And David Shannon in his *The Great Depression* refers to a speech made by Congressman George Huddleston of Alabama on January 5, 1932 before a subcommittee on manufacturing, in which the Representative insisted that "men are actually starving by the thousands today, children are being stunted by lack of food, old people are having their lives cut short." It is surely not strange that attitudes formed during days when starvation was for some a fact and for others a threat should lead many in the abundant today to eat too much, and many to become obese.

It is useful to remember that these days are not altogether over, even in overfed, prosperous America. In 1967 we still have some ill-fed and actually underfed groups in the United States: Negro cotton farm workers displaced by mechanization of cotton-picking and replacement of cotton by corn crops in Alabama and Mississippi; migrant farm workers—on the Eastern stream, mostly Negroes, and on the West Coast stream, mostly Mexicans; Indian denizens of certain reservations; groups of Alaskan Eskimos and Indians; and some of the poorest inhabitants of our big-city slums.

That social attitudes may in turn affect the prevalence of obesity in a particular community is strongly indicated by some of the results of the Midtown Manhattan Study. This study was originally designed to be a comprehensive survey of the epidemiology of mental illness. One hundred and ten thousand individuals—all the adults between 20 and 59 years of age who occupied a certain residential area in New York City—were the group investigated. A major focus of the survey was the relationship between social class and mental illness, and an important discovery was the striking relationship between socio-economic status and obesity. Moore, Stunkard, and Srole examined the correlation between weight-to-height relationship and socio-economic status and found that it was high, particularly in women. The prevalence of obesity was seven times higher among women reared in the lowest social-class category as compared with those raised in the highest category.

This finding was later independently confirmed by Ernest Abramson who stated, "In an investigation of body weight in Swedish women, we found that women from the highest income group did not increase in weight after the age of 35, while women from lower income groups increased in weight up to over 60 years of age."

Moore, Stunkard, and Srole were understandably elated over the finding in regard to the class-conditioned character of obesity presented by the Midtown Manhattan Study data. It, they believe,

> has profound implications for theory and therapy. For it means that whatever its genetic and biochemical determinants, obesity in man is susceptible to an extraordinary degree of control by social factors. It suggests that a broad-scale assault on the problem need not await further understanding of the physiological determinants of obesity.

What they look to is "a program of education and control designed to reproduce certain critical influences to which society has already exposed its upper-class members."

I must confess to being a little less sanguine than my Philadelphia friends. For one thing, I am not as sure of the interpretation of their study as they are. This is in part because my own results, among an admittedly much smaller group of adolescents, in a more homogeneous community (Newton, Massachusetts), did not show much correlation between obesity and social class (in spite of their demonstrating once again the familial character of obesity). This may mean—and the Swedish results tend to suggest it—that social pressures are most useful as regards the control of "creeping" middle-age obesity in hitherto nonobese subjects, while they exert little influence on obesity among the young.

Another variable may be that in New York the different ethnic groups are characterized at the same time by different tendencies to obesity and by different socio-economic background. Few people would deny that white Protestants in New York City belong to a higher social class on the average than the Puerto Ricans. Their body types are anthropologically different and it is not unreasonable to think that there may be differences in susceptibility to obesity. Within the white group, Anglo-Saxon Episcopalians are at the same time richer and more ectomorphic than Germanic Lutherans, and hence a comparison between two subgroups does—in part for genetic reasons—appear to confirm the primacy of the environment.

Finally, my study showing a strong bias in college admissions against obese boys and even more against obese girls makes me wonder whether a cause-and-effect relationship is not also involved: to stay with the ladies (who show by far the strongest correlation between overweight and social class in the Manhattan study), an obese girl has only one-third as much chance to get into a "prestige" college, the college of her choice, or indeed any college, as a nonobese girl. She is thus likely to go down in socio-economic status. Decreased likelihood of advancing socially through marriage is also an obvious penalty which the obese girl—the ugly duckling of our age—has to pay. She may thus be lower-class because she is obese, as much as or rather than, be obese because she is lower-class.

This is not to say that I would not welcome a large-scale program based on education, on the creation of recreational facilities, and on the recognition of existing social pressures to try to control our mounting prevalence of obesity. Understanding of existing attitudes is essential if such a mass program is to succeed. (We shall see that it is equally essential if one is going to deal intelligently with a single individual.) People who are not fat have attitudes, mostly hostile, toward those who are. People who are fat have attitudes, mostly self-deprecatory, toward themselves. And when an entire segment of society—the most prosperous citizens, in this instance, of a large urban community—give obesity a strong negative value, its members, within the limits of their genetic possibilities and latitude of choosing their mode of life, control their obesity better than people who despise it less.

Study Questions

1. Does the author state his case inductively or deductively? State the syllogism which governs the essay.
2. Which of the parts of the syllogism does Mayer devote most of the essay to proving?

3. Mainly, how does Mayer prove his argument—with examples, statistics, or what?
4. Do you think this method of proof serves his purpose well? Why or why not?
5. Do you feel Mayer's essay is clear and concise or do you find it somewhat confusing in places? Give an example to back up your response.

Evil: The Root of the Problem   HELEN E. ELLIS

At least since man began to form societies, he has been concerned about evil. He has attempted to define what constitutes evil, what kinds of evil are crimes against man, what are sins against God, what are both. He has conceived a moral system, a definition of the good and the bad. In all ages, however, he has allowed superstition to influence and pervert his morality by designating as "good" or "evil" uncontrollable aspects of nature. The shape of one's body, his ethnic heritage, the place of his birth are all as outside the realm of morality as is weather. They belong to the amorality of nature itself. As yellow grass is not bad and green grass good, so yellow skin is not bad and white skin good. Both grass and skin, because they exist within nature, exist outside morality; for morality is a concept man intellectualizes. His mind determines what is the good and the evil, what is positive and what negative within his society. What his mind can ultimately designate as good or evil are abstracts or concepts. For example, hatred is an emotion, an abstract, since we cannot see it or touch it but can only see or touch its results. We can see the twisted face which reflects inner hate; we can see and touch the harmed body or other physical consequence of hate. Murder, then, though it is evil in itself, also is the result of evil —of hate or fear or some other emotion which gave rise to the act of murder.

Marshall McLuhan's statement that "the medium is the message" applies as strongly to evil as to communication media: "Consequences of any medium— that is, of any extension of ourselves—result from the new scale that is introduced into our affairs by each extension of ourselves."* In other words, the consequences of any extension of ourselves are caused by any extension of ourselves. Certainly an act of evil is an extension of ourselves, so we might say that an act of evil is caused by an act of evil, which emanates from evil. The point here is simply to say that evil might be viewed as a spiral which circles

Reprinted by permission.
*Marshall McLuhan, *Understanding Media: The Extensions of Man* (New York: New American Library, 1964), p. 23.

inward to the greatest evil, which is not only the acme of all evils but the "medium" or evil itself. I am not, however, about to propose that man himself is the greatest of evils, but rather to say that all evil, as well as all good, arises from man himself; thus of necessity there exists in man the potential both for the greatest evil and the greatest good, which can be realized as man extends himself through his acts.

What man has considered to be the greatest evil has depended on the nature of his society. In a society in which water is scarce, the greatest evil might be to drink more than one's share of the available supply. In a society based on the freedom to live, murder might be the greatest evil. Dante, in his *Divine Comedy*, assigned the betrayers or traitors to benefactors to the lowest circle of the Inferno. Shakespeare's King Lear claimed that the greatest evil is filial ingratitude. Goethe's Faust committed the greatest evil by demanding access to all knowledge. The Ten Commandments rank as the greatest evil the placing of other gods before the one God. All of these evils, however, as well as such common ones as rape, theft, and other acts of inhumanity, can be seen to have a common element, what we might call a first cause or greatest evil from which they result. Each of them arises from man's egoism.

It is necessary first to consider the difference between the "egoist" and the "egotist." An egoist is a person who believes that his own needs and desires are the legitimate motives for all his acts. An egotist, on the other hand, is merely a person who exaggerates his own importance. It can be seen that the words are not synonymous, but that the concept of egotism is contained within the larger, more inclusive word "egoism." I would suggest that the greatest of all evils is the concept of egoism, the centering of all of life around oneself. We can see how all evils arise from the egoist doctrine. To betray one's benefactor, for example, is to put one's own interests before those of others. To be ungrateful to one's parents is to put one's own concerns first; to desire all knowledge is to distort by magnification one's individual capacity and right; to break the First Commandment is to put oneself before God and thus make of oneself a god. All of the evil extensions of man in our society—war, poverty, prejudice, pollution, crime—are the messages that result from the medium: egoism. All of them can be traced to this one belief in the supreme value of oneself.

The philosopher Nietzsche, who denounced morality as "the mob instinct," called for a superman who could put his own vision ahead of all other considerations, and for its achievement could take any action, even annihilation of his fellow man. The superman he envisioned was the greatest evil incarnate, the absolute egoist. Judeo-Christian morality recognizes the greatest of evils as egoism when it admonishes man to "do unto others as you would have them do unto you." To perfectly comply with this injunction would be to achieve the opposite of the greatest evil—the greatest good. Only by learning to be other-directed can man overcome his egoism. Only by analyzing his motives for every act can man dig out the truth of his own evil and, by recognizing it, overcome it. Only when all people can admit that their membership in the brotherhood of man is equal only to that of all others can the greatest evil be eradicated. Only then will all evil end.

Study Questions

1. What syllogisms underlie the material presented in the introduction?
2. What is the sequential argument used to lead to the conclusion "the greatest evil is egoism"? What part of that argument does the largest portion of the essay attempt to demonstrate?
3. The conclusion of the essay is also built around a syllogism. What is it? Does it pertain to evil, good, or morality in general? Is it valid? Why is it the major syllogism of the essay, even if it is not developed in the argument proper?
4. List all words which the writer defines in the essay. Are these definitions essential? Which of them is most important to the essay?
5. Is the main-idea sentence of this essay explicitly stated? If so, underline it. If not, write a sentence which you think states the writer's main idea.

Race: A Study in Superstition   JACQUES BARZUN

Suppose for a moment that the word and concept "Race" were wholly alien to our thought and vocabulary, and that someone to whom it was familiar were trying to tell us what it meant. How could he go about it? He might begin by saying that a race was a group of people of all ages and sexes who were found in one place and resembled one another. We should certainly object to the definition as being too vague. How large is "one place" and what does "resemblance" mean? In some ways all men resemble one another; but in another way, no two individuals are alike. Even supposing that our interlocutor mentioned a white skin and light hair as the signs denoting a given race, we should find it difficult to agree on the precise point where white skin ends and dark begins among individuals. The Berbers of North Africa are blue-eyed and lighter-skinned than the Sicilians, and as Shaw has pointed out, a really *white* man would be a horrible sight. The same difficulty would arise about light hair or brown eyes; indeed, all the characteristics of the human body that might be named as criteria would be found in actuality to merge into a finely graded series which one can break up into groups only by being arbitrary and saying, "I shall call this man white, and that one, a shade darker, black." Moreover, we should find that, contrary to common opinion, no set of fixed characteristics occurs in human beings as a constant distinguishing mark of race. So-called Nordics have long skulls, but so have many so-called Negroes, the Eskimos, and the anthropoid apes. The "Mongolian" birth-spot occurs among the whites, and the Ainos of Japan frequently show features that should class them as "Nordics."

This lack of uniformity is bad enough but we could also stump our informant with another query. What if the striking differences of skin and hair and eyes were more striking than significant? A knowledge of the normal life of men in society suggests that a Japanese scientist is in many ways more like an American scientist than either is like a manual laborer of his own color. In other words, it is fallacious to consider human beings as mere arrangements of organs, apart from their functions, their habits, and their minds.

If we voiced this objection, the word "Mind" would probably recall to our friend the great differences among the shapes of the human skull, thought to be related to mental differences, and expressible in index numbers. But if we forced him to be a little clearer about what is meant by *dolichocephalic* and *brachycephalic* and what can be inferred from this classification of skulls ... we should soon find ourselves in a maze of contradictions fit to make us despair of discovering a reliable token of race.

True, another word than Mind is for many people the clue to race. That word is Blood. For the French and German racists "blood" is an infallible oracle giving answers to all questions. Conversations with intelligent Nazis convinces one that for them the phrase *"Mein Blut spricht"* is no figure of speech. In their minds, blood is synonymous with race, with conscience, with honesty, with artistic judgment, and with a sense of their own superiority. To more prosaic minds blood is merely a tissue which is carried in a serous fluid and which circulates through the body. The blood of neither parent is directly communicated to the offspring and the properties of any individual's blood are not ascertainable without fairly complicated tests, which, according to competent serologists, have nothing to do with determining race. It seems difficult to form a clear idea of what the world is talking about when it says "Race." What next? Well, one might frame a definition by borrowing from animal husbandry: a race is the total number of descendants from common ancestors, that is, all the offspring from one pair of progenitors. Adam and Eve are the traditional human pair in Christendom, but they hardly help if one is looking for distinct races in mankind. One pair of ancestors would obviously make us all of one race. How account for the "striking differences" that caught our attention earlier? It is not usual for "white" parents to give birth to "Hindu" children. The divergence between a supposed original pair of ancestors and their offspring must have occurred somewhere. The influence of environment readily suggests itself as a cause of modification. In other words, we arrive naturally at the climate-theory of races, which has had a long and troubled history. It includes all explanations from accounting for a dark skin by the heat of the sun to interpreting German philosophy as a result of fog and heavy annual rainfall. At this juncture two questions arise: How do "striking characters" get transmitted from parent to progeny? and What are the results of mixing strikingly different groups?

The answer to the first question is the subject of a whole science, Genetics, and its most competent students are the most hesitant to give categorical answers. Some of the facts of heredity are known, but these are few compared to the questions that one could ask. This is not the place and I have not the competence to deal with the technical problems of heredity. What few general remarks can be made will be found further on, together with the simple conclusion that the idea of race as it is used in politics and social life will not be tenable until we know something definite about the transmission of non-physical traits. To build racial anthropologies without a comprehensive genetics is like starting a house with the roof. This self-evident proposition has, nevertheless, not deterred even the best scientific minds of this and the preceding century. That is why we cannot stop the discussion of race here, but must show in detail how absurd and unsubstantial its manifold dogmas are.

We are no nearer finding out what a race is by asking biology than we are by measuring skulls or judging at sight on the basis of pigmentation. The remaining methods are even less promising. First comes history. We can arbitrarily go back to the time of the Germanic invasions in the fourth and fifth centuries A.D. and find in the struggle of peoples after the Fall of Rome the origin of modern races. We shall then juggle with the names of Celts, Gauls, Iberians, Ligurians, Helvetii, Belgae, Brythons, Latins, Franks, Normans, Saxons, Goths, Angles, Jutes, Lombards, and Burgundians. But when it comes to determining who these were, where they lived, whether they survived, what they looked like, and whether in our day the French writer, Rémy de Gourmont, is a Gaul or a Norman—one man's guess is nearly as good as another's. Next we can try nationalism. We can assert, with Sir Arthur Keith, that a race and a nation are synonymous; that several hundred years of a common history and a common way of life have welded people of divergent physiques into one race. That definition hardly defines. Under it, the "renegade Englishman," Houston Stewart Chamberlain, who elected Germany as his Fatherland, would be of German race. The language spoken is an equally unsatisfactory criterion. By that token Henry James and Joseph Conrad would be of the same race, though one was born in New York and the other in the Ukraine. Some people are bilingual, and the race of a headwaiter would be beyond conjecture.

As for "centuries of common history," that is a familiar metaphor, but it is inexact as a statement of fact. No human being lives through centuries of common "history" and what anyone picks up of the past through education or common report varies with social class, education, and intelligence. The "common way of life" is equally fallacious, except in self-contained, one-class communities; and this is true in spite of the tremendous power over mass emotions which the press, the cinema, and the radio have acquired in recent times. They are powerful agents of assimilation but they have not yet created distinct breeds of men. The fact that one can make all Western Europeans believe for a time in atrocity stories or flying saucers is no test of their belonging to the same race. It only proves them to be men by proving them to be gullible. We are still far from our original goal, which was to understand what the separate, unmixable races of men might be.

But if we give up the pursuit on our own account, we must still see what men who have written about race think it is. Their ideas form, not a definition of race, for they disagree among themselves, but a mode of thought to which I give the name race-thinking and which is easily recognizable.

Race-thinking does not consist merely in believing a particular theory about human races, and to refute the believer in Aryan or Nordic supremacy would not suffice to show up the error that underlies the notion of a Nordic or Aryan race. It would only let the disillusioned racist fall into the arms of the Celticist, the Yellow-Peril fanatic, or the dolichocephalic anthropologist. What must be uprooted is the passion for labeling and classifying groups on insufficient evidence. The remarkable wish to generalize and impute individual traits to masses of people with whom we have no acquaintance is an everyday occurrence. "The Japanese are a crafty and imitative race." "Isn't that typically American?" "That is a Jewish trait." "Nordic self-control." Why do we all feel an inward satisfaction in mouthing these groundless platitudes? Why does it take conscious restraint to keep from doing it? Some answers will be suggested throughout this book. At this point it is needful only to note that if one cliché or theory is destroyed by facts, the mind that entertained it is not proof against adopting another. The strength or weakness of the notion does not affect the liability of the mind to repeating its error. In short, race-thinking is a habit. It is not confined to the anthropologists and ethnologists, the historians and publicists who make up systems or preach discrimination; race-thinking occurs whenever someone, in a casual or considered remark, implies the truth of any of the following propositions:

1. That mankind is divided into unchanging natural types, recognizable by physical features, which are transmitted "through the blood" and that permit distinctions to be made between "pure" and "mixed" races.
   Example: "The races amongst whom the Greeks planted themselves were in some cases on a similar level of culture. Where the natives were still backward or barbarous, they came of a stock either closely related to the Greek or at least separated from it by no great physical differences. Amalgamation with the native races was easy and it involved neither physical nor intellectual degeneracy as its consequence. Of the races with which the Greeks came in contact the Thracian was far from the highest in the scale of culture; yet two of the greatest names in the Great Age of Athens are those of men who had Thracian blood in their veins, Cimon and the historian Thucydides." (E. M. Walker, *Encyclopaedia Britannica*, 14th ed., X, 766.)

2. That the mental and moral behavior of human beings can be related to physical structure, and that knowledge of the structure or of the racial label which denotes it provides a satisfactory account of the behavior.
   Example: "In March last [the book] was subjected to a brief but pungent critique by Du Bois-Reymond, the celebrated Perpetual Secretary of the Academy of Sciences in Berlin. . . . He thus exposes himself to the suspicion —which, unhappily, is not weakened by his other writings—that the fiery Celtic blood of his country occasionally runs away with him, converting

him for the time into a scientific Chauvin." (John Tyndall, *Fragments of Science*, I, 385.)

3. That individual personality, ideas, and capacities, as well as national culture, politics, and morals, are the products of social entities variously termed race, nation, class, family, whose causative force is clear without further definition or inquiry into the connection between the group and the spiritual "product."

Example: "Yet there is in Celtdom a certain literary feeling which does not exist in Anglo-Saxondom. It is diffused, no doubt, and appreciative rather than creative, and lacking in the sterner critical spirit which is so necessary to all creative work; still it is there, and it is delighted with the rolling sound of the noble phrase. . . . So far then, as a man three-parts Celt, I was by nature inclined to the work of words." (Arthur Machen, *Far Off Things*, 86.)

These three types of race-thinking naturally merge into one another. Few writers limit themselves to any one type, and mankind at large uses all three with equal readiness according to the occasion. The formal rejection of the fallacy in one guise does not protect against its other guises. When race seems inappropriate, nation does the same work, and from nation the shift is easy to the family, class, college, or vague "tradition." We thus get not only the Celtic or the Jewish mind, but the German or the Greek mind, and also the bourgeois and the Harvard mind, and beyond this (as we find in biographies, novels, and plays), the X-, Y-, or Z-family mind which is made to account for the hero's personality, achievements, and failings.

This critique of a common practice may seem a denial of the obvious fact that people who belong to the same family, nation, climate, class, or "race" have a tendency to think alike, perhaps even to look alike. No such denial is made or implied. What is asserted and implied is that *these similarities, if they exist, must be shown.* They must not be merely presumed. The particular individual of whom the group quality is predicated must be studied in his own person and in his relation to the group before the "explanatory" label can be affixed. The need to do this is obvious. The mind's tendency is to assume greater simplicity and regularity in nature than actually exists. Possibly, if we could study environment, descent, nation, climate, and class like natural objects, and if they stayed put, again like natural objects, we might draw tenable conclusions about their role in shaping human character. But we are nowhere near this stage of investigation, and the race-thinker, whatever his affiliation, does not even conceive the lack. He takes ready-made the names by which we refer to the supposed factors and from the name deduces arbitrarily what he wishes to find: the Mongolians are crafty; the Dutch have no sense of humor; brachycephalic people are excitable; the Aryan is a born leader. Finally, persuaded by his own glibness, the race believer comes to see only those instances that seem to bear out his preconceived notion. He may not consciously suppress evidence against his thesis, but he becomes blind to its existence and immune to its presentation by others.

The race-formula is applied to groups and individuals and to the quick and the dead. As a classical scholar has pointed out in treating of the familiar "character" of ancient peoples—Greek equipoise, Roman gravity, and so forth: "Our reverence for scientific method has made us the more prone to pick out a single characteristic of a people as a convenient label for a pigeon-hole and then ignore other possible descriptions. We talk glibly of the Greek mind, the medieval mind, and the like—as if there has ever been more than one kind of mind—and we forget that it is merely environment that emphasizes one fashion at a given time, in thought as in dress, without, however, obliterating other fashions. Certainly the prevailing temper or trait is illuminating, but it must not so focus our attention upon itself as to exclude other attitudes or traits which in their aggregate may be more significant." (M. Hadas, *Classical Journal*, Oct., 1935, 18.)

The connection between race-thinking and scientific method is especially paradoxical. One would think that the so-called scientific habit of thought would encourage care in dealing with details and differences. It should seem as though the object under consideration, be it a man or a group, would be looked at from all sides, seen as it really is. The very opposite has happened. The inclination is to lump individuals together on the most superficial, unverified grounds of similarity and describe them en masse. We class, as it were, all white powders as bicarbonate of soda and dispense them on that convenient principle. When such a mode of thought becomes quasi-universal, sinks out of the conscious mind to reappear in everybody's mouth as the most obvious of truths, then it is no exaggeration to term it a superstition on a par with the belief in witchcraft and horoscopes.

To sum up: a satisfactory definition of race is not to be had. The formulas in common use do not really define or do not accord with the facts, so that a prudent man will suspend judgment until genetics can offer a more complete body of knowledge. But to expect prudence in thinking about subjects charged with political emotion is folly too; and so we find the racists of the past 150 years leaping over the initial obstacle to race-theorizing, making assumptions to suit their object and failing to define their terms, just like the man in the street who borrows their language without questioning its validity.

Study Questions

1. Though Barzun devotes considerable time and space to the demonstration of two major points, he begins his essay without an introduction. Outline or write one that might serve as an appropriate beginning to his argument.
2. In the summing up, he begins with two statements that are actually conclusions to the two sequential arguments that are developed in the essay. What are those arguments and which part of the essay is devoted to each?
3. Barzun points out that prejudice or "race-thinking" is often the result

of fallacious reasoning. What specific fallacies does he discuss and how does he prove that the thinking that entertains them is illogical?

4. Where and how does Barzun use definition and division as a structural device for part of his essay?

5. In other parts of his essay, he uses other structural methods we have studied. What are they, and how do they help organize his material?

6. Barzun's argument is not only about "race" and "race-thinking." He also proposes a way in which both can be avoided. What is the mode of thinking he advocates? What material in the body of the essay and conclusion suggests that Barzun is pessimistic about the likelihood of finding this kind of behavior in man? What do you think Barzun's definition of man or of man's social behavior would be?

A Modest Proposal   JONATHAN SWIFT

*For Preventing the Children of Poor People in Ireland
from Being a Burden to Their Parents or Country,
and for Making Them Beneficial to the Public*

It is a melancholy object to those who walk through this great town or travel in the country, when they see the streets, the roads, and cabin doors, crowded with beggars of the female-sex, followed by three, four, or six children, all in rags and importuning every passenger for an alms. These mothers, instead of being able to work for their honest livelihood, are forced to employ all their time in strolling to beg sustenance for their helpless infants, who, as they grow up, either turn thieves for want of work, or leave their dear native country to fight for the Pretender in Spain, or sell themselves to the Barbadoes.

I think it is agreed by all parties that this prodigious number of children in the arms, or on the backs, or at the heels of their mothers, and frequently of their fathers, is in the present deplorable state of the kingdom a very great additional grievance; and therefore whoever could find out a fair, cheap, and easy method of making these children sound, useful members of the commonwealth would deserve so well of the public as to have his statue set up for a preserver of the nation.

But my intention is very far from being confined to provide only for the children of professed beggars; it is of a much greater extent, and shall take in the whole number of infants at a certain age who are born of parents in effect as little able to support them as those who demand our charity in the streets.

As to my own part, having turned my thoughts for many years upon this important subject, and maturely weighed the several schemes of other projectors, I have always found them grossly mistaken in their computation. It is true, a child just dropped from its dam may be supported by her milk for a solar year, with little other nourishment; at most not above the value of two shillings, which the mother may certainly get, or the value in scraps, by her lawful occupation of begging; and it is exactly at one year old that I propose to provide for them in such a manner as instead of being a charge upon their parents or the parish, or wanting food and raiment for the rest of their lives, they shall on the contrary contribute to the feeding, and partly to the clothing, of many thousands.

There is likewise another great advantage in my scheme, that it will prevent those voluntary abortions, and that horrid practice of women murdering their bastard children, alas, too frequent among us, sacrificing the poor innocent babes, I doubt, more to avoid the expense than the shame, which would move tears and pity in the most savage and inhuman breast.

The number of souls in this kingdom being usually reckoned one million and a half, of these I calculate there may be about two hundred thousand couple whose wives are breeders; from which number I subtract thirty thousand couples who are able to maintain their own children, although I apprehend there cannot be so many under the present distresses of the kingdom; but this being granted, there will remain an hundred and seventy thousand breeders. I again subtract fifty thousand for those women who miscarry, or whose children die by accident or disease within the year. There only remain an hundred and twenty thousand children of poor parents annually born. The question therefore is, how this number shall be reared and provided for, which, as I have already said, under the present situation of affairs, is utterly impossible by all the methods hitherto proposed. For we can neither employ them in handicraft or agriculture; we neither build houses (I mean in the country) nor cultivate land. They can very seldom pick up a livelihood by stealing till they arrive at six years old, except where they are of towardly parts; although I confess they learn the rudiments much earlier, during which time they can however be looked upon only as probationers, as I have been informed by a principal gentleman in the county of Cavan, who protested to me that he never knew above one or two instances under the age of six, even in a part of the kingdom so renowned for the quickest proficiency in that art.

I am assured by our merchants that a boy or a girl before twelve years old is no salable commodity; and even when they come to this age they will not yield above three pounds, or three pounds and half a crown at most on the Exchange; which cannot turn to account either to the parents or the kingdom, the charge of nutriment and rags having been at least four times that value.

I shall now therefore humbly propose my own thoughts, which I hope will not be liable to the least objection.

I have been assured by a very knowing American of my acquaintance in London, that a young healthy child well nursed is at a year old a most delicious, nourishing, and wholesome food, whether stewed, roasted, baked, or boiled; and I make no doubt that it will equally serve in a fricassee or a ragout.

I do therefore humbly offer it to public consideration that of the hundred and twenty thousand children, already computed, twenty thousand may be reserved for breed, whereof only one fourth part to be males, which is more than we allow to sheep, black cattle, or swine; and my reason is that these children are seldom the fruits of marriage, a circumstance not much regarded by our savages, therefore one male will be sufficient to serve four females. That the remaining hundred thousand may at a year old be offered in sale to the persons of quality and fortune through the kingdom, always advising the mother to let them suck plentifully in the last month, so as to render them plump and fat for a good table. A child will make two dishes at an entertainment for friends; and when the family dines alone, the fore or hind quarter will make a reasonable dish, and seasoned with a little pepper or salt will be very good boiled on the fourth day, especially in winter.

I have reckoned upon a medium that a child just born will weigh twelve pounds, and in a solar year if tolerably nursed increaseth to twenty-eight pounds.

I grant this food will be somewhat dear, and therefore very proper for landlords, who, as they have already devoured most of the parents, seem to have the best title to the children.

Infant's flesh will be in season throughout the year, but more plentiful in March, and a little before and after. For we are told by a grave author, an eminent French physician, that fish being a prolific diet, there are more children born in Roman Catholic countries about nine months after Lent than at any other season; therefore, reckoning a year after Lent, the markets will be more glutted than usual, because the number of popish infants is at least three to one in this kingdom; and therefore it will have one other collateral advantage, by lessening the number of Papists among us.

I have already computed the charge of nursing a beggar's child (in which list I reckon all cottagers, laborers, and four fifths of the farmers) to be about two shillings per annum, rags included; and I believe no gentleman would repine to give ten shillings for the carcass of a good fat child, which, as I have said, will make four dishes of excellent nutritive meat, when he hath only some particular friend or his own family to dine with him. Thus the squire will learn to be a good landlord, and grow popular among the tenants; the mother will have eight shillings net profit, and be fit for work till she produces another child.

Those who are more thrifty (as I must confess the times require) may flay the carcass; the skin of which artificially dressed will make admirable gloves for ladies, and summer boots for fine gentlemen.

As to our city of Dublin, shambles may be appointed for this purpose in the most convenient parts of it, and butchers we may be assured will not be wanting; although I rather recommend buying the children alive, and dressing them hot from the knife as we do roasting pigs.

A very worthy person, a true lover of his country, and whose virtues I highly esteem, was lately pleased in discoursing on this matter to offer a refinement upon my scheme. He said that many gentlemen of this kingdom, having of late destroyed their deer, he conceived that the want of venison might be well supplied by the bodies of young lads and maidens, not exceeding fourteen years of age nor under twelve, so great a number of both sexes in every county being now ready to starve for want of work and service; and these to be disposed of by their parents, if alive, or otherwise by their nearest relations. But with due deference to so excellent a friend and so deserving a patriot, I cannot be altogether in his sentiments; for as to the males, my American. acquaintance assured me from frequent experience that their flesh was generally tough and lean, like that of our schoolboys, by continual exercise, and their taste disagreeable; and to fatten them would not answer the charge. Then as to the females, it would, I think with humble submission, be a loss to the public, because they soon would become breeders themselves: and besides, it is not improbable that some scrupulous people might be apt to censure such a practice (although indeed very unjustly) as a little bordering upon cruelty; which, I confess, hath always been with me the strongest objection against any project, how well soever intended.

But in order to justify my friend, he confessed that this expedient was put into his head by the famous Psalmanazar, a native of the island Formosa, who came from thence to London above twenty years ago, and in conversation told my friend that in his country when any young person happened to be put to death, the executioner sold the carcass to persons of quality as a prime dainty; and that in his time the body of a plump girl of fifteen, who was crucified for an attempt to poison the emperor, was sold to his Imperial Majesty's prime minister of state, and other great mandarins of the court, in joints from the gibbet, at four hundred crowns. Neither indeed can I deny that if the same use were made of several plump young girls in this town, who without one single groat to their fortunes cannot stir abroad without a chair, and appear at the playhouse and assemblies in foreign fineries which they never will pay for, the kingdom would not be the worse.

Some persons of a desponding spirit are in great concern about that vast number of poor people who are aged, diseased, or maimed, and I have been desired to employ my thoughts what course may be taken to ease the nation of so grievous an encumbrance. But I am not in the least pain upon that matter, because it is very well known that they are every day dying and rotting by cold and famine, and filth and vermin, as fast as can be reasonably expected. And as to the younger laborers, they are now in almost as hopeful a condition. They cannot get work, and consequently pine away for want of nourishment to a degree that if at any time they are accidentally hired to common labor, they have not strength to perform it; and thus the country and themselves are happily delivered from the evils to come.

I have too long digressed, and therefore shall return to my subject. I think the advantages by the proposal which I have made are obvious and many, as well as of the highest importance.

For first, as I have already observed, it would greatly lessen the number of Papists, with whom we are yearly overrun, being the principal breeders of the nation as well as our most dangerous enemies; and who stay at home on purpose to deliver the kingdom to the Pretender, hoping to take their advantage by the absence of so many good Protestants, who have chosen rather to leave their country than to stay at home and pay tithes against their conscience to an Episcopal curate.

Secondly, the poorer tenants will have something valuable of their own, which by law may be made liable to distress, and help to pay their landlord's rent, their corn and cattle being already seized and money a thing unknown.

Thirdly, whereas the maintenance of an hundred thousand children, from two years old and upwards, cannot be computed at less than ten shillings a piece per annum, the nation's stock will be thereby increased fifty thousand pounds per annum, besides the profit of a new dish introduced to the tables of all gentlemen of fortune in the kingdom who have any refinement in taste. And the money will circulate among ourselves, the goods being entirely of our own growth and manufacture.

Fourthly, the constant breeders, besides the gain of eight shillings sterling per annum by the sale of their children, will be rid of the charge of maintaining them after the first year.

Fifthly, this food would likewise bring great custom to taverns, where the vintners will certainly be so prudent as to procure the best receipts for dressing it to perfection, and consequently have their houses frequented by all the fine gentlemen, who justly value themselves upon their knowledge in good eating; and a skillful cook, who understands how to oblige his guests, will contrive to make it as expensive as they please.

Sixthly, this would be a great inducement to marriage, which all wise nations have either encouraged by rewards or enforced by laws and penalties. It would increase the care and tenderness of mothers toward their children, when they were sure of a settlement for life to the poor babes, provided in some sort by the public, to their annual profit instead of expense. We should see an honest emulation among the married women, which of them could bring the fattest child to the market. Men would become as fond of their wives during the time of their pregnancy as they are now of their mares in foal, their cows in calf, or sows when they are ready to farrow; nor offer to beat or kick them (as is too frequent a practice) for fear of a miscarriage.

Many other advantages might be enumerated. For instance, the addition of some thousand carcasses in our exportation of barreled beef, the propagation of swine's flesh, and improvement in the art of making good bacon, so much wanted among us by the great destruction of pigs, too frequent at our tables, which are no way comparable in taste or magnificence to a well-grown, fat, yearling child, which roasted whole will make a considerable figure at a lord mayor's feast or any other public entertainment. But this and many others I omit, being studious of brevity.

Supposing that one thousand families in this city would be constant customers for infants' flesh, besides others who might have it at merry meetings, particularly weddings and christenings, I compute that Dublin would take off annually about twenty thousand carcasses, and the rest of the kingdom (where probably they will be sold somewhat cheaper) the remaining eighty thousand.

I can think of no one objection that will possibly be raised against this proposal, unless it should be urged that the number of people will be thereby much lessened in the kingdom. This I freely own, and it was indeed one principal design in offering it to the world. I desire the reader will observe, that I calculate my remedy for this one individual kingdom of Ireland and for no other that ever was, is, or I think ever can be upon earth. Therefore let no man talk to me of other expedients: of taxing our absentees at five shillings a pound: of using neither clothes nor household furniture except what is of our own growth and manufacture: of utterly rejecting the materials and instruments that promote foreign luxury: of curing the expensiveness of pride, vanity, idleness, and gaming in our women: of introducing a vein of parsimony, prudence, and temperance: of learning to love our country, in the want of which we differ even from Laplanders and the inhabitants of Topinamboo: of quitting our animosities and factions, nor acting any longer like the Jews, who were murdering one another at the very moment their city was taken: of being a little cautious not to sell our country and conscience for nothing: of teaching landlords to have at least one degree of mercy toward their tenants: lastly, of putting a spirit of honesty, industry, and skill into our shopkeepers; who, if a resolution could now be taken to buy only our native goods, would immediately unite to cheat and exact upon us in the price, the measure, and the goodness, nor could ever yet be brought to make one fair proposal of just dealing, though often and earnestly invited to it.

Therefore I repeat, let no man talk to me of these and the like expedients, till he hath at least some glimpse of hope that there will ever be some hearty and sincere attempt to put them in practice.

But as to myself, having been wearied out for many years with offering vain, idle, visionary thoughts, and at length utterly despairing of success, I fortunately fell upon this proposal, which, as it is wholly new, so it hath something solid and real, of no expense and little trouble, full in our own power, and whereby we can incur no danger in disobliging England. For this kind of commodity will not bear exportation, the flesh being of too tender a consistence to admit a long continuance in salt, although perhaps I could name a country which would be glad to eat up our whole nation without it.

After all, I am not so violently bent upon my own opinion as to reject any offer proposed by wise men, which shall be found equally innocent, cheap, easy, and effectual. But before something of that kind shall be advanced in contradiction to my scheme, and offering a better, I desire the author or authors will be pleased maturely to consider two points. First, as things now stand, how they will be able to find food and raiment for an hundred thousand useless mouths and backs. And secondly, there being a round million of creatures in human figure throughout this kingdom, whose sole subsistence put into a common stock would leave them in debt two millions of pounds sterling, adding those who are beggars by profession to the bulk of farmers, cottagers, and laborers, with their wives and children who are beggars in effect; I desire those politicians who dislike my overture, and may perhaps be so bold to attempt an answer, that they will first ask the parents of these mortals whether they would not at this day think it a great happiness to have been sold for food at a year old in the manner I prescribe, and thereby have avoided such a perpetual scene of misfortunes as they have since gone through by the oppression of landlords, the impossibility of paying rent without money or trade, the want of common sustenance, with neither house nor clothes to cover them from the inclemencies of the weather, and the most inevitable prospect of entailing the like or greater miseries upon their breed forever.

I profess, in the sincerity of my heart, that I have not the least personal interest in endeavoring to promote this necessary work, having no other motive than the public good of my country, by advancing our trade, providing for infants, relieving the poor, and giving some pleasure to the rich. I have no children by which I can propose to get a single penny; the youngest being nine years old, and my wife past childbearing.

Study Questions

1. Swift begins his essay with a number of reasons why children are not, at the time, useful to society. Make a list of these reasons.
2. In the section beginning "I shall now therefore humbly propose my own thoughts, which I hope will not be liable to the least objection," Swift outlines a scheme which he suggests would not only aid the Irish economy but also improve general conditions in Ireland and benefit both children and parents. List the kinds of proof that he offers to support his scheme, quoting an example of each.
3. State the syllogism present in the paragraph beginning "Infant's flesh will be in season throughout the year, but more plentiful in March."
4. This essay is a satire, a work which attacks human behavior through ridicule. What is the object of Swift's attack?
5. In the essay there are a number of examples of irony (statements which mean something different from what they say). Find several examples of such statements and rewrite them to state the author's true meaning.
6. Formulate the syllogism which governs the entire essay, stating both premises and the conclusion in your own words.

To His Coy Mistress　　　　　　　ANDREW MARVELL

Had we but world enough, and time,
This coyness lady were no crime.
We would sit down, and think which way
To walk, and pass our long love's day.
Thou by the Indian Ganges' side　　　　　5
Should'st rubies find: I by the tide
Of Humber would complain. I would

Love you ten years before the Flood:
And you should if you please refuse
Till the conversion of the Jews.   10
My vegetable love should grow
Vaster than empires, and more slow.
An hundred years should go to praise
Thine eyes, and on thy forehead gaze.
Two hundred to adore each breast: 15
But thirty thousand to the rest.
An age at least to every part,
And the last age should show your heart.
For lady you deserve this state;
Nor would I love at lower rate.   20
     But at my back I always hear
Time's winged chariot hurrying near:
And yonder all before us lie
Deserts of vast eternity.
Thy beauty shall no more be found;   25
Nor, in thy marble vault, shall sound
My echoing song: then worms shall try
That long preserv'd virginity:
And your quaint honor turn to dust;
And into ashes all my lust.   30
The grave's a fine and private place,
But none I think do there embrace.
     Now therefore, while the youthful hue
Sits on thy skin like morning dew,
And while thy willing soul transpires   35
At every pore with instant fires,
Now let us sport us while we may;
And now, like am'rous birds of prey,
Rather at once our time devour,
Than languish in his slow-chapt pow'r.   40
Let us roll all our strength, and all
Our sweetness, up into one ball:
And tear our pleasures with rough strife,
Thorough the iron gates of life.
Thus, though we cannot make our sun   45
Stand still, yet we will make him run.

Study Questions

1. Marvell's poem is structured around an "if . . . then" form of argu-
    ment. Sum up in one sentence the main argument he states in the
    first twenty lines.

2. In lines 21–32, he refutes the "if" part of the argument. Express in one sentence his refutation.
3. What proofs does he give to support his refutation?
4. In lines 33–46, the poet arrives at a conclusion. Summarize his conclusion in one statement.
5. Using your answers to questions 1, 2, and 4, restate the argument of the poem as a valid syllogism.
6. Marvell chose to state his argument in a poem rather than in an essay. Why do you suppose he did so? How is the effect of the argument enhanced by its form?
7. Using the sequential argument, construct what might have been the recipient's reply.

Was the World Made for Man?   MARK TWAIN

*Alfred Russell Wallace's revival of the theory that this earth is at the centre of the stellar universe, and is the only habitable globe, has aroused great interest in the world.—*LITERARY DIGEST

For ourselves we do thoroughly believe that man, as he lives just here on this tiny earth, is in essence and possibilities the most sublime existence in all the range of non-divine being—the chief love and delight of God.—Chicago INTERIOR *(Presb.)*

I seem to be the only scientist and theologian still remaining to be heard from on this important matter of whether the world was made for man or not. I feel that it is time for me to speak.

I stand almost with the others. They believe the world was made for man, I believe it likely that it was made for man; they think there is proof, astronomical mainly, that it was made for man, I think there is evidence only, not proof, that it was made for him. It is too early, yet, to arrange the verdict, the returns are not all in. When they are all in, I think they will show that the world was made for man; but we must not hurry, we must patiently wait till they are all in.

Now as far as we have got, astronomy is on our side. Mr. Wallace has clearly shown this. He has clearly shown two things: that the world was made for man, and that the universe was made for the world—to stiddy it, you know. The astronomy part is settled, and cannot be challenged.

We come now to the geological part. This is the one where the evidence is not all in, yet. It is coming in, hourly, daily, coming in all the time, but naturally it comes with geological carefulness and deliberation, and we must not be impatient, we must not get excited, we must be calm, and wait. To lose our tranquillity will not hurry geology; nothing hurries geology.

It takes a long time to prepare a world for man, such a thing is not done in a day. Some of the great scientists, carefully ciphering the evidences furnished by geology, have arrived at the conviction that our world is prodigiously old, and they may be right, but Lord Kelvin is not of their opinion. He takes a cautious, conservative view, in order to be on the safe side, and feels sure it is not so old as they think. As Lord Kelvin is the highest authority in science now living, I think we must yield to him and accept his view. He does not concede that the world is more than a hundred million years old. He believes it is that old, but not older. Lyell believed that our race was introduced into the world 31,000 years ago, Herbert Spencer makes it 32,000. Lord Kelvin agrees with Spencer.

Very well. According to these figures it took 99,968,000 years to prepare the world for man, impatient as the Creator doubtless was to see him and admire him. But a large enterprise like this has to be conducted warily, painstakingly, logically. It was foreseen that man would have to have the oyster. Therefore the first preparation was made for the oyster. Very well, you cannot make an oyster out of whole cloth, you must make the oyster's ancestor first. This is not done in a day. You must make a vast variety of invertebrates, to start with—belemnites, trilobites, Jebusites, Amalekites, and that sort of fry, and put them to soak in a primary sea, and wait and see what will happen. Some will be a disappointment—the belemnites, the Ammonites and such; they will be failures, they will die out and become extinct, in the course of the nineteen million years covered by the experiment, but all is not lost, for the Amalekites will fetch the homestake; they will develop gradually into encrinites, and stalacites, and blatherskites, and one thing and another as the mighty ages creep on and the Archaean and the Cambrian Periods pile their lofty crags in the primordial seas, and at last the first grand stage in the preparation of the world for man stands completed, the oyster is done. An oyster has hardly any more reasoning power than a scientist has; and so it is reasonably certain that this one jumped to the conclusion that the nineteen million years was a preparation for *him*; but that would be just like an oyster, which is the most conceited animal there is, except man. And anyway, this one could not know, at that early date, that he was only an incident in a scheme, and that there was some more to the scheme, yet.

The oyster being achieved, the next thing to be arranged for in the preparation of the world for man was fish. Fish and coal—to fry it with. So the Old Silurian seas were opened up to breed the fish in, and at the same time the great work of building Old Red Sandstone mountains eighty thousand feet high to cold-storage their fossils in was begun. This latter was quite indispensable, for there would be no end of failures again, no end of extinctions—millions of them—and it would be cheaper and less trouble to can them in the rocks than keep tally of them in a book. One does not build the coal beds and eighty thousand feet of perpendicular Old Red Sandstone in a brief time—no, it took twenty million years. In the first place, a coal bed is a slow and troublesome and tiresome thing to construct. You have to grow prodigious forests of tree-ferns and reeds and calamites and such things in a marshy region; then you have to sink them under out of sight and let them rot; then you have to turn the streams on them, so as to bury them under several feet of sediment, and the sediment must have time to harden and turn to rock; next you must grow another forest on top, then sink it and put on another layer of sediment and harden it; then more forest and more rock, layer upon layer, three miles deep —ah, indeed it is a sickening slow job to build a coal-measure and do it right!

So the millions of years drag on; and meantime the fish culture is lazying along and frazzling out in a way to make a person tired. You have developed ten thousand kinds of fishes from the oyster; and come to look, you have raised nothing but fossils, nothing but extinctions. There is nothing left alive and progressive but a ganoid or two and perhaps half a dozen asteroids. Even the cat wouldn't eat such.

Still, it is no great matter; there is plenty of time, yet, and they will develop into something tasty before man is ready for them. Even a ganoid can be depended on for that, when he is not going to be called on for sixty million years.

The Paleozoic time limit having now been reached, it was necessary to begin the next stage in the preparation of the world for man, by opening up the Mesozoic Age and instituting some reptiles. For man would need reptiles. Not to eat, but to develop himself from. This being the most important detail of the scheme, a spacious liberality of time was set apart for it—thirty million years. What wonders followed! From the remaining ganoids and asteroids and alkaloids were developed by slow and steady and painstaking culture those stupendous saurians that used to prowl about the steamy world in those remote ages, with their snaky heads reared forty feet in the air and sixty feet of body and tail racing and thrashing after. All gone, now, alas—all extinct, except the little handful of Arkansawrians left stranded and lonely with us here upon this far-flung verge and fringe of time.

Yes, it took thirty million years and twenty million reptiles to get one that would stick long enough to develop into something else and let the scheme proceed to the next step.

Then the pterodactyl burst upon the world in all his impressive solemnity and grandeur, and all Nature recognized that the Cenozoic threshold was crossed and a new Period open for business, a new stage begun in the preparation of the globe for man. It may be that the pterodactyl thought the thirty million years had been intended as a preparation for himself, for there was nothing too foolish for a pterodactyl to imagine, but he was in error, the preparation was for man. Without doubt the pterodactyl attracted great attention, for even the least observant could see that there was the making of a bird in him. And so it turned out. Also the makings of a mammal, in time. One thing we have to say to his credit, that in the matter of picturesqueness he was the triumph of his Period; he wore wings and had teeth, and was a starchy and wonderful mixture altogether, a kind of long-distance premonitory symptom of Kipling's marine:

> 'E isn't one o' the reg'lar Line, nor 'e isn't one of the crew,
> 'E's a kind of a giddy harumfrodite—soldier an' sailor too!

From this time onward for nearly another thirty million years the preparation moved briskly. From the pterodactyl was developed the bird; from the bird the kangaroo, from the kangaroo the other marsupials; from these the mastodon, the megatherium, the gaint sloth, the Irish elk, and all that crowd that you make useful and instructive fossils out of—then came the first great Ice Sheet, and they all retreated before it and crossed over the bridge at Bering Strait and wandered around over Europe and Asia and died. All except a few, to carry on the preparation with. Six Glacial Periods with two million years between Periods chased these poor orphans up and down and about the earth, from weather to weather—from tropic swelter at the poles to Arctic frost at the equator and back again and to and fro, they never knowing what kind of weather was going to turn up next; and if ever they settled down anywhere the whole continent suddenly sank under them without the least notice and they had to trade places with the fishes and scramble off to where the seas had been, and scarcely a dry rag on them; and when there was nothing else doing a volcano would let go and fire them out from wherever they had located. They led this unsettled and irritating life for twenty-five million years, half the time afloat, half the time aground, and always wondering what it was all for, they never suspecting, of course, that it was a preparation for man and had to be done just so or it wouldn't be any proper and harmonious place for him when he arrived.

And at last came the monkey, and anybody could see that man wasn't far off, now. And in truth that was so. The monkey went on developing for close upon five million years, and then turned into a man—to all appearances.

Such is the history of it. Man has been here 32,000 years. That it took a hundred million years to prepare the world for him is proof that that is what it was done for. I suppose it is. I dunno. If the Eiffel Tower were now representing the world's age, the skin of paint on the pinnacle-knob at its summit would represent man's share of that age; and anybody would perceive that that skin was what the tower was built for. I reckon they would, I dunno.

Study Questions

1. This essay makes use of a special variety of argument known as the *reductio ad absurdum*, in which an opponent's ideas are developed in such a way as to show their absurdity. On the basis of this essay, construct the syllogism apparently used by Twain's contemporaries to prove that the world was indeed made for man. Is that syllogism absurd? Why or why not? To what extent is a *non sequitur* or *post hoc* fallacy involved in that syllogism?

2. The body of the essay discusses two kinds of evidence (in effect, two reasons) for believing that the world was made for man. The astronomical evidence is disposed of in one brief paragraph, while the geological evidence is discussed in great detail. Does the essay therefore seem out of balance? Why or why not?

3. At the time the essay was written (about 1900) there appeared to be good evidence for believing that the earth was the only inhabited planet in the universe, though this assumption has been increasingly challenged in recent years. If it could be *proved* that the earth was the only inhabited planet, would this proof provide evidence that the world was made *for* man? Why or why not?

4. What humorous and/or satirical details does Twain include to make the argument seem especially absurd?

5. The concluding paragraph is built around an analogy. If that analogy is valid, the argument that the world was made for man is totally absurd. How valid is the analogy?

The Bomb and Man's Consciousness   W. H. AUDEN

If what I read in the newspapers is true, then I know this about nuclear weapons: (1) If an atomic war were to start tomorrow, within 20 minutes or so 100 million people in the United States and 500 million in Russia would be dead. (2) The decision to use nuclear bombs would be taken by a tiny handful of persons. The rest of us would not and could not be either consulted or warned. (3) Whether any one individual would be among the dead or the survivors would be a pure matter of chance. If the bombs were dropped in the winter, I should be vaporized, for in the winter I live in Manhattan; if in summer, when I live in Austria, a neutral country, the missiles would sail harmlessly over my head. (4) Whether these weapons will ever be used and, if so, when, how and by whom, are questions neither I nor anybody else can answer.

Consequently, the existence of these devices has no effect upon my daily life, either practically or emotionally. As a human being, I know that I must die, but I do not know when or how. Implosion is merely one more item added to the list of possible future causes of my death, more dramatic, maybe, but statistically less probable than an automobile accident, a coronary or a cancer. I am too concerned over things which are happening in the present, like the insane multiplication and misuse of the automobile or the revolting nervous vulgarity of our affluent mass society, and over things which seem certain to happen in the near future, like the overpopulation of the earth, to worry much about an event which may never happen.

As a symbol, on the other hand, the existence of nuclear weapons is of great significance. Highlighting a development which began with the invention of the steam engine, they have made everybody conscious of a radical change in the relation between man and nature. Life has always been uncertain, but until recently there were two causes for this uncertainty: natural catastrophes, like famines, floods, plagues, legally called Acts of God, and acts of human choice, restraint of princes, malice domestic, piracy on the high seas, etc.

Today in the technologically advanced countries—and it is only a matter of time before it will be the case everywhere—we have little to fear from nature; our only serious problem is man, who can now do, or get nature to do for him, what he is not yet capable of understanding. His mastery over nature has, as it were, brought man back to the same point at which he stood when he was utterly helpless before her. Primitive tribes also held that all problems were, ultimately, human problems, for how nature behaved to them depended, they believed, upon whether their actions were pleasing or displeasing to the gods.

For a historical instant, between, say, 1815 and 1914, a tiny group of well-educated and well-off persons in Europe and America, dazzled by the early achievements of technology, persuaded themselves that there was no human problem; that, once full mastery over nature was won, all problems would vanish.

This emotional faith in Progress, the belief that all change must inevitably be change for the better, was complemented by the intellectual faith of nineteenth-century scientists in the objective truth of their discoveries, their belief that, as C. S. Lewis says:

by inferences from our sense experience (improved by instruments) we could "know" the ultimate physical reality more or less as, by maps, pictures and travel books, a man can "know" a country he has not visited, and that in both cases the "truth" would be a sort of mental replica of the thing itself.

Historical events since 1914 have destroyed the belief in inevitable progress. It is clear to all that knowledge, including knowledge of himself, and the power that knowledge confers, do not in any way affect man's will; they merely increase his capacity to do what he wills, for good or evil, and what he has actually chosen to do during the past 50 years suggests that, as theologians have always asserted, his will is inclined to evil.

Similarly, their own researches have compelled scientists to the conclusion that "objective" truth about physical reality is not scientifically obtainable. As Werner Heisenberg has written:

It would not be too crude an oversimplification to say that *for the first time in the course of history modern man on this earth now confronts himself alone,* and that he no longer has partners or opponents. . . . When we speak of the picture of nature in the exact science of our age, we do not mean a picture of nature so much as a *picture of our relationships with nature.* . . .

Science no longer confronts nature as an objective observer, but sees itself as an actor in the interplay between man and nature. The scientific method of analyzing, explaining and classifying has become conscious of its limitations, which arise out of the fact that by its intervention science alters and refashions the object of investigation. In other words, method and object can no longer be separated. *The scientific world-view has ceased to be a scientific view in the true sense of the word.*

What conclusions, then, may we draw from knowing that our power to do evil is now virtually unlimited, and that we no longer have any partners or opponents other than ourselves? Firstly, I think, it renders invalid the traditional analogy between moral law and criminal law. Criminal law is imposed law, which can be broken. It forbids me, for example, to commit a robbery but, if I choose, I can commit one. If I do, there are three possible consequences. I may be caught and punished, but the particular punishment inflicted upon me will depend upon the criminal code under which I happen to be living; it has no intrinsic relation to the nature of my crime. I may be caught but be a person of such influence that I can bribe the police or the judge so that I am either not charged or acquitted. Or I may fail to get caught; at the present time, I understand, if I commit a robbery in New York City, the chances of getting away with it are about three to one in my favor.

If we think of Ethics as a set of imposed rules, then it is obvious that man can break them with absolute impunity. If the word "ethics" has any meaning, then we must agree with Wittgenstein, "Ethics does not treat of the world. Ethics must be a condition of the world, like logic." The laws of ethics, that is to say, must be like the laws of physics and chemistry, laws we can, out of ignorance or willfulness, defy but cannot break, any more than I can break the laws of biochemistry by getting drunk or the law of gravity by jumping out of the window, and the consequence of defying them must be as inevitable and as intrinsically linked to their natures as a hangover or a broken leg. To state moral laws in the imperative is simply a matter of pedagogical technique, just as a mother says to her child, "Stay away from that window!" because the child is as yet ignorant of what will happen if it falls out of it.

Unfortunately, while we very soon learn what will happen if we jump out of windows and have no desire to break our legs, in relation to the laws of ethics, to the necessity, let us say, of loving our neighbor as ourselves, we all too often behave either like madmen who imagine that, unlike other folks, they are magicians who can fly, or like suicides who wish to destroy themselves out of spite or despair. Essentially, loving my neighbor means recognizing that his existence is as real as my own. In primitive static societies, people living a hundred miles apart were unaware of each other's existence, so that the question of loving each other did not arise.

Today, as we all know, nothing that happens in any part of the world is without its impact on the whole. It is no easier than it ever was wholeheartedly to believe in the existence of others, but the consequences of refusal become plainer every day. "Your life and death are with your neighbor," said St. Anthony. Nuclear weapons have made it clear that this is now true in a quite literal sense.

The realization that the scientific picture is a picture of human relationships with nature has already had one happy result. Though still afraid, and with reason, of the practical uses to which scientific knowledge may be put, we have been freed from that fear, which haunted our forefathers, that science might discover something that would invalidate all traditional teaching about human nature. Every time some important discovery was made, by Copernicus or Darwin or Freud or Einstein, there was a hullaballoo: conservatives feared that anarchy in faith and morals would result, while radicals drew theological and moral inferences which the discovery itself did not warrant.

Science now permits us to say that "objective" nature, the world which alone is "real" to us as the one in which we are born, love, hate, work, reproduce and die is the world given us by our senses, a world in which the sun crosses the sky from east to west, the night heaven is a vault over our heads studded with stars, a world of three-dimensional space where the human body is the standard by which objects are judged big or small, where objects have defined boundaries and are either at rest or in motion. Scientific knowledge about macroscopic or subatomic events may enable us to perform many acts we could not perform before, but it is still as inhabitants of this human world that we perform them.

To say that in nature man now encounters neither a partner nor an opponent is really to say that now he and not nature decides what the relationship between them is to be, and in this matter we are slow to realize what it implies. If nothing in the universe is responsible for us, then we are responsible for everything in the universe, just as in the Book of Genesis Adam was made responsible for dressing and tilling the Garden of Eden. So long as man was helpless before the forces of nature, in fact nature's slave, it was natural that he should think of her as an opponent and dream of a day when their relative positions would be reversed, he would be master and she slave.

We are still not prepared to abandon this attitude, although some of the evil consequences to ourselves of treating her as a slave are already apparent. Much has been written, for example, about the effects of ruthless exploitation of nature, thoughtless disturbances of her ecology, indiscriminate use of antibiotics, etc., but we are still loath to change our ways. The time has come when we must choose to treat nature not as a slave but as a partner, or, more accurately, perhaps, as a loving father treats his children. We have first to admit that every created thing has as much right to its kind of existence as we have to ours, and then go on to ask what, with our help, it could become but cannot by its own unaided efforts.

The model for our right relation to nature should be that of the good trainer of animals. It seems obvious to me, for instance, that a well-trained sheepdog has more realized its "dog nature" than a wild one, just as a spoiled lapdog or one terrified by ill usage has had its "dogginess" debased. This means, of course, reintroducing the notion of teleology, for a long time now a dirty word with scientists, but they will get over the shock. Our world will be a safer and healthier place when we can admit that to make an atomic bomb is morally to corrupt a host of innocent electrons below the age of consent.

Study Questions

1. Auden writes, "If nothing in the universe is responsible for us, then we are responsible for everything in the universe. . . ." Rewrite this statement as a syllogism. Does this statement summarize Auden's central argument?

2. Point out where Auden uses comparison as a method of organization.

3. The writer makes one statement which he labels an "oversimplification." Do you agree? Why or why not?

4. What is "teleology"? How does it relate to Auden's argument?

5. Auden's last statement is a witty summary of his main thought. Is humor out of place here? Why or why not?

PRELIMINARY WORKSHEET

1. Topic   _____

2. Statement of most important reason for your belief   _____

   _____

   _____

   _____

3. Write a categorical syllogism with three propositions in positive form

       a.   major premise

   _____

   _____

   _____

   _____

       b.   minor premise

   _____

   _____

   _____

   _____

       c.   conclusion

   _____

   _____

   _____

   _____

4. Support your major premise with details   _____

   _____

   _____

   _____

   _____

5. Support your minor premise with details   _____

   _____

_____

_____

_____

_____

6. Utilize a method of development (comparison, for example) _____

_____

_____

_____

_____

7. Supplementary information for introduction _____

_____

_____

_____

_____

8. Concluding material _____

_____

_____

_____

_____

EVALUATION GUIDE

Name

Topic

Introduction

    1.   State the subject of the argument. _____

_____

_____

_____

2. What is the author trying to prove about the subject? _____

_____

_____

_____

3. Analyze the sequential argument that serves as the basis for the paper.

   a. major premise: _____

   _____

   b. minor premise: _____

   _____

   c. conclusion: _____

   _____

1. Is the sequential argument a valid syllogism? If not, why not?

_____

_____

_____

2. How does the writer prove the major premise? Is the proof adequate? Is it convincing? _____

_____

_____

_____

3. What methods of development are used to support the minor premise?

_____

_____

_____

4. How does the author acknowledge the argument of the opposition?

_____

_____

_____

Conclusion

1. Does the conclusion draw together all the aspects of the argument and restate them in a forceful manner? _____

_____

2. Does the author convince you that his position is a reasonable one? If not, why not? _____

_____

_____

_____

_____

_____

Rating

___ This paper should be rewritten completely or in part.

___ This paper is acceptable but needs some minor revisions.

___ This is an outstandingly good paper.

Appendix: Guidelines for Documentation of Sources

The following sample footnotes and bibliography satisfy the requirements of the *MLA Style Sheet* (published by the Modern Language Association of America) and are therefore suitable for the work done in most colleges and universities. Any instructor is free, of course, to modify form as he wishes; in all cases the student should follow the directions of the instructor under whom the paper is being written. The student should always, however, observe the two primary rules of documentation:

1. references must be clear and exact
2. form must be consistent

Footnotes

A.   Typed footnotes should be single spaced at the bottom of the page on which the reference is made. Triple space between the final line of your text and the first footnote; double space between footnotes.

B.   Sample footnotes follow, indicating the indentations of lines, order of contents, and punctuation:

[1]Louis A. Allison, *Writing Your Term Paper* (Boston: Houghton Mifflin, 1967), p. 216.

[2]*Ibid.*, p. 59.

[3]Stanislav Bevske and Edward Milhouse, *Theories of Evolution* (New York: Wiley, 1961), p. 64.

[4]Emily Dickinson, *Selected Poems*, ed. Henry Wigglesworth (New York: Harper, 1972), p. 193.

[5]Louis A. Allison, *Library Resources for the Layman* (Boston: Houghton Mifflin, 1970), p. 80.

[6]Bevske and Milhouse, p. 48.

[7]Allison, *Library Resources for the Layman*, p. 36.

[8]Georges Tomaine, *History of French Architecture*, trans. Thomas Pippin (New York: Harcourt, 1943), VII, 131.

[9]William Smithers, "Symbolists in the Nineteenth Century," *Famous Literary Essays* (New York: Macmillan, 1951) pp. 301–303.

[10]Howard Attleboro, "Extrasensory Perception," *Encyclopaedia Britannica* (1964), V, 721.

[11]*Ibid.*, p. 720.

[12]Mary L. Stebbins, "Sensory Perception, Without the Extra," *Psychology Today*, XX (March, 1971), 43.

[13]"Better Read than Dead," *Life*, XXXII (December 29, 1972), 51.

[14]Sen. Humbert Humbert, "Weed Out Injustice," *New York Times*, Oct. 2, 1957, sec. IV, p. 8.

[15]Tomaine, V, 25.

[16]"Usurpers of the Throne," *Encyclopedia Nova Zembla* (1969), XX, 532.

[17]James Wiggins et al., eds., *Voices of Destiny* (New York: Random House, 1956), II, 31.

[18]Frances Xavier, "Pleasure Dome," *Essays in Honor of Caspar Milquetoast*, ed. Jon Dough et al. (Xanadu: Coleridge Press, 1803), p. 56.

Bibliography

A bibliography is simply a list of the published sources you consulted. It should be arranged in alphabetical order on a separate page at the end of your paper. In the samples below note the arrangement of the author's name, the indentation of the second and all succeeding lines, and the punctuation:

Allison, Louis A. *Writing Your Term Paper*. Boston: Houghton Mifflin, 1967.

————. *Library Resources for the Layman*. Boston: Houghton Mifflin, 1970.

Attleboro, Howard. "Extrasensory Perception." *Encyclopaedia Britannica* (1964), V, 720–723.

Bevske, Stanislav and Edward Milhouse. *Theories of Evolution*. New York: Wiley, 1961.

"Better Read than Dead." *Life*, XXXII (December 29, 1972), 51.

Dickinson, Emily. *Selected Poems*, ed. Henry Wigglesworth. New York: Harper, 1972.

Humbert, Sen. Humbert. "Weed Out Injustice." *New York Times*, Oct. 2, 1957, sec. IV, p. 8.

Smithers, William. "Symbolists in the Nineteenth Century." *Famous Literary Essays*. New York: Macmillan, 1951.

Stebbins, Mary L. "Sensory Perception, Without the Extra." *Psychology Today*, XX (March, 1971), 40–48.

Tomaine, Georges. *History of French Architecture*, tran. Thomas Pippin. 8 vols. New York: Harcourt, 1943.

"Usurpers of the Throne." *Encyclopedia Nova Zembla* (1969), XX, 529–532.

Wiggins, James et al., eds. *Voices of Destiny*. 2 vols. New York: Random House, 1956.

Xavier, Frances. "Pleasure Dome." *Essays in Honor of Caspar Milquetoast*. ed. Jon Dough et al. Xanadu: Coleridge Press, 1803.

Index